Introduction to Scholarship in Modern Languages and Literatures

SECOND EDITION

Edited by Joseph Gibaldi

The Modern Language Association of America
New York 1992

Library of Congress Cataloging-in-Publication Data

Introduction to scholarship in modern languages and literatures /
edited by Joseph Gibaldi.
p. cm.
Includes bibliographical references and index.
ISBN 0-87352-385-7 (cloth) ISBN 0-87352-386-5 (paper)
1. Philology, Modern—Research. I. Gibaldi, Joseph, 1942–
PB35.I57 1992
407'.2—dc20 91-42873

Published by The Modern Language Association of America
10 Astor Place, New York, New York 10003-6981

CONTENTS

Preface

THIS book has a publication history that spans nearly half a century and includes four previous similar collections. The Modern Language Association's Committee on Research Activities (now incorporated into the MLA Publications Committee) initiated the project with a report entitled "The Aims, Methods, and Materials of Research in Modern Languages and Literatures," which first appeared in *PMLA* (67 [Oct. 1952]: 3–37). Subsequent members of the committee continued the enterprise by periodically sponsoring new collections of essays written by distinguished scholars and intended to introduce students to scholarship in the field of language and literature. Over the next several decades, at approximately ten-year intervals, the MLA published two editions of the pamphlet *The Aims and Methods of Scholarship in Modern Languages and Literatures* (1962; 1970) and the first edition of *Introduction to Scholarship in Modern Languages and Literatures* (1981). Continuing this tradition, the association offers this volume as an introduction to linguistic and literary study for the next decade.

The essays presented in this volume are both retrospective and prospective. The authors discuss the nature, value, philosophy, and underlying assumptions of their subjects; outline the history of relevant scholarship; survey major issues and approaches of the past, present, and foreseeable future; and conclude with suggestions for further reading and a complete list of works cited. Although the essays inevitably reflect the special interests of their authors, each author has made a genuine effort to be evenhanded and wide-ranging and to describe the field from an international point of view. Further, since mapping intellectual terrain is not as precise a science as mapping physical terrain is, readers will probably notice some unavoidable overlapping among essays. Such overlappings, though, may prove illuminating and provocative as they serve to reinforce and qualify. At the same time, despite the volume's inclusive and comprehensive orientation, some specialists will doubtless find omissions in coverage. While no volume could ever hope to touch on all the myriad activities pursued by linguistic and literary scholars, this book seeks to address as many of the prevalent scholarly activities in the field as possible.

The sentiments I expressed in the concluding paragraph of my preface to the 1981 edition hold even greater relevance to the present work: "The dimension and complexity of our assignment make it difficult for us to hope to repeat the success of the . . . predecessors of this collection. We must remain content, therefore, to hope that the volume will serve reasonably faithfully as a kind of mirror, reflecting the activities and endeavors of scholars in modern languages and literatures, and as a kind of lamp, guiding readers to what seem the more promising paths for future linguistic and literary study."

JG

ACKNOWLEDGMENTS

THE preparation of this book entailed various stages of planning, consultation, and evaluation and required the support and assistance of a large number of persons, including members of the sponsoring committee, the MLA headquarters staff, and the association at large, many of whose members served as advisers and as consultant readers of outlines and manuscripts drafted for the volume. The committee members who planned and have overseen the development of the book include Germaine Brée, King-Kok Cheung, Manthia Diawara, Betty S. Flowers, Debra Fried, Barbara Gelpi, Eric P. Hamp, Vincent B. Leitch, Shirley G. Lim, Juan López-Morillas, Carmen C. McClendon, Richard K. Priebe, Kenneth M. Roemer, Marilyn R. Schuster, Walter H. Sokel, Hans R. Vaget, Guadalupe Valdés, and Edward M. White. Among others who have lent the project valuable support as well as invaluable scholarly, editorial, and administrative expertise are the following: Judith H. Altreuter, Janet L. Anderson, Richard W. Bailey, Russell Berman, Don Bialostosky, Jo Ann Boydston, Richard Brod, Marshall Brown, Claire Cook, Amy S. Cooper, Robert C. Davis, Phyllis Franklin, Judy Goulding, Stephen Greenblatt, Alice O. Hadley, Elizabeth Holland, A. Joseph Hollander, Andreas Huyssen, Barbara Johnson, Dominick LaCapra, Rebecca Hunsicker Lanning, David E. Laurence, Michael Lieb, Alan Liu, Elaine Marks, Robert K. Martin, Donald A. McQuade, Alicia Mahaney Minsky, Helene Moglen, Stephen North, Martha Nussbaum, Stephen T. Olsen, Donald H. Reiman, Steven Scher, James A. Schulz, Peter Shillingsburg, David C. Smith, Janet Swaffar, Elizabeth Traugott, Catharine E. Wall, Adrienne M. Ward, Anita Wenden, Kenneth G. Wilson, and Anne E. Yanagi.

Language and Composition

EDWARD FINEGAN

Linguistics

LANGUAGES, LANGUAGE, AND LINGUISTICS

LINGUISTICS has been called the most scientific of the humanities and the most humanistic of the sciences. Using both humanistic and scientific modes of inquiry, it is a field that defines languages and Language as its domain. The term *languages*—with a small *l*—denotes particular symbolic systems of human interaction and communication (e.g., English, Spanish, Korean, Sanskrit). *Language*—with a capital *L*—refers to characteristics common to all languages, especially grammatical structure. While some linguists consider Language the proper domain of the field, most study particular languages and view the field broadly.

All language varieties—that is, all dialects (standard and nonstandard, regional and national) and all registers (written and spoken, from pidgins to poetry and from motherese to legalese)—contribute equally to our knowledge of languages, and every variety is equally shaped by the laws of Language. For some linguists, languages are quick studies in the social structures of human communities and the mainstay of social interaction; for others, Language is primarily a window on facets of the mind. For all, languages and Language are puzzles whose patterns are not yet adequately described, let alone explained, in social or psychological terms or, indeed, in neurological or biological terms.

The principal objects of linguistic investigation are the structural properties of languages and the variation in linguistic form across communities, situations, and time. Ideally, the goal of linguistics is to account for both the invariant and varying structures of languages, for language acquisition and language change, and ultimately to provide an account of what links language structures and the communicative, social, and aesthetic uses to which they are put. As Deborah Tannen writes, "Linguistics . . . can be scientific, humanistic, and aesthetic. It must be, as we are engaged in examining the eternal tension between fixity and novelty, creativity within constraints" (*Talking* 197).

A central concern of linguistic analysis is grammar. Grammarians focus on the structural characteristics of languages and, often, on universal grammar, which encompasses the principles and structures common to all grammars. Following nineteenth-century comparative and historical linguists, modern structuralists treat grammars as autonomous systems and view them abstractly, independently of their communicative functions, their social contexts, and their aesthetic deployment. Typically, structural grammarians analyze sentences and parts of sentences rather than discourse or texts, and they do so strictly in terms of form.

Another major focus of linguistic analysis is language use, particularly the ways in which linguistic structures reflect and sustain social relations and social situations. Linguists interested in language use focus on structural variation and seek to explain differences by examining communicative and situational contexts and the social relations among participants. They take discourse rather than sentences as their domain, in part because the choice of a structure (e.g., active voice over passive voice or the pronunciation of *-in* over *-ing*) cannot be explained without reference to the discourse and context of that structure. Discourse can be spoken, written, or signed, of course, and it can be produced by interacting interlocutors (as in conversation and interviews) or by solitary speakers or writers with specific addressees (as in personal letters) or generalized addressees (as in radio broadcasts and scholarly articles).

A pair of examples may help clarify matters. Structural grammarians aim to characterize the relation between active-voice sentences ("The author persuasively argues the thesis in a dazzling central chapter.") and passive-voice sentences ("The thesis is persuasively argued by the author in a dazzling central chapter."); their work focuses on the arrangement of syntactic elements within the sentence and on the formal relation between active and passive structures (a topic to which I return later). Structural grammarians do not ask which contexts favor one form over the other in a discourse. Functional grammarians (one type of linguist interested in language use), however, account for the choice between actives and passives by appealing to such phenomena as parallel structures in successive sentences, the linear organization of given and new information, and textual coherence. In functional analyses—for instance, of the syntactic and distributional patterns of over four hundred relative clauses ("the car that she borrowed") transcribed from tape-recorded conversations—researchers typically conclude that their findings strongly support

> a position which views grammar . . . not as autonomous or as independent from issues of pragmatics, semantics, and interaction, but rather as necessarily including the entire interactional dimension of the communicative situation in which conversationalists constitute the people and things they want to talk about.
>
> (Fox and Thompson 315)

As the second example, consider the variant pronunciations of English *-ing* words like *studying*. Structural linguists would note that *-in'* and *-ing* are alternative pronunciations having the same referential meaning (*failin'* an exam is no less painful than *failing* one). Sociolinguists (with their focus on language use) would note that, while all speakers use both these forms, they do so with different proportions of the variants, depending on their social filiations and the context of their discourse; even within a small strip of conversation, a single speaker may say both *-ing* and *-in'*. Sociolinguists aiming to uncover the patterns linking *-in'* and *-ing* to social groups and social situations have found in Norwich, England (Trudgill, *Social*), and New York City (Labov) that women use more *-ing* pronunciations than men and likewise that people with higher socioeconomic status use more *-ing* pronunciations than people with lower socioeconomic status do in comparable situations. Thus, *-in'* and *-ing* are social *dialect* features because they mark gender and socioeconomic status; they are characteristic of particular social groups.

These same variants of pronunciation also index situations of use in Norwich and New York, with *-ing* occurring more frequently in formal situations than in informal ones. This variation across situations makes these pronunciations *register* features as well as dialect features, and it is curious that the same variable marks both speakers and situations, especially since such joint functioning of linguistic features seems to be the rule rather than the exception. Similar patterns of distribution characterize other features in these and other English-speaking communities, and features of other language communities function in much the same way. Social stratification of linguistic variables is known in Argentine and Panamanian Spanish, Brazilian Portuguese, the French of Montreal and of Lyons, and in several German-speaking communities. Interaction between social dialect variation and register variation probably can also be found in these communities, as in Norwich and New York. Such interrelated patterning between social dialect and register variation challenges sociolinguistic theorists to provide an explanation. (See Baron in this volume.)

Because the myriad shapes of human languages—from Swahili and Sioux to French and Finnish—must conform to the constraints of the human language faculty, the explanation for the existence of between four and six thousand languages and countless dialects, as well as for the disparate forms of, say, dinner-table conversation and an epic poem, must lie outside the uniform character of the brain. It is a truism that an infant capable of acquiring any one language is equally capable of acquiring any other; after all, no physiological characteristics predispose one to the acquisition of a particular language. Rather, a body of contingent facts—when and where one is born and with whom one is raised; the complex social, economic, political, and religious history of one's community—molds the particular language and dialect one acquires. An adequate linguistics must account for both the variant and invariant structures of languages, as well as for their use as indexes of social groups and communicative situations. Otherwise, as Dell Hymes notes, we fail to see what communities have achieved within the realm of possibilities delimited by the brain's language faculty (see *Foundations*).

THE SUBFIELDS OF LINGUISTICS

There are many frameworks for language analysis, and, though individual analyses are faulted for eclecticism, the field of linguistics is itself eclectic. One observation that drives much current grammatical theorizing is the stunning efficiency and uniformity with which children acquire a native tongue, and speculation abounds on the contributions of nature and nurture—the roles played by the hypothesized innate language structures of the brain and by the social and cultural contexts of acquisition, including the "input" available to children. (On language acquisition and language learning, see Kramsch in this volume.) Like the authors of certain linguistic treatises of seventeenth-century Europe, grammarians today are struck more by similarities across languages than by the obvious but superficial differences between languages, and much current theory addresses aspects of grammar that are thought to be common to all languages. Such language universals, if they prove to be innate, could explain the efficiency and uniformity of first-language acquisition. Thus the aim of many linguists is to design a model of the representation of language in the mind, delimiting the universal features of grammatical structure and characterizing the parameters that could lead to actual and potential differences across languages; that is, these linguists strive to provide a characterization of the notion "possible human grammar."

Other linguists have different goals, and grammar is only part of what they aim to account for. For these linguists, grammatical analysis that does not consider what communities make of their language is too limited and mechanistic; they argue that formal, autonomous grammars overlook socially and humanistically significant variation within and across communities. This difference in viewpoint, which currently divides the field of linguistics, is captured in the dichotomy between grammatical competence and communicative competence.

For Noam Chomsky, grammatical competence is "the speaker-hearer's knowledge of his language" (*Aspects* 4). Echoing Ferdinand de Saussure's distinction between langue and parole (see his *Course*), Chomsky distinguishes between competence and performance (more recently between "internalized" and "externalized" language). Although earlier he seemed principally to want to exclude slips of the tongue and other errors from linguistic description by relegating them to performance, his exclusions ignore far more than errors. For Chomsky, externalized language is language as it exists in utterances and discourse, as it can be observed in use. Internalized language, in contrast, is a property of the mind or brain, and thus it cannot be observed directly: it is "some element of the mind of the person who knows the language, acquired by the learner, and used by the speaker-hearer" (*Knowledge* 22). Chomsky's linguistics excludes real-world language: language in use (externalized language) "appears to play no role in the theory of language"; indeed, "languages in this sense are not real-world objects but are artificial, somewhat arbitrary, and perhaps not very interesting constructs." Linguistics, for Chomsky, treats only internalized language, and in that sense it is "part of psychology, ultimately biology" (*Knowledge* 26–27).

Of course, many linguists regard language use as the basis for all that is known of language, and they view language variation as an essential part of the competence of speakers and a legitimate object of linguistic analysis. Linguists studying language use honor it as the raison d'être of grammatical systems, particular and universal, and believe that variation not only reflects social identity but helps to create and maintain it. To these linguists, Chomsky does not represent the field at large; he is simply an advocate for the school that aims to determine the innate and universal characteristics of grammar.

In an alternative conceptualization, John J. Gumperz and Dell Hymes define the object of linguistic analysis—in marked contrast to Chomsky's grammatical competence—as communicative competence: "what a speaker needs to know to communicate effectively in culturally significant settings" (vii). For these linguists,

> language usage—i.e., what is said on a particular occasion, how it is phrased, and how it is coordinated with nonverbal signs—cannot simply be a matter of free individual choice. It must itself be affected by subconsciously internalized constraints similar to grammatical constraints. (vi)

Linguists who focus on communicative competence "deal with speakers as members of communities, as incumbents of social roles, and seek to explain their use of language to achieve self-identification and to conduct their activities" (vi).

For the student of literature, communicative competence is of greater concern than grammatical competence, which focuses only on sentences and fails to address discourse. But grammatical competence is also important for literary analysis because verbal art exploits the same grammatical structures as other language varieties. If Chomsky's views were not popular, it would go without saying that an adequate conception of language must attend to both grammatical and communicative competence.

Within these broad approaches, most linguists pursue relatively narrow goals in their research, often within one of the numerous subfields of linguistics. Some of these subfields reflect particular levels of grammatical analysis such as sound systems and syntax, while others reflect distinct methodological approaches such as acoustic phonetics and computational linguistics. Still a third set combines different objects of analysis with different methodologies; these include historical linguistics, sociolinguistics, psycholinguistics, and discourse analysis. Grammatical analysis has held center stage in linguistic analysis for millennia (but compare Lunsford's comments in this volume concerning the historical importance of rhetoric). Today grammar treats sounds and their patterning (phonetics and phonology), the organization of semantic and grammatical elements within words (morphology), the arrangement of words into structured strings (syntax), and the complex systems of lexical and sentential meaning (semantics). Between grammar and use is the subfield of pragmatics, which treats the relation between linguistic form and its contextualized use and interpretation in communicative acts.

Neither psycholinguistics nor computational linguistics can be even minimally characterized in this essay, except to note that psycholinguistics ranges widely, from first-and second-language acquisition (as treated in Kramsch's essay in this volume) to the mental processing of words, sentences, and texts, and that it overlaps with applied linguistics in such arenas as bilingualism and reading. Increasingly, too, psycholinguistics has clinical applications, for example with dyslexia and Alzheimer's disease. Computational linguistics is less a full-fledged subfield than a cover term for a wide range of computer-utilizing studies, from the modeling of grammatical theories to the statistical analysis of natural-language texts. Computers also have promising applications in lexicography (see Sinclair), but their vaunted use for machine translation remains disappointing, primarily because a sufficiently explicit understanding of languages still evades us and the requisite contextual information remains inadequately formalized. (For computer applications to literary texts, Hockey and Miall provide useful overviews; see also issues of the journal *Literary and Linguistic Computing.*)

Historical linguistics, the nineteenth-century springboard for modern linguistics, uses a variety of methods to trace the evolution of languages and relate them to one another "genetically." It employs two principal models: the family-tree model (in which offshoots of parent tongues evolve over time) and the wave model (which reflects the influence of languages on one another when they are in contact). From the family-tree model we understand Latin to be the historical predecessor (the parent language) of Spanish, French, Italian, Portuguese, and Rumanian, among others, and we see Proto-Germanic (of which we have no records) to be the parent of English, German, Dutch, Norwegian, Swedish, Danish, and the defunct Gothic, among others. From the wave model we understand the influence of French on English after the Norman invasion in AD 1066 and of the neighboring Baltic languages on one another in the Baltic sprachbund (borrowed from the German word for "speech league").

Historical linguistics has provided knowledge of the Indo-European family of languages, including the Germanic, Italic, Hellenic, and Celtic branches on the one side and the Slavonic, Baltic, Indo-Iranian, Armenian, and Albanian branches (as well as the extinct Anatolian and Tocharian) on the other. It has also given us a grasp of other language families and established the genetic independence of languages sometimes thought to be related (e.g., Chinese and Japanese). Much work remains to be done in identifying the genetic relations among the native languages of Africa, the Americas, Australia, and Papua New Guinea and in distinguishing between inherited and borrowed similarities. Despite the central role of historical studies in the development of linguistics, the subfield does not now enjoy the prominence it once did (see Watkins). Still, the last decade has witnessed an exciting revival of valuable historical work even on languages as well combed as English and French. Much of this new work falls into one of four broad approaches: it reanalyzes earlier stages of a grammar in the light of what is now understood about structure, typology, and universals (on English, see the works by Kroch and Lightfoot; on Romance, see those by Fleischman and Harris); it applies current models of social dialect and register variation to the competing forms of earlier periods in an effort to explain change (see Weinreich, Labov, and Herzog; Biber and Finegan; Romaine, *Socio-historical*); it seeks to establish general patterns of semantic development in grammatical and lexical forms (see Traugott; Traugott and Heine); or it traces the grammaticalization of forms arising frequently in the discourse patterns of conversation (see Hopper; Givón; Traugott and Heine).

Sociolinguists have a wide spectrum of interests, including urban dialects, ethnic and socioeconomic language varieties, gender-related language characteristics, register variation and stylistics, the ethnography of communication, and traditional dialect geography. More than a few sociolinguists pursue applied interests, including literacy and the relation between forms of discourse and their uses in political and social control (see Baron in this volume; Andersen; Gee; Macdonell). Situational variation and stylistics are also gaining increased attention from sociolinguists. As the complex relation between dialects and registers is addressed, sociolinguists and literary scholars are likely to find their shared interests growing.

Discourse analysis, sometimes considered part of sociolinguistics, is a loosely defined subfield that has no specific methodology. By definition it focuses not on sentences but on texts, socially and contextually framed. As Tannen says, discourse analysis "does not entail a single theory or coherent set of theories [nor does it] describe a theoretical perspective or methodological framework at all. It simply describes the object of study: language beyond the sentence." For Tannen, as for many linguists, the name "discourse analysis" says "nothing more or other than the term 'linguistics': the study of language" (*Talking* 6–7). But, as we have seen, not all linguists agree that language beyond the sentence is the proper domain of the field, and discourse analysis has a separate name and identity in part to legitimate certain types of language analysis and to encompass sociological and anthropological work on language. Despite Tannen's equation of linguistics and discourse analysis, it is principally discourse analysis that has brought attention to texts and to context (see Greetham and Scholes in this volume).

In conclusion, a few words about semantics and pragmatics: Semantics has from time to time been ruled in and out of linguistics. In the first half of the century, structural grammarians like Leonard Bloomfield argued that including semantics would entail the study of all knowledge and thereby threaten linguistics as an independent discipline. Today semantics is defined narrowly and viewed as part of grammar, which is after all a system relating sound and meaning. Falling within the purview of semantics are the structure of the lexicon and the elements of lexical meaning, as well as the ways in which the meaning of a sentence is not merely the sum meaning of its words.

Pragmatics mediates semantic meaning and contextualized interpretation. A sentence like "Can you pass me the salt?" is semantically a yes-no question concerning the ability of the addressee to pass the addressor the salt, but its contextualized interpretation will likely be as an indirect request of the addressee to pass the salt to the speaker, and pragmatics explores the mechanisms of such interpretation. Besides studying such indirect speech acts, pragmatics looks at a wide range of sociolinguistic matters, from the expression of politeness and the use of respect vocabulary to conversational structure and performative utterances (those that in specifiable conditions effectuate what they say: "You're under arrest"; "I now pronounce you husband and wife"). The subject matter of pragmatics includes investigation of the situations in which performative utterances accomplish their work and of the manner in which interlocutors understand the intended force of an utterance (see Levinson for a useful survey).

PREMISES OF LINGUISTIC ANALYSIS

Before we consider the structural levels of language, several widely accepted premises of linguistics are worthy of mention. First, most linguists recognize that linguistic symbols are essentially arbitrary—that no inherent relation exists between things and their names in various languages. The word for "cat" differs from language to language, and so do the words for the vocal noises cats make, though an occasional hint of a culturally filtered echo inhabits words like *meow*. The same arbitrariness might be claimed for the order of events in the world and the order of linguistic expressions representing them, although rhetorical strategies may favor sequences of expressions that mirror actual chronology, as in narratives. Even so, to say that linguistic symbols are essentially arbitrary is not to say that they lack iconicity altogether. The child who reports, "My mother is taking a long, loong, looong shower," reflects the intuitive value of iconic expression as much as the poet's crafted onomatopoeia does. But despite increasing recognition of iconic elements in word and clause formation, the essential arbitrariness of basic linguistic symbols remains intact. (For recent work on syntactic iconicity, see Haiman.)

Second, linguistics aims to be a descriptive field, not a prescriptive one. Linguists describe the structures of human language and the uses to which those structures are put; they do not (as linguists) prescribe what those structures ought to be in some ideal world or judge their use in the real world. In fact, linguists have been belligerently neutral on questions of language value. (On descriptivism and prescriptivism, see Baron; Finegan; and Milroy and Milroy.)

Third, since Saussure in the early twentieth century, linguists take description of a language at one point in time (synchronic description) to be basic to all other analysis. Historical (or diachronic) analysis with its focus on language change compares two or more synchronic descriptions. Diachrony, like synchrony, can focus on texts or sentences or words or sounds, and it can appeal for explanation to factors that are structural, psychological (e.g., perceptual), or social (e.g., language contact). Synchrony cannot appeal to diachrony for explanation, though history can often shed light on how the facts that need explaining came to be as they are.

GRAMMATICAL ANALYSIS

Phonology. Not all the sounds of a language are structurally significant in that language (i.e., not all differences of sound will signal a difference in meaning). A given pair of sounds existing in two languages may represent different structural units in one language but not in the other. Thus both English and French have oral and nasal vowels, but nasalization cannot signal a difference in meaning between two otherwise identical English words, whereas in French it can (and does). For example, English has a rule that nasalizes vowels when they precede nasal consonants (written *m, n, ng*). Compare the pronunciations of *lamb, ban, bong* with *lap, bad, bog*. Because vowel nasalization is regular (i.e., rule-governed) in English, the occurrence of a nasalized vowel is predictable (i.e., any vowel preceding a nasal consonant will be nasalized), and thus nasalization cannot serve to differentiate words. The nasalization rule makes it impossible for English to have a pair of words such as *bãm* and *bam* or *lõte* and *lote*, where only the first of each pair has a nasalized vowel. In French, however, nasalization is not rule-governed; rather, it is a feature of individual words that can signal a meaning difference in contrasting pairs such as [ɔ̃t] and [ɔt] (*honte* 'shame'; *hotte* 'hutch'). (Don't be misled by the spelling: children acquiring French have no spelling to guide them!) Nasalization, then, is a significant feature of French, capable of making a contrast between words. Children (and adults) learning French must note, in their mental dictionaries, nasal and oral vowels for each word (*lin* [lɛ̃] 'flax' is not the same as *lait* [lɛ] 'milk'), whereas an English-speaking child systematically nasalizes vowels by rule and doesn't need to identify nasalized vowels word by word.

Another example is provided by English and Korean, which both have the same three oral consonants articulated by closure of the lips: the aspirated *p* of *pill* (pronounced with an audible breath of air, strong enough to blow out a match, and represented phonetically as [p^h]), the unaspirated *p* of *spill* (represented as [p]), and the *b* of *bill* (represented as [b]). These three articulations have only two representations in the mental lexicon of English speakers (i.e., as /p/ or /b/). The aspirated [p^h] of *pill* does not need to be distinguished from an unaspirated [p] in a speaker's lexicon because all English speakers have internalized a rule that aspirates every /p/ that begins a word (as well as /p/'s in certain other positions; the same rule also aspirates /t/ and /k/ sounds in parallel positions). But no conceivable rule could specify whether /p/ or /b/ occurs in an English word. Therefore /p/ sounds and /b/ sounds must be distinguished from each other English word by English word. In Korean, by contrast, the occurrence of aspirated [p^h] and unaspirated [p] is not determined by rule, so speakers must note for each word whether it has [p^h] or [p]. The occurrence of [b] in Korean, however, is rule governed: [b], but never [p], occurs between vowels or other voiced sounds (and hence [b] could never occur at the beginning or end of a word).

Thus, Korean and English subsume the same three sounds in two structural units of their phonological systems, but they do so quite differently. In English, the units are /p/ and /b/, with [p^h] and [p] merely rule-governed variants of /p/. In Korean, the units are /p/ and /p^h/, with [b] merely a rule-governed variant of /p/. In other words, English attaches significance to whether a consonant is voiced (like [b] and [z]) or voiceless (like [p] and [s]), but it treats aspiration as insignificant. Korean attaches significance to whether a consonant is aspirated or unaspirated but treats voicing as not significant. As a consequence, English can have the words *bill* and *pill* (the latter with rule-assigned aspiration), but it does not have *pill* without aspiration (as pronounced in *spill*). Korean distinguishes *p^hul* 'grass' from *pul* 'fire'; it has *pap* 'law' and *mubap* 'lawlessness' but could not have *mupap* because of the rule that voices /p/ between vowels. Learners of a foreign language tend to transfer their native distributional patterns of rule-governed variants to the target language; thus, an English speaker learning French is heard to pronounce *Pierre* and *petit* with the aspirated [p^h] that English (but not French) uses at the beginning of a word, while a French learner of English may fail to provide the aspiration to words that begin with /p/ in English. This tendency to apply the phonological rules of one's native language to another language is part of what creates a foreign accent.

In sum, languages have inventories of significant phonological units (phonemes) such as /p/ and rules for generating required but nonsignificant "phonetic" variants. Distinguishing underlying "emic" units from "etic" realizations is at the heart of structural linguistics, and the notions of "emic" and "etic," which have been borrowed into folklore and anthropology through the work of Claude Lévi-Strauss, constitute part of the definition of structuralism in other fields. (For more on the cross-disciplinary use of linguistic constructs, see Gunn in this volume.)

Every language also has constraints on how consonants and vowels can be joined to form syllables. Japanese, for example, has three basic syllable types. If C represents a consonant and V a vowel, Japanese permits V and CV syllables (e.g., *a* and *ga*), as well as CVC syllables provided that the second consonant is a nasal (as in *hon* 'book'). English, by contrast, permits not only V, CV, and CVC syllable types but also syllables beginning with two consonants (*plate* and *grit*) and three consonants (as pronounced in *split, stream*, and *squid*). With three consonants, however, the first must be /s/; the second /p/, /t/, or /k/; and the third /l/, /r/, or /w/. English permits many other syllable types, including relatively complex ones like CCCVCCC representing words like *squirts* and *squelched* (where *ch* represents a single consonant sound and *ed* represents [t]). Renewed interest in syllables has contributed to a new "metrical phonology." With its focus on stress patterning and other rhythmic phenomena, metrical phonology has reawakened interest in literary uses of meter and rhythm among linguists (see Kiparsky and Youmans).

Morphology and Morphosyntax. At a level higher than sounds and syllables, grammars make reference to morphemes, which are sequences of sounds associated with a meaning (DOG, SEE) or grammatical function (third-person singular present-tense marker -S as in *sees* or progressive marker -ING as in *seeing*). Unlike a desk dictionary, whose entries are typically words, the mental lexicon of a speaker also lists morphemes (many of which, like DOG, SEE, and KANGAROO are likewise words). As the speaker's counterpart to a published dictionary, a mental lexicon has entries that lack etymologies and illustrative citations but specify certain other information about a morpheme: which phonemes it contains and in which order (as a basis for pronunciation), semantic information (for meaning), and syntactic information about word class (part of speech) and which classes it can co-occur with (e.g., plural -s affixes to nouns but not to adjectives). For a verb, the lexicon contains information about its syntactic-semantic frame; for example, *give*, as in "Alice gave Sarah the book," takes three noun phrases (or "arguments"): an agent giver (Alice), a patient given (the book), and a recipient (Sarah). Much remains to be discovered about how mental lexicons are organized so as to make their contents accessible for online sentence production and comprehension: obviously the alphabetical organization of dictionaries is neither available to speakers nor adequate for such purposes.

As it happens, much of the information needed to structure grammatical sentences could be specified either in the lexicon or in the syntax of a speaker's grammar. In just which of these components particular information actually resides remains unclear in many instances. Like traditional grammatical analyses, recent theory favors placing a greater burden on the lexicon, with a consequent reduction in the complexity of the syntactic component. This theoretical shift has made morphology and morphosyntax major subfields of grammar.

Generative Syntax. For the past three decades, the most influential ways of characterizing sentences structurally have employed a "generative" approach, whereby a lexicon and a set of rules for organizing its elements into the sentences of a language can be specified explicitly (i.e., mechanically, computationally, autonomously—without reference to contingent facts about the world or the particular situations of use).

Although phonological, syntactic, and semantic components of generative grammars have been recognized for some time, each component has been viewed as part of a unified, integrated system. Thus, the syntactic component generates a structure that receives an interpretation for meaning by the operations of the semantic component and an interpretation for pronunciation by the operations of the phonological component. In this standard generative model, the syntactic component is the centerpiece. It comprises a lexicon of the sort described above and a set of phrase-structure rules of the general form S → NP VP (i.e., a sentence consists of a noun phrase followed by a verb phrase). Phrase-structure rules generate deep (or underlying) structures known as "phrase markers" (the familiar "tree diagrams," illustrated in fig. 1). As figure 1 shows, phrase markers specify a linear order of constituent elements (determiner precedes noun), as well as a hierarchical order (prepositional phrase has two constituent parts, preposition and noun phrase).

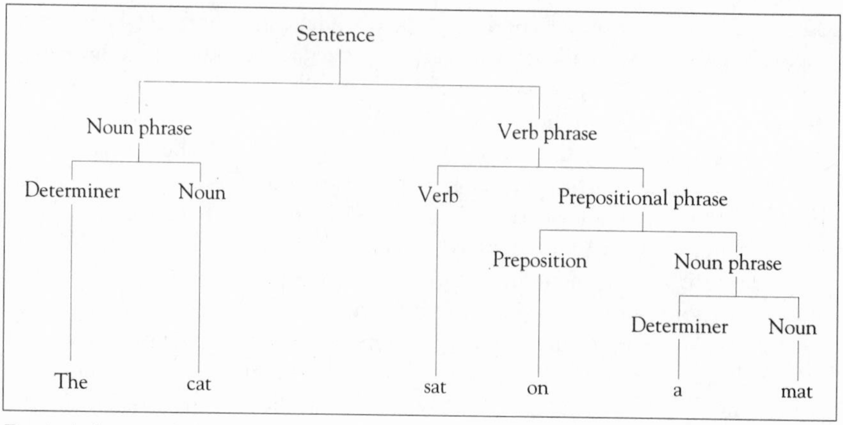

Fig. 1. A phrase marker.

In the generative-transformational grammar of the 1960s and early 1970s, operations called transformations restructured deep phrase markers into "surface" phrase markers (the structure of actual spoken and written sentences). Transformations were formulated for language-specific structures such as the English passive or the French relative clause. Some transformations were required for grammaticality; others were optional, since grammatical sentences resulted whether or not the transformations operated. Passivization was an optional transformation: both "The critics panned her first novel" and "Her first novel was panned by the critics" are grammatical. Reflexivization was obligatory: "Larry pitied himself" (on which the reflexive transformation has operated) is grammatical, but "Larry pitied Larry" (on which it has not) is ungrammatical (where Larry and Larry have identical referents). Transformations accounted for much stylistic variation in both prose and poetry, and linguistic style could be described by reference to an author's preferences among optional transformations. Within a view of style essentially as the dress of thought, a characteristic fondness for particular modes of expression could be identified with particular authors (see the essays in Freeman).

Besides having distinct levels such as phonology and syntax, recent generative models (e.g., government-binding theory) have conceptually distinct modules that operate independently but interactively within a level. The interaction of the modules produces what in earlier models was generated by a set of procedures unified as a transformation (e.g., the passive transformation). As conceptualized, these modules operate at sufficiently abstract levels to be applicable across languages, and their interaction with one another creates the syntactic patterns of sentences. In this view, what makes one language different from another is a relatively small number of "parameters" in each module whose values are set by exposure to a particular language during the process of acquisition. Thus, a child's principal grammatical task is simply to set these parameters to reflect the structures of the language being acquired; the parameters and the range of potential values are innately specified. If this conception of grammatical structure is correct, it will go a long way toward explaining the breathtaking accomplishment represented by every child's first-language acquisition.

Generative grammarians using the government-binding model have proposed a set of modules as alternatives to the unified system of rules and transformations of standard transformational grammar. One module treats case assignment (not the morphological cases familiar to students of inflected languages like German, Russian, or Latin but a highly abstract case system); another module assigns semantic roles to nouns; a third handles government. For example, the earlier English passive transformation, as Chomsky later decomposed it (*Lectures*), consists of four procedures: moving the object noun phrase following the verb to the subject position preceding it, moving the initial subject noun phrase to a position after the verb and making it the object of the added preposition *by*, altering the verb to a past participle, and inserting an appropriate form of the auxiliary verb *to be*.

Serious problems occur with such a transformation, however. For one thing, as formulated, the English passive is unrelated to passive constructions in other languages. More important, permitting such specific transformations would license other similar transformations in the model, thereby granting grammars extraordinary power and freedom. Because acquiring a language is easier when fewer options are available to the child acquiring it, generative theories favor the most limited grammar compatible with the facts. Space restrictions here preclude a description of how passives would be treated in current generative models, but the English-specific points in the transformation above have been relegated to individual lexical items and are no longer handled by the syntax. Significantly, too, passive structures are not generated by specific movement and insertion procedures, as in the standard transformational analysis. Instead, various general principles applicable to all languages operate independently of one another to "license" certain structures, and the confluence of various modules can produce passive structures (see Jaeggli).

The modular approach to grammar arose partly because early transformational grammar was largely English-based, and it assumed that what held true of English would, mutatis mutandis, hold true of all languages. But as grammarians turned to French, Spanish, Italian, Dutch, Japanese, Chinese, and other languages, much of the putative generality of English-based analyses crumbled, and many middle-level generalizations fell (including the notion of structure-specific and language-specific transformations) and were replaced by general principles of wider applicability. As a result of these theoretical realignments, current grammatical descriptions are declarative rather than procedural, and they rely heavily on the features of individual verbs and nouns as specified in the mental lexicon.

Typology. Related to the subject of linguistic generality is typology, and a few words about typological approaches may be useful. Typologists are interested in shared patterns of structural features that are independent of language contact and of genetic relatedness among languages. If, say, English, German, Dutch, Danish, Norwegian, and Swedish exhibit certain characteristics that don't appear in other languages (e.g., dental suffixes to mark the past tense, as in English *thanked* and German *dankte*), these features may (as in this case) be inherited from a common ancestor language and, as such, be germane to genetic relatedness but not necessarily to typology. Likewise, in the Baltic sprachbund mentioned earlier, Greek, Rumanian, Albanian, and Bulgarian share a number of structural features, although they belong to different branches of Indo-Euopean, whose member languages do not generally possess those features. One such feature is the loss of the infinitive such that, instead of expressions like "give me to drink," these languages have the equivalent of "give me that I drink": Greek "ðos mu na pjo," Albanian "a-më të pi," Bulgarian "daj mi da pija," and Rumanian "dă-mi să beau" (examples from Comrie, *World's* 10). Rumanian does not share this feature with the other Romance languages, nor does Bulgarian share it with the other Slavonic languages, nor Greek with Ancient Greek. Instead, the similarities arise from mutual contact among neighboring languages, and therefore they are not of direct interest to typologists.

Even independently of contact and genetic relatedness, significant correlations among structures exist across languages—for example, between the order of objects and verbs, on the one hand, and of other constituents such as nouns and adjectives, on the other. In languages where the verb follows the object (OV languages, such as Japanese and Persian), there is a strong tendency for adjectives, genitives, and relative clauses to precede nouns and for prepositions to follow them (in which case they are called "postpositions"). In languages with the complementary pattern in which objects follow verbs (VO languages, such as Welsh, Irish, and Classical Arabic), nouns tend to precede adjectives, genitives, and relative clauses, and there are prepositions. Japanese is a canonical OV language with all the expected patterns: adjectives and relative clauses preceding nouns (*omoshiroi hon* 'an interesting book'; *anata ga katta hon* 'the book you bought'); genitives preceding nouns (*Taroo no hon* 'Taro's book'); and postpositions (*Tookyoo ni* 'to Tokyo'). Other languages are less canonical. English is mixed, with relative clauses following their head nouns and with prepositions, as expected for VO languages, but with adjectives generally preceding nouns ("subversive intent"), a characteristic of OV languages, while genitives can precede or follow ("Auden's apologies" and "the modernity of Emerson"). The relations among such word-order patterns, universal grammar, and the parameters of individual languages constitute a central puzzle for syntactic typology.

Functional Syntax. Before leaving syntax and typology, I return briefly to functional grammar, which highlights certain fundamental empirical and philosophical issues remaining unsettled in linguistics today. One fundamental empirical question that suggests the depth of the disagreement is the concept of sentence. As axiomatic as the idea seems in most current (and traditional) grammar (compare the phrase marker of fig. 1), some functional grammarians and discourse analysts assert that its centrality rests on a literate bias and that its empirical status as a unit of analysis must be examined alongside competing notions such as clause, paragraph, and topic chain (Hopper 132). Some theorists argue that analysis of sentences should be nothing more than a methodological preliminary to the analysis of discourse (Givón). Others take the stronger position that sentences may be "a secondary emergence," resulting from "a rhetorical amalgamation of clauses" or from collaborative discourse making (Hopper 131).

The philosophical issues involve the disputed status of innate grammatical structures cast in the image of the seventeenth-century rationalists. As suggested above, generative grammarians posit innate grammatical structures whose putative configuration has changed somewhat in response to changing theoretical models but whose bedrock Cartesian notion of innate knowledge remains stable. For the functionalists, however, grammar is emergent rather than innate; it is the (developmental and evolutionary) product of discourse created in particular communicative contexts. These competing ideologies, as Paul Hopper has noted, correspond to the two major intellectual currents of the day: structuralism "with its belief in and attention to a priori structures of consciousness and behavior" and hermeneutics "with its equally firm conviction that temporality and context are continually reshaping the elusive present" (133).

Semantics. As important and central to language as semantics is, sentence semantics can barely be mentioned here, while lexical semantics can only be named. Besides their grammatical relations within a clause as subject, object, and indirect object, noun phrases have semantic roles such as agent, patient, instrument, recipient, locative, and temporal (see Fillmore). In "Alice gave Eric the prize in Atlanta yesterday," *Alice* is an agent, *Eric* a recipient, *prize* a patient, *Atlanta* a locative, and *yesterday* a temporal. Such semantic roles do not have fixed connections to grammatical relations: not every agent is a subject, nor is every object a patient. In English, grammatical subjects can have any of several semantic roles: as agent in "The jailer opened the gate with the key"; as instrument in "The key opened the gate"; as patient in "The gate opened"; as locative in "Maine suffers extremes of hot and cold"; and as temporal in "Tuesday is our busiest day." English is exceptional in permitting such a wide range of semantic roles as subjects. Many other languages, including even close relatives like German, permit fewer semantic roles as grammatical subjects, and the direct equivalents of certain sentences given above would therefore be ungrammatical in those languages.

SOURCES OF LINGUISTIC DATA

As a consequence of different focuses and subfields, preferred sources of linguistic data also differ. Field work involving elicitation sessions with bilingual or monolingual speakers of the language being analyzed is a classic source of data for grammatical, lexical, and phonological data. Supported by gestures and simple props, elicitation sessions consist basically of questions and answers, and they produce phrases, clauses, and sentences, rather than discourse, as data. For some linguists, introspection suffices; they ask themselves and others about the grammaticality of imagined (and sometimes farfetched) sentences. For still others, natural-language texts, from historical records to transcribed conversations, serve as data. Narratives, an important source of discourse data, are available in many forms. For naturally occurring speech, portable audio and video recorders make it possible to gather data anywhere, from African villages and Native American reservations to urban street corners and suburban shopping malls, and it can be collected by formal or subtle interview techniques or by participant observation. Psycholinguists, especially those interested in sentence processing, construct experimental situations in which consultants (sometimes unwittingly) perform linguistic tasks that provide special data. To investigate language acquisition, some linguists engage in lengthy and detailed taping and transcription of children's discourse, while others use little more than introspection and logic. Thus linguists take as data any form of written, spoken, or signed language, whether naturally occurring or elicited; and some linguists, especially those in the generative framework, take intuitions and judgments of grammaticality as data. Linguists working with various sources of data have been called field linguists, bush linguists, armchair linguists, street linguists, and so on. Because particular sources of data are naturally skewed in one direction or another, each source needs to be supplemented by others, for only when complementary sources of data produce compatible findings can investigators be confident about the validity of their analyses, as William Labov has noted.

STANDARDS AND STYLES, REGISTERS AND DIALECTS

Standard languages and dialects are familiar notions to readers of this volume. From a historical point of view, standard languages are simply dialects that have undergone certain processes of standardization, whereby a designated dialect is elaborated in form to meet an expanded range of functions and is then codified in dictionaries and grammars. The standardized variety is used in the legal, medical, educational, and other professional affairs of a nation, as well as in the mass media. Linguists reject the folk view that nonstandard dialects are corruptions of the standard variety and instead view all dialects of a language (including the standard variety) as descendants of a single ancestor tongue, the standard simply being the variety selected—for political, social, economic, and other nonlinguistic reasons—for development as a vehicle of wider communication, especially in writing.

The concept of register is less familiar than that of dialect, and it can be introduced by considering multilingual speech communities, whose linguistic repertoires comprise varieties drawn from several languages. In multilingual communities, particular languages tend to serve particular domains of use: one language in the home, another in business or education, a third in religious ceremonies (e.g., Yiddish, English, and Hebrew among older New York City Jewish families; Spanish, English, and Latin among Latinos in Los Angeles thirty years ago). Thus, within multilingual communities marked linguistic variation can exist from situation to situation. The same is true in monolingual communities, which also mark different communicative situations with different language varieties. The term *registers* refers to language varieties characteristic of particular situations of use, and the linguistic features of those registers reflect the communicative, situational, and social circumstances surrounding their use. At the very least, a change of topic (e.g., from the national pastime to the national debt) will necessitate a change in vocabulary, but registers can differ from one another in as many ways as languages differ, though less strikingly, of course. Registers are less studied by linguists than dialects are (and they are often less salient to speakers), although some registers (e.g., motherese, legalese, conversation, and advertising) have been thoroughly analyzed (see Ferguson; Crystal and Davy; Levi and Walker; Ghadessy).

Linguists' registers are akin to literary analysts' genres, but the two are not altogether equivalent. Although the genres of literary language, from a linguistic point of view, are not different in principle from other registers, literary language has received special attention from linguists (see Freeman; Jakobson; Kiparsky; Leech and Short; Pratt; and Sebeok; see also Culler in this volume). Approaches differ: some linguists analyze prose fiction, others poetic verse; some treat syntax, others meter; and so forth. One recent approach to English prose style tracks functionally related sets of linguistic features in fiction, essays, and letters over the past four centuries and finds parallel evolution in all three registers (Biber and Finegan). For example, just as first-person and second-person pronouns, interrogative sentences, contractions, hedges (e.g., *sort of, kind of*), and several other linguistic features characterize conversation and tend to co-occur frequently in that register but not in, say, typical academic articles, so other sets of linguistic features co-occur with regularity in other kinds of discourse (see Biber for details). Three such feature sets have been associated with literate versus oral styles, where *literate* means characteristic of typical written styles but does not necessarily entail writing (e.g., scholarly monographs and lectures) and *oral* means characteristic of spoken styles but does not necessarily entail speech (e.g., conversations and personal letters).

The linguistic features of each set share communicative and conventional functions that account for their co-occurrence in particular kinds of texts. For example, frequent nouns and prepositions, longer words, and lexical variety typically characterize language that is informative in purpose. Frequent relative clauses and a marked absence of time and place adverbs (*now* and *yesterday; here* and *above*) typify relatively context-independent discourse. Personal involvement is signaled by first-person and second-person pronouns and by various devices such as contractions and ellipsis that condense expression. Sometimes two feature sets represent opposite poles of a single situational dimension. For

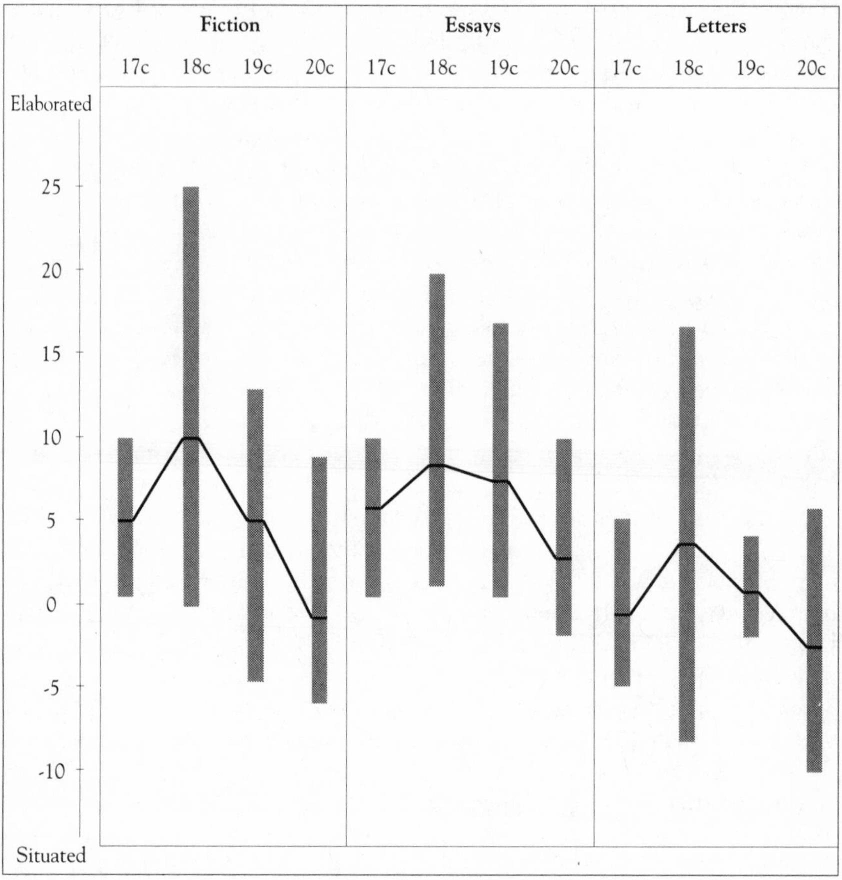

Fig. 2. The movement of three English-language registers along the elaborated-situated dimension during the past four centuries. Solid lines connect the mean values for each register. Adapted from Biber and Finegan.

example, with respect to informational versus involved purposes, texts typically show relatively frequent use of one set of defining features or the other but not both. In the historical study of English fiction, essays, and letters mentioned above, the linguistic features representing three dimensions were tracked: informational versus involved purposes, explicit reference versus context dependence, and abstract versus concrete style.

Because the frequencies of the defining features of a dimension determine a characterization of each text along that dimension, texts of any period and any register can be compared with those of other periods and registers. The past four centuries have witnessed a drift of English fiction, essays, and letters from relatively explicit, or "elaborated," to relatively more context-dependent, or "situated," reference, as shown in figure 2 (where solid lines show average values for each century and the length of the vertical bars represents the range of texts).

This drift reflects, among other things, a decrease in the number of relative clauses and nominalizations (e.g., *establishment, sincerity*) and an increase in the number of time and place adverbs that characterize texts of these registers. Note in figure 2, however, that the eighteenth century bucks the trend and exhibits more explicit referencing strategies (i.e., more elaboration) than the seventeenth century does. While some eighteenth-century writers advanced the trend toward more situated forms of reference in fiction and letters, others (staunch neoclassicists like Samuel Johnson) wrote prose works with higher levels of elaborated reference than writers of the preceding or the two following centuries did. The other two dimensions, which are not illustrated here, display the same overall patterns: prose moved from relatively more informational to relatively more involved and from relatively abstract to relatively nonabstract. In sum, the patterns along all three dimensions indicate that English prose has become increasingly "oral" since the seventeenth century, although eighteenth-century prose was on average exceptionally "literate."

THE FUTURE OF LINGUISTICS

Linguistic analysis has thrived on dichotomies, oppositions, contrasts; the field has exhibited a tendency to see things in black and white, as "either/or" rather than "more or less." But the dichotomies of the past are proving inadequate to accommodate the depth and range of observations confronting linguists now, and a recent trend has been to analyze language more in terms of "squishes," of tendencies instead of absolutes, and to view language forms along parameters of continuous variation. Tightly constrained models (e.g., dichotomies between grammatical and ungrammatical structures or between speech and writing) fail to accommodate observations of actual language use. In this connection, the use of computers has had two notable effects on linguistic analysis. On the one hand, computers show clearly how inadequate many rules of grammar really are: when programmed into a completely obedient and perfectly dumb computer, the output of such rules is quite feeble compared with natural discourse and is often ungrammatical. On the other hand, when large bodies of text are analyzed by computational techniques, the continuous variability of language along multiple situational dimensions becomes more comprehensible, the patterns behind the data less opaque.

To return to a question raised earlier in this essay, we can ask whether linguistic analysis should be undertaken from essentially social or essentially psychological perspectives. To some extent, of course, this is an empirical question: Are the shapes of sentences and of discourse determined solely by psychological factors or solely by social factors? But if we assume, as many linguists do, that both psychological and social factors are critical to valid language analysis, the contest between these points of view can be seen as partly political: What are the implications of limiting linguistics to the study of Language (with a capital *L*), of discounting differences among languages and dialects and ignoring the contingent effects of history and cultural evolution? Is it what we as human beings share linguistically that joins us in the human community, or is humanity equally defined by the ways in which communities differ from one another? Alternatively, what are the implications of giving prominence to contingent factors, to existing and potential social structures, to examining discourse as empowering or disenfranchising? Is rhetoric merely the dress of thought, or are languages and thoughts mutually implicated? Some linguists believe that Language must first be studied acontextually, in an idealized state analogous to the physicist's vacuum. Others are persuaded that a linguistics devoid of context and a view of Language devoid of variation do violence to the social nature of languages and shunt aside questions of social justice and of epistemology, ignoring the role of languages as primary instruments of social construction and shared knowledge; further, autonomous views of grammar clearly tend to ignore verbal art and leave it with an impoverished linguistic foundation.

This essay expresses the viewpoint that language is essentially social *and* essentially psychological and that neither languages nor Language can be understood without attention to both. The grammatical representations that underlie language use surely reside in the brain and will one day be given a neurological account. Just as surely, the neurology of language has taken form under the influence of the structures and functions of social intercourse. Presumably (some would say "obviously") communication and social interaction have helped Language evolve into its current shape in the brain, languages and dialects evolve into their myriad forms across speech communities, and registers develop to meet the peculiar challenges of an endless array of communicative situations. For today's linguistics to focus exclusively on either one or the other of these fundamentally important aspects of language would certainly limit progress in the field as a whole. For any branch of linguistics to attempt to define the others out of court would be shortsighted, if not foolhardy.

Suggestions for Further Reading

The World's Major Languages, by Bernard Comrie, is a useful reference work, containing chapters on forty languages, including Spanish, French, Portuguese, Italian, German, Dutch, English, Russian, Japanese, Chinese, and Arabic; each chapter provides useful information about the structure of the language and its writing system, as well as something of its history and social setting; Comrie has separately collected those chapters treating the major languages of western Europe, while Martin Harris and Nigel Vincent have collected and augmented the chapters on the Romance languages. Peter Trudgill's *Language in the British Isles* covers English in various aspects and the Celtic languages (which are not covered in Comrie), as well as Channel Island French, Romani, and others. Charles A. Ferguson and Shirley Brice Heath provide coverage of American Indian languages (which are not treated by Comrie); New World Spanish; other languages used in the United States, including German and French; and the registers of law, medicine, and education.

Geoffrey Leech and Michael H. Short take a quite different approach to stylistics than that of Douglas Biber and Edward Finegan illustrated in this chapter; Leech and Short focus primarily on the qualitative, whereas Biber and Finegan mix quantitative analysis and qualitative interpretation. Roger Fowler gives a useful introduction to stylistic issues, while Michael Toolan, analyzing Faulkner's *Go Down Moses*, also includes informative chapters on the current state of stylistics. Reflecting a 1958 symposium at which Roman Jakobson delivered extensive closing remarks on poetics and stylistics, Thomas A. Sebeok's *Style in Language* remains a classic collection of essays, while Donald C. Freeman's volume includes more recent pieces. Paul Kiparsky and Gilbert Youmans offer a collection of original articles on rhythm and meter.

Gunther Kress's essay is a brief review of critical discourse analysis; the works of both Roger Andersen and Diane Macdonell exemplify critical language studies at greater length; Tony Crowley applies critical techniques to the notion of standard English. Kenji Hakuta's *Mirror of Language* and Suzanne Romaine's *Bilingualism* are good on bilingualism. Deborah Tannen's *Linguistics in Context* is a wide-ranging and accessible collection of lectures on humanistic approaches to linguistic analysis delivered in 1985 by various scholars at institutes sponsored by the Linguistic Society of America, Teachers of English to Speakers of Other Languages, and the National Endowment for the Humanities. The excitement of the debate between autonomous grammarians and functionalists is palpable in a special issue of *Language and Communication* (ed. Harris and Taylor). In *The Politics of Linguistics*, Frederick J. Newmeyer defends an autonomous view; Terence Moore and Christine Carling are critical. Also critical is Claude Hagège's *Dialogic Species*, a best-seller in France, now available in an English translation. On discourse analysis, the works by Deborah Schiffrin, Michael Stubbs, and Teun van Dijk are all useful. John Haiman's collection records the proceedings of a 1983 symposium on iconicity in syntax.

Several introductory linguistics texts are available, including one by Elizabeth Closs Traugott and Mary Louise Pratt expressly for students of literature; Edward Finegan and Niko Besnier provide a more recent treatment not specifically geared to literary interests, as do William O'Grady et al. David Crystal's one-volume *Encyclopedia*, as lavishly illustrated as a coffee-table book, offers good coverage for a range of more popular language topics, while his *Dictionary* is clear and useful. Exceptional breadth and currency is provided in the 750 entries of the *International Encyclopedia of Linguistics*, edited by William Bright in four volumes; it contains articles on hundreds of languages and language groups, as well as on specialized linguistic topics (government-binding theory, parts of speech, phonology), topics of literary interest (stylistics, poetics, ethnopoetics), and a few individual scholars (Jakob Grimm, Roman Jakobson). Comrie's *Language Universals and Linguistic Typology* is an accessible treatment of that topic; John A. Hawkins makes typological comparisons between German and English. Beyond basic texts, *Linguistics: The Cambridge Survey*, edited by Newmeyer, is recommended, although some of its essays are of moderate difficulty.

Among journals, *Language*, published by the Linguistic Society of America, is highly respected; it and the *Journal of Linguistics*, published by Cambridge University Press for the Linguistics Association of Great Britain, represent the field most widely. *Linguistic Inquiry* treats a wide range of topics in formal grammar. Covering discourse analysis are *Discourse Processes*, representing various perspectives but with psychological ones predominant, and *Text*, with a more social orientation. *Language Variation and Change*, a recent entry, promises to represent both social and historical aspects of language variation. *Language in Society* has a strong ethnographic representation. *Language and Style* represents the mutual interests of linguistics and literature. *Literary and Linguistic Computing* publishes computer-related analyses of texts.

University of Southern California

Works Cited

Andersen, Roger. *The Power and the Word: Language, Power and Change.* London: Paladin, 1988.

Baron, Dennis E. *Grammar and Good Taste: Reforming the American Language.* New Haven: Yale UP, 1982.

Biber, Douglas. *Variation across Speech and Writing.* Cambridge: Cambridge UP, 1988.

Biber, Douglas, and Edward Finegan. "Drift and the Evolution of English Style: A History of Three Genres." *Language* 65 (1989): 487–517.

Bright, William, ed. *International Encyclopedia of Linguistics.* 4 vols. New York: Oxford UP, 1992.

Chomsky, Noam. *Aspects of the Theory of Syntax.* Cambridge: MIT P, 1965.

———. *Knowledge of Language: Its Nature, Origin, and Use.* New York: Praeger, 1986.

———. *Lectures on Government and Binding: The Pisa Lectures.* Dordrecht: Foris, 1981.

Comrie, Bernard. *Language Universals and Linguistic Typology.* 2nd ed. Chicago: U of Chicago P, 1989.

———, ed. *The Major Languages of Western Europe.* London: Routledge, 1990.

———, ed. *The World's Major Languages.* New York: Oxford UP, 1987.

Crowley, Tony. *Standard English and the Politics of Language.* Urbana: U of Illinois P, 1989.

Crystal, David. *The Cambridge Encyclopedia of Language.* Cambridge: Cambridge UP, 1987.

———. *A Dictionary of Linguistics and Phonetics.* 3rd ed. Oxford: Blackwell, 1991.

Crystal, David, and Derek Davy. *Investigating English Style.* London: Longman, 1969.

Ferguson, Charles A., ed. *Special Language Registers.* Spec. issue of *Discourse Processes* 8.4 (1985): 391–454.

Ferguson, Charles A., and Shirley Brice Heath, eds. *Language in the USA.* Cambridge: Cambridge UP, 1981.

Fillmore, Charles J. "The Case for Case." *Universals in Linguistic Theory.* Ed. Emmon Bach and Robert T. Harms. New York: Holt, 1968. 1–88.

Finegan, Edward. *Attitudes toward English Usage: The History of a War of Words.* New York: Teachers Coll. P, 1980.

Finegan, Edward, and Niko Besnier. *Language: Its Structure and Use.* San Diego: Harcourt, 1989.

Fleischman, Suzanne. *The Future in Thought and Language: Diachronic Evidence from Romance.* Cambridge: Cambridge UP, 1982.

Fowler, Roger. *Linguistic Criticism.* Oxford: Oxford UP, 1986.

Fox, Barbara A., and Sandra A. Thompson. "A Discourse Explanation of the Grammar of Relative Clauses in English Conversation." *Language* 66 (1990): 297–316.

Freeman, Donald C., ed. *Essays in Modern Stylistics.* London: Methuen, 1981.

Gee, James Paul. *Social Linguistics and Literacies: Ideology in Discourses.* London: Falmer, 1990.

Ghadessy, Mohsen, ed. *Registers of Written English: Situational Factors and Linguistic Features.* London: Pinter, 1988.

Givón, T[almy]. *Syntax: A Functional-Typological Introduction.* Amsterdam: Benjamins, 1984.

Gumperz, John J., and Dell Hymes, eds. *Directions in Sociolinguistics: The Ethnography of Communication.* New York: Holt, 1972; Oxford: Blackwell, 1986.

Hagège, Claude. *The Dialogic Species: A Linguistic Contribution to the Social Sciences.* Trans. Sharon L. Shelly. New York: Columbia UP, 1990. Trans. of *L'homme de paroles.* Paris: Arthème Fayard, 1985.

Haiman, John, ed. *Iconicity in Syntax.* Amsterdam: Benjamins, 1985.

Hakuta, Kenji. *Mirror of Language: The Debate on Bilingualism.* New York: Basic, 1986.

Harris, Martin. *The Evolution of French Syntax: A Comparative Approach.* London: Longman, 1978.

Harris, Martin, and Nigel Vincent, eds. *The Romance Languages.* New York: Oxford UP, 1988.

Harris, Roy, and Talbot Taylor, eds. Spec. issue of *Language and Communication* 11 (1991): 1–114.

Hawkins, John A. *A Comparative Typology of English and German: Unifying the Contrasts.* Austin: U of Texas P, 1986.

Hockey, Susan. *A Guide to Computer Applications in the Humanities.* Baltimore: Johns Hopkins UP, 1980.

Hopper, Paul. "Emergent Grammar and the A Priori Grammar Postulate." Tannen, *Linguistics* 117–34.

Hymes, Dell. *Foundations in Sociolinguistics.* Philadelphia: U of Pennsylvania P, 1974.

Jaeggli, Osvaldo A. "Passive." *Linguistic Inquiry* 17 (1986): 587–622.

Jakobson, Roman. *Verbal Art, Verbal Sign, Verbal Time.* Ed. Krystyna Pomorska and Stephen Rudy. Minneapolis: U of Minnesota P, 1985.

Kiparsky, Paul. "The Role of Linguistics in a Theory of Poetry." *Language as a Human Problem.* Ed. Morton Bloomfield and Einar Haugen. New York: Norton, 1974. 233–46.

Kiparsky, Paul, and Gilbert Youmans, eds. *Phonetics and Phonology: Rhythm and Meter.* Orlando: Academic, 1989.

Kress, Gunther. "Critical Discourse Analysis." *Annual Review of Applied Linguistics* 11 (1991): 84–99.

Kroch, Anthony S. "Reflexes of Grammar in Patterns of Language Change." *Language Variation and Change* 1 (1990): 199–244.

Labov, William. *Sociolinguistic Patterns.* Philadelphia: U of Pennsylvania P, 1972.

Leech, Geoffrey, and Michael H. Short. *Style in Fiction: A Linguistic Introduction to English Fictional Prose.* London: Longman, 1981.

Levi, Judith N., and Anne Graffam Walker, eds. *Language in the Judicial Process.* New York: Plenum, 1990.

Levinson, Stephen C. *Pragmatics.* Cambridge: Cambridge UP, 1983.

Lightfoot, David W. "Syntactic Change." Newmeyer, *Linguistics* 1: 303–23.

Macdonell, Diane. *Theories of Discourse: An Introduction.* Oxford: Blackwell, 1986.

Miall, David S., ed. *Humanities and the Computer: New Directions.* Oxford: Oxford UP, 1990.

Milroy, James, and Lesley Milroy. *Authority in Language: Investigating Language Prescription and Standardisation.* 2nd ed. London: Routledge, 1991.

Moore, Terence, and Christine Carling. *Understanding Language: Towards a Post-Chomskyan Linguistics.* London: Macmillan, 1982.

Newmeyer, Frederick J., ed. *Linguistics: The Cambridge Survey.* 4 vols. Cambridge: Cambridge UP, 1988.

———. *The Politics of Linguistics.* Chicago: U of Chicago P, 1986.

O'Grady, William, Michael Dubrovolsky, and Mark Aronoff. *Contemporary Linguistics: An Introduction.* New York: St. Martin's, 1989.

Pratt, Mary Louise. *Toward a Speech Act Theory of Literary Discourse.* Bloomington: Indiana UP, 1977.

Romaine, Suzanne. *Bilingualism.* Oxford: Blackwell, 1989.

———. *Socio-historical Linguistics: Its Status and Methodology.* Cambridge: Cambridge UP, 1982.

Saussure, Ferdinand de. *Course in General Linguistics.* Trans. Wade Baskin. New York: McGraw, 1966.

Schiffrin, Deborah. *Discourse Markers.* Cambridge: Cambridge UP, 1987.

Sebeok, Thomas A., ed. *Style in Language.* Cambridge: MIT P, 1960.

Sinclair, J[ohn] M., ed. *Looking Up: An Account of the COBUILD Project in Lexical Computing and the Development of the Collins COBUILD English Language Dictionary.* London: Collins, 1987.

Stubbs, Michael. *Discourse Analysis: The Sociolinguistic Analysis of Natural Language.* Chicago: U of Chicago P, 1983.

Tannen, Deborah, ed. *Linguistics in Context: Connecting Observation and Understanding.* Norwood: Ablex, 1988.

———. *Talking Voices: Repetition, Dialogue, and Imagery in Conversational Discourse.* Cambridge: Cambridge UP, 1989.

Toolan, Michael. *The Stylistics of Fiction: A Literary-Linguistic Approach.* London: Routledge, 1990.

Traugott, Elizabeth Closs. "On the Rise of Epistemic Meanings in English: An Example of Subjectification in Semantic Change." *Language* 65 (1989): 31–55.

Traugott, Elizabeth Closs, and Bernd Heine, eds. *Approaches to Grammaticalization.* 2 vols. Amsterdam: Benjamins, 1991.

Traugott, Elizabeth Closs, and Mary Louise Pratt. *Linguistics for Students of Literature.* New York: Harcourt, 1980.

Trudgill, Peter, ed. *Language in the British Isles.* Cambridge: Cambridge UP, 1984.

———. *The Social Differentiation of English in Norwich.* Cambridge: Cambridge UP, 1974.

van Dijk, Teun, ed. *Handbook of Discourse Analysis.* 4 vols. New York: Academic, 1985.

Watkins, Calvert. "New Parameters in Historical Linguistics, Philology, and Culture History." *Language* 65 (1989): 783–99.

Weinreich, Uriel, William Labov, and Marvin I. Herzog. "Empirical Foundations for a Theory of Language Change." *Directions for Historical Linguistics: A Symposium.* Ed. W. P. Lehmann and Yakov Malkiel. Austin: U of Texas P, 1968. 95–188.

DENNIS BARON

Language, Culture, and Society

ONCE interconnected under the broad term *philology*, literary and linguistic scholarship became divorced for much of the twentieth century, with departments of language and literature tending to emphasize literary culture at the expense of the equally important study of language. Yet the more recent focus on theory in the humanities—together with the analysis and redefinition of the literary canon, the development of women's studies and gender studies, speculation on pedagogy and the role of the computer, and an interdisciplinary interest in writing process and product—has led to a reintegration of linguistics into the curriculum as an essential discipline offering insight into basic questions of orality and literacy, the cultural significance of language, and human social behavior in general. Linguistics, too, has changed during recent years, moving outward from phonological and syntactic theory and a concentration on idealized forms of language to a broader concern with language acquisition, second-language teaching, and the study of language in its social setting (see, for example, the essays by Finegan and Kramsch, in this volume).

Along with bipedal locomotion and the opposable thumb, the phenomenon we call language is often cited as a defining characteristic of the human species. So strong is this identification of language with human nature that anthropologists study hominid fossils looking for evolutionary clues to the origins of speech. Some humans, however, seem reluctant to share language with other species: great and still unresolved controversies have arisen over the past two decades as experimenters began claiming success in teaching primates to communicate symbolically. There is a tendency to treat language as the personal property not only of the species but of the individual as well. So commonplace now is the notion that language functions to express the psychological nuances of personality, and so striking is the idiosyncrasy of language in our daily experience—the amusing twists and turns of a child learning to speak, the anonymous but unmistakable voice of a friend on the answering machine, the psychoanalytic insights language offers the therapist, the stylistic fingerprint of an accomplished novelist—that we may easily forget that language is above all a social phenomenon.

There are no groups of humans who do not use language to communicate, and some evidence suggests that language cannot develop in individuals isolated from social groups. In addition, living languages change over time, and while each linguistic innovation must originate at the level of the individual language user, a variant form must also be accepted at the level of the group for it to become a part of the language. Language change and the development of language standards are features not only of time passing but of conscious innovation and social conditioning as well. It is the larger culture that determines language attitudes and validates linguistic norms; that ignores variation, condemns it as an error, or celebrates it as a creative insight; and that sorts the users of language into the average or the chosen or the damned.

Convinced that language both reflects and influences culture and society, humanistic linguists and their colleagues in anthropology, education, law, philosophy, psychology, public policy, and sociology have begun to examine the social context of language use, producing studies that range from global theories of orality and literacy, to national language policy and planning, to local annotated descriptions of turn-taking in conversations. Perhaps the most interesting of these developments for students of language and literature explore the clash between majority and minority language rights that is often aggravated in the selection of an official language; the roles of standard and nonstandard dialects in school and the workplace; the problem of literacy in both developing and technologically advanced societies; and the vexed question of language and gender. We must consider as well the ongoing controversy over the ethical position of the linguist as an agent affecting language attitudes, language planning, and language change. There are, of course, many important, even central, areas that an essay such as this, which is necessarily limited in scope, must regrettably ignore in order to present a coherent introduction to the general topic.

LANGUAGE AND NATION

Language use carries not only the idiosyncratic stamp of the individual but the mark of the nation as well. Consequently, language becomes both a primary vehicle for the transmission of group culture and a badge of national identification. Perhaps the most commonly cited example of the relation between language and culture is the number and variety of words for *snow* in the Eskimo, or, more properly, the Inuit, language. Inuit has words for falling snow, snow on the ground, encrusted snow, and some twenty others, while English speakers, for whom snow has less central a cultural position, have a rather more limited set of terms. We must avoid the common assumption, however, that language inevitably limits perception. Inuit is no better adapted than English for expressing snow terms, nor is English more civilized than Inuit, or somehow better suited to the abstractions and divagations of literary theory. Both languages express what their speakers wish or need to express, and an English speaker can refer to powder, crusty snow, packing snow for snowballs or for building forts, and sooty mounds of snow piled up by plows at street corners as readily as an Inuit can deconstruct the supposed *cinéma vérité* of Robert Flaherty's documentary *Nanook of the North* (1922).

Languages carve up the color spectrum differently—the English shades of dark and light blue are two distinct colors in Russian. They also disagree on the linguistic spectrum. The very definition of languages is influenced by social or political factors as well as linguistic ones. Though to an external observer, Danish, Swedish, and Norwegian may constitute mutually understandable Scandinavian dialects, they are classified as separate languages by their speakers, who prefer that distinct tongues separate their distinct political units. In contrast, the Chinese consider the mutually incomprehensible spoken varieties of Cantonese, Mandarin, Hakka, Hunan, North and South Min, Wu, and so forth not as separate languages but as dialects of an all-embracing, culturally unifying Chinese (see Halliday, McIntosh, and Strevens).

In extreme cases, the power of language to signal ethnicity can be deadly. According to the Old Testament (Judges 12.4–6), when the Ephraimites tried to cross the Jordan into Gilead, Jephthah asked them to say the Hebrew word *shibboleth*, literally and appropriately "stream in flood." Because they were unable to pronounce the *sh* sound, the Ephraimites failed the password test and were killed. So powerful is the story that the word *shibboleth* has come in English to mean any test, linguistic or otherwise, that can reveal a person's identity or allegiance.

Reaction to groups whose language is different or unfamiliar is not always so negative, though it is frequently as unsubtle and very often entails significant consequences. While a number of the Europeans who came to what they called the New World in the fifteenth and sixteenth centuries regarded the American natives as entirely without language and therefore subhuman (a view typified in the portrayal of Caliban, the "cannibal" in Shakespeare's *Tempest*), others identified the speakers of what were perceived to be brave new tongues as descendants of the lost tribes of Israel or as purely innocent and rational beings whose enviably transparent language was an uncorrupted, transcendental reflex of the natural world. In the long run, though, neither of these idealistic views of the American languages prevailed. Instead, the realities of colonial occupation ensured the dominance of European languages at the expense of the indigenous ones, which were absorbed, destroyed, or permanently relegated to secondary status (see Greenblatt for a detailed account of the initial European reactions to New World language).

In elaborations of the age-old assumption that language reflects national identity, the German philosopher Johann Gottlieb Fichte and the philologist Wilhelm von Humboldt asserted the natural superiority of their language in contrast to the failings of more primitive forms of speech in nationalistic essays that drew legitimate charges of racism from their critics. In a more scientific attempt to state the language-nation connection, the twentieth-century American linguists Edward Sapir and Benjamin Lee Whorf maintained that because language controls the individual's perception of reality, no two languages perceive the natural world in exactly the same way. While linguists today reject the strong, deterministic form of the Sapir-Whorf hypothesis, which would render translation, borrowing, and linguistic innovation virtually impossible, they do acknowledge a weaker version of the theory arguing that language influences perception (see Kramsch in this volume). Confirming experiments have shown, predictably, that it is easier to understand and remember phenomena for which linguistic patterns already exist than it is to deal with entities or concepts for which there are no words. But as literary artists have long understood, the inconvenience of the unknown may be a temporary phenomenon: the human imagination quickly adapts new data to old language patterns or invents ways to deal with new situations.

If language is a prison house, occasionally preventing us from noticing the details of the reality outside us, it is also a vital means by which we harness that reality, making it our own. European explorers in the Western Hemisphere transported Old World names for the flora, fauna, and geography they encountered (*corn, robin, creek*), or they borrowed native terms (*peyote, skunk, woodchuck*) or words from other colonial languages (*hoosegow, lariat, prairie*), or they innovated (*bluebird, bluff, prairie oyster*), just as today's physicists and astronomers translate their complex equations and predictions into *quarks, quasars*, and *black holes*. John Keats may have been nodding when in "On First Looking into Chapman's Homer" he depicted "stout Cortez" rather than Balboa discovering the Pacific Ocean, but the explorers also made mistakes, naming the *turkey bird* as such because they thought it came from the East (similarly, the French called it *d'Inde*, the bird "from India," which survives in the modern French term for the great fowl, *dinde*). And they mistakenly named the natives of the Americas because the first explorers thought they had found a western passage to India.

In addition to its most basic functions of communication and expression, language takes on symbolic value as the embodiment of a culture. It has come to represent the most potent symbol of group identity and local or nationalistic pride. It is also a prime element in cultural myth and group cohesion, whether the group is narrowly defined (the jargon of computer programmers, the argot of criminals) or broadly (the presumed democratic character of classical Greek; the self-proclaimed rationality of French; the sacred nature of Hebrew, Arabic, and Sanskrit). With language perceived to represent the spirit of a group or a nation, it functions at a political as well as a social level. National literature comes to epitomize the values of society—even when it is critical of those values—and the language in which it is written takes on a sacred as well as a secular character, so that tampering with the literary language may be viewed as anything from a misdemeanor, a minor disturbance to the public order, at one extreme, to nothing short of revolutionary, at the other. The usage critics of English frequently recommend jail sentences, or even capital punishment, for writers brash enough to use, for example, *hopefully* as a sentence adverbial (*Hopefully, this will all be over soon*), a construction that, though widespread, is relatively recent (the earliest *OED* citation is 1932, but the form is rare until the 1960s), or *gift* as a transitive verb (*She gifted him with a necktie*), which has a four-hundred-year history in Standard English writing but is often condemned as wrong today. While no one seriously proposes to hang the violators of English usage conventions, opposition to linguistic innovation and variation is not always rhetorical. In the early 1900s, students and faculty members at the University of Athens protested publicly in order to stop a performance of Aeschylus's *Oresteia* in modern, demotic Greek, and violent demonstrations at the university protesting a modernized translation of the New Testament led to several deaths.

Language and ethnicity, which remain strongly connected in the popular mind, have often been the objects of political manipulation. Despite the myth of the Tower of Babel, which postulates a single, Edenic language and longs for its return, multilingualism is and probably has always been the basic human condition. There are virtually no monolingual states in the world today. Nonetheless, monolingualism is an ideal toward which many societies have gravitated, for a combination of ideological and practical reasons. And in some cases, monolingualism has been imposed—with varying degrees of success—on a linguistically diverse polity (see Calvet; Grillo; Wardhaugh, *Languages*).

The concept of one nation, one language arose in the West as European nation-states developed out of the remnants of the Roman Empire and vernacular languages started to replace Latin as the vehicles of government, education, and literature in the Middle Ages and the Renaissance. In the 1790s, the French government began its formal policy of spreading Parisian French and banning local languages and dialects in order to unify and rationalize the republic under one language, a slow process that was not "completed" until after World War I, though pockets of resistance remain today (Weber). As such, the effort was to create the French people and nation by giving them the French language, resulting in the commonplace notion that to be French is to speak French. Similarly, the complexity of the *questione della lingua*, an ongoing debate in Italy from the time of Dante to the present, rests on the assumption that defining the language is a necessary precursor to establishing the nation. Such assumptions oversimplify linguistic reality: rivalry persists between northern and southern varieties of Italian, and the degree of variation in modern French prompts a thriving business for usage guides in that language.

THE OFFICIAL-LANGUAGE QUESTION

No modern law makes French the official language of France. Nonetheless, France has passed (though it later relaxed) laws to curtail the use of minority languages, and current legislation prohibits the borrowing of foreign words into French. Other nations have considered purifying their languages of what they conceive to be foreign contamination, though usually without much success, at least so far as the informal, spoken language is concerned. In the nineteenth century, and again during the Nazi era, Germany sought to nationalize its language through the creation or revival of native terms to replace foreign borrowings. Reaching outward rather than turning inward, in the late 1920s

Kemal Attaturk romanized the Turkish alphabet as part of his plan to westernize and modernize Turkey.

The establishment of a unifying national language in states whose boundaries encompass several linguistic groups is frequently accompanied by formal or informal restrictions on the use of minority languages (and, occasionally, majority languages). The Turks banned the word *Kurd* from their language, renaming this large ethnic group "Mountain Turks" in a futile attempt to render them invisible and thus less troublesome to the central government. England was successful in actively suppressing Irish, Scots, and Welsh for several centuries at home (and, of course, Cornish and Manx, which have disappeared entirely), while at the same time spreading English as the language of education and administration in its Asian and African colonies. After independence, the Republic of Ireland sought to reverse the decline of Gaelic, giving it official status, establishing Irish-language schools, and offering bounties to families pledging to use the language at home. These efforts have not succeeded in reviving the language.

The Soviet Union alternated between policies of Russification and support for local languages; unrest among Soviet nationalities frequently manifested itself in demands for local language rights. After two centuries, Canadian policies of Anglicization have been reversed and French language rights have been restored at the insistence of the Québecois, though other minority languages in Canada, such as Ukrainian or Urdu, are not similarly protected, a situation that aggravates linguistic tensions in the country. In New Zealand, too, some local languages are treated better than others. The indigenous Maori language is now being taught in English-language schools as part of a reawakened appreciation of the national heritage, though Auckland, which has the largest Polynesian-speaking community in the world, pays no special attention to the linguistic needs of this largely impoverished immigrant group.

In former European colonies, the question of choosing an official language or languages has often brought conflict. The language friction that persists in Canada (as well as similar linguistic strife that developed when two distinct language communities were yoked to form the national state of Belgium in the nineteenth century and when multilingual India gained independence from Britain in 1947) is frequently cited as a warning by supporters of official English in the United States, though observers point out that linguistic violence generally occurs when language rights are suppressed, not when they are guaranteed. Furthermore, despite the presence of large numbers of minority-language speakers throughout its history, the United States without official-language legislation has managed to create what other countries with official-language policies have failed to establish, a society in which upward of ninety-six percent of the population speaks the unofficial national language, English, according to 1980 census figures. Nonetheless, there have been calls to make English (or, occasionally, *American*) the official language of the United States since the nation's founding. Supporters of official English in the United States have argued from both ideological and nativistic grounds, though the stridency of the nativists has often dissuaded more mainstream Americans from supporting restrictive language legislation.

The idea of one nation speaking one language appeals to many Americans who consider discrimination based on race, ethnicity, religion, or gender abhorrent. An official language would create a political and cultural bond among Americans of diverse origins, so the ideological argument goes (bolstering cries for such a bond are 1980 census figures showing that one in seven Americans speaks a language other than English or lives in a home where someone else speaks such a language). Furthermore, official English, according to its advocates, would ensure the continuity of the democratically constituted society whose principles were first articulated in English and can best be understood in that language (official-language supporters, who seem committed to a strong version of the Sapir-Whorf hypothesis, have a natural bias against translation).

In contrast, nativists have supported the official-English movement as part of their two-century-old program to curb immigration and keep the United States ethnically homogeneous. They reacted in the eighteenth and nineteenth centuries against the German presence in the nation, labeling the German language as undemocratic and regarding German speakers as racially distinct from other Americans, as well as lazy, clannish, ignorant, religiously unacceptable, and excessively fertile. German speakers were even accused of causing Pennsylvania's hard winters. Similar unfounded charges have been repeated for each new wave of immigrants who appeared to threaten the stability of those unhyphenated Americans who had finally assimilated after several generations of struggle. Nativists later opposed the influx of immigrants from central and southern Europe between 1880 and World War I.

Today's nativists again warn that the newest immigrants, speakers of Asian languages and Spanish, will turn the United States into an unmanageable, polyglot nation, despite evidence showing that the children of nonanglophones continue to adopt English at an impressive rate. On the local level, English-only advocates propose ordinances requiring that signs be in the Roman alphabet, that grocers pass English tests to satisfy health codes, and that municipal libraries be prohibited from purchasing foreign language materials. They support state official-language laws as well as an amendment to the United States Constitution making English the official language of the nation.

Australia, a largely immigrant country like the United States, is attempting to resolve its multilingual frictions by supporting pluralism after many years of a whites-only, English-only policy. Nonanglophones are encouraged to learn English while retaining their native language. At the same time, English speakers, who remain a clear majority of the population, are encouraged to acquire a second language. Such a policy, known as English Plus, has been proposed for the United States as well, though minority-language retention and foreign language education have typically been unsuccessful in this country on a large scale.

Language policy in the United States, while not formally defined, has always assumed the priority of English in all areas of government, education, and commerce. In addition, as the sociolinguist Joshua Fishman and his colleagues have shown (*Rise and Fall*), language legislation has generally remained the province of the states, the federal government intervening only when the rights of minority-language speakers have been seriously compromised. For example, a number of states outlawed foreign language instruction below the ninth grade in the period during and immediately after World War I. In the landmark cases *Meyer v. Nebraska* (1923) and *Farrington v. Tokushige* (1927), involving the Fourteenth and Fifth amendments, respectively, the United States Supreme Court ruled such legislation unconstitutional. The federal Voting Rights Act of 1965 struck down discriminatory English-literacy tests and protected the rights of nonanglophone citizens to vote in their native language. In the case of *Lau v. Nichols* (1974), the Supreme Court banned what had long been the common practice of schools to ignore the non-English-speaking students in their classrooms. Ordering no specific remedy, the Court instructed school districts to come up with plans to assure non-English-speaking children an education equivalent to that provided their anglophone peers. The ruling has resulted in controversial programs of bilingual education.

It is possible that the official-language question in the United States will come to a head in the 1990s. In the past few years, more than two-thirds of the states have considered some form of official-English legislation, and a number of states have adopted official-English laws, though their effect remains unclear. Nor is it entirely certain what might happen to government language policy should an English Language Amendment (ELA) to the federal Constitution be adopted. Legal practice assumes that in the case of a conflict, more recent legislation has precedence over earlier statutes and legal decisions. It is possible that an ELA would be purely symbolic, producing little or no visible change in the way the American government interacts with its citizens. At the other extreme, the amendment could neutralize earlier minority-language protections based on the Fifth and Fourteenth amendments or on other federal legislation, thereby restricting the use of languages other than English in the United States. It is certain, in any case, that an ELA, if passed, would be subjected to numerous court tests before its effects became clear.

Minority-language rights will become a highly visible problem as the European Community moves toward unification and as Eastern Europe moves out of the Soviet sphere of influence, as it seems to be doing. The United Nations Charter and a number of subsequent international agreements such as the Helsinki Accord have stressed the importance of native-language education, particularly in the early grades, for so-called guest workers and for native linguistic minorities. The provision of social, medical, legal, and other governmental services for these groups in their own languages will prove a controversial challenge as well. It is likely that research in the area of language and nation will concentrate in the next few years on the areas of official-language planning, second-language instruction, and the dynamics of multilingualism.

LANGUAGE VARIETY AND STANDARD LANGUAGE

Debate over an official language raises another complex issue: Whose variety of English (or French, or Spanish, or Hindi) is to be official? Language changes over time, but it also varies over geographical and social space. Linguists have long studied geographical variation through an examination of written texts and, where possible, through the administration of oral questionnaires and the recording of the spoken language in its natural context. Such research frequently concentrates on the speech of older people in rural areas in order to record forms of a language that may be in danger of dying out. More recently, linguists have come to study social variation as well, looking for usage attributable to class, race, and gender. The sociolinguist William Labov demonstrated the linguistic insecurity of the American lower middle class (*Social Stratification*). In their anxiety to climb the social ladder, members of this class consider correct English a badge of success. Consequently, in their speech they often employ forms that they perceive as prestigious but that are in reality nonprestige forms, errors, or hypercorrections. According to Labov, those at the top—the upper-middle-class speakers whom others try to emulate—exhibit a low degree of language anxiety, as do those at the bottom of the social scale, who he argues have little hope of breaking out of the trap of poverty.

In *Language in the Inner City* Labov also contributed greatly to the study of Black English, demonstrating that what had frequently been dismissed as error-laden nonlanguage was actually a logical, rule-governed, and effective form of communication. More recently, the study of minority dialects of English has focused on their origins and their variety, together with the difficulties speakers of nonstandard varieties of English may encounter when faced with the academic English of the American school system (see, e.g., Smitherman; Baugh).

Initially it was assumed that Black English arose on Southern plantations as slaves learned an imperfect version of their masters' language. Some dialectologists, tracing features of Black English to seventeenth-century East Anglia, went so far as to argue that it was no different from Southern white English. However, many experts now believe in the creole origins of Black English. That is to say, they find in Black English a substratum of West African languages with an overlay of English. This evidence suggests the development of Black English in African slave-trading ports, on slave ships coming to America, or on plantations. In all three, slaves from different language backgrounds were mixed together to hamper communication and lessen the chances for revolt. Defeating the intentions of the traders and owners, the slaves forged a pidgin, or contact, language, an amalgam of their different languages and dialects that served in a limited way to meet their most immediate communication needs. According to the theory, the pidgin eventually expanded, or became creolized, assuming the more general functions of language (including rhetorical and literary use) and becoming more and more like English, the language from which the creole eventually drew most of its grammar and vocabulary (in Haiti, where the administrative language was French, the slaves developed a French–West African creole).

Despite the general acceptance of the creole theory, in recent years sociolinguists have been finding less evidence of creolization in the historical record. Walt Wolfram is one of several researchers in this area calling for a refinement and reevaluation of the accounts of the origins of Black English. Linguists now recognize as well that there are many varieties of Black English, related to age, social class, and the context of communication. Research in the next decade will examine these varieties and their relation to the notion of standard English. Labov (*Increasing Divergence*) has warned, however, that black and white varieties of English are diverging as the social distance between the races increases, particularly at the lower levels of American society. Although Labov's claim has received much publicity in the popular press, the validity of the data on which it is based has been questioned (see, for example, the well-taken comments of Butters as well as those of Wolfram). The perceived distance between Black and white English is widely regarded as one reason for the failure of many minority children in American schools, and linguists are likely to pay more attention in the years to come both to the divergence hypothesis as proposed by Labov and to ways in which language education in schools can help bridge this gap.

The question of language variety leads inevitably to the question of standard language, the spoken or written dialect of a distinct class of language users that in many societies is promoted by the schools and the culture in general as a model to be emulated by all. In some cases, as with French and Italian, language academies were set up as long ago as the sixteenth century to adjudicate usage disputes and to promulgate dictionaries and grammars of acceptable speech and writing. Speakers of English have traditionally resisted the formation of a language academy, preferring to derive their standards indirectly from literature, from language commentaries, and from a loosely defined approximation of what they see as educated usage (see Heath).

The word *standard* as a measurement of correctness or perfection first appeared in English in the fifteenth century, but it was not connected with language until the eighteenth, when it was applied to Greek and French, languages whose reputed superiority was frequently held up for users of English to envy. *Standard* was not joined to English until the nineteenth century (the first *OED* citation is from 1836), though such expressions as the *King's English*, the *King's language*, and *Received English* do occur before that, giving evidence for an early and ongoing concern with correct, good, or approved English. However, the strong association of the term *standard* with precisely defined and regulated weights and measures, as well as with monetary systems, creates the illusion that standard language has scientific validity, that it can be defined and copied, like the standard meter or kilogram, and that it has the same currency for everyone.

It is commonly supposed, for one thing, that a standard of usage exists for English, and for other languages as well, that all agree on, a standard that may be described with some precision, reduced to a few simple rules, and imposed on an entire nation, if not the whole English- or French- or Russian-speaking world. As a concession to the varieties of English used in such diverse areas as Australia, Britain, Canada, India, Ireland, New Zealand, Nigeria, and the United States, we usually—though sometimes reluctantly—acknowledge the existence of regional or national spoken and written standards (see Kachru for a discussion of English varieties in Asia). Arabic similarly recognizes regional or national standards as well as the more universal literary standard of the Koranic language. But whether we are dealing with standards or Standard, we are invariably thwarted by the problem of definition.

Try as they have, linguists have achieved nothing even closely approximating an exhaustive description of the varieties of English or any other modern language. Nor have they arrived at an understanding of the complex nature of language standards and the degree of variability permissible within what can be broadly termed acceptable usage. Put simply, the grammars and dictionaries of language are all open-ended. No matter how many correct ways of saying things we manage to collect, many are missed, and more still have yet to be invented.

Ever since the publication of Claude Favre Vaugelas's *Remarqves svr la langve françois*, in 1659, the question of good usage in French has produced volumes of debate. Recent studies (for example, Harmer) suggest that after two centuries of centrally controlled language education, variation in French is as common as ever. Similarly, speakers of English seldom agree on what they mean by Standard English, beyond an identification of it with a vague prestige norm, and though the schools are frequently blamed for a failure to inculcate good English usage, there is little agreement on how acceptable language use is to be enforced. Instead, it is generally easier to reach a consensus on what is *not* standard—for example, double negatives (*I don't got none*), errors in subject-verb agreement (*they was*) or in the concord of pronouns with their referents (*Everyone put on their coat*).

Frequently, the usage experts find themselves on opposite sides of an issue. In his *Desk-Book of Errors in English* (1907), the lexicographer Frank Vizetelly proscribed the common time-telling expression *a quarter of seven* on the grounds that it literally means "one and three-quarters"—that is, "seven divided by four." Vizetelly favored the phrase *a quarter to seven* as more correct. Taking an opposite though equally absurd position based on the same restriction of language to the literal, the grammarian Josephine Turck Baker in her book *Correct English* (also 1907) contended that *to* means "in the direction of" or "toward" and insisted that *a quarter to seven* can therefore only mean "one quarter of an hour in the direction of seven," or *six fifteen*. Baker chose as the only correct way to tell time the one rejected by Vizetelly. This standoff leaves the perplexed seeker after Standard English to select between two equally illogical expressions. Neither expert mentioned *a quarter till seven*, a common variant that is still generally snubbed by the usage critics as dialectal, nor did they have the foresight to predict that the more neutral *six forty-five* would become the form most appropriate to today's digital timepieces.

As the linguist and usage critic Bergen Evans has shown, rules of correctness seem made to be broken. It is impossible to deny the existence of acceptable variation in English even in so apparently standard an area as subject-verb agreement. In British English, collective nouns like *band* (as in *rock band*), *government*, and *corporation* are treated as plurals, while Americans employ them in the singular. Even within the United States there is disagreement over the status of *data*, scrupulously construed as a plural by number-crunching researchers unwilling to seem ignorant of Latin but more freely treated as a singular among the general population. Other Latin plurals—for example, *media* and *phenomena*—are frequently construed as English singulars, and many unclassical academics use the Latin genitive *vitae*, from *curriculum vitae*, "course of life," as the equivalent of *vita* or *resume* (this latter form also appears in our dictionaries of Standard English as the variously accented *resumé* and *résumé*).

Variation in pronoun concord is permitted as well. Evans illustrates this by citing the unquestionably binding, if grammatically discordant, language of the United States Constitution: "Each House shall keep a journal of its proceedings, and from time to time publish the same, excepting such parts as may in *their* judgment require secrecy" (art. 1, sec. 5, subsec. 3; emphasis added). *Their* is no slip of the federalist quill. Rather, it is clear evidence—one of countless examples cited by the chroniclers of English—of the perfectly standard process whereby meaning overrides formal grammatical rules.

Even so stigmatized a word as *ain't* has its defenders, and its place in informal, Standard English speech, an undeniable fact but one whose mention in *Webster's Third New International Dictionary* (1961) brought a hostile reaction from language critics. It would seem that the complaints against variant pronunciation, morphology, syntax, or diction that are chronically lodged by language watchers in the popular press frequently signal that the offending form is either threatening to become standard or has already become so.

As vague as the standard for a language like English or French may be, the power of standard language is undeniable, and it often proves an insurmountable social barrier to those who cannot grasp it. While mastery of the standard language is seldom sufficient by itself to ensure economic success, it is often a prerequisite for achieving such success. This is clear in developed or developing nations, where access to the civil service, education, the courts, the media, and the business community depends on fluency in the official standard, which may be a different dialect or an entirely different language from that spoken in one's home.

In the 1970s there was considerable debate in American linguistic and educational circles over what was called, in a controversial pamphlet issued in

1971 by the Conference on College Composition and Communication, the "students' right to their own language." Arguing that each variety of a language is a legitimate vehicle for communication and expression, the authors of the pamphlet charged that to deny students the right to their dialect or native language was a form of linguistic discrimination that robbed them of their fundamental humanity. Such a view remains an important corrective to the notion that there is one, and only one, right linguistic way to do things in speech and writing. Of late, however, it has come to be tempered with the equally compelling perception that possession of the standard language, or the "language of wider communication," as it is sometimes called, represents a form of economic and social empowerment, that denial of access to the standard language produces a form of enslavement. *Empowerment* has become a catch phrase, and confusion over the linguistic obligations of the schools is rampant, with linguists, education specialists, and lawmakers still trying to sort out theory and practice. In the *Ann Arbor School* decision (also called the *King* decision) in 1979, the United States District Court for the Eastern District of Michigan ordered the Ann Arbor School Board to use the latest linguistic and pedagogical knowledge to ensure that all students possessed the ability to speak, read, and write Standard English (see Chambers; Smitherman, *Black English*). The confusion over standard language may result in absurd situations that place disadvantaged students in even further educational jeopardy. For example, attempts to institute one English-Spanish bilingual program in New York City were thwarted by the insistence of Hispanic parents that the schools use standard Castilian Spanish rather than the local Puerto Rican variety with which their children were familiar. As a result, the children were forced to learn Spanish as a foreign language, as well as English. It will be up to the language specialists of the 1990s to ascertain the effectiveness of second-language teaching and to contribute to the resolution of the problems of majority- and minority-language education.

ORALITY AND LITERACY

Literacy is a protean term, changing with the times and charged with political meaning. To be literate means to be educated or, more narrowly, to be able to read and write. There was a time when to be literate required mastering Latin, and perhaps Greek as well. A *literate person* can simply indicate someone who is "cultured" or "educated," and its opposite very often refers disparagingly to someone who does not know as much as we do, or who disagrees with our point of view. What *literacy* has come to signify now, when it is used in such common expressions as the *literacy crisis*, is an essential skill, one that allows the individual to function at the lowest level of competence needed to get along in life (this concept is also called *functional literacy* and refers to such minimal skills as reading recipes or tool manuals and filling out job applications). More optimistic perhaps is the view of *literacy* as the ability of the individual to participate productively in the national culture and economy.

More specifically, and more practically, linguistic empowerment focuses on the development of literacy—reading and writing education. To these traditional literacies, others have lately been added: *mathematical literacy* (sometimes called *numeracy*, with its own opposite, *innumeracy*), *psychological literacy, economic literacy, musical literacy, science literacy, computer literacy*, and even *television literacy*, which some might find a contradiction in terms. Capping these off is E. D. Hirsch's umbrella term *cultural literacy*, which has mesmerized educators and social critics in the United States seeking a clearly defined, shared curriculum in order to rejuvenate a culture, or at least an educational system, that they perceive as both fragmented and failing. At the same time, cultural literacy has generated strong opposition to its reliance on a narrow, traditional body of elite Western knowledge (sometimes disparagingly called "the books of dead white men"), a canon that ignores the contributions to language and culture of women, minorities, the oppressed classes, the East, and the Third World—in short, of most of humanity (see Scholes in this volume).

Robert Pattison and Harvey Graff, the latter in *The Legacies of Literacy*, have outlined the history of views of literacy in order to demonstrate that it is no less than the way a culture looks at the problems of language and, as such, varies according to time and place. Jack Goody and Walter Ong have suggested ways in which the shift from oral to print-based forms of communication alters both social organization and human consciousness and the literacy produced thereby. That position is disputed by Brian Street and Ruth Finnegan, who attack the notion that orality and literacy are polar opposites. Taking her cue from composition studies, Deborah Brandt convincingly treats literacy as process, both pluralistic and contextualized rather than monolithic and objectifying; such a position has important consequences for reading and writing instruction. Paulo Freire places literacy in the political context of class struggle, while Graff (*Literacy Myth*) shows that mastering literacy is no guarantee of socioeconomic success, and J. Elspeth Stuckey has argued her view of literacy as a tool that society uses to maintain stratification and exclude certain groups from the centers of power. And a number of scholars have attempted to predict the effects of the computer revolution on the literacy of the future, suggesting, for example, that the linear consciousness imposed by books will shift to a more vertical, associative way of reading. Their questions range from the future-shock type (Will there be books in 2001?) to more productive explorations of cognition and linguistic production.

The literacy debate focuses scholarly interest from a wide range of fields on a broad range of language-related topics. Although the debate is heated, and is likely to remain so, it promises to produce some valuable scholarship in the next decade as linguists, cognitive psychologists, educators, and computer scientists explore literacy theory and examine the practical issues of reading and writing instruction.

LANGUAGE AND GENDER

The questions of what literacy is and whose language is to be standard hinge to a great extent on the distribution of power and prestige in a given society. They raise, as well, the related issue of language and gender, another example of language in its social context that evokes cultural values and power relationships.

Since the early 1970s, language specialists have been examining the connections among language, sex, and gender to determine whether men and women use language differently and to remedy the sex bias perceived in English and other languages. Some researchers initially suggested that women and men favored distinct subsets of vocabulary (women used more color and fabric terms; men knew the names of tools). Others found women's language more tentative, favoring trivializing adjectives and such self-effacing constructions as tag questions (The theory is cute, isn't it?). Further investigation showed that vocabulary tends to be a function of experience: those who work with colors and textiles, or with wood and machinery, whether male or female, know the appropriate terms. And self-effacing constructions may be used by those in a subordinate role in an interchange, or by those simply assuming one, noblesse oblige, regardless of their sex.

The complexities of language use have made it difficult to sort language out on the basis of sex alone. While language is conditioned by social factors, and they in turn may be conditioned by sex bias, it has yet to be convincingly demonstrated that the biological distinctions of sex have context-independent linguistic reflexes. For example, even voice pitch, which may seem an obvious sex-linked language characteristic, does not pattern categorically: not all men have low voices; not all women have high ones. Nonetheless, a stereotype of men's and women's language, based to a great extent on cultural assumptions about their biological and social roles, has persisted over many centuries. It is clear, too, that the sexes are frequently portrayed in popular as well as canonical literature as using language differently, and their differential access to language has lately been the subject of discussion in critical circles.

Since classical times, grammarians (who were generally men) have tried to ensure the dominance of the linguistic masculine in their patriarchally organized cultures. For example, the use of the term *gender* to identify certain morphological classes of nouns in Indo-European languages has been remarkably influential, though attempts to trace gender categories to biology have proved futile. Grammarians assigned priority to the class of nouns categorized as "masculine" in declension, giving the "feminine" and "neuter" nouns, though often more numerous, lesser status in the grammatical pecking order. They supported, as well, a system of generic reference in which a masculine noun or pronoun is used in representing not only masculine but mixed-sex groups—for example, *Everyone loves his mother; Man is a thinking animal; A doctor should try to cure his patients.* In Italian, girls are *le ragazze*, but the addition of the tiniest infant boy to a group of 99,999 girls requires a masculine plural noun: *i ragazzi*. One language reformer earlier in this century argued that gender was an unnecessary category in English and proposed eliminating the feminine and neuter personal pronouns in favor of a generalized *he, his, him*.

The notion of women's speech has also been encumbered by views of women as subordinate to men. And because in the Genesis story the expulsion of the first couple from the Garden of Eden is attributed to Eve's use of language, women's speech and writing have often been discouraged or deliberately suppressed. For several centuries it was common to find the very word *woman*, from the Old English *wif* + *mann*, literally "female person," derived from "woe to man" on the authority of Genesis. More secularly minded etymologists, anxious to discover biology rather than Scripture reflected in language, traced *woman* to *womb* + *man*—that is, "wombed person"—despite the fact that *womb* in English initially meant "belly" or "stomach," thus naming an organ common to the two sexes. Still others, fixating on social organization rather than genetic determination, accepted the word's true derivation from *wif* but incorrectly saw in *wife* a reflection of woman's presumed social function as "weaver."

Because Eve is physically derived from Adam in the Old Testament story of Genesis, or at least in one of the two creation myths retold in Genesis, women's words are also frequently supposed to derive from men's. Hence a woman who writes is still sometimes referred to as an *authoress* or *poetess*, words that suggest dilettantism or secondary status. Other masculine-feminine pairs imply a similar status gap between the sexes: *governor-governess*, *major-majorette*, *master-mistress*. Linguists have further observed a general semantic derogation of nouns that refer to women in English and other languages. Many negative terms for women originated as positive or neutral: *whore* from an Indo-European root meaning "dear"; *courtesan*, "a member of the court"; *wench*, "a child of either sex." The word *harlot* referred only to men until the sixteenth century.

The English system of honorifics has developed asymmetrically, with a bias perceived to favor men: the title *Mr.* is neutral with regard to marital status in men, while *Miss* and *Mrs.* generally signal it in women. Title use in English is complicated by the fact that the feminine terms are sometimes age-graded, *Miss* being used for younger women, *Mrs.* for older ones. Furthermore, the words may mask marital status; *Miss* is used by many professional women who are married, while *Mrs.* is often retained by widowed or divorced women. Ms., a title probably derived from the marriage-neutral use of *Miss* that was advocated by some feminists in the early twentieth century, was added to the paradigm as early as 1932 in the United States to restore gender balance, though it did not become popular until the 1970s. Even though it has become increasingly common, Ms. remains controversial—more so among usage critics and the American literary establishment than among the general business community, which recognizes the practical value of the term—and there is some indication that it has simply come to replace *Miss* in the usage of many unmarried women.

In addition to the title paradigm, advocates of sex neutrality in language have targeted the English pronoun system, the word *man* used in general reference to people, and compound nouns ending in *-man* on the grounds that masculine bias in language reinforces discrimination in employment and has a demonstrable effect on self-image. In the past 130 years, more than eighty proposals have been offered for a common-gender pronoun to replace the generic masculine *he* or the more fairly coordinate though often cumbersome *he or she*. *Thon* and the variations of *heer, hiser*, and *himer* were occasionally used in public and were included in a number of dictionaries. Because it is extremely difficult to introduce an artificially concocted word into something so basic to a language as the pronoun system, no epicene pronoun is likely to succeed for English. However, the singular *they*, generally frowned on in formal writing, remains the most common alternative to the more and more discordant universal masculine.

As the *Oxford English Dictionary* notes, English is the only Germanic language that did not develop separate words to refer to *man* as "adult male" and *man* as "person, human being." Conflation of the two functions of the word produces confusion as well as bias, and many style manuals now recommend that writers employ a nonambiguous word like *person* when that is the sense intended. Proposed alternatives to compound nouns ending in *-man* frequently employ *-person*—for example, *chairperson*—or they simply clip *man* from the stem, as in *chair*. In other instances, masculine-feminine pairs may be neutralized: *steward* and *stewardess* become *flight attendant; actor* and *actress* coalesce as *actor; waiter* and *waitress* are replaced by *server, waitperson* or *wait*, or occasionally by such coinages as *waitron*, with its pseudo-Latin plural, *waitri*.

Attention to the problem of sexist language has affected the style of edited nonfiction English prose, particularly in the United States, and may ultimately be a determinant in the course of the language in the late twentieth century. In support of its stand against sex discrimination in employment, the United States government issued a revised, gender-neutral official list of job titles. The style books of major American publishing houses, professional societies, and the media all root out sex bias to various degrees, eliminating generic masculines, warning writers not to refer to women as *girls*, some changing adjectives like *seminal* to *influential* or nouns like *seminar* to *study group*. Feminist writers occasionally propose fairly radical rewritings of English words to draw attention to linguistic discrimination and to correct it. French and German writers have also explored their languages, which preserve grammatical gender in their noun systems, to identify and correct the sexism inherent in language use and analysis. While it is possible to argue that consciously changing language—a difficult task in itself—is no guarantee that social attitudes will follow, it is impossible to deny that language does influence how people think. Certainly, raising the linguistic consciousness of speakers and writers can and does produce results, though not always the results desired by language reformers. Research in the area of language and gender will continue to focus on the practical issues of reform, though it already shows clear signs of developing theoretical notions of linguistic empowerment of the sort that dominate literacy studies as well.

LANGUAGE TEACHING, PLANNING, AND LINGUISTIC ETHICS

As we have seen, linguists and other language specialists not only observe language in its natural habitat; they frequently make recommendations for its improvement. They may be formally charged with the task of refitting an oral language in a developing nation for the technical and communicative functions of a modern, literate culture. Or they may concern themselves with improving language education in the schools of industrialized countries. In some cases, they may seek to put some aspect of language—for example, the systems of spelling or gender reference—on a more rational or less discriminatory footing. Such work can be controversial. In 1906 President Theodore Roosevelt issued an executive order requiring that all federal government agencies adopt the reformed, simplified spelling developed by the language experts of the Simplified Spelling Board, but there was so much opposition to his demand that, speaking more softly, he withdrew the order. Closer to our own day, a small number of MLA members, resentful of what they saw to be unjustified editorial meddling, resigned from the organization on its publication of Francine Wattman Frank and Paula A. Treichler's authoritative and scrupulously researched recommendations for gender-neutral academic writing. In any case, English spelling reform, which continues to be advocated by a number of amateurs and even some professionals, seems doomed to failure, while calls for removing language bias in formal contexts have made significant headway among scholars and other professional and business writers.

Another frequently unrewarding task that linguists take on is that of educating the public about the true nature of language. In 1921 H. C. Wyld, on assuming the Chair of Philology at Oxford, lamented that "the general ignorance concerning [the science of language] is so profound that it is very difficult to persuade people that there really is a considerable mass of well-ascertained fact, and a definite body of doctrine on linguistic questions." Wyld went on to charge that while many people find questions of language fascinating, their opinions about it are "incredibly and hopelessly wrong." He concluded, "There is no subject which attracts a larger number of cranks and quacks than English Philology" (10).

Wyld's comments are certainly as true today as they ever were. One area where ignorance of "the science of language" generally proves troublesome is in the training of language teachers. Despite repeated calls for the increased involvement of linguists in the education of language teachers, their role in that process remains problematic. As Claire Kramsch demonstrates later in this volume, linguistic knowledge is often prized in the development of second-language instruction. Unfortunately, the facts of language continue to be undervalued in the training of first-language teachers (that is, teachers of English to speakers of English, teachers of French to speakers of French, and so on), who find themselves in the uncomfortable position of having to serve as language arbiters without adequate preparation to do so.

Language teachers have always received both praise and blame from the general public for their traditional role in maintaining language standards. Their opinions on correct grammar and usage are sought out, yet at the same time their judgments are feared or resented. One typical comment—which precludes further communication—should be familiar to language teachers: "Oh, you're an English (French, Latin, Japanese) teacher. I guess I'd better watch my grammar." Paradoxically, though they are considered language experts, the linguistic education of language teachers is often rudimentary, consisting of little more than a single course in descriptive grammar or history of the language, and they are consequently hard put to make the linguistic judgments required of them. Moreover, the contributions of linguistic theory to teacher training have often seemed unnecessarily abstract, indirect, or even at odds with the teaching mission (consider, for example, the failure of transformational-generative grammar to make an impact on the language teaching curriculum in the 1960s and 1970s). Clearly, teacher education and curriculum development remain areas in which linguists and language teachers must learn to address each other with greater circumspection and effectiveness.

Linguists are often mocked by language commentators in the popular press for a supposed lack of standards. The charge that linguists are obsessively permissive about language use, that they have no standards of their own and encourage others to abandon standards as well, wrongly conflates two separate issues: the scope of linguistic investigation and the contexts of language use. Assuming that language is by nature both complex and variable, linguists argue that, just as no language is inherently better than any other, the standard form of a language is not in essence superior to any other variant. It is simply the particular variety of the language that, through fiat or accident, has become the elite, prestige, or official form of communication. Such a view in no way demotes the standard, nor does it suggest that linguists abandon standard language in their own writing. Indeed, linguists are keenly aware of the contextual appropriateness of language, and when they write, they adhere to standards of formal, edited prose and expect their students to do the same.

In addition to serving as occasional objects of journalistic obloquy, linguists may disagree among themselves about their roles. Some linguists charge in the scholarly literature that their colleagues ignore the facts of language in favor of theories that fail to explain language phenomena adequately. They argue that an undue focus on standard language ignores language variety, particularly that of the nonelite, presenting an unbalanced picture of linguistic operations and placing users of nonstandard varieties at a disadvantage (see Finegan in this volume). They further charge that interfering with the language use of others, a process often characterized in negative terms as linguistic engineering, is a violation both of scientific objectivity and a kind of Hippocratic admonition to do no harm. In contrast, other linguists insist they have a distinct obligation to help nonstandard speakers learn the form of speech and writing associated with power and success. They maintain, as well, that it is naive to strive for objectivity in language investigation, since we must use language to study language and since the very examination of linguistic features interferes with the phenomenon under study. They warn that if linguists, whose job it is to know the history and structure of language, do not involve themselves in issues of language standardization as well as in schemes for language modernization or improvement, these matters will be left in the hands of politicians and amateurs (Wyld's "cranks and quacks") whose interests are conceivably less enlightened and whose insights into language operations are certain to be less acute (see, for example, Greenbaum, *Good English*).

It is not likely that either side of this ethical debate will prevail in the near future. In fact, it may be that both points of view are necessary correctives to any single view of language: after all, it is disagreement among experts, rather than consensus, that keeps us all honest and promotes further investigation. More important, perhaps, than achieving consensus, is the increasing recognition that we must acknowledge and better understand the impact of the language opinions of linguists and nonlinguists alike. As Richard Bailey reminds us, ideas about language based on myth and misinformation are as real and as powerful as those based on fact: both affect the way that language is perceived and used, both affect the way that users of language are treated, and both are appropriate objects of further study for the linguist.

Suggestions for Further Reading

Some good general introductions include such textbooks as Richard A. Hudson's *Sociolinguistics* and Ronald Wardhaugh's *Introduction to Sociolinguistics* and the updated collection of essays edited by John J. Gumperz and Dell Hymes, as well as the sociolinguistics volume *Linguistics: The Cambridge Survey*, edited by Frederick J. Newmeyer. J. Maxwell Atkinson and John Heritage have edited a basic collection of essays on conversational analysis.

Language and Nation. Wardhaugh (*Languages*) and Louis-Jean Calvet discuss the effects of imposing English and French at home in Great Britain and France and in colonies and former colonies abroad. Einar Haugen's classic study of Norwegian language planning was published in 1966, and the three-volume collection edited by Istvan Fodor and Claude Hagège contains essays on language reform and standardization in many other countries. Sidney Greenbaum (*English Language*) surveys linguistic attitudes in English-speaking nations, and Richard W. Bailey and Manfred Görlach examine the variety and spread of English throughout the world.

The Official-Language Question. Joshua Fishman et al. (*Language Loyalty*) discuss, as their subtitle indicates, the maintenance and perpetuation of non-English mother tongues by American ethnic and religious groups; Fishman et al. (*Ethnic Revival*) update this classic work. Arnold M. Leibowitz focuses on official- and minority-language legislation and case law in the United States. Calvin Veltman convincingly demonstrates the adoption of English by minority-language speakers in the United States. Heinz Kloss and Dennis Baron (*English-Only Question*) trace the official-English question and the status of minority languages in the country for the past two centuries, while Kenji Hakuta discusses changing theories of bilingualism. And James Crawford discusses the history and effectiveness of American bilingual education programs.

Language Variety and Standard Language. Basic studies in attitudes toward variation and standardization in English include Edward Finegan's *Attitudes* and Baron's *Grammar and Good Taste* and *Declining Grammar.* No student of the subject can ignore William Labov's work on linguistic insecurity and on Black English. Two collections of essays (Ferguson and Heath; Trudgill) discuss the language situation in the United States and Great Britain, respectively. John Earl Joseph examines language standardization for a variety of languages. The first volume of the *Dictionary of American Regional English (DARE)*, edited by Frederic G. Cassidy, appeared in 1987; the second volume is scheduled to appear in 1992. *DARE* contains the most up-to-date survey of lexical variation in the United States, with computer-generated maps indicating frequency of occurrence of variant forms. *Webster's Dictionary of English Usage* provides a detailed summary of usage controversies against a background of historical citations and offers sensible advice for the perplexed.

Orality and Literacy. In the past decade, scholarly treatments of literacy have appeared at an impressive rate. In addition to the basic works listed in the essay are several recommended volumes. William V. Harris examines literacy in the Greek and Roman world, Michael T. Clanchy traces the shift from mistrust of the written word to an increasing dependence on it in thirteenth-century England, and Robert Allan Houston sketches a history of literacy in early modern Europe. The collection edited by Richard W. Bailey and Robin Melanie Fosheim for the MLA contains essential essays on the users, uses, and politics of literacy. Collections by David R. Olson, Nancy Torrance, and Angela Hildyard, by Suzanne de Castell, Allan Luke, and Kieran Egan, and by Andrea A. Lunsford, Helene Moglen, and James Slevin address the alleged literacy crisis from a variety of critical perspectives.

Language and Gender. This area, too, has seen a great deal of publication activity in recent years. Casey Miller and Kate Swift convincingly demonstrate in *Words and Women* the bias against women to be found in the ways English is used, and offer in *The Handbook of Nonsexist Writing* a detailed set of suggestions for neutralizing the bias. Cheris Kramarae attributes differences in the language of men and women to the relative power they exert in social situations. The collection edited by Barrie Thorne, Kramarae, and Nancy Henley discusses the issue of sexism in language from a variety of social science and philosophical perspectives. Baron in *Grammar and Gender* surveys the treatment of gender issues in works about language—dictionaries, grammars, etymologies, and general commentaries—showing how stereotypes of sex roles have influenced the way we look at language. Deborah Tannen argues that because American women and men live in different worlds, their conversation, or lack of it, resembles cross-cultural communication. And Francine Wattman Frank and Paula A. Treichler offer a carefully reasoned theoretical context for sex-neutral language, together with specific recommendations for unbiased academic writing.

University of Illinois, Urbana

Works Cited

Atkinson, J. Mawxell, and John Heritage, eds. *Structures of Social Action: Studies in Conversation Analysis.* Cambridge: Cambridge UP, 1984.

Bailey, Richard W. *Images of English: A Cultural History of the Language.* Ann Arbor: U of Michigan P, forthcoming.

Bailey, Richard W., and Manfred Görlach, eds. *English as a World Language.* Ann Arbor: U of Michigan P, 1983.

Bailey, Richard W., and Robin Melanie Fosheim, eds. *Literacy for Life: The Demand for Reading and Writing.* New York: MLA, 1983.

Baker, Josephine Turck. *Correct English: How to Use It.* Baltimore: Sadler-Rowe, 1907.

Baron, Dennis. *Declining Grammar and Other Essays on the English Vocabulary.* Urbana: NCTE, 1989.

———. *The English-Only Question: An Official Language for Americans?* New Haven: Yale UP, 1990.

———. *Grammar and Gender.* New Haven: Yale UP, 1986.

———. *Grammar and Good Taste: Reforming the American Language.* New Haven: Yale UP, 1982.

Baugh, John. *Black Street Speech: Its History, Structure, and Survival.* Austin: U of Texas P, 1983.

Brandt, Deborah. *Literacy as Involvement: The Acts of Writers, Readers, and Texts.* Carbondale: Southern Illinois UP, 1990.

Butters, Ronald. *The Death of Black English: Divergence and Convergence in Black and White Vernaculars.* Frankfurt am Main: Lang, 1989.

Calvet, Louis-Jean. *La guerre des langues et les politiques linguistique.* Paris: Payot, 1987.

Cassidy, Frederic G., ed. *The Dictionary of American Regional English.* Vol. 1: A–C. Cambridge: Harvard UP, 1987.

Castell, Suzanne de, Allan Luke, and Kieran Egan, eds. *Literacy, Society, and Schooling: A Reader.* Cambridge: Cambridge UP, 1986.

Chambers, John W., Jr., ed. *Black English: Educational Equity and the Law.* Ann Arbor: Karoma, 1983.

Clanchy, Michael T. *From Memory to Written Record: England 1066–1307.* London: Arnold, 1979.

Conference on College Composition and Communication. *Students' Right to Their Own Language.* Chicago: NCTE, 1971.

Crawford, James. *Bilingual Education: History, Politics, Theory, and Practice.* Trenton: Crane, 1989.

Evans, Bergen. *Comfortable Words.* New York: Random, 1961.

Ferguson, Charles A., and Shirley Brice Heath, eds. *Language in the USA.* Cambridge: Cambridge UP, 1981.

Fichte, Johann Gottlieb. *Addresses to the German Nation.* Trans. R. F. Jones and G. H. Turnbull. Chicago: Open Court, 1922.

Finegan, Edward. *Attitudes toward English Usage: The History of a War of Words.* New York: Teachers Coll. P, 1980.

Finnegan, Ruth. *Literacy and Orality: Studies in the Technology of Communication.* Oxford: Blackwell, 1988.

Fishman, Joshua A., et al. *Language Loyalty in the United States: The Maintenance and Perpetuation of Non-English Mother Tongues by American Ethnic and Religious Groups.* Hague: Mouton, 1966.

Fishman, Joshua A., et al. *The Rise and Fall of the Ethnic Revival: Perspectives on Language and Ethnicity.* Berlin: Mouton, 1985.

Fodor, Istvan, and Claude Hagège, eds. *Language Reform: History and Future.* Hamburg: Buske, 1983–84.

Frank, Francine Wattman, and Paula A. Treichler. *Language, Gender, and Professional Writing: Theoretical Approaches and Guidelines for Nonsexist Usage.* New York: MLA, 1989.

Freire, Paulo. *The Politics of Education: Culture, Power, and Liberation.* Trans. Donald Macedo. South Hadley: Bergin, 1985.

Goody, Jack. *The Logic of Writing and the Organization of Society.* Cambridge: Cambridge UP, 1986.

Graff, Harvey. *The Legacies of Literacy: Continuities and Contradictions in Western Culture and Society.* Bloomington: Indiana UP, 1987.

———. *The Literacy Myth: Literacy and Social Structure in the Nineteenth-Century City.* New York: Academic, 1979.

Greenbaum, Sidney, ed. *The English Language Today.* Oxford: Pergamon, 1985.

———. *Good English and the Grammarian.* London: Longman, 1988.

Greenblatt, Stephen J. "Learning to Curse: Aspects of Linguistic Colonialism in the Sixteenth Century." *First Images of America: The Impact of the New World on the Old.* Ed. Fredi Chiappelli, Michael J. B. Allen, and Robert L. Benson. 2 vols. Berkeley: U of California P, 1976. 2: 561–80.

Grillo, R. D. *Dominant Languages: Language and Hierarchy in Britain and France.* Cambridge: Cambridge UP, 1989.

Gumperz, John J., and Dell Hymes, eds. *Directions in Sociolinguistics: The Ethnography of Communication.* 2nd ed. Oxford: Blackwell, 1986.

Hakuta, Kenji. *Mirror of Language: The Debate on Bilingualism.* New York: Basic, 1986.

Halliday, M. A. K., Angus McIntosh, and Peter Strevens."The Users and Uses of

Language." *The Varieties of Present-Day English.* Ed. Richard W. Bailey and Jay L. Robinson. New York: Macmillan, 1973. 9–37.

Harmer, Lewis Charles. *Uncertainties in French Grammar.* Cambridge: Cambridge UP, 1973.

Harris, William V. *Ancient Literacy.* Cambridge: Harvard UP, 1989.

Haugen, Einar. *Language Conflict and Language Planning: The Case of Modern Norwegian.* Cambridge: Harvard UP, 1966.

Heath, Shirley Brice. "A National Language Academy? Debate in the New Nation." *Linguistics* 189 (1977): 9–43.

Hirsch, E. D., Jr. *Cultural Literacy: What Every American Needs to Know.* Boston: Houghton, 1987.

Houston, Robert Allan. *Literacy in Early Modern Europe: Culture and Education, 1500–1800.* London: Longman, 1988.

Hudson, Richard A. *Sociolinguistics.* Cambridge: Cambridge UP, 1980.

Humboldt, Wilhelm von. *On Language: The Diversity of Human Language-Structure and Its Influence on the Mental Development of Mankind.* Trans. Peter Heath. Cambridge: Cambridge UP, 1988.

Joseph, John Earl. *Eloquence and Power: The Rise of Language Standards and Standard Languages.* Oxford: Blackwell, 1987.

Kachru, Braj B. *The Alchemy of English: The Spread, Function, and Modes of Non-native Englishes.* Oxford: Pergamon, 1986.

Kloss, Heinz. *The American Bilingual Tradition.* Rowley: Newbury, 1977.

Kramarae, Cheris. *Women and Men Speaking.* Rowley: Newbury, 1981.

Labov, William. *The Increasing Divergence of Black and White Vernaculars: Introduction to the Research Reports.* Philadelphia: U of Pennsylvania, manuscript, 1985.

———. *Language in the Inner City.* Philadelphia: U of Pennsylvania P, 1972.

———. *The Social Stratification of English in New York City.* Washington: Center for Applied Linguistics, 1966.

Leibowitz, Arnold M. *Federal Recognition of the Rights of Minority Language Groups in the United States.* Rosslyn: Natl. Clearinghouse for Bilingual Educ., 1982.

Lunsford, Andrea A., Helene Moglen, and James Slevin, eds. *The Right to Literacy.* New York: MLA, 1990.

Miller, Casey, and Kate Swift. *The Handbook of Nonsexist Writing: For Writers, Editors, and Speakers.* New York: Lippincott, 1980.

———. *Words and Women.* New York: Anchor-Doubleday, 1975.

Newmeyer, Frederick J., ed. *Language: The Socio-cultural Context.* Vol. 4 of *Linguistics: The Cambridge Survey.* Cambridge: Cambridge UP, 1988.

Olson, David R., Nancy Torrance, and Angela Hildyard, eds. *Literacy, Language, and Learning: The Nature and Consequences of Reading and Writing.* Cambridge: Cambridge UP, 1985.

Ong, Walter. *Orality and Literacy: The Technologizing of the Word.* London: Methuen, 1977.

Pattison, Robert. *On Literacy: The Politics of the Word from Homer to the Age of Rock.* New York: Oxford UP, 1982.

Sapir, Edward. *Language: An Introduction to the Study of Speech.* New York: Harcourt, 1921.

Smitherman, Geneva. *Black English and the Education of Black Children and Youth.* Detroit: Wayne State U, Center for Black Studies, 1981.

———. *Talkin and Testifyin: The Language of Black America.* Boston: Houghton, 1977.

Street, Brian. *Literacy in Theory and Practice.* Cambridge: Cambridge UP, 1984.

Stuckey, J. Elspeth. *The Violence of Literacy.* Portsmouth: Boynton, 1991.

Tannen, Deborah. *You Just Don't Understand: Women and Men in Conversation.* New York: Morrow, 1990.

Thorne, Barrie, Cheris Kramarae, and Nancy Henley, eds. *Language, Gender and Society.* Rowley: Newbury, 1983.

Trudgill, Peter, ed. *Language in the British Isles.* Cambridge: Cambridge UP, 1984.

Veltman, Calvin. *Language Shift in the United States.* Berlin: Mouton, 1983.

Vizetelly, Frank. *Desk-Book of Errors in English.* New York: Funk, 1907.

Wardhaugh, Ronald. *An Introduction to Sociolinguistics.* Oxford: Blackwell, 1986.

———. *Languages in Competition: Dominance, Diversity, and Decline.* Oxford: Blackwell, 1987.

Weber, Eugen. *Peasants into Frenchmen: The Modernization of Rural France 1870–1914.* Stanford: Stanford UP, 1976.

Webster's Dictionary of English Usage. Springfield: Merriam, 1989.

Whorf, Benjamin Lee. *Language, Thought, and Reality: Selected Writings of Benjamin L. Whorf.* Ed. John B. Carroll. Cambridge: MIT P, 1956.

Wolfram, Walt. "Re-examining Vernacular Black English." *Language* 66 (1990): 121–33.

Wyld, H. C. *English Philology in English Universities.* Oxford: Clarendon–Oxford UP, 1921.

CLAIRE J. KRAMSCH

Language Acquisition and Language Learning

THE inclusion of language acquisition and learning in the second edition of this volume is a noteworthy event, for many readers probably do not engage in second-language research but pursue literary or linguistic studies and teach language classes. For those readers, I would like to place the field of research I describe here in its proper relation to the teaching they do.

Foreign language pedagogy has long been guided, directly or indirectly, by theories of language and learning. These theories have given rise to various methods or approaches, which have found their way into textbooks and syllabi and, in bits and pieces, into teachers' practices. H. H. Stern gives an exhaustive account of the history of language teaching and its relation to the theoretical thought of various disciplines. Until recently, however, language teachers have not based their teaching consistently on theoretical research. Most of them learned their craft on the job, teaching the way they were taught and the way their teachers were taught. Both literature scholars and linguists were convinced that learning a language was only a matter of memory, repetition, and hard work and of acquiring skills that students would then learn to use by going to the country where the language was spoken. Language teachers knew nothing of how people learn languages or of why some learners fail and others succeed.

My own career is a case in point. Trained in German literature and philology and called on to teach German language classes, I remember my despair at not understanding the most elementary principles of language use. I had to teach conversation classes but did not understand the systematics of conversation; I had to teach texts but had not been told what a text is; I had to correct errors but did not know why errors had been made. I remember my amazement one day in the early 1970s when I happened on studies in conversation and discourse analysis, and I immersed myself in the new field of second-language-acquisition research. Everything I taught started making sense. Everything I researched fell into place.

I began to see that literature and language scholars and teachers have much to learn from each other. Literature scholars can broaden their critical tools by applying to literary texts the same methods of discourse analysis that language-acquisition scholars use for analyzing the production of public discourses, including the discourse of the language classroom itself. At the same time, language-acquisition scholars can broaden their reflection on language learning to include not just the functional uses of language but also the figurative uses as presentation and representation of reality (Widdowson, *Stylistics*). Moreover, literature scholars can bring to language teaching their unique training in the critical analysis of texts.

I would tell the novice language teacher, Go beyond the textbook you teach and learn about the way language is spoken and used. The literature you study and the language you teach are grounded in language as social practice, and "language has its rules of use without which rules of grammar would be useless" (Hymes 278). Read work in psycholinguistics and sociolinguistics as well as in linguistic approaches to literature. Understand the foreign culture you teach not only through its literature but also through its social sciences and ethnography. Deepen your knowledge of your students' own culture by reading similar studies about the United States or Canada, both in English and in the foreign language. The better you understand language and language use, the better you will be able to transmit to your students the critical knowledge you have gained by being a participant observer and researcher of that unique educational setting, the foreign language classroom. In the field of language acquisition, theory and practice enrich each other (see Ferguson).

It is important to distinguish between a teaching perspective and a learning perspective on language acquisition. Whereas teachers are mainly concerned with relating student performance to teacher input in a principled way, a learning perspective describes the process of attempting to acquire a second language. Before teachers can devise effective activities and techniques for the classroom, they must first understand how people learn languages. Thus language-acquisition research adopts primarily a learning perspective, and only in this light does it consider implications for language teaching.

LANGUAGE ACQUISITION AND LEARNING

The capacity to learn one's native tongue and then another language or several more is a unique property of the human species that has not ceased to amaze parents, linguists, and language teachers. How do children manage to produce an infinite number of sentences with the finite means of available grammars? What is the relation between their cognitive and their linguistic development? What makes learning a second language as an adult different? And then, as Michael H. Long has asked, Does second language instruction make a difference? If the answer from second-language-acquisition research is yes, then we must determine exactly what we can and should teach at what level for what purpose.

These questions have not only inspired scholars in linguistics, psychology, sociology, and education to pursue research in language acquisition, they have fueled political passions as well. In various countries, scholars' research results are used (or misused) as a basis for such policy decisions as the maintenance or abolition of bilingual and immersion programs, the restoration of high school and college foreign language requirements, and the governance structure of language and literature departments. Beyond academia, language-acquisition research helps us understand the links between language, literacy, and sociocultural identity, as well as the interrelations of foreign language teaching, national interests, and international peace and understanding (Kramsch).

The terms *language acquisition* and *language learning* have come to designate first- and second-language acquisition, respectively. According to a distinction popularized by Stephen Krashen, whose work I discuss later, the term *acquisition* is meant to capture the way children learn their native language in naturalistic settings, while the term *learning* refers to the conscious applications of rules in the study of a second language in instructional settings. However, this dichotomy is not so clear-cut. After all, adults can also "acquire" a second language in naturalistic settings, and a certain amount of "acquisition" also takes place in classrooms.

Another distinction is made between a *second language* and a *foreign language*. A second language is one learned by outsiders within a community of native speakers, such as English as a second language (ESL) taught in the United States. A foreign language is a subject learned in an instructional setting removed from the relevant speech community, such as French in United States high schools. Second-language-acquisition research is uncertain about the nature and the degree of difference between second-language learning and foreign language learning.

Since the 1970s scholars have considered a variety of questions under the generic category of second-language-acquisition (SLA) research. For instance, are the processes of first- and second-language acquisition—or of second- and foreign language acquisition—similar? If so, for which learners, under which conditions, at which stage of acquisition? How much consciousness and which cognitive operations are involved? To what extent, if at all, is learning a language like learning, say, how to ride a bike?

HISTORIC OVERVIEW

First- and second-language acquisition are relatively recent domains of inquiry. At a time when language study was closely linked to philology and phonetics, Europeans scholars such as Henry Sweet, Harold Palmer, Otto Jespersen, and Wilhelm Vietor attempted to apply the findings of the linguistic sciences to language teaching. Despite developments in linguistic thought in the 1920s and 1930s, however, no theoretical foundation was established for language teaching before 1940, and questions about what it means to acquire, learn, and know a language did not get addressed before the 1960s.

Until the 1960s, theories of language acquisition were subsumed under general theories of learning, and the prevalent theory was behaviorism. Children were thought to learn their native language by imitation and reinforcement. It was believed that learning a language, whether one's native tongue (L1) or a second language (L2), was the result of imitating words and sentences produced by adult native speakers. Foreign language learning was assumed to be most successful when the task was broken down into a number of stimulus-response links, which could be systematically practiced and mastered one by one, such as verb conjugation or noun declension. The major concern was how to teach language so that it could be acquired as a set of habits. Learning a second language was seen as a process of replacing old habits with new ones, so errors were considered undesirable.

The subsequent work of Noam Chomsky, particularly his *Syntactic Structures*, led researchers to question behaviorist explanations of language acquisition. Chomsky made it clear that learning a language is not the acquisition of a set of habits. Rather, children are born with what he called a "language-acquisition device," a uniquely human mental organ or cognitive capacity to acquire language. Children learn their native tongue not by deficient imitation of the full-fledged adult system but by a dynamic process of formulating abstract rules based on the language they hear.

Around the same time that Chomsky initiated research into the mental processes at work in the acquisition of a first language, Robert Lado's classic work *Linguistics across Cultures* focused attention on the errors that second-language learners make. Lado claimed that "we can predict and describe the patterns that will cause difficulty in learning, and those that will not cause difficulty, by comparing systematically the language and the culture to be learned with the native language and culture of the student" (vii). He outlined procedures for making such comparisons in phonology, grammar, and vocabulary and in the cultural aspects of a language. Lado's research, linked with the audiolingual method of language teaching, had a far-reaching effect on language-teaching practice. A later series of texts on contrastive structure, such as William G. Moulton's *Sounds of English and German*, directly applied Lado's work. Teachers were encouraged to teach pronunciation, for example, by isolating particular German sounds like *Miete* and *Mitte* and contrasting them with English sounds like *bean* and *bin*.

Lado's work also exemplifies the way second-language learning has influenced linguistic research. Written in the heyday of structural linguistics and behaviorist theory, it became associated with a movement in applied linguistics called contrastive analysis, which claims that the principal barrier to second-language acquisition is the interference of the L1 system with the L2 system. Linguists distinguish here between transfer and interference. Similarities between two languages cause "positive transfer," such as extending the use of the pronoun in "it is raining" to the French "il pleut." Differences cause "negative transfer," generally known as "interference," such as expanding that use to Spanish and saying "el llueve" instead of "llueve." The question remained, What exactly was being transferred? Contrastive analysis, in its strong structuralist form, was refined by Robert J. Di Pietro in his book *Language Structures in*

Contrast and then abandoned in the late 1970s; it is only now regaining momentum in a different form.

The 1960s saw a boom of empirical studies that explored the mental processes of second-language learners. An influential article published by S. Pit Corder in 1967, entitled "The Significance of Learners' Errors," proposed that both L1 and L2 learners make errors to test certain hypotheses about the language they are learning. In the following dialogue, for example, a child tests a series of hypotheses regarding the formation of past tenses:

> MOTHER: Did Billy have his egg cut up for him at breakfast?
> CHILD: Yes I showeds him.
> MOTHER: You what?
> CHILD: I showed him.
> MOTHER: You showed him?
> CHILD: I seed him.
> MOTHER: Ah, you saw him.
> CHILD: Yes, I saw him. (167)

According to Corder, errors should be viewed not as regrettable mishaps but as necessary steps in the learning process. This approach was in opposition to the idea of language learning as presented in the contrastive-analysis hypothesis. In 1973, a milestone study by Heidi Dulay and Marina Burt showed that only 3% of the errors made by Spanish-speaking children learning English could be attributed to interference from their native language, whereas 85% were developmental errors that children learning Spanish as their native tongue also seemed to make. This study, by suggesting that not all language performance is derived from external input, suddenly changed the direction of language-learning research. Although not all researchers agreed with Dulay and Burt's findings, SLA research virtually stopped looking at transfer phenomena; rather, it started observing and systematically recording the errors made by second-language learners as they acquire grammatical structures—minimal units of sound (phonemes) and meaning (morphemes) and selected syntactic structures.

Together with Corder's study, Larry Selinker's "Interlanguage" is considered to mark the beginning of SLA research. Selinker showed that learners create their own systematic "interlanguage" through their errors. His argument, which I describe later, corroborated Daniel Slobin's findings in studies of children who were learning their native tongue. Children seemed to have not only a biological faculty to learn language but a psychological one as well. Slobin proposed that children are not born with substantive "knowledge"; instead, they have a set of procedures, or operating principles, that they follow to establish the relevance and the relative importance of the input they receive. Throughout the 1970s, scholars like Elaine Tarone, Uli Frauenfelder, and Larry Selinker (Tarone et al.), Jack C. Richards, and Evelyn Hatch attempted to demonstrate the systematic structure of a learner's interlanguage by analyzing learners' errors. Krashen's studies of learners' natural development led him to formulate a series of hypotheses that became influential in the next decade. I return to these studies later.

By the late 1970s, then, it became clear that both interference from L1 and natural development processes are at work in the acquisition of L2 in naturalistic settings. Indeed, scholars found that learners acquire a language according to what Corder had termed "a built-in syllabus," with quite specific learning and communicating strategies. But transfer did seem to occur on various levels. The 1980s saw, in addition to continued natural-development studies, a resurgence of interest in transfer studies. The first volume to deal comprehensively with transfer phenomena in language acquisition was *Language Transfer in Language Learning*, edited by Susan M. Gass and Larry Selinker.

All SLA research since the 1970s has been characterized by a major shift in focus to the learner and the affective and cognitive processes involved in language learning. Instead of concentrating almost exclusively on the existence or absence of certain grammatical forms in learners' language, psycholinguists have turned their attention to the strategies learners use to learn the forms and to communicate intended meanings. The interest of scholars like James Cummins and Lily Wong Fillmore in the way learners match forms and meanings led researchers to investigate those factors that account for variability in acquisition among learners. Some of these factors are internal to the learner, such as general cognitive and intellectual abilities and affective states; others involve the interaction of the learners with their environment (input from teacher, peers, native speakers).

In the early years of SLA research, the language under study was mostly English, acquired in naturalistic settings. The overwhelming spread of English as an international language generated a great deal of empirical research on learners of English as a second language in the United States, Canada, and Great Britain. This research was followed by studies of the acquisition of other languages in naturalistic settings, such as in the Français langue étrangère in France and the Deutsch als Fremdsprache in Germany, two societies that had to meet the communicative needs of masses of immigrant workers.

However, learning a language in the country where that language is spoken and learning a language in a general educational setting in one's native country are two different contexts that respond to different learners' needs. Hence, interest in examining the educational and, specifically, the classroom conditions of language learning in schools has grown. Many scholars are well-known for their work on ESL classrooms: Richard Allwright and Michael P. Breen in Great Britain; Willis J. Edmondson in Germany; Herbert W. Seliger and Michael H. Long, Teresa Pica and Cathy Doughty, Craig Chaudron, and Leo van Lier in the United States. Merrill Swain and Sharon Lapkin have examined French immersion classes in Canada. Other scholars have started observing foreign language classrooms: J. P. B. Allen, Maria Fröhlich, and Nina Spada in Canada developed a communication-oriented observation scheme; Gabriele Kasper recorded teacher-induced errors in German classes in Denmark; and recent doctoral dissertations in the United States have observed the influence of instruction patterns and task variation on student interaction in Spanish and French classes, respectively.

WHAT IS SECOND-LANGUAGE ACQUISITION RESEARCH?

Definition of the Field

According to Rod Ellis, the term *SLA research* refers to studies designed to investigate "the subconscious or conscious process by which a language other than the mother tongue is learnt in a natural or a tutored setting" (6). It covers both second-language acquisition and foreign language learning. SLA research is an interdisciplinary field. Its research methods are taken primarily from psycholinguistics, that is, the study of the relation between linguistic behavior and the psychological processes (memory, perception, attention) that underlie it. The work of Thomas G. Bever on speech perception and speech processing, George A. Miller on language and communication, Kenneth Goodman on reading, and Roy O. Freedle and John B. Carroll on language comprehension and the acquisition of knowledge have greatly influenced the way SLA studies have been conducted. SLA research now increasingly draws also on other fields, such as pragmatics, sociolinguistics, and discourse analysis, that study the way language reflects and shapes the social context in which it is used. For example, the work of M. A. K. Halliday on language as social semiotic, William Labov on the social context of language, John J. Gumperz on discourse strategies, and Teun van Dijk on discourse processes have had a strong effect on pragmatic strands of SLA research.

Two other terms are used with respect to SLA research: *applied linguistics* and *educational linguistics*. Some controversy has arisen about the scope of these two fields, but they generally refer to what Charles A. Ferguson calls "the application of the methods and results of linguistic science to the solution of practical language problems" (82). Language learning is one such problem. In contrast to theoretical linguistics, which seeks to understand the nature of language, applied linguistics contributes to a theory of first- and second-language learning as a psychological and social activity and as a subset of human behavior. SLA research, which arose out of the realization that language learning involves more than just linguistic phenomena, can thus be viewed as a subdiscipline under the larger umbrella of applied linguistics. It is emerging in the United States as the designation for all research about L2 learning.

Theoretical Frameworks

The common focus of all second-language research is the language learner, that is, the processes by which a learner acquires, stores, organizes, and uses knowledge of the language for successful communication. Within the short history of the field, researchers have investigated these processes and drawn theoretical hypotheses from four major perspectives that coexist today: linguistics, cognitive psychology, sociolinguistics, and social psychology.

The linguistic perspective, which varies according to the particular linguistic theory it relies on, focuses on the differences among languages or on universal characteristics of language and the human capacity for language learning. Contrastive analysis was intended to account for and predict L2 learner difficulties on the basis of differences in linguistic characteristics of two or more languages. In its strongest form, contrastive analysis is no longer used, but as the notion of L1 transfer has become more sophisticated and as social and cultural differences in language learning have received increased interest, contrastive-analysis research has proved valid for investigating the acquisition of sociolinguistic and pragmatic competence in a foreign language. For example, Robin C. Scarcella investigates interferences in "discourse accent"—the use of conversational features (e.g., turn taking, interrupting) from one's first language in the same way in one's second language. Shoshonna Blum-Kulka, Juliane House, and Gabriele Kasper study the way learners use speech acts inappropriately in the target language, such as saying "please" as a response to "thank you" in English. Jenny Thomas elucidates the different types of pragmatic failures made by learners of a foreign language, from using the wrong rejoinder for an intended meaning to misinterpreting the social and cultural context in which a verbal exchange is taking place.

Another linguistic approach seems promising for future research, although it is still scant on evidence. Based on the assumption that Chomsky's language-acquisition device functions in both first- and second-language acquisition, this approach attempts to find out which constraints limit the hypotheses a learner can make about specific structures of the language to be acquired. These constraints are due not only to transfers from the surface structure of the first language and to the nature of the language heard in the environment but to innate and universal linguistic principles, called universal grammar, that apply to all languages. Gass tested how learners from various first-language backgrounds formed relative clauses in English on three types of tasks: a grammaticality judgment task, a sentence-combining task, and a free-composition task. She found that, for learners of all languages, a phrase such as "the child that was hit by him" was easier to process than "the woman to whom he sent the book" or "the woman whose child went across the river," a result suggesting the existence of a universal principle of "accessibility hierarchy" in ease of acquisition. Also within a universal-grammar framework, other SLA researchers investigate how, at a deep abstract level, different languages give different values to certain aspects or parameters of universal principles. For example, Suzanne Flynn examined the particular difficulties Japanese learners of English have because of deep syntactic differences between the two languages.

A second perspective in second-language research is that of cognitive psychology. Barry McLaughlin, a major researcher of cognitive processes in language learning, made the useful distinction between automatic and controlled processes to explain the differences between proficient and less proficient learners. According to cognitive theory, "learning a language is acquiring a complex cognitive skill" that involves "the gradual accumulation of automatized subskills and a constant restructuring of internalized representations as the learner achieves increasing degrees of mastery" (*Theories* 148). Learners of French first gain automatic knowledge of the forms of the *imparfait* and the *passé composé*, slowly build for themselves a representation of when to use one or the other, and then revise and restructure this representation to match the way native speakers use these tenses in speaking and writing. Claus Faerch and Gabriele Kasper distinguish between declarative knowledge, which consists of internalized rules and memorized chunks of the language, and procedural knowledge, which consists of knowing how to accumulate, automatize, and restructure the forms and their use in communication. Experimentation based on observation, introspection, and retrospection has yielded insights into the strategies and procedures used by learners. The work of Ellen Bialystok, Maria Fröhlich, and John Howard and of Elaine Tarone on communication strategies, of Rod Ellis on systematic and nonsystematic variability in interlanguage, and of J. Michael O'Malley and Anna U. Chamot on learning strategies are all important milestones in SLA research done within a psycholinguistic framework. The now classic study by N. Naiman, Maria Fröhlich, H. H. Stern, and A. Todesco on the "good language learner" has been expanded by Anita Wenden and Joan Rubin, and Lily Wong Fillmore's study of the social and cognitive strategies used by Spanish children learning English has had a far-reaching effect on cognitive approaches to SLA.

Investigation of the way learners use language for communication has also been carried out within a sociolinguistic framework, the third perspective. It studies the relation between language acquisition and its social context—in the classroom, the community, or written texts. A sociolinguistic approach has suggested that second-language acquisition is analogous to processes involved in pidginization and creolization, where people who do not share a common language develop a language with a reduced range of structures and uses, like the pidgin variety of English spoken in New Guinea. John Schumann hypothesized that pidginization is a result of the social and psychological distance between the learner and the target culture, which might account for the desire to acculturate or not and, hence, to learn the language. For example, the Heidelberger Forschungsprojekt Pidgin-German, reported on by Wolfgang Klein and Norbert Dittmar, studied the acquisition of German syntax by forty-eight Spanish and Italian immigrant workers in Germany who received no formal language instruction. It showed that the syntactic development of their interlanguage was indeed related to several factors, such as age and length of education, but the highest correlation was found between syntactic development and leisure contact with Germans, an indication that social proximity is a critical factor in successful language acquisition.

As a subset of sociolinguistics, a discourse-analysis approach to SLA, led by Hatch, studies the speech adjustments native speakers make when they enter into verbal contact with nonnative speakers or learners. By observing this "foreigner talk" and also by watching phenomena of turn taking and conversational correction, researchers of language classrooms hope to achieve a better understanding of the interactional constraints on language acquisition, especially in classrooms. Along with the quantitative research methods more typical of sociolinguistics, classroom research has started to adopt ethnographic methods of inquiry that include case studies, diary studies, introspective and retrospective accounts, recall protocols, and long-term association of the researcher with his or her subjects.

Besides cognitive and discourse processes, SLA is interested in the affective factors that shape a learner's acquisition of a second language. A fourth perspective comes therefore from social psychology, which focuses on the influence of situational factors and individual differences on language learning. Howard C. Gardner and Wallace E. Lambert's innovative work on attitudes and motivation in language learning and Howard Giles and J. Byrne's intergroup approach to second-language acquisition have had a widespread effect on the field. H. Douglas Brown is well-known for his work on affective variables. Additional studies such as those of David R. Krathwohl, Benjamin Bloom, and Bertram B. Masia on the affective domain, Leslie M. Beebe on risk taking, and Kathleen Bailey on competitiveness and anxiety in language learning are examples of the large body of research devoted to personality factors in language acquisition.

The four theoretical perspectives sketched above testify to the disciplinary diversity of SLA. Guided by hypotheses based on linguistic, cognitive, sociolinguistic, and social psychological theory, it looks at data from actual learner performance and attempts to build models of language learning that can both explain and predict successful performance. I turn now to a few empirical studies and some of the models proposed.

Empirical Studies

Taking as their point of departure raw data collected or elicited from learners in natural or instructional settings, SLA studies examine the performance of several learners at a single point in time (cross-sectional studies) or of one learner over a period of time (longitudinal studies). These observations are then screened for consistencies and variations and interpreted.

Selinker's interlanguage study, which is based on evidence collected by other researchers from learners in natural and instructional settings, posited that language learning proceeds in a series of transitional stages, as learners acquire more knowledge of the L2. At each stage, they are in control of a language system that is equivalent to neither the L1 nor the L2—an interlanguage. Selinker suggests that five principal processes operate in interlanguage: (1) language transfer, such as German time-place order after the verb in the English interlanguage of German speakers; (2) overgeneralization of target-language rules, such as in the sentence "What did he intended to say?"; (3) transfer of training, such as the confusion of *he* and *she* because of the overuse of *he* in textbooks and drills; (4) strategies of L2 learning, such as the simplification in "Don't worry, I'm hearing him"; (5) strategies of L2 communication, such as the avoidance of grammatical form to fulfill the more pressing needs of communication in "I was in Frankfurt when I fill application."

Selinker's study has triggered many debates about what this interlanguage is. First, identifying the errors made in the learner's interlanguage is difficult. For example, is "I fill application" an error of pronunciation, morphology (lack of awareness of the past tense), or syntax (lack of awareness of concordance of tenses)? a learning or a communication strategy? Furthermore, linguists disagree about what constitutes the initial state of a learner's interlanguage. From a cognitive perspective, second-language learners do not start with a clean slate: they already have, from their first language, a range of cognitive and communicative abilities that enable them to understand structures they have never encountered. As sociolinguists point out, the concept of the L2 native speaker is an ideal or standard construct that has no social reality. Even native speakers are not equally proficient on topics they don't know, in social settings they are unfamiliar with, and in speech genres they have not been educated in.

The question is, then, Is interlanguage a unitary construct, or do learners have various competencies at various times for various tasks in various situations? Further questions under discussion are, Can interlanguage become fossilized at some intermediary stage, or does it remain amenable to change, and under what conditions does change occur?

To answer some of these questions, SLA research has conducted descriptive studies around three general questions: What does it mean to know a language? What are the processes involved in learning a language? What learning conditions favor or impede language acquisition? These studies are all predicated on the view that learning a language means not only learning forms and structures but learning how to use these forms accurately and appropriately in various social settings.

What does it mean to know a language? Michael P. Breen and Christopher N. Candlin have argued that knowing a foreign language means having the ability to express, interpret, and negotiate intended meanings, a definition that goes far beyond using the right grammatical rule or the right item of vocabulary. Others have attempted to define the various components of communicative competence. For example, studies by Michael Canale and by Canale and Swain have identified four distinct aspects that do not automatically overlap: grammatical competence, or the ability to understand and produce grammatically correct sentences; discourse competence, or the ability to connect sentences in stretches of discourse and to form a meaningful whole out of a series of utterances; sociolinguistic competence, or the ability to conform to socially and culturally appropriate norms of verbal behavior; and strategic competence, which enables the learner to function in a way that compensates for deficiencies in the other three competencies.

What are the processes involved in learning a language? We have seen that a large body of work is devoted to the strategies learners employ to comprehend and produce spoken language (see Faerch and Kasper; Fillmore, Kempler, and Wang). An equally large body of research focuses on reading in a second language. Building on the work of psychologists and cognitive scientists like Walter Kintsch, and Richard C. Anderson and David A. Ausubel, SLA researchers have shown how second-language readers use information-processing strategies to create meaning out of the words on the page. They develop and activate cognitive schemata, or mental representations, that allow them to anticipate incoming information and link it to other representations they might already have. Forming these schemata is more complex than deciphering the surface form of the words is. Once they have acquired an automatic recognition of the forms, second-language readers need to restructure their schemata to fit the newly emerging meanings. Patricia L. Carrell's and Margaret Steffensen's studies of learners of English as a second language, Elizabeth Bernhardt's and Janet Swaffar's studies of learners of German, and James Lee's study of learners of Spanish in the United States have shown how misrepresentations can occur if learners do not reorganize their initial schemata or if they cannot develop the culturally relevant schemata. For instance, American college students misread a German text about the "death of forests" (*Waldsterben*) as a text about the "end of the world" (*Weltsterben*), and North American readers adequately decoded but culturally misconstrued an English account of an Indian wedding.

What learning conditions favor or impede language acquisition? Many studies examine the learners themselves and the influence of age, intelligence, aptitude, motivation, and personality. With respect to age, Eric H. Lenneberg's 1967 study introduced the idea that during a certain critical period language acquisition takes place naturally and effortlessly. With the onset of puberty, it was claimed, the plasticity of the brain begins to disappear and lateralization of the language function in the left hemisphere of the brain is completed. Thus adults have greater difficulty learning languages. The critical-period hypothesis has been seriously called into question in recent years. Although children are quicker than adolescents to acquire those linguistic skills necessary for rapid socialization and integration into the target group (including nativelike pronunciation), adolescents, who have greater cognitive skills, outperform children in grammatical and lexical accuracy. Adults, too, have greater cognitive abilities that help them acquire primary levels of language proficiency more rapidly than children do. Researchers like Seliger have therefore suggested multiple critical periods ("Implication"). For example, there may be one critical period for the acquisition of nativelike pronunciation and another for the acquisition of grammar.

One of the best-known studies of motivation in second-language learning was carried out by Gardner and Lambert, who over a period of twelve years studied foreign language learners in Canada, the United States, and the Philippines in an attempt to determine how attitudinal and motivational factors affect language-learning success. They distinguished two kinds of motivation: instrumental and integrative. Instrumental motivation is motivation to attain instrumental goals, such as furthering a career, reading technical material, or going to the target country; integrative motivation is motivation to integrate oneself within the culture of the second-language group and to be part of that society. Gardner and Lambert found that integrative motivation generally accompanied higher scores on proficiency tests in a foreign language.

Besides exploring learner-dependent conditions of acquisition, SLA scholars have also investigated the effects of the learning environment itself. Interaction between children and caretakers seems to play an important role in L1 acquisition. For example, the discourse "scaffolding" provided by adults in their conversations with children (Child: "Hiding." Adult: "Hiding? What's hiding?" Child: "Balloon hiding.") might help these children acquire the syntactic structures of full grammatical sentences in their first language. In a similar manner, as Seliger ("Practice") and Long ("Native Speaker") have argued, interaction with other speakers of the language seems to play a crucial role in the acquisition of syntactic and lexical structures by L2 learners, by providing them with what Krashen calls "comprehensible input" and the opportunity to negotiate the meaning of that input (*Second Language*).

In the past, language researchers have tried to study ways in which classroom instruction and other learning environments can be manipulated for more efficient language acquisition. Until the 1970s, attempts were made to establish the relative merits of one pedagogical "method" over another (e.g., grammar-translation vs. audiolingual vs. communicative). However, as Janet Swaffar, Katherine Arens, and Martha Morgan demonstrated in an influential study in 1982, such comparisons proved futile. Too many uncontrollable variables made it impossible to separate a given method from the personal variations introduced by the teacher and a given group of learners. Furthermore, these comparisons were interested only in the linguistic product, not in the learner's underlying processes of acquisition. By contrast, recent studies, under the rubric "classroom research," look at small pieces of the SLA picture. Pica, for example, classifies the types of corrections or repairs made in language classrooms; she also investigates the types of tasks given to the learners and the appropriateness of those tasks in fostering communicative goals. Susan M. Gass and Evangeline M. Varonis examine gender differences in the way classroom discourse is managed; Long looks at modifications in teacher talk ("Questions").

Model Building

Several of the studies mentioned above have generated models or hypotheses that are the object of heated debates. One of these is Krashen's monitor model, which is based on data from untutored and tutored second-language acquisition. Proposed for the first time in 1977 and developed subsequently in 1981 and

1982, the model offers a prime example of the lively controversies that dominate the field at the present time (see Krashen's "Monitor Model"; *Principles; Second Language*). From his and others' studies of the modifications that parents and caretakers make when talking to young children, Krashen made three observations: (1) Caretakers talk in a simplified manner to make themselves understood. (2) Their input is only roughly tuned to the children's linguistic knowledge, containing many structures the children already know but also some not yet acquired. (3) Their speech refers to the here and now of the immediate environment.

With these observations from a limited sample, Krashen posited his two widely debated hypotheses. In the first, the "acquisition-learning hypothesis," learners are said to make use of two different kinds of linguistic knowledge: explicit or learned knowledge (with conscious application of learned rules) and implicit or acquired knowledge (with unconscious application of use patterns learners have "picked up," so to speak). According to Krashen, learning and acquisition are two distinct, nonoverlapping systems of knowledge. Learning is achieved through the monitor, the device that learners use to oversee their language performance and edit it in accordance with the formal rules of the language. However, since Krashen views acquisition, not learning, as the primary process for the development of communicative competence, the value of formal language instruction is called into question by his model.

The second hypothesis is the "input hypothesis." Learners are said to learn the language automatically when they are exposed to comprehensible input containing linguistic structures that are just beyond their present level of mastery and when they don't feel threatened by the learning environment, that is, when their "affective filter" is down. Both hypotheses have had widespread repercussions among researchers and teachers alike. They have triggered a large body of research related to the nature of the input, the concept of comprehensibility, and the factors that contribute to making this input comprehensible.

Despite the popularity of Krashen's model and its marked effect on language teaching methodology in the United States, many researchers feel that it is inaccurate. In 1978, McLaughlin and Bialystok, both noted for their work on cognitive processes in language learning, were the first to refute Krashen's model. McLaughlin, who was trained as a psychologist, rephrased Krashen's conscious versus unconscious dichotomy into a more accurate description of controlled versus automatic processes in language learning (see his "Monitor Model"). He argued later that second-language learning involves "the gradual integration of subskills [that] as controlled processes initially dominate and then become automatic" (*Theories* 139). McLaughlin suggests that the distinction between consciousness and unconsciousness is located on a continuum.

Opposing Krashen's learning and acquisition model, Bialystok, a trained linguist, offered a distinction between explicit and implicit linguistic knowledge (see her "Theoretical Model"). In the explicit category are the facts a person knows about language and the ability to articulate those facts. Implicit knowledge is information that is automatically and spontaneously used in language tasks. Both types of knowledge exist on a continuum, and they are linked to each other by connecting inferencing processes. McLaughlin and Bialystok each argued that the cognitive processes involved in second-language acquisition are much more complex than Krashen would like us to believe.

Since the 1970s, the monitor model has continued to provoke discussion. Long, who has done extensive research on interaction in ESL classrooms, insists that "instruction makes a difference" and that learned knowledge can indeed become acquired knowledge. Swain, known for her studies of French immersion programs in Canada, argues not that input is comprehensible per se but that it is made comprehensible through communicative interaction and is thus linked to "comprehensible output." Applying these findings to classroom practice, Wilga M. Rivers calls comprehension and production the "interactive duo" (see "Comprehension"). She maintains that to acquire a language, learners need to produce it actively, not just be exposed to it. For the time being, the usefulness of Krashen's hypotheses may lie less in their ability to predict language acquisition than in the metaphorical framework they provide for conceptualizing language-learning processes.

Other scholars have attempted to build models of language acquisition from empirical data. Whereas the monitor model hardly accounts for language-learner variability in language learning, Schumann's acculturation model or pidginization hypothesis tries to explain the variations introduced by affective and social factors. From data collected through diary studies, questionnaires, and interviews with learners, in particular from one adult Spanish speaker's acquisition of English in the United States, Schumann claims that similar psychosocial processes underlie both the formation of pidgins and spontaneous second-language acquisition. His Hispanic subject in the United States, Alberto, who was exposed to a high degree of social distance from English speakers, failed to progress very far in learning English. Alberto's English was characterized by many of the forms observed in pidgins, such as "no + verb" negatives, uninverted interrogatives, and the absence of possessive and plural inflections. Early language learners and immigrant workers, who have to acquire the dominant language for special purposes, develop a simplified variety of language called pidgin, which both satisfies their communicative needs and reflects their social and cultural distance vis-à-vis the target culture.

Set within a sociopsychological framework, Giles and Byrne's accommodation model of language learning shares certain premises with Schumann's acculturation model, but for Giles and Byrne what affects second-language acquisition is not the actual social distance between the learner's social group and the target-language community but the group members' *perception* of this distance and their definition of themselves and others. This model, like Schumann's, illustrates attempts by SLA researchers to explain individual variance in learners through motivation, societal context, and the learners' objectives in that context. Neither the acculturation nor the accommodation model alone explains how environmental and learner-internal processes interact and how they affect the rate and success of second-language acquisition. Several other models of language acquisition have been proposed, in particular by Ellis and McLaughlin (*Theories*).

The developments in SLA research reveal a great diversity of approaches and research tools that, in turn, reflects the variety of issues under study. In addition to questions common to first- and second-language acquisition research, such as competence versus performance and conscious versus unconscious learning, issues in second-language learning include the effects of learner personality and experience and all the variational factors of context and social interaction. To date, no comprehensive theory captures all the various contexts of occurrence, products, and processes involved in second-language acquisition. Indeed, some researchers believe, with Charles A. Ferguson and Thomas Huebner, that it is not even advisable to strive for such a theory at the present time, since it could potentially trivialize the field with a single paradigmatic view.

For the moment, the various models and hypotheses are useful as research heuristics, and the cross-disciplinary debates they engender are healthy and intellectually fruitful. The effect of SLA research on language instruction has to be sought not so much for the direct clues it gives teachers about what and how to teach but, rather, for the understanding it gives them about the enormous complexity of second-language acquisition processes. As Patsy M. Lightbown remarks, "Language acquisition research can offer no formulas, no recipes, but it is an essential component of teacher education, because it can give teachers appropriate expectations for themselves and their students" (183). In conclusion, I briefly discuss some of these expectations.

PRACTICAL IMPLICATIONS FOR LANGUAGE TEACHING AND LEARNING

SLA research has considerably changed our thinking about the way people learn to listen, speak, read, and write in a second language. Three major goals for language teachers have emerged from SLA research: focus on the learner, emphasize learning processes and communication strategies, and provide interaction with the social context.

When the communicative revolution in language teaching started in Europe in the early 1970s, it was based on an analysis of learners' needs and purposes and the threshold of competence deemed necessary for speakers to function within the European community. Since then, research in this country has shed some light on what learners can and cannot be expected to do at various levels of competence. For example, Corder's and Selinker's work on learners' errors make teachers realize how futile it can be to correct every single error on the spot and to attempt to prevent the learners from making errors at all cost. Since making errors is evidence that the learner is hypothesizing and testing the system, a more flexible pedagogy is called for, one that encourages risk taking and experimentation with the language according to the communicative demands of the moment. This idea doesn't mean that errors should never be corrected. Teachers who choose not to rephrase a student's utterance in a correct manner but to let the error pass uncorrected, focusing on the message rather than on the form, can still keep their ears attuned to patterns of errors and then deal with them globally at a later time.

Even within the various levels of proficiency established in the guidelines issued by the American Council on the Teaching of Foreign Languages, teachers should expect great variability among learners. Students differ not only in what they have been taught but in their types and degrees of literacy, motivation, and anxiety, their age, and their relation to the speech community whose language their are learning. Focusing on the learner rather than on the textbook or the method means that the teacher finds out the individual differences among learners, such as the students' different interests or learning styles, and consciously varies the activities to match—with some activities reflecting a more analytic, deductive approach and some a more analogic, inductive way of learning. Studies by Kathleen Bailey and Leslie M. Beebe show that learner anxiety has many sources: the fear of getting a bad grade, of not saying what you mean, of understanding the words but not the intentions, of having to speak in front of twenty other students, of not only entering a new culture but having to help the teacher run the lesson as smoothly as possible. These studies help teachers confront their own fears as they try to deal with those of their students.

By emphasizing learning processes over linguistic products, SLA research makes teachers aware of the procedures by which learners organize knowledge and generate meaning from the forms they learn: how learners compare and contrast the new information with their existing cognitive schemata, how they build and test hypotheses, how they construct their own interlanguage to fit their immediate and long-term communicative needs. The work of McLaughlin can help teachers realize how much "cognitive restructuring" goes on in the minds of their students, and it can temper teachers' surprise if the output students produce on tests doesn't always correspond to the input they were given. In fact, the teacher's task is to give students the opportunity to rephrase, restructure, and reorganize the content and the form of dialogues and readings. Thus, comprehension questions that merely require students to lift the right responses from a text do nothing to help them restructure, or make sense of, the text. Instead, brainstorming techniques and advance organizers are among the many reading strategies that have been suggested in recent years, for example by Swaffar, to help students learn.

Recent research on communication strategies has direct applications for the teaching of speaking and reading. Learners can no longer expect to understand and be understood by others in conversation on the basis of their knowledge of grammar and vocabulary alone. Conversation has its social rules without which rules of grammar would be useless, and these rules are often different in the foreign language; they have to be observed and learned. In the same manner, learners should not be disappointed if they understand all the words on the page yet still don't know what the text is about. Meaning is a matter not of decoding signs but of establishing connections, making inferences, drawing conclusions, and constructing the appropriate schemata.

The work by Canale and Swain on communicative competence should make teachers aware of the importance of strategic competence in both speaking and reading. Communication strategies can and should be taught explicitly during classroom activities: how to interrupt another speaker, how to switch topics during group work, how to begin a conversation when acting out the dialogue, how to end the conversation. These and other tactics are the social glue of face-to-face encounters that speakers need to conduct conversations and develop fluency in the language.

Recognizing the importance of the social context of communication means that learners are encouraged to view language learning not only as the acquisition of a body of factual knowledge that can be displayed on a test but as an interactional process in which learning the forms and using them in communication are inseparable. SLA research shows that this interaction is central to the learning process: interaction of learners with peers, teachers, native speakers, and written texts. Fillmore's work on differences among learners can inspire teachers to pass on to their students some of the social and cognitive strategies successful learners use: "Join a group and act as if you understand what's going on, even if you don't; get some expressions you understand, and start talking; make the most of what you've got; work on big things first, save the details for later" (209). Teaching language as social interaction calls for a diversification of classroom formats, such as group and pair work, to maximize opportunities for interactions of various kinds. It also calls for an increased use of "authentic" materials, whose social meaning lies beyond the illustration of grammatical rules.

Finally, as the pragmatics strand of SLA research has shown, culture is inscribed in the very discourse that learners acquire. Teachers and learners must recognize that no language is innocent and that, along with the language, they teach and are taught a style of interaction and of knowledge presentation that characterizes the culture of a given speech community or educational institution. A critical view of language in discourse should help learners understand the links not only between the language and the culture they are learning but also between their own language and culture.[1]

Suggestions for Further Reading

For detailed studies of some of the key issues under investigation in SLA, the most useful edited volumes are those by Susan M. Gass and Carolyn G. Madden, *Input in Second Language Acquisition*; Gass and Larry Selinker, *Language Transfer in Language Learning*; and Gass, Madden, Dennis Preston, and Selinker, *Variation in Second Language Acquisition*. Two excellent reviews of the work done in SLA research can be found in Rod Ellis, *Understanding Second Language Acquisition*, and Leslie M. Beebe, *Issues in Second Language Acquisition*, as well as in influential articles by Michael H. Long, Patsy M. Lightbown, and Charles A. Ferguson and Thomas Huebner. Kenji Hakuta, *Mirror of Language: The Debate on Bilingualism*, gives a well-balanced and dispassionate state-of-the-art review of research on that hotly debated topic. Classics in the general field of applied linguistics include two books by British linguists, S. Pit Corder and J. P. B. Allen, *The Edinburgh Course in Applied Linguistics*, and Henry G. Widdowson, *Explorations in Applied Linguistics*.

To get a broader outlook on the issues of language learning and teaching, prospective scholars will find it extremely useful to read Jerome Bruner, *Actual Minds, Possible Worlds*; James Wertsch, *Culture, Communication and Cognition*; John J. Gumperz, *Discourse Strategies*; Shirley Brice Heath, *Ways with Words*; and Dell Hymes, "On Communicative Competence," as well as any of the numerous volumes in the series Advances in Discourse Processes (ed. Roy O. Freedle) that offer an interdisciplinary perspective on all aspects of language learning and use.

H. H. Stern's *Fundamental Concepts of Language Teaching* is the standard reference work for all foreign language teachers, along with Wilga M. Rivers, *Teaching Foreign Language Skills*; Sandra Savignon, *Communicative Competence: Theory and Classroom Practice*; and H. Douglas Brown, *Principles of Language Learning and Teaching*. The United States proficiency orientation in language teaching is best illustrated in Alice Omaggio, *Teaching Language in Context*.

There are five major journals: *TESOL Quarterly* and *Modern Language Journal* contain an easily readable mix of empirical research and pedagogic articles; *Applied Linguistics*, *Studies in Second Language Acquisition*, and *Language Learning* contain more difficult theoretical and empirical studies.

Of professional interest are the *Proficiency Guidelines*, published by the American Council for the Teaching of Foreign Languages (ACTFL); Helen Kornblum's *Directory of Professional Preparation Programs in TESOL in the United States*, and the publications of the Center for Applied Linguistics in Washington, D.C.

University of California, Berkeley

Note

[1] I am grateful to Carl Blyth, Heidi Byrnes, and Janet Swaffar, as well as to the many anonymous reviewers, for their helpful comments on earlier drafts of this essay.

Works Cited

Allen, J. P. B, Maria Fröhlich, and Nina Spada. "The Communicative Orientation of Language Teaching: An Observation Scheme." *On TESOL '83: The Question of*

Control. Ed. Jean Handscombe, Richard A. Orem, and Barry Taylor. Washington: TESOL, 1984. 231–52.

Allwright, Richard. *Observation in the Language Classroom.* New York: Longman, 1988.

American Council for the Teaching of Foreign Languages. *ACTFL Proficiency Guidelines.* Hastings-on-Hudson: ACTFL, 1986.

Anderson, Richard C., and David A. Ausubel, eds. *Readings in the Psychology of Cognition.* New York: Holt, 1965.

Bailey, Kathleen. "Competitiveness and Anxiety in Adult Second Language Learning: Looking at and through the Diary Studies." Seliger and Long 67–103.

Beebe, Leslie M., ed. *Issues in Second Language Acquisition: Multiple Perspectives.* Rowley: Newbury, 1987.

———. "Risk-Taking and the Language Learner." Seliger and Long 39–66.

Bernhardt, Elizabeth. "Reading in the Foreign Language." *Listening, Reading, and Writing: Analysis and Application.* Ed. Barbara Wing. Middlebury: Northeast Conference, 1986. 93–115.

Bever, Thomas G. "Perceptions, Thought, and Language." Freedle and Carroll 99–112.

Bialystok, Ellen. "A Theoretical Model of Second Language Learning." *Language Learning* 28 (1978): 69–83.

Bialystok, Ellen, Maria Fröhlich, and John Howard. *Studies in Second Language Teaching and Learning in Classroom Settings: Strategies, Processes and Functions.* Toronto: Ontario Inst. for Studies in Education, 1979.

Blum-Kulka, Shoshonna, Juliane House, and Gabriele Kasper, eds. *Cross-Cultural Pragmatics: Requests and Apologies.* Advances in Discourse Processes 31. Ed. Roy O. Freedle. Norwood: Ablex, 1990.

Breen, Michael P. "The Social Context for Language Learning—A Neglected Situation?" *Studies in Second Language Acquisition* 7 (1985): 135–58.

Breen, Michael P., and Christopher N. Candlin. "The Essentials of a Communicative Curriculum in Language Teaching." *Applied Linguistics* 1 (1980): 89–112.

Brown, H. Douglas. "Affective Variables in Second Language Acquisition." *Language Learning* 23 (1973): 231–44.

———. *Principles of Language Learning and Teaching.* 2nd ed. Englewood Cliffs: Prentice, 1987.

Bruner, Jerome. *Actual Minds, Possible Worlds.* Cambridge: Harvard UP, 1987.

Canale, Michael. "From Communicative Competence to Communicative Language Pedagogy." *Language and Communication.* Ed. Jack C. Richards and Richard Schmidt. London: Longman, 1983. 2–27.

Canale, Michael, and Merrill Swain. "Theoretical Bases of Communicative Approaches to Second Language Teaching and Testing." *Applied Linguistics* 1 (1980): 1–47.

Carrell, Patricia L. "Three Components of Background Knowledge in Reading Comprehension." *Language Learning* 33 (1979): 183–207.

Chaudron, Craig. *Second Language Classrooms.* Cambridge: Cambridge UP, 1988.

Chomsky, Noam. *Syntactic Structures.* The Hague: Mouton, 1957.

Corder, S. Pit. "The Significance of Learners' Errors." *International Review of Applied Linguistics in Language Teaching* 5 (1967): 161–69.

Corder, S. Pit, and J. P. B. Allen, eds. *The Edinburgh Course in Applied Linguistics.* Oxford: Oxford UP, 1974.

Cummins, James. "Cognitive/Academic Language Proficiency, Linguistic Interdependence, the Optimal Age Question, and Some Other Matters." *Working Papers on Bilingualism* 19 (1979): 197–205.

Di Pietro, Robert J. *Language Structures in Contrast.* Rowley: Newbury, 1971.

Dulay, Heidi, and Marina Burt. "Natural Sequences in Child Second Language Acquisition." *Language Learning* 24 (1974): 37–53.

Edmondson, Willis J. "Some Problems concerning the Evaluation of Foreign Language Classroom Discourse." *Applied Linguistics* 1 (1980): 271–87..

Ellis, Rod. *Understanding Second Language Acquisition.* New York: Oxford UP, 1986.

Faerch, Claus, and Gabriele Kasper, eds. *Strategies in Interlanguage Communication.* London: Longman, 1983.

Ferguson, Charles A. "Language Teaching and Theories of Language." *Language Teaching, Testing, and Technology: Lessons from the Past with a View toward the Future.* Georgetown Univ. Round Table on Languages and Linguistics. Ed. James E. Alatis. Washington: Georgetown UP, 1989. 81–88.

Ferguson, Charles A., and Thomas Huebner. *Foreign Language Instruction and Second Language Acquisition Research in the United States.* Occasional Papers 1. Washington: Natl. Foreign Lang. Center, 1989.

Fillmore, Charles J., D. Kempler, and W. Wang, eds. *Individual Differences in Language Ability and Language Behavior.* New York: Academic, 1979.

Fillmore, Lily Wong. "Individual Differences in Second Language Acquisition." Fillmore, Kempler, and Wang 203–28.

Flynn, Suzanne. "Similarities and Differences between First and Second Language Acquisition: Setting the Parameters of Universal Grammar." *Acquisition of Symbolic Skills.* Ed. D. R. Rogers and J. A. Sloboda. New York: Plenum, 1983. 485–99.

Freedle, Roy O., and John B. Carroll, eds. *Language Comprehension and the Acquisition of Knowledge.* New York: Wiley, 1972.

Gardner, Howard C., and Wallace E. Lambert. *Attitudes and Motivation in Language Learning.* Rowley: Newbury, 1972.

Gass, Susan M. "Language Transfer and Universal Grammatical Relations." *Language Learning* 29 (1979): 327–44.

Gass, Susan M., and Carolyn G. Madden, eds. *Input in Second Language Acquisition.* Rowley: Newbury, 1985.

Gass, Susan M., Carolyn G. Madden, Dennis Preston, and Larry Selinker, eds. *Variation in Second Language Acquisition.* 2 vols. Clevedon: Multilingual Matters, 1989.

Gass, Susan M., and Evangeline M. Varonis. "Sex Differences in NNS/NNS Interactions." *Talking to Learn: Conversation in Second Language Acquisition.* Ed. Richard Day. Rowley: Newbury, 1986. 327–51.

Gass, Susan M., and Larry Selinker, eds. *Language Transfer in Language Learning.* Rowley: Newbury, 1983.

Giles, Howard, and J. Byrne. "An Intergroup Approach to Second Language Acquisition." *Journal of Multilingual and Multicultural Development* 3 (1982): 17–40.

Goodman, Kenneth. "Reading: A Psycholinguistic Guessing Game." *Language and Reading, An Interdisciplinary Approach.* Ed. D. V. Gunderson. Washington: CAL, 1970. 107–19.

Gumperz, John J. *Discourse Strategies.* Cambridge: Cambridge UP, 1983.

———, ed. *Language and Social Identity.* Cambridge: Cambridge UP, 1983.

Hakuta, Kenji. *Mirror of Language: The Debate on Bilingualism.* New York: Basic, 1986.

Halliday, M. A. K. *Language as Social Semiotic: The Social Interpretation of Language and Meaning.* London: Arnold, 1978.

Hatch, Evelyn. "Acquisition of Syntax in a Second Language." *Understanding Second and Foreign Language Learning: Issues and Approaches.* Ed. Jack C. Richards. Rowley: Newbury, 1978. 34–70.

———, ed. *Second Language Acquisition: A Book of Readings.* Rowley: Newbury, 1978.

Heath, Shirley Brice. *Ways with Words: Language, Life, and Work in Communities and Classrooms.* Cambridge: Cambridge UP, 1983.

Hymes, Dell. "On Communicative Competence." *Sociolinguistics.* Ed. J. B. Pride and Janet Holmes. Harmondsworth, Eng.: Penguin, 1972. 269–93.

Kasper, Gabriele. *Pragmatische Aspekte in der Interimsprache. Eine Untersuchung des Englischen fortgeschrittener deutscher Lerner.* Tubingen: Narr, 1981.

Kintsch, Walter. *The Representation of Meaning in Memory.* Hillsdale: Erlbaum, 1974.

Klein, Wolfgang, and Norbert Dittmar. *Developing Grammars: The Acquisition of German Syntax by Foreign Workers.* New York: Springer, 1979.

Kornblum, Helen. *Directory of Professional Preparation Programs in TESOL in the United States: 1989–1991.* Alexandria: TESOL, 1989.

Kramsch, Claire. *New Directions in the Teaching of Language and Culture.* Occasional Papers 3. Washington: Nat. Foreign Lang. Center, 1989.

Krashen, Stephen. "The Monitor Model for Adult Second Language Performance." *Viewpoints on English as a Second Language.* Ed. Marina Burt, Heidi Dulay, and Mary Finocchiaro. New York: Regents, 1977. 152–61.

———. *Principles and Practice in Second Language Acquisition.* Englewood Cliffs: Prentice, 1982.

———. *Second Language Acquisition and Second Language Learning.* New York: Prentice, 1981.

Krathwohl, David R., Benjamin Bloom, and Bertram B. Masia. *Taxonomy of Educational Objectives. Handbook H: Affective Domain.* New York: McKay, 1964.

Labov, William. "The Study of Language in Its Social Context." *Studium Generale* 23 (1970): 30–87.

Lado, Robert. *Linguistics across Cultures: Applied Linguistics for Language Teachers.* Ann Arbor: U of Michigan P, 1957.

Lee, James F. "Comprehending the Spanish Subjunctive: An Information Processing Perspective." *Modern Language Journal* 71 (1987): 50–57.

Lenneberg, Eric H. *Biological Foundations of Language.* New York: Wiley, 1967.

Lightbown, Patsy M. "Great Expectations: Second Language Research and Classroom Teaching." *Applied Linguistics* 6 (1986): 173–89.

Long, Michael H. "Does Second Language Instruction Make a Difference?" *TESOL Quarterly* 17 (1983): 359–82.

———. "Native Speaker/Non-native Speaker Conversation and the Negotiation of Comprehensible Input." *Applied Linguistics* 4 (1983): 126–41.

———. "Questions in Foreigner Talk Discourse." *Language Learning* 31 (1981): 135–57.

McLaughlin, Barry. "The Monitor Model: Some Methodological Considerations." *Language Learning* 28 (1978): 309–32.

———. *Theories of Second-Language Learning.* London: Arnold, 1987.

Miller, George A. *Language and Communication.* New York: McGraw, 1951.

Moulton, William G. *The Sounds of English and German.* Contrastive Structure Series. Ed. Charles A. Ferguson. Chicago: U of Chicago P, 1962.

Naiman, N., Maria Fröhlich, H. H. Stern, and A. Todesco. *The Good Language Learner.* Research in Education Series 7. Toronto: Ontario Inst. for Studies in Education, 1978.

Omaggio, Alice. *Teaching Language in Context: Proficiency-Oriented Instruction.* Boston: Heinle, 1986.

O'Malley, J. Michael, and Anna U. Chamot. *Learning Strategies in Second Language Acquisition.* Cambridge: Cambridge UP, 1989.

Pica, Teresa. "Second-Language Acquisition, Social Interaction, and the Classroom." *Applied Linguistics* 8 (1987): 2–22.

Pica, Teresa, and Cathy Doughty. "Input and Interaction in the Communicative Language Classroom: A Comparison of Teacher-Fronted and Group Activities." Gass and Madden 115–32.

Richards, Jack C. *Error Analysis: Perspectives on Second Language Acquisition.* London: Longman, 1974.

Rivers, Wilga M. "Comprehension and Production in Interactive Language Teaching." *Modern Language Journal* 70 (1986): 1–7.

———. *Teaching Foreign Language Skills.* 2nd ed. Chicago: U of Chicago P, 1981.

Savignon, Sandra. *Communicative Competence: Theory and Classroom Practice.* Reading: Addison, 1983.

Scarcella, Robin C. "Discourse Accent in Second Language Performance." Gass and Selinker 306–26.

Schumann, John. *The Pidginization Process: A Model for Second Language Acquisition.* Rowley: Newbury, 1978.

Seliger, Herbert W. "Does Practice Make Perfect? A Study of Interaction Patterns and L2 Competence." *Language Learning* 27 (1977): 263–75.

———. "Implication of a Multiple Critical Periods Hypothesis for Second Language Learning." *Second Language Acquisition Research.* Ed. William Ritchie. New York: Academic, 1978. 11–19.

Seliger, Herbert W., and Michael H. Long, eds. *Classroom-Oriented Research in Second Language Acquisition.* Rowley: Newbury, 1983.

Selinker, Larry. "Interlanguage." *International Review of Applied Linguistics in Language Teaching* 10 (1972): 209–31.

Slobin, Daniel. "Cognitive Prerequisites for the Development of Grammar." *Studies in*

Child Language Development. Ed. Charles Ferguson and Daniel Slobin. New York: Holt, 1973. 175–208.

Steffensen, Margaret. "Register, Cohesion, and Cross-Cultural Reading Comprehension." *Applied Linguistics* 7 (1986): 71–85.

Stern, H. H. *Fundamental Concepts of Language Teaching.* Oxford: Oxford UP, 1983.

Swaffar, Janet. "Readers, Texts, and Second Languages: The Interactive Process." *Modern Language Journal* 72 (1988): 163–73.

Swaffar, Janet, Katherine Arens, and Martha Morgan. "Teacher Classroom Practices: Redefining Method as Task Hierarchy." *Modern Language Journal* 66 (1982): 24–33.

Swain, Merrill, and Sharon Lapkin. *Evaluating Bilingual Education: A Canadian Case Study.* Avon: Multilingual Matters, 1982.

Tarone, Elaine. "Communication Strategies, Foreigner Talk, and Repair in Interlanguage." *Language Learning* 30 (1980): 417–31.

Tarone, Elaine, Uli Frauenfelder, and Larry Selinker. "Systematicity/Variability and Stability/Instability in Interlanguage Systems." *Papers in Second Language Acquisition* 4 (1976): 93–134.

Thomas, Jenny. "Cross-Cultural Pragmatic Failure." *Applied Linguistics* 4 (1983): 91–112.

van Dijk, Teun, ed. *Handbook of Discourse Analysis.* 4 vols. New York: Academic, 1985.

van Lier, Leo. *The Classroom and the Language Learner: Ethnography and Second Language Classroom Research.* London: Longman, 1988.

Wenden, Anita, and Joan Rubin. *Learner Strategies in Language Learning.* Englewood Cliffs: Prentice, 1987.

Wertsch, James. *Culture, Communication and Cognition: Vygotskian Perspectives.* Cambridge: Cambridge UP, 1985.

Widdowson, Henry G. *Explorations in Applied Linguistics.* Oxford: Oxford UP, 1979.

———. *Stylistics and the Teaching of Literature.* London: Longman, 1975.

ANDREA A. LUNSFORD

Rhetoric and Composition

THE story of rhetoric and composition told in these pages grows, as it must, out of my own personal and professional experience: as a PhD candidate—and now a professor—in a discipline that has only recently recognized a formal specialization in rhetoric and composition. In the twenty years or so since I began the PhD program, rhetoric and composition, as areas of inquiry and research, have claimed a place in English studies, though that place is by no means uncontested.

How did I come to embark on studies that would lead me to the heart of this contest? By the late 1960s, I had earned a BA and MA in English (meaning at that time "literature"), written a thesis on Faulkner, and taken a job at a new community college. My first major assignment: design a writing program.

I worked very hard at this task, for I wanted badly to teach the students crowding into my classroom, students who would later be called "nontraditional" or "mature," students who represented rich diversity—in age, class, ethnicity—students, I quickly began to learn, I was vastly underprepared to teach. I thought often of Sisyphus and rolled the rock of my classes uphill, lecturing on the "readings" and doing grammar drills, but with less and less confidence. Like most of my friends, I had been trained in close reading of literary texts, and this training was a valuable asset as I concentrated on reading and interpreting student texts. But how to talk about the relation between the texts we were reading and those we were trying to write? And how to *teach* students how to write such texts? These topics had never come up in my training. But now I was doing it (more or less), and *it* was remarkably hard. Then one day I opened the mail to find what was for me a new book: the 1971 edition of *Classical Rhetoric for the Modern Student*, by Edward P. J. Corbett. Here was a world I knew nothing of, a world that offered answers to some of my many questions, most of all a world that took the teaching of writing as its intellectual goal.

On that day I became a student of rhetoric and composition, though I knew only vaguely and intuitively that this field offered the conceptual, theoretical, and political ground for teaching that I was looking for—one that was radically democratic; that valued what was "other"; that blurred the boundaries between disciplines, between the genres of reading, writing, and speaking, between theory and practice, between research and teaching; and that tended carefully to its effects in the world beyond as well as in the academy. These characteristics, I argue, are largely responsible for the remarkable growth of composition and rhetoric during the last quarter century as well as for the vitality, the sense of excitement and playful purpose that animates the field today.

At the time, I knew only that I had a lot of reading to do. As I explored the books Corbett's text led me to, I discovered a growing body of literature on composition, beginning with Richard Braddock, Richard Lloyd-Jones, and Lowell Schoer's 1963 *Research in Written Composition.* I learned to recognize the names that increasingly dotted my new territorial map: Wallace Douglas, Janet Emig, John Gerber, William Irmscher, James Kinneavy, Ken Macrorie, Robert Zoellner. And I began to explore the terra incognita surrounding my small island, to try to discover where this field of study came from. I found that over two thousand years ago, a series of Greek thinkers (including Aspasia, Socrates, Isocrates, Plato, and Aristotle) posed—and debated—two seemingly simple questions: How is it that people use language to understand and persuade one another? What are the ethical responsibilities of those engaged in such language use? I learned also that these questions lie at the center of rhetoric, one of the world's oldest disciplines and the basis of much within English studies today, including composition.

As old as the discipline of rhetoric, I also learned, is the dispute over its definition and role. From Plato, who often equated rhetoric with "quackery" and with making what is only apparent seem "real," to the widespread contemporary use of the term to mean propaganda or lies or both, *rhetoric* has been associated, at best, with the "dress of thought" and, at worst, with bombast, manipulation, and coercion. In this view, rhetoric is merely a set of techniques or tricks. But countering such definitions have been many others—from Aristotle's "the faculty of observing in any given case the available means of persuasion" (24), to Quintilian's art of the "good [wo]man skilled in speaking" (12.355), to Kenneth Burke's "use of language as a symbolic means of inducing cooperation in beings that by nature respond to symbols" (Rhetoric *and* Grammar 567)—definitions that rest on a conception of rhetoric not as technique but as art.

Throughout Western history, then, varying conceptualizations of rhetoric have played on and against one another, creating a dynamic and often highly productive tension. Today this tension can be seen at work in the encounter among varying stories told about rhetoric: the tropological, or "figured," story told by literary theory, in which rhetoric is most often equated with a set of linguistic ornaments and schemes; the pseudoscientific story told by analytic philosophy, in which rhetoric is equated with nonrational or emotional aspects of discourse; the ecological story told by anthropology and some branches of the social sciences, in which rhetoric serves an epistemic, or knowledge-making, function; the essentially commercial story told by much of the mass media, in which rhetoric plays the role of the archetypal snake oil seller.

TOWARD DEFINITION

Those in rhetoric and composition argue for a definition of rhetoric as, in Susan Miller's words, "a plastic art, one that cannot describe, or change, without being changed itself" (*Rescuing* 148). Given the shifting boundaries of such change and the tension implicit in competing definitions and roles, rhetorical scholarship concerns itself with the nature of and relation among the elements in any given language act—speaker (sender, encoder, agent, writer), listener (receiver, audience, decoder, reader), text (message, sign), and context (scene, site, situation)—as well as with the ethical, emotional, rational, and situational appeals that interanimate language or discourse events. In terms of language, rhetoricians may be said to study who is doing what to or with whom in what place(s) for what reason(s) and toward what end(s).

Inextricably related to these concerns are the material conditions of discourse. In this regard, the history of rhetoric traces the development of the arts of oral discourse, the mingling of oral and literate practices, and the spread of literacy and its technologies. At its inception, of course, rhetoric was primarily an oral art, and this focus on orality—on speeches, sermons, and other verbal forms—lingered well into the age of print literacy. As material conditions changed, however, allowing for cheaper and easier production and dissemination of texts, writing and written discourse were fully inscribed in both private and public life.

The history of rhetoric, like all histories, is a story, and one that is being rewritten and reinvented today, particularly by feminist rhetoricians (Jarratt; Swearingen) and by those interested in rereading the Sophistic contribution to rhetoric (Enos; Neel). The history of composition studies, though much smaller in scope (250 years as opposed to 2,500) is no less fraught with controversy: we can find widely differing accounts of this history in work by Albert Kitzhaber, William Riley Parker, S. Michael Halloran, James Berlin, Sharon Crowley, Nan Johnson, and Robert Connors. For all their differences, however, most scholars agree that composition studies evolved in conjunction with changes in the social and material conditions affecting discourse production, particularly in the late eighteenth and nineteenth centuries, conditions that allowed for more and more print literacy; for worlds of words written, not spoken—in short, for textuality.

In American universities, composition was linked first with the oral arts of rhetoric and moral philosophy, later with departments of English, which eventually replaced the classical languages at the center of the curriculum (Graff). For many reasons, composition in these early universities dealt primarily with pragmatic uses of language, with grammar, and with the teaching of written "themes." These goals often seemed at odds with or irrelevant to the study of high literature, and thus the relationship between literature and composition, to say the very least, continued to be a troubled one well into this century. The questioning of New Critical tenets, the critique of English studies offered by Marxists, feminists, and poststructuralists, and the attempts of a group of scholars (Corbett; Kinneavy; Winterowd; Booth; Lauer) to ground composition in an expanded theory of rhetoric slowly created a space for composition and rhetoric in the academy, though not necessarily within English departments (Hairston; Slevin). In fact, readers of this essay may attend schools that offer rhetoric as a specialty within the English department but include composition studies only insofar as the work of the field informs a writing center or a freshman composition course. Other schools may offer an undergraduate major and graduate specialization in composition studies but include little if any of the history of rhetoric. At still other schools, a separate rhetoric department exists, and at yet others the writing program exists outside any departmental structure.

Wherever they may be institutionally situated, scholars in composition today study written discourse in a wide variety of settings, from the home, community, and public arena, to the academy and other institutions as well as professional workplaces. Thus, while rhetoric is interested in building and testing theories of persuasion primarily through the symbol system of language, composition is concerned with the way written texts come to be and the way they are used in the home, school, workplace, and public worlds we all inhabit.

METHODS

As fields of study, rhetoric and composition are thus closely allied, often overlapping, but not synonymous. Both areas of research, however, are of necessity strongly cross-disciplinary, a characteristic they share with other fields that have grown in prominence during the last twenty-five years (such as cognitive science or cultural studies). This cross-disciplinarity is perhaps most evident in the range of research methods scholars of rhetoric and composition typically employ.

Historical Research

Much work in rhetoric seeks to establish—or to disrupt or dispute—histories of the rhetorical tradition, relying on both traditional and "new" methods of historicizing. Where, when, and for what purposes did an art of language use arise in the Western world or in the Middle and Far East? How is the rhetorical tradition in any era related to epistemology and ideology? How did the tradition evolve in England, in Scotland, in Europe, in North America? How has the art of rhetoric manifested itself in the discourse practices of *any* time and place?

Answers to these questions have been offered—and hotly contested—by scholars in rhetoric. Indeed, little agreement exists on *a* story of rhetoric, of *a* rhetorical tradition—and many parts of those stories and that tradition remain largely unexplored. While we know something of rhetoric's history in terms of the Athenian citizenry (an elite all-male group), for example, scholars are only beginning to explore the uses of rhetoric among women and other disenfranchised groups in the classical world. In America, scholars have charted some of the course of rhetoric in higher education, but much less in public and professional discourse. And even the work on rhetoric's role in higher education is limited to colleges populated almost exclusively by white middle- and upper-class males.

Thus much historical scholarship in rhetoric currently demonstrates the ways in which "histories" of rhetoric provide only narrow or partial stories (Jarratt; Enos; Johnson; Crowley; Murphy). In addition, scholars of rhetoric and composition increasingly seek to cross both disciplinary and cultural boundaries. Charles Bazerman's study of discursive practices in physics (*Shaping Written Knowledge*), his ongoing exploration of the discourse community growing up around the concept of electricity (beginning roughly in 1600 and continuing to the present day), and Ann Blakeslee's analysis of developing discourse conventions in *Physics Review* and *Physics Review Letters* represent two examples of cross-disciplinary work. The International Society for the History of Rhetoric stands as an embodiment of cross-cultural study. This scholarly organization, with members from twenty countries, meets biennially to explore the history of rhetoric in all its constituent cultures. The 1989 meeting (held at the University of Göttingen), for instance, featured Roichi Okabe speaking on the influence of Western rhetoric in Japan, Lilia Metodieva on the Bulgarian rhetorical tradition, and Colette Nativel on the topic La théorie de l'imitation au XVII siècle en rhétorique et en peinture. The society's journal, *Rhetorica*, currently publishes articles in English, French, Italian, and Spanish and aims to establish an international forum on the history, nature, functions, and scope of rhetoric. Both the journal and the society's meetings offer exciting opportunities for moving beyond Anglo- or Eurocentric conceptions of rhetoric and for enacting cross-cultural rhetorical research.

Theoretical Research

Since the time of Socrates, Plato, and Aristotle, scholars interested in theory building have sought to articulate principles or models that can account for or describe how language allows meaning to arise. In contemporary North America, Kenneth Burke offers perhaps the most highly complex, elegant theory of language persuasion and motivation, based on his concepts of absence, negativity, identification, and consubstantiality (see in particular *A Rhetoric of Motives, A Grammar of Motives*, and *Language as Symbolic Action*). Belgian rhetoricians Chaim Perelman and L. Olbrechts-Tyteca situate their theory of human persuasion, most fully articulated in *The New Rhetoric*, in the history of argument; they are interested especially in an exploration and expansion of the concept of audience. James Kinneavy's *Theory of Discourse* focuses instead on texts, dividing the textual world according to aims (persuasive, expressive, expository, literary) and modes (descriptive, evaluative, narrative, classificatory). More recently, Linda Flower and her colleagues, concentrating on the writer, have attempted to build a social cognitive theory of composing. Other researchers have worked to build an adequate theory of invention (R. Young; Lauer), of revision (Sommers; Murray), or of reciprocity between writers and readers (Nystrand).

Space limitations allow for only the barest sketch of theoretical research in rhetoric and composition, but perhaps more important than a survey are those points of conflict in the theoretical arena. Certainly one of the most troubled issues regards the adequacy and relevance of earlier theories (particularly those developed during the classical period) to modern discourse. Positions on this question range from enthusiastic adaptation of classical theory (Weaver; Corbett; Vickers; Sloan), to reworkings of that theory (Burke; Toulmin; Winterowd), to outright rejection (Knoblauch and Brannon; Berthoff; Berlin). But if earlier theoretical constructs seem inadequate to account for current discourse practices, so do most contemporary theories, none of which, for instance, encompasses thus far the profound impact of new technologies on writers, readers, and the texts they produce. Nor have contemporary theorists yet managed to capture the full importance of context to any language act, to escape the constraints of ethnocentricity, or to create a theory of rhetoric or of composing flexible enough to allow for the full range of difference in gender, race, class, and culture.

Empirical Research

Nowhere is the methodological conversation more alive with controversy than in the area of empirical research. Since methods used in historical and theoretical research are of long standing in the humanistic disciplines, arguments may rage over the quality of such research or over exactly how best to conduct it, but few scholars question the basic value of historical or theoretical inquiry. Not so with empirical research, however, no doubt partially because some empirical methodologies are characteristic of disciplines outside the humanities, notably the sciences and social sciences. Its strongly cross-disciplinary nature allows rhetoric and composition to draw on diverse methodologies, but it doesn't guarantee that all approaches will be equally accepted by all. Hence the current debate over the efficacy of quantitative and qualitative empirical methods. Those who tend to favor quantitative studies—those which yield to numerical analysis (Witte; Bamberg; Hillocks)—point out that their conclusions can be fully tested and rest on, at the very least, statistical significance. Those who favor qualitative studies, by contrast, point out that human discourse and human persuasion cannot be reduced to controlled experiments with numerical counterparts and that more helpful by far are the "thick descriptions" provided by detailed case studies and ethnographies such as those of Janet Emig, Shirley Brice Heath, and Linda Brodkey. Such an easy opposition between quantitative and qualitative methods, however, seems needlessly reductive, since both kinds of methods can shed light on questions raised by scholars in rhetoric and composition. As a result, many researchers argue for the use of multilayered research designs that may combine, for instance, statistical analysis of a large-scale survey, in-depth case studies of several respondents to the survey, and discourse analysis of documents written by the respondents.

When Lisa Ede and I set out to explore collaborative writing, for example, we began by surveying a random sample of professionals and later conducted case studies and discourse-based interviews. And even then, we decided to widen our angle of vision by including historical analysis as well as pedagogical applications (*Singular Texts/Plural Authors*). For students entering the field of rhetoric and composition, the plethora of research methods—and the heated controversy surrounding their reliability and use—may seem daunting. And, indeed, if researchers had to be equally proficient at using every method, the task would be more than daunting. Luckily, several factors militate against this difficulty. First, much empirical research in rhetoric and composition is carried out collaboratively, with researchers bringing varying areas of expertise to any given project. As a result, few if any researchers want or need to be proficient in the full range of empirical methodologies available. Considerably more manageable is to become familiar enough with the range of methods to read studies based on the use of such methods and to evaluate the results of these studies.

MAJOR RESEARCH QUESTIONS

Methodologies, of course, are only as interesting or as important as the questions they study. For scholars of rhetoric and composition, those questions may most readily be mapped by reference to the coordinates of discourse—writers, readers, texts, contexts—that together allow meaning to arise.

Questions about Writers

What exactly is going on in the act of writing, so much of which is invisible, unavailable for observation? This question has generated an impressive body of research during the last quarter century alone, research closely tied to what is often called the "process movement" in rhetoric and composition. Paralleling similar moves in many other disciplines, from physics to anthropology, this movement shifted the researcher's gaze from the isolated, acontextualized written product to those processes through which the product was created, a shift in this case from the text to the writer. From Janet Emig's landmark study of the composing processes of high school writers and the elegant studies of children's writing behaviors (Dyson; Graves; Harste, Woodward, and Burke; Hilgers) to detailed studies of professional writers at work (Doheny-Farina; Odell and Goswami; Heath), researchers have illuminated the complex web of activities writers engage in as they work.

A Case or Two in Point

Early efforts aimed at creating a model of the writing process are exemplified by Linda Flower and John Hayes's 1981 "Cognitive Process Theory of Writing" (370). The question informing this early essay was: "How does cognition guide composing?" To provide a tentative answer to the question, Flower and her colleagues asked writers (novices as well as experienced professionals) to report aloud on what they were doing as they were writing, carefully recording every-

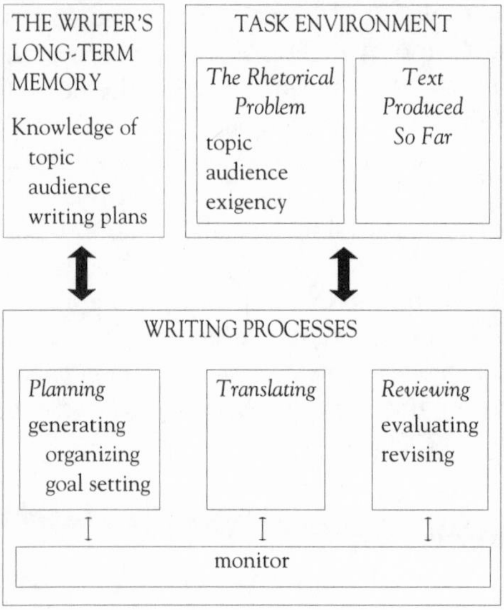

Fig. 1. Flower and Hayes's 1981 model.

Adapted from Linda Flower and John R. Hayes, "A Cognitive Process Theory of Writing," *College Composition and Communication* 32 (1981): 370. © 1981 by the National Council of Teachers of English. Used with permission.

thing these writers said and wrote and then poring over the transcripts of the "protocols" thus produced. Out of a series of such studies grew these researchers' first model, a tentative picture of composing (fig. 1).

As other scholars have responded to this model, Flower has moved to a more speculative kind of inquiry designed to elaborate on and interrogate ways of representing the writing process. A 1989 article, "Studying Cognition in Context," offers her most recent conceptual map (fig. 2). As readers of this volume may well imagine, such attempts to provide speculative conceptual maps or formal models of writing have stirred considerable controversy, especially as they suggest claims for wide generalizability or as they may valorize certain ways of writing (see, e.g., Brooke's "Control in Writing: Flower, Derrida, and Images of the Writer"). Moreover, Flower's ongoing research project, as she is the first to note, rests on studies of American writers only. To broaden perspectives, Alan Purves and his colleagues have been studying writers in eleven countries, aiming to amass a fully international sample of writing and writing behaviors (*Writing across Languages and Cultures: Issues in Contrastive Rhetoric*). While such global research is in its infancy, these studies have already yielded provocative findings regarding differences in the ways writers in varying cultures gather and use information, structure arguments, and evaluate discourse. For those interested in arguing for or against "universals" of writing, as well as those interested in international communication, such research is of great interest.

Until recently, most studies of writers and writing processes rested on largely unexamined assumptions about the nature of the writing subject. *Writer* was defined operationally as "this one who is writing." Along with the radical destabilization of the subject in literary theory, philosophy, and psychology, however, researchers in rhetoric and composition have begun to explore the term *writer* itself, tracing the way it has been defined and realized throughout history and engaging in debate over how these issues impinge on current theory and practice in rhetoric and composition (see Miller; Phelps; Harkin and Schilb; Ede and Lunsford). Such stories aim to explore the constructed nature of the "writer" as well as to describe individual writers at work.

Questions about Readers

In defining *rhetoric* as "the study of misunderstanding and its remedies," I. A. Richards called attention to the importance of readers (or interpreters) in any language act (3). Following this lead, researchers in rhetoric and composition have studied what readers do in an attempt to illuminate both cognitive and social aspects of reading. In particular, scholars have built on work in psychology (Collins and Adams; Kintsch; Kintsch and van Dijk; deBeaugrande) and in literary studies (Iser; Fish; Bleich; Gadamer; Derrida) by providing detailed accounts of readers reading and by exploring the relation between reading and writing.

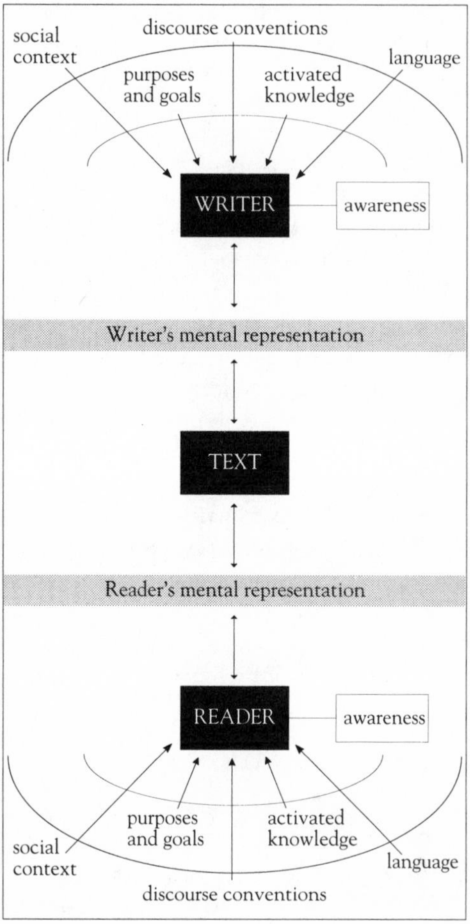

Fig. 2. Flower's 1989 map.

Adapted from Linda Flower et al., *Reading-to-Write: Exploring a Cognitive and Social Process* (New York: Oxford UP, 1990) 13. © 1990 by the Center for the Study of Writing. Used with permission of Oxford University Press, Inc.

A Case or Two in Point

In what specific ways, Elizabeth Flynn wondered, does gender affect reading? With this question in mind, Flynn began studying her own student readers, recording and analyzing their responses to pieces of literature and looking carefully for patterns that might be related to gender. What she found affirmed what feminist colleagues have long argued: that sex and gender roles have a profound influence on ways of reading (and interpreting) and, further, that we as a society are ill-prepared to allow for such differences in our communities, homes, schools, or workplaces ("Gender and Reading," further elaborated in Flynn and Schweickart). On the basis of her case study, Flynn concluded tentatively:

> Reading is a silent, private activity and thus perhaps affords women a degree of protection not present when they speak. Quite possibly the hedging and tentativeness of women's speech are transformed into useful interpretive strategies—receptivity and yet critical assessment of the text—in the act of reading. A willingness to listen, a sensitivity to emotional nuance, an ability to empathize

> with and yet judge, may be disadvantageous in speech but advantageous in reading. We may come to discover that women have interpretive powers that have not been sufficiently appreciated. (286)

Flynn's essay points up one major problem with early research in rhetoric and composition: its pervasive tendency to report on writers and readers as if they were all fairly similar in experience and outlook. Researchers rushed to study the composing processes of student writers—as though "student" was a stable concept, as though students were all alike. Because of what might be called this regression toward the mean in much composition research, scholars are now reexamining prior conclusions and assumptions, aided by a growing body of rich case studies and ethnographies of writers and readers that reveal—and celebrate—difference.

Martin Nystrand and his colleagues are among those who use case studies as a means of documenting the relationship between writers and readers, between writing and reading within the conceptual framework of reciprocity theory. Nystrand argues that "written discourse is not the well-oiled engine of written speech production nor the well-regulated cybernetic system of cognitive scripts and well-formed, permissible text types. It is the social process whereby literate individuals 'write on the premises of the reader and read on the premises of the writer' " (18). A major task of researchers in this field is to enrich our understanding of the "reciprocal" social processes linking writers and readers.

Questions about Texts

As the foregoing discussion has suggested, scholars in rhetoric and composition have sought to broaden definitions of research (to include methods associated with the social sciences and sciences) and of writers and readers (to include students of all ages and writers and readers in widely varying settings). Nowhere is this resistance to traditional definitional boundaries more evident than in the area of texts, the pieces of discourse researchers choose to study. Rejecting the long-standing implicit definition of text as "literary," researchers in this field include in their purview *written discourse of any kind*: student texts; business and other professional texts, including advertising; scientific and technical texts; electronic texts; the texts of civic and public as well as of private life. If it exists as a written document, the great likelihood is that someone in composition and rhetoric is studying it.

True to their eclectic traditions, such researchers use principles of analysis derived from a number of different fields. From literary studies they adapt methods of close reading; from linguistics and stylistics they borrow syntactic analysis, speech-act analysis, and principles of semiotics; from philosophy they take propositional, syllogistic, and informal logical analysis; from anthropology they borrow ethnographic and field study techniques that allow for contextualization of pieces of discourse. Rhetorical analysis itself, of course, has a long history and a number of expert recent practitioners, from Richard McKeon and Richard Weaver to Kenneth Burke, Edwin Black, and Wayne Booth. The aim of such multifaceted analysis is to construct as rich and thick a description as possible of any particular textual world.

A Case or Two in Point

Insisting that student texts both deserve and reward careful scholarly attention, Mina Shaughnessy sought to map the textual world of the underprepared college writer. From the beginning of the open-admissions program at the City University of New York, through her ringing "Diving In" address to the MLA (which received a standing ovation in San Francisco in 1975), to the publication of *Errors and Expectations* (1977) and her untimely death in 1979, Shaughnessy led the way in demonstrating the complex reasoning that lies behind the most apparently garbled of student syntax. In doing so, she shifted the gaze in English studies from the fixed point of literary language and made a space in which scholars of rhetoric and composition could work. Among the most provocative of such work has been that of David Bartholomae, whose essays (such as "Inventing the University" and "The Study of Error") and text (*Facts, Artifacts, and Counterfacts*, coauthored with Anthony Petrosky) have served to define a philosophy and pedagogy for basic writing, one that in recent years has engendered a lively debate over its ideological and epistemological—and, of course, political—assumptions.

Two other brief examples will, I hope, suggest the broad range of textuality scholars in rhetoric and composition study. While I could point in almost any direction, I choose here to mention two other textual worlds that have been traditionally ignored by researchers in English: personal and private discourse and civic or organizational writing. Jacqueline Jones Royster takes the first as her field of study, concentrating particularly on the intellectual tradition of black women in America and tracing the development and perpetuation of that tradition in letters, diaries, and other pieces of personal or private discourse. In the public area of civic discourse, Sandra Stotsky has pioneered the study of public letter writing, most recently in an analysis of letters to legislators and texts produced by the League of Women Voters.

This expanding definition of *text* brings more clearly into focus the collaborative nature of most texts, whether written by a first-year student who draws on class discussion and late-night conversations with friends, an insurance executive who makes final changes to and signs a report to stockholders, or a computer programmer who draws on the work of several staff writers in developing a new software. Thus just as rhetorical and literary theory has radically destabilized the concepts of *author* and *reader*, so rhetoric and composition studies destabilize the concept of *text*, opening it up and hence bringing into view many kinds of discourse formally excluded from examination.

Questions about Contexts

As a *techne*, rhetoric has always been concerned with principles of use: How will any pieces of discourse be put to use—by particular people in particular times and in particular locations? Thus rhetoric, more than many disciplines, has attended to "situatedness," or to what Burke calls the scenic properties of discourse as well as the "ratios" existing among scene and the other coordinates of text, writer, and reader. Attending to context thus means observing the ways in which discourse is embedded in local cultures and studying the isomorphic relation between discourse and culture, or "scene." For scholars in rhetoric and composition, several scenes are currently of particular interest: the local context of the classroom and the broader contexts of the academy, the workplace, and the community. Studies of classroom contexts seek to define optimal conditions for learning to write through experimental studies of instructional strategies, methods of evaluation, types of assignments, and teacher and student attitudes toward learning and writing. Other studies probe the nature of the "community" that may be established in a classroom and examine the ways in which such community building may be said to liberate or to oppress learners.

A Case or Two in Point

Scholars of rhetoric and composition have been especially interested of late in studying classroom contexts that recognize—and value—difference. A number of studies focus on the ways in which collaborative contexts can invite exploration of gender, race, and ethnic differences. Such differences, however, are most often visible; they yield to direct observation. What, however, of those minorities who are largely invisible? That is a question examined in depth by Sarah Sloane and Judy Doenges, who focus on one particular invisible minority—lesbian and gay students. In a series of case studies, Sloane and Doenges demonstrate that the classroom context for such students often offers a deadly double bind: the "community" values self-exploration, the creation of "authentic voice," but all too often implicitly silences the authentic voices of this group of students.

Classroom contexts are themselves obviously embedded in the culture of the academy, and just as obviously scholars in rhetoric and composition wish to explore the nature of that relation. In a series of articles, Mike Rose argues that student writers (and particularly underprepared student writers) and the classroom contexts they inhabit are themselves constructed by an academy that is exclusionary and positivistic ("Remedial Writing Courses"; "Language of Exclusion"). Rose's work on academic contexts led to his 1989 *Lives on the Boundary*. In this book Rose blends autobiography, case studies, and discourse analysis in a moving and trenchant description of the academy's haves and have-nots. In doing so, he offers an implicit yet compelling rebuttal of "cultural literacy," as expounded by E. D. Hirsch, as a national goal.

Rose is joined in his analysis of academic institutions by a number of other scholars, including Patricia Bizzell, James Berlin, and Ira Shor. Though their work differs in method and focus, all share Rose's interest in examining the ideology of both the academy and of rhetoric and composition studies. Other researchers, such as Art Young, Elaine Maimon, Anne Herrington, and Toby Fulwiler, focus on the ways writing is used in disciplines across the university and on how writing may best be used to enhance learning in all academic areas.

Writers and readers inhabit a number of contexts beyond the academy, and these contexts are also of great interest to those in rhetoric and composition. Most strongly associated with explorations of home, workplace, and community contexts is Shirley Brice Heath. Beginning with a study of language at home (*Telling Tongues*) and continuing through her award-winning study of discourse in two Piedmont communities (*Ways with Words*) to her current study of contexts varying from the Little League to the factory floor, Heath has challenged scholars to recognize (and study) the complex web of contextual forces in which any piece of discourse is always inscribed. Following Heath's lead are scores of researchers investigating other contextual frames for discourse, ranging from day care (Anne Haas Dyson, "Case Study") to elder-care facilities (Janet Emig, personal correspondence), from the black church (Beverly Moss) to the international insurance corporation (Geoffrey Cross), from Tunisian communities (Keith Walters, "Women") to Samoan villages (Elinor Ochs) or the barrio (Ralph Cintron, "Literacy"; "Use"). Such cultural contexts offer researchers an opportunity to examine discourse in situ and thus to gain a richer understanding of the symbolic motives surrounding any language act.

RHETORIC AND COMPOSITION AND A LITERATE DEMOCRACY

Questions about writers, readers, texts, and contexts demonstrate how far flung and various are the lands surrounding the small island of rhetoric and composition on which I stood some two decades ago. They also suggest to me, at least, that this loose confederation of conceptual countries is linked by a mutual concern for literacy or, more accurately, for literacies. At the nexus of rhetoric and composition's terministic screen (Burke, *Language as Symbolic Action*), literacy encompasses highly theoretical concerns about the relation between thought, language, and action as well as historical concerns about the organization and development of literacy and pragmatic concerns about how literate behaviors are nurtured and practiced. The study of literacy inevitably shades theory into pedagogy, research into practice; it cuts across lines of class, age, race, and gender, reaching out to all. But for these very reasons, the study of literacy inevitably raises political questions: How will literacy be defined and measured? Who will have access to full and multiple literacy? Who will be denied? Who is responsible for literacy?

These questions are being answered in radically different ways by different elements in our society, from the White House and statehouse to the prison house. Consider, as an example from the academy, this scene: A large public institution establishes selective admissions based on ACT scores (the ACT calls for no writing). Its first-year students take one required composition course or, in some cases, a term of noncredit course work in a writing workshop or writing center before being admitted to the one required course. These courses, which constitute the "service" component of the English department, are taught by part-time instructors and graduate students, many of whom are new to the discipline and to the classroom. At the end of one year, roughly forty percent of the first-year students are gone; the percentage for minority students is even higher. The part-time instructors rotate into similar jobs at nearby institutions; the graduate student teaching assistants continue their studies, prepare to write theses and dissertations on traditional literary topics, and pick up whatever tips they can about how to teach the next round of first-year students. Meanwhile, the students who survive sign up for subsequent courses in which they will be expected, on the basis of no further instruction and very little practice, to perform as skilled writers and readers.

This is a troubling scene, and one that is still far too familiar to too many of us. It is troubling precisely because of the answers it implicitly gives to the questions I have raised concerning literacy. This scene, after all, defines literacy reductively, as a set of narrowly defined skills that can be taught by almost anyone and in the most inhospitable of situations; its reductive definition acts as exclusionary gatekeeper; and it assigns responsibility to a marginalized group, thus seriously undercutting the significance of the task at hand.

Whether their research focuses on women's contributions to Renaissance rhetoric, the interpretive strategies basic writers bring to texts, or the argumentative structure of Chinese myths, scholars of rhetoric and composition are vitally concerned with the scenes of literacy. They seek to build scenes on their own campuses that will present answers to questions regarding literacy in ways very different from the hypothetical institution described above. They want, moreover, to press beyond the boundaries of their campuses, to create scenes that encompass those in the public schools, in neighborhood and community-based organizations, and in the workplace. They wish, in short, to break down the walls of the ivory tower, bridge the surrounding moat, and establish conversation in the public square.

Much exciting contemporary work in rhetoric and composition attempts to sketch in such a scene: Jan Swearingen's analysis of public literacy in the ancient world (*Rhetoric*), Michael Halloran and Greg Clark's studies of nineteenth-century public discourse, Marilyn Cooper and Michael Holzman's collection of essays *Writing as Social Action*, Deborah Brandt's cogent argument in *Literacy as Involvement*, Richard Lanham's calls for electronic democratization of text, Mike Rose's stress on community action and participation in *Lives on the Boundary*, or many of the essays in *The Right to Literacy*, edited by Andrea A. Lunsford, Helene Moglen, and James Slevin. These scholars and the many others I have referred to in this essay have, over the last two and a half decades, created an intellectual space in which scholars of rhetoric and composition can study scenes of literacy and literate behaviors. This space is large and loosely bounded, informed by cross-disciplinary, transinstitutional, multivoiced, and deeply democratic principles. The scholars who inhabit this space are committed to the exploration of what it means to be fully literate in the twenty-first or any other century, what it means—in practical and social as well as theoretical terms—to create worlds from words written, spoken, or read.[1]

Suggestions for Further Reading

Students interested in pursuing the research questions discussed in this essay might best begin by moving in two directions at once: conducting a retrospective study of their own writing and reading histories, trying to map the development of their own literate behavior; and reading in several of the field's major journals (*College Composition and Communication, College English, Journal of Advanced Composition, Philosophy and Rhetoric, Rhetorica, Rhetoric Review, Rhetoric Society Quarterly, Writing Instructor*, or *Written Communication*, for instance). These journals will alert readers to areas of controversy as well as to new publications and upcoming professional meetings. Attending such meetings provides one potent means of joining the scholarly conversation: the Conference on College Composition and Communication attracts over three thousand participants and features hundreds of sessions; smaller gatherings, such as the Wyoming Conference on Freshman and Sophomore English, the Penn State Conference on Rhetoric and Composition, or the relatively new Graduate Student Conference, offer more intimate forums for exploration and debate.

Of course, readers of this essay may elect, as I did years ago, to choose one text and follow the leads it provides. If so, the new third edition of Edward P. J. Corbett's *Classical Rhetoric for the Modern Student* is available, and this work still provides an excellent introduction to the classical tradition. Further, it can now be read side by side with Patricia Bizzell and Bruce Herzberg's recent collection of excerpted primary rhetoric texts (*The Rhetorical Tradition*). In addition, several general overviews of the field are available, including Erika Lindemann and Gary Tate, *An Introduction to Composition Studies*; Tate, *Teaching Composition: Twelve Bibliographical Essays*; and Michael G. Moran and Ronald F. Lunsford, *Research in Composition and Rhetoric: A Bibliographic Sourcebook*. Finally, four texts provide widely varying perspectives on rhetoric and composition studies and are provocative precisely because of their differences: Susan Miller's *Rescuing the Subject*, Jasper Neel's *Plato, Derrida, and Writing*, Stephen M. North's *Making of Knowledge in Composition*, and Louise Wetherbee Phelps's *Composition as a Human Science*.

Reading about a field, studying work in that field, can go a long way toward making a reader part of its conversation. Prospective researchers in rhetoric and composition, however, must finally respond to Mina Shaughnessy's call, must move beyond the safe territory of reading, and dive in to the research questions regarding writers, readers, texts, and contexts that beckon compellingly from the edge of their own intellectual horizons. A major goal of this essay has been to indicate the directions in which those horizons might stretch.

Ohio State University

Note

[1]I am indebted to many, many friends and colleagues who have helped me think systemically about our field and particularly to Joe Gibaldi, Alicia Mahaney, Lisa Ede, Cheryl Glenn, Erika Lindemann, and two MLA reviewers for their careful reading and criticisms of this essay and to Scott Leonard, Patricia Kelvin, Heather Graves, and Carrie Leverenz for their unstinting assistance in assembling the list of works cited in preparing this manuscript.

Works Cited and Recommended

Aristotle. *The* Rhetoric *and the* Poetics *of Aristotle.* Trans. W. Rhys Roberts and Ingram Bywater. 1954. New York: Modern Lib., 1984.

Bamberg, B. J. "Composition Instruction Does Make a Difference: A Comparison of High School Preparation of College Freshmen in Regular and Remedial English Classes." *Research in the Teaching of English* 12 (1978): 47–59.

Bartholomae, David. "Inventing the University." *When a Writer Can't Write: Studies in Writer's Block and Other Composing Problems.* Ed. Mike Rose. New York: Guilford, 1985. 134–65.

———. "The Study of Error." *College Composition and Communication* 31 (1980): 253–68.

Bartholomae, David, and Anthony Petrosky. *Facts, Artifacts, and Counterfacts: Theory and Method for a Reading and Writing Course.* Upper Montclair: Boynton, 1986.

Bazerman, Charles. *Shaping Written Knowledge: The Genre and Activity of the Experimental Article in Science.* Madison: U of Wisconsin P, 1988.

Berlin, James A. *Rhetoric and Reality: Writing Instruction in American Colleges, 1900–1985.* Carbondale: Southern Illinois UP, 1987.

———. *Writing Instruction in Nineteenth-Century American Colleges.* Carbondale: Southern Illinois UP, 1984.

Berthoff, Ann E. *Forming, Thinking, Writing: The Composing Imagination.* Upper Montclair: Boynton, 1982.

———. *The Making of Meaning: Metaphors, Models, and Maxims for Writing Teachers.* Upper Montclair: Boynton, 1981.

Bizzell, Patricia. "Arguing about Literacy." *College English* 50 (1988): 141–53.

———. "Cognition, Convention, and Certainty: What We Need to Know about Writing." *Pre/Text* 3 (1982): 213–43.

———. "College Composition: Initiation into the Academic Discourse Communities." *Curriculum Inquiry* 12 (1982): 191–207.

———. "The Ethos of Academic Discourse." *College Composition and Communication* 29 (1978): 351–55.

———. " 'Inherent' Ideology, 'Universal' History, 'Empirical' Evidence, and 'Context-Free' Writing: Some Problems with E. D. Hirsch's *The Philosophy of Composition.*" *MLN* 95 (1980): 1181–202.

———. "On the Possibility of a Unified Theory of Composition and Literature." *Rhetoric Review* 4 (1986): 174–80.

———. "William Perry and Liberal Education." *College English* 46 (1984): 447–54.

Bizzell, Patricia, and Bruce Herzberg. *The Rhetorical Tradition: Readings from Classical Times to the Present.* Boston: Bedford–St. Martin's, 1990.

Black, Edwin. *Rhetorical Criticism: A Study in Method.* New York: Macmillan, 1965.

Blakeslee, Ann. "The Rhetoric of Two Physics Journals." Eighth Annual Penn State Conference on Rhetoric and Composition. July 1989.

Bleich, David. *The Double Perspective.* New York: Oxford UP, 1988.

———. *Readings and Feelings: An Introduction to Subjective Criticism.* Urbana: NCTE, 1975.

Booth, Wayne C. *The Company We Keep: An Ethics of Fiction.* Berkeley: U of California P, 1988.

———. *Modern Dogma and the Rhetoric of Assent.* Chicago: U of Chicago P, 1974.

———. "The Rhetorical Stance." *College Composition and Communication* 14 (1963): 139–45.

———. *The Rhetoric of Fiction.* Chicago: U of Chicago P, 1961.

Braddock, Richard, Richard Lloyd-Jones, and Lowell Schoer. *Research in Written Composition.* Champaign: NCTE, 1963.

Brandt, Deborah. *Literacy as Involvement: The Acts of Writers, Readers, and Texts.* Carbondale: Southern Illinois UP, 1990.

Brodkey, Linda. *Academic Writing as Social Practice.* Philadelphia: Temple UP, 1987.

———. "On the Subjects of Class and Gender in 'The Literacy Letters.' " *College English* 51 (1989): 125–41.

Brooke, Robert. "Control in Writing: Flower, Derrida, and Images of the Writer." *College English* 51 (1989): 405–17.

Burke, Kenneth. A Grammar of Motives *and* A Rhetoric of Motives. 1945 and 1950. Cleveland: World, 1962.

———. *Language as Symbolic Action.* Berkeley: U of California P, 1966.

Cintron, Ralph. "Literacy in Mexican-American Families." Conference on College Composition and Communication. St. Louis, Mar. 1988.

———. "The Use of Oral and Written Language in the Homes of Three *Mexicano* Families." Diss. U of Illinois, Chicago, 1990.

Collins, Allan, John Seely Brown, and Kathy M. Larkin. *Inference in Text Understanding.* Champaign: U of Illinois, Urbana, 1977.

Collins, Allan, and Marilyn Jager Adams. *Reasoning from Incomplete Knowledge.* Research Rept. 3019. Cambridge: Bolt, 1975.

———. "A Schema-Theoretic View of Reading." *Theoretical Models and Processes of Reading.* Ed. Harry Singer and Robert Ruddell. 3rd ed. Newark: Intl. Reading Assoc., 1985.

Connors, Robert J. "The Rhetoric of Explanation: Explanatory Rhetoric from Aristotle to 1850." *Written Communication* 1 (1984): 189–210.

———. "The Rhetoric of Explanation: Explanatory Rhetoric from 1850 to the Present." *Written Communication* 2 (1985): 49–72.

———. "The Rise and Fall of the Modes of Discourse." *College Composition and Communication* 32 (1981): 444–55.

Cooper, Marilyn, and Michael Holzman, eds. *Writing as Social Action.* Portsmouth: Boynton, 1989.

Corbett, Edward P. J. *Classical Rhetoric for the Modern Student.* 3rd ed. New York: Oxford UP, 1990.

———."The Usefulness of Classical Rhetoric." *College Composition and Communication* 14 (1963): 162–64.

Cross, Geoffrey. "Editing in Context: An Ethnographic Exploration of Editor-Writer Revision at a Midwestern Insurance Company." Diss. Ohio State U, 1988.

Crowley, Sharon. "The Current-Traditional Theory of Style: An Informal History." *Rhetoric Society Quarterly* 16 (1986): 233–50.

———. "The Evolution of Invention in Current-Traditional Rhetoric." *Rhetoric Review* 3 (1985): 146–62.

deBeaugrande, Robert. "Psychology and Composition." *College Composition and Communication* 30 (1979): 50–57.

———. "Writer, Reader, Critic: Comparing Critical Theories as Discourse." *College English* 46 (1984): 533–59.

———. "Writing and Meaning: The Context of Research." *Writing in Real Time: Modelling Production Processes.* Ed. Ann Matsuhashi. Norwood: Ablex, 1986.

Derrida, Jacques. *Dissemination.* Trans. Barbara Johnson. Chicago: U of Chicago P, 1981.

———. *Limited, Inc.* Trans. Samuel Weber and Jeffrey Mehlman. Rev. ed. Evanston: Northwestern UP, 1988.

———. *Of Grammatology.* Trans. Gayatri C. Spivak. Baltimore: Johns Hopkins UP, 1976.

———. *Writing and Difference.* Trans. Alan Bass. Chicago: U of Chicago P, 1978.

Doheny-Farina, Stephen. "Writing in an Emerging Organization: An Ethnographic Study." *Written Communication* 3 (1986): 158–85.

Douglas, Wallace. "Rhetoric for the Meritocracy." Ohmann 97–132.

Dyson, Anne Haas. "A Case Study Examination of the Role of Oral Language in the Writing Process of Kindergartners." *DAI* 47 (1986): 2001A.

———. *Collaboration through Writing and Reading.* Urbana: NCTE, 1989.

Ede, Lisa S., and Andrea A. Lunsford. *Singular Texts/Plural Authors: Perspectives on Collaborative Writing.* Carbondale: Southern Illinois UP, 1990.

Emig, Janet. *The Composing Processes of Twelfth Graders.* Urbana: NCTE, 1971.

Enos, Richard L. "The Composing Process of the Sophists: New Directions for Composition Research." Occasional Paper. Center for the Study of Writing at the Univ. of California, Berkeley, and Carnegie Mellon Univ., 1989.

Fish, Stanley. *Is There a Text in This Class? The Authority of Interpretive Communities.* Cambridge: Harvard UP, 1980.

Flower, Linda. *Studying Cognition in Context: Introduction to the Study.* Center for the Study of Writing Technical Rept. 21. Univ. of California, Berkeley, and Carnegie Mellon Univ., 1989.

Flower, Linda, and John R. Hayes. "A Cognitive Process Theory of Writing." *College Composition and Communication* 32 (1981): 365–87.

Flynn, Elizabeth A. "Composing as a Woman." *College Composition and Communication* 39 (1988): 423–35.

———. "Composing 'Composing as a Woman': A Perspective on Research." *College Composition and Communication* 41 (1990): 83–89.

———. "Gender and Reading." *Gender and Reading: Essays on Readers, Texts, and Contexts.* Ed. Elizabeth A. Flynn and Patrocinio P. Schweickart. Baltimore: Johns Hopkins UP, 1986. 267–88.

Fulwiler, Toby. "How Well Does Writing across the Curriculum Work?" *College English* 46 (1984): 113–25.

———. "Showing, Not Telling, at a Writing Workshop." *Rhetoric and Composition: A Sourcebook for Teachers and Writers.* Ed. Richard L. Graves. Upper Montclair: Boynton, 1984. 338–46.

———. "Understanding Bad Writing." *College English Journal* 15 (1984): 54–59.

———. "Writing and the Alternative Curriculum." *Illinois English Bulletin* 74 (1986): 7–13.

Gadamer, Hans-Georg. *Philosophical Hermeneutics.* Trans. David E. Linge. Berkeley: U of California P, 1976.

Gerber, John C. *The College Teaching of English.* Ed. John C. Gerber. New York: Appleton, 1965.

———. "Loomings." Conference on College Composition and Communication. St. Louis, Mar. 1975. ERIC ED 103 893.

———. "The 1962 Summer Institutes of the Commission on English: Their Achievement and Promise." *PMLA* 78 (1963): 9–25.

Graff, Gerald. *Professing Literature: An Institutional History.* Chicago: U of Chicago P, 1987.

Graves, Donald H. *Balance the Basics: Let Them Write.* Ford Foundation Rept. 1987.

———. *A Researcher Learns to Write.* Exeter: Heinemann, 1984.

Hairston, Maxine. "Breaking Our Bonds and Reaffirming Our Connections." *College Composition and Communication* 36 (1985): 272–82.

Halloran, S. Michael. "Rhetoric in the American College Curriculum: The Decline of Public Discourse." *Pre/Text* 3 (1982): 245–69.

Halloran, S. Michael, and Greg Clark. "Theory and Practice in Nineteenth Century American Rhetoric: The Transformation of Oratorical Culture." *Oratorical Culture in America.* Ed. Greg Clark and S. Michael Halloran. Carbondale: Southern Illinois UP, forthcoming.

Harkin, Patricia, and John Schilb, eds. *Contending with Words: Composition and Rhetoric in a Postmodern Age.* New York: MLA, 1991.

Harste, Jerome, Virginia Woodward, and Carolyn L. Burke. *Language Stories and Literacy Lessons.* Portsmouth: Heinemann, 1984.

Heath, Shirley Brice. *Telling Tongues: Language Policy to Mexico, Colony to Nation.* New York: Teachers Coll. P, 1972.

———. *Ways with Words: Language, Life, and Work in Communities and Classrooms.* Cambridge: Cambridge UP, 1983.

Herrington, Anne. "Writing to Learn: Writing across the Disciplines." *College English* 43 (1981): 379–87.

Hilgers, T. L. "How Children Change as Critical Evaluators of Writing: Four Three-Year Case Studies." *Research in the Teaching of English* 20 (1986): 36–55.

———. "Toward a Taxonomy of Beginning Writer's Evaluative Statements on Written Composition." *Written Communication* 1 (1984): 365–84.

———. "Training College Composition Students in the Use of Free-Writing and Problem-Solving Heuristics for Rhetorical Invention." *Research in the Teaching of English* 14 (1980): 293–307.

———. "Young Writers Facing a New Collaborative Writing Task." *Journal of Research in Childhood Education* 2 (1987): 108–16.

Hillocks, George, Jr. *Research on Written Composition: New Directions for Teaching.* Urbana: ERIC Clearinghouse on Reading and Communication Skills, 1986.

Hirsch, E. D., Jr. *Cultural Literacy: What Every American Needs to Know.* Boston: Houghton, 1987.

Irmscher, William F. *Teaching Expository Writing.* New York: Holt, 1979.

Iser, Wolfgang. *The Act of Reading: A Theory of Aesthetic Response.* Baltimore: Johns Hopkins UP, 1978.

Isocrates. *Isocrates.* Trans. George Norlin. Loeb Classical Library. Vol. 1. 1928. Cambridge: Harvard UP, 1980.

Jarratt, Susan. "The First Sophists and the Political Implications of *Techne.*" Conference on College Composition and Communication. Seattle, Mar. 1989.

———. "The First Sophists as the Precursors of Humanism: Expanding the Limits of Literacy." Conference on College Composition and Communication. Atlanta, Mar. 1987.

———. "Rationalism and the Irrational in Histories of the First Sophists." Seventh Biennial Conference of the Intl. Soc. for the History of Rhetoric. Göttingen, 26–29 July 1989.

———. "Toward a Sophistic Historiography." *Pre/Text* 8 (1987): 9–28.

Johnson, Nan. "English Composition, Rhetoric, and English Studies at Nineteenth-Century Canadian Colleges and Universities." *English Quarterly* 20 (1987): 296–304.

———. *Nineteenth-Century Rhetoric: Theory and Practice in North America.* Carbondale: Southern Illinois UP, 1991.

———. "Origin and Artifact: Classical Rhetoric in the Modern Composition Class." *English Quarterly* 19 (1986): 207–15.

———. "Rhetoric and Belles Lettres in the Canadian Academy: An Historical Analysis." *College English* 50 (1988): 861–73.

Kinneavy, James. *A Theory of Discourse.* Englewood Cliffs: Prentice, 1971.

Kintsch, Walter. "Learning from Text." *Cognition and Instruction* 3 (1986): 87–108.

Kintsch, Walter, and T. A. van Dijk. "Toward a Model of Text Comprehension and Production." *Psychological Review* 85 (1978): 363–94.

Kitzhaber, Albert R. "Rhetoric in American Colleges, 1855–1900." Diss. U of Washington, 1953.

Knoblauch, C. H., and Lil Brannon. *Rhetorical Traditions and the Teaching of Writing.* Upper Montclair: Boynton, 1984.

Lanham, Richard. "The Extraordinary Convergence: Democracy, Technology, Theory, and the University Curriculum." *South Atlantic Quarterly* 89 (1990): 27–50.

———. *Literacy and the Survival of Humanism.* New Haven: Yale UP, 1983.

Lauer, Janice M. "Issues in Rhetorical Invention." *Essays on Classical Rhetoric and Modern Discourse.* Ed. Robert J. Connors, Lisa S. Ede, and Andrea A. Lunsford. Carbondale: Southern Illinois UP, 1984. 127–39.

Lauer, Janice M., Gene Montague, Andrea A. Lunsford, and Janet Emig, eds. *Four Worlds of Writing.* 3rd ed. New York: Harper, 1990.

LeFevre, Karen Burke. *Invention as a Social Act.* Carbondale: Southern Illinois UP, 1987.

Lindemann, Erika. *A Rhetoric for Writing Teachers.* 2nd ed. New York: Oxford UP, 1987.

Lindemann, Erika, and Gary Tate. *An Introduction to Composition Studies.* New York: Oxford UP, 1991.

Lunsford, Andrea A., Helene Moglen, and James Slevin, eds. *The Right to Literacy.* New York: MLA, 1990.

Macrorie, Ken. *Telling Writing.* 2nd ed. Rochelle Park: Hayden, 1970.

———. *Uptaught.* Rochelle Park: Hayden, 1970.

Maimon, Elaine P. "Collaborative Learning and Writing across the Curriculum." *WPA* 9 (1986): 9–15.

———. "Knowledge, Acknowledgment, and Writing across the Curriculum: Toward an Educated Community." *The Territory of Language: Linguistics, Stylistics, and the Teaching of Composition.* Ed. Donald A. McQuade. Carbondale: Southern Illinois UP, 1986.

Maimon, Elaine P., et al., eds. *Reading in the Arts and Sciences.* Boston: Little, 1985.

McKeon, Richard. *Rhetoric: Essays in Invention and Discovery.* Ed. Mark Blackman. Woodbridge: Ox Bow, 1987.

Metodieva, Lilia. "G. Serovosk's Rhetorical Figures." Seventh Biennial Conference of the Intl. Soc. for the History of Rhetoric. Göttingen, 26–29 July 1989.

Miller, Susan. *Rescuing the Subject.* Carbondale: Southern Illinois UP, 1989.

———. *Textual Carnivals.* Carbondale: Southern Illinois UP, 1991.

Moran, Michael G., and Ronald F. Lunsford, eds. *Research in Composition and Rhetoric: A Bibliographic Sourcebook.* Westport: Greenwood, 1984.

Moss, Beverly J. "Showing Authority in the Black Church." Conference on College Composition and Communication. Seattle, Mar. 1989.

Murphy, James J. *Renaissance Eloquence: Studies in the Theory and Practice of Renaissance Rhetoric.* Berkeley: U of California P, 1983.

———. *Rhetoric in the Middle Ages: A History of Rhetorical Theory from Saint Augustine to the Renaissance.* Berkeley: U of California P, 1974.

———, ed. *The Rhetorical Tradition and Modern Writing.* New York: MLA, 1982.

———. *A Short History of Writing Instruction from Ancient Greece to America.* Davis: Hermagoras, 1990.

———. *Three Medieval Rhetorical Arts.* Berkeley: U of California P, 1971.

Murray, Donald. "Internal Revision: A Process of Discovery." *Research on Composing: Points of Departure.* Ed. Charles R. Cooper and Lee Odell. Urbana: NCTE, 1978. 85–103.

———. "Teaching the Other Self: The Writer's First Reader." *College Composition and Communication* 33 (1982): 140–47.

———. *Write to Learn.* New York: Holt, 1984.

Nativel, Colette. "La théorie de l'imitation au XVII siècle en rhétorique et en peinture." Seventh Biennial Conference of the Intl. Soc. for the History of Rhetoric. Göttingen, 26–29 July 1989.

Neel, Jasper. *Plato, Derrida, and Writing.* Carbondale: Southern Illinois UP, 1988.

North, Stephen M. *The Making of Knowledge in Composition: Portrait of an Emerging Field.* Upper Montclair: Boynton, 1987.

Nystrand, Martin. *The Structure of Written Communication: Studies in Reciprocity between Writers and Readers.* Orlando: Academic, 1986.

Ochs, Elinor. *Culture and Language Development: Language Acquisition and Language Socialization in a Samoan Village.* Cambridge: Cambridge UP, 1988.

Odell, Lee, and Dixie Goswami, eds. *Writing in Non-academic Settings.* New York: Guilford, 1985.

Ohmann, Richard M. *English in America: A Radical View of the Profession.* New York: Oxford UP, 1976.

Okabe, Roichi. "The Impact of Western Rhetoric in the East: The Case of Japan." Seventh Biennial Conference of the Intl. Soc. for the History of Rhetoric. Göttingen, 26–29 July 1989.

Parker, William Riley. "Where Do English Departments Come From?" *College English* 28 (1967): 339–51.

Perelman, Chaim, and L. Olbrechts-Tyteca. *The New Rhetoric.* Notre Dame: U of Notre Dame P, 1969.

Phelps, Louise Wetherbee. *Composition as a Human Science: Contribution to the Self-Understanding of a Discipline.* New York: Oxford UP, 1988.

Purves, Alan C., ed. *Writing across Languages and Cultures: Issues in Contrastive Rhetoric.* Newbury Park: Sage, 1988.

Quintilian. *The Institutio Oratoria of Quintilian.* Vol. 4. London: Heinemann, 1977. 4 vols.

Richards, I. A. *The Philosophy of Rhetoric.* New York: Oxford UP, 1965.

Rose, Mike. "The Language of Exclusion: Writing Instruction at the University." *College English* 47 (1985): 341–59.

———. *Lives on the Boundary: The Struggles and Achievements of America's Underprepared.* London: Collier-Macmillan, 1989.

———. "Remedial Writing Courses: A Critique and a Proposal." *College English* 45 (1983): 109–28.

Royster, Jacqueline Jones. "Perspectives on the Intellectual Tradition of Black Women Writers." Lunsford, Moglen, and Slevin 103–12.

Shaughnessy, Mina P. "Diving In: An Introduction to Basic Writing." *College Composition and Communication* 27 (1976): 234–39.

———. *Errors and Expectations: A Guide for the Teacher of Basic Writing.* New York: Oxford UP, 1977.

Shor, Ira. *Freire for the Classroom: A Sourcebook for Liberatory Teaching.* Portsmouth: Boynton, 1987.

Slevin, James F. "Connecting English Studies." *College English* 48 (1986): 543–50.

Sloan, Thomas. "Reinventing *Inventio.*" *College English* 51 (1989): 461–73.

Sloane, Sarah, and Judy Doenges. "An Invisible Minority Finds a Voice in the Writing Classroom." Conference on College Composition and Communication. Seattle, Mar. 1989.

Sommers, Nancy. "Revision and the Composing Process: A Case Study of College Freshmen and Experienced Adult Writers." *DAI* 39 (1979): 6145A.

———. "Revision Strategies of Student Writers and Experienced Adult Writers." *College Composition and Communication* 31 (1980): 378–88.

Stotsky, Sandra. *Civic Writing in the Classroom.* Social Studies Development Center, Indiana Univ. Bloomington: ERIC/ChESS and ERIC/RCS, 1987.

———. "The Decline of the Civic Ethic." *Connecting Civic Education and Language Education: The Contemporary Challenge.* Ed. Stotsky. New York: Teachers Coll. P, 1991. 1–35.

———. "Writing in a Political Context: The Value of Letters to Legislators." *Written Communication* 9 (1987): 394–410.

Swearingen, C. Jan. "Inez de la Cruz." Roundtable, The Greatest Rhetorician Who Ever Lived. Conference on College Composition and Communication. Seattle, Mar. 1989.

———. *Rhetoric and Irony: Western Literacy/Western Lies.* New York: Oxford UP, 1991.

Tate, Gary, ed. *Teaching Composition: Twelve Bibliographical Essays.* Fort Worth: Texas Christian UP, 1987.

Toulmin, Stephen. *The Uses of Argument.* Cambridge: Cambridge UP, 1958.

Vickers, Brian. *In Defense of Rhetoric.* New York: Oxford UP, 1988.

Walters, Keith. "Language, Logic, and Literacy." Lunsford, Moglen, and Slevin 173–88.

———. "Women, Men, and Linguistic Variation in the Arab World." *Perspectives on Arabic Linguistics III: Papers from the Third Annual Symposium on Arabic Linguistics.* Ed. Bernard Comrie and Mushira Eid. Philadelphia: Benjamins, 1991. 199–229.

Weaver, Richard. *Language Is Sermonic.* Ed. Richard L. Johannesen, Rennard Strickland, and Ralph T. Eubanks. Baton Rouge: Louisiana State UP, 1970.

Winterowd, W. Ross. *Composition/Rhetoric: A Synthesis.* Carbondale: Southern Illinois UP, 1986.

———. *The Culture and Politics of Literacy.* New York: Oxford UP, 1989.

Witte, Stephen P. "Pre-Text and Composing." *College Composition and Communication* 38 (1987): 397–425.

———. "Topical Structure and Revision." *College Composition and Communication* 34 (1983): 313–41.

———. "Toward a Model for Research in Written Composition." *Research in the Teaching of English* 14 (1980): 5–17.

Young, Art. "Rebuilding Community in the English Department." *ADE Bulletin* 77 (1984): 13–21.

Young, Art, and Toby Fulwiler, eds. *Writing across the Disciplines: Research into Practice.* Upper Montclair: Boynton, 1986.

Young, Richard E. "Paradigms and Problems: Needed Research in Rhetorical Invention." *Research on Composing: Points of Departure.* Ed. Charles R. Cooper and Lee Odell. Urbana: NCTE, 1978. 29–48.

Young, Richard E., Alton L. Becker, and Kenneth L. Pike, eds. *Rhetoric: Discovery and Change.* New York: Harcourt, 1970.

Zoellner, Robert. "Talk-Write: A Behavioral Pedagogy for Composition." *College English* 30 (1969): 267–320.

Literary Studies: Text, Interpretation, History, Theory

D. C. GREETHAM

Textual Scholarship

TEXTUAL scholarship is practiced informally by many people. Anybody who has detected a misprint in a book is a textual critic, as is anyone who has noticed that a TV or videotape version of a film may be different from the theatrical release or anyone who has played the party game of "telephone." All these forms of transmission—plus music, painting, sculpture, and any other medium in which form carries a message—involve attempts to transmit that message to a receptor. It is the business of textual scholars to determine, scientifically and technically, speculatively and intuitively, how successfully the transmission has been made and then to decide whether to do anything with this information. Will the reader who discovered the misprint not only correct it mentally but also change the reading in the text itself, write to the publisher and complain, or even edit another version of the text? The recent contention between John Kidd and Hans Walter Gabler over Gabler's edition of James Joyce's *Ulysses* (see Rossman) began with Kidd conducting at first an informal, then a more rigorous, reading of Gabler's text, and has ended with Kidd's reediting *Ulysses* himself, just as Samuel Johnson reedited Shakespeare in part because of a dissatisfaction with Alexander Pope's edition or as the editors working under the auspices of the MLA's Center for the Editing of American Authors (CEAA) or Center (later Committee) on Scholarly Editions (CSE) reedited American and British literature because of a dissatisfaction with earlier, impressionistic, belletristic editing of that literature. Thus, much textual criticism, that part of textual scholarship concerned with evaluating readings, is founded on a suspicion or "mistrust of texts," as Eugène Vinaver, medievalist and editor of Malory, has put it (352). Textual scholarship is always querulous, interrogative, incredulous, and dissatisfied, and it is perhaps the exemplary discipline for today's "hermeneutics of suspicion."

DEFINING TEXTUAL SCHOLARSHIP

Textual scholarship is more than just "criticism," however, and it is best defined as the general term for all the activities associated with discovering, describing, transcribing, editing, glossing, annotating, and commenting on texts. While literary texts (or, at least, texts composed of words) are the most familiar objects of textual scholarship, the textual scholar may study any means of textual communication—a painting, a sculpture, a novel, a poem, a film, a symphony, a gesture. All these media have meaning or form, and it is in part the textual scholar's aim to preserve (or, if necessary, to re-create) this meaning or form, in the face of the laws of physical decay. As G. Thomas Tanselle has movingly put it:

> What every artifact displays is the residue of an unequal contest: the effort of a human being to transcend the human, an effort continually thwarted by physical realities. Even a document with a text of the sort not generally regarded as art—a simple message to a friend, for example—illustrates the immutable condition of written statements: in writing down a message, one brings down an abstraction to the concrete, where it is an alien, damaged here and there through the intractability of the physical. (*Rationale* 64–65)

This articulation of the idealist view of textual scholarship would be challenged by those scholars who believe not that the physical is alien to a text but that it is the text's only condition; however, such idealism is always a useful corrective to the popular assumption that texts and the works they represent are created and sustained in a culture unmediated by the act of transmission. Of course, the relative value given to different types of transmission varies from culture to culture: an extreme example is the *Mahābhārata*'s condemnation to hell of those who commit the Vedic texts to writing, which has inevitably had the result of making such Sanskrit manuscripts very rare (see Rocher, in Greetham, *Scholarly Editing*). Similar distinctions (and similar problems) arise in adopting either the ethnolinguistic model of folk literature transmission (where the linguistic features, the words embodying specific performances, are the object of study) or the literary model (which attempts to reconstruct the putative original by examining its variants). Despite these complications, if we perceive that expression—on parchment or paper, in stone or clay, in sound waves or electronic pulses—may in certain circumstances be regarded as only a contigent reduction of the abstract to the inadequacies of the concrete and if we therefore see textual scholarship as the means whereby some of these inadequacies may be temporarily overcome, then the textual scholar has a heavy responsibility. Ontological distinctions may, of course, be made among the various media in which texts are transmitted, for in the plastic arts the concrete form and the ideal work of which it is a manifestation appear to occupy, or at least compete for, the same space—since there is no work other than the plastic representation. Nonetheless, scholars may have different views on how the abstract ideal may best be presented or codified, even in the apparently intractable plastic media. For example, the recent arguments over the damage or improvement sustained by the cleaning of the Sistine Chapel frescoes rest on whether the removal of various upper layers of the frescoes will enhance or destroy our understanding of Michelangelo's intentions. Thus, much recent textual speculation has moved beyond a narrow consideration of the textuality of individual media to attempts at a unified field theory for all texts in whatever mode of transmission. My concerns here are more local—the verbal texts of literature and the possible reconstruction of their abstract forms out of the concrete manifestations—and

I acknowledge that any edition, like any other transmission of the verbal text, can only ever be contingent and temporary.

HISTORY OF TEXTUAL SCHOLARSHIP

Early History

These matters of abstract message and concrete form are serious issues, and textual scholarship has always taken itself seriously. Until comparatively recently, the archival, philological, and editorial work associated with textual scholarship was regarded as one of the essential skills of any critic or scholar and was practiced by such diverse figures as Saint Jerome, Erasmus, Alexander Pope, Samuel Johnson, and A. E. Housman, all of whom either produced formal editions or achieved recognition for their analysis of textual cruxes.

Textual scholarship is, moreover, the oldest scholarly activity in the West, attested to by the sixth-century-BC Athenian attempts to arrest the decline of the Homeric texts and by the third-century-BC formation of the two rival scholarly libraries in Alexandria and Pergamum (Sandys, vol. 1, chs. 7–8). In these early years the basic assumptions underlying all subsequent textual scholarship were soon established. Thus, when Peisistratus (c. 560–27 BC) had an official copy of Homer compiled for the Panathena festival, he was acknowledging that any act of transmission introduces corruptions in a text, especially in the oral transmission practiced by the rhapsodes who recited the Homeric poems. This acknowledgment was formalized in the twentieth century with the often cited principle of "universal variation," which postulates that even a seemingly innocent act like photocopying produces detectable textual changes. Similarly, when Ptolemy Soter named Zenodotus of Ephesus as the first chief librarian at Alexandria, it was determined that the multiple holdings of the library (eventually about 700,000 rolls) were to be used in "collation"; that is, variant readings in different texts of the same work were to be compared to establish the original, authorial intention—according to the principle of "analogy." In the idealist atmosphere of Alexandria, this principle—the search for form behind the corrupt remains of transmission—complemented the Aristotelian empiricism of the linguists and grammarians of the library, reflecting the textual assumption that such a putative ideal version did lie behind the variant "remaniements" of the surviving documents and that this ideal could be speculatively reconstructed by an editor sensitive to genuine, as opposed to spurious, Homeric (or Shakespearean or Miltonic or Joycean) usage. This principle motivates both the twentieth-century eclectic, intentionalist movement, with its attempts to reconstruct a single-state "text that never was" (representing the author's final intentions) out of corrupt documentary remains, and the similar bibliographical concept of "ideal copy," the most perfect state of a work as originally intended by its printer or publisher following the completion of all intentional changes, although not necessarily actualized in any extant copy of the book (Gaskell, *Introduction* 321). In literary traditions where little or nothing remains in the author's hand (the norm until the Renaissance), one can appreciate why this desire to overcome the scribal or compositorial corruptions was seductive. Conversely, when the Pergamanians—rivals to the Alexandrians—invoked "anomaly" rather than analogy as their preferred linguistic and textual ethic, this persuasion was dependent on a Stoic acceptance of the inevitable decadence of all temporal, earthly phenomena as a result of humanity's fallen condition, with the corollary that the Alexandrian construction of the ideal was both impious and impossible. The grammarians and linguists of Pergamum therefore determined that individual performance rather than ideal usage should be the standard for adjudication and commentary. For textual scholars who followed this principle the only honest recourse in editing multiple-text works was to select a document that, on philological or other grounds, seemed best to represent authorial intention and, thereafter, to follow the readings of that document with absolute fidelity. This principle is endorsed in twentieth-century "best text" theory, which has dominated editing in Old French literature for seventy-five years or so, and it is still common in other European vernaculars.

So right at the beginning, the terms of the textual debate were set. Classical scholars asked the same questions still being asked today: How and where do we find our texts, and what system do we use to record what we find? (archival research and enumerative bibliography); How do we compare multiple copies of the same work? (collation and stemmatics, the genealogy of texts); How do we describe the physical embodiment of the text in roll or book? (codicology, descriptive and analytical bibliography); How do we transcribe the writing in the text? (paleography and diplomatics); How do we tell what is genuine and what is spurious? (textual criticism and textual editing); How do we decide what our audience needs to know about the text? (annotation, glossing, and textual commentary). All these matters are components of the general discipline of textual scholarship, and they have all been practiced to one degree or another in the days since the Alexandrians and the Pergamanians.

This early flowering of textual scholarship had two other important results. First, the exegetical, lexicographical, metrical, and grammatical studies produced by these scholars (particularly in Pergamum) for the elucidation of texts began to achieve an independent life. But when published separately, they were usually adorned with *lemmata* (headwords to each note) linking them to the text itself. This cross-referencing helped to preserve the text referred to from further corruption, since the commentary would fit only a particular edition. Today, the New Variorum Edition of Shakespeare prints both the act-scene-line numbers of the Globe edition and the "through-line" numbers or continuous lineation of the Norton First Folio facsimile to ensure the same sort of fit. Second, the Alexandrians and Pergamanians, simply by the attention they brought to certain texts, conferred canonical status on them. (Pergamum, for example, was the first to extend the canon from poetry to prose.) The status of the "big three" dramatic authors—Aeschylus, Sophocles, and Euripides—and the losses sustained by other authors owe much to the early librarians' decision that there should be *x* number of tragic poets, *y* number of lyric poets, and so on and that these authors' texts should be the ones copied and studied. Similarly, in our own time, the MLA has influenced the received canon by promoting editions sponsored or supported by the CEAA and its successor, the CSE, a project that has had canonical results (if only to reinforce a preexisting canon). The first series of editions from CEAA inevitably reflected the scholarly canon of the time (the 1960s), and they were criticized (e.g., by Wilson) precisely for being too "scholarly" and for thus excluding the general reader unable to negotiate the editorial paraphernalia. But another exclusion also resulted from this reflection of contemporary academic taste: the canon included the "great white fathers" of American literature—such as Emerson, Melville, Thoreau, and Whitman—and omitted other authors. To date, the CSE has certified only two volumes by women authors (Woolf and Cather) and nothing by nonwhites. Similarly, the CEAA-CSE seals awarded to "approved" editions can have a canonical effect, although the CSE is careful to emphasize that a seal is given to *an*, rather than *the*, approved edition. Even with this demurral, the CSE and the seals it awards were until very recently identified with specific methodologies or ideologies. The concentration on nineteenth-century Anglo-American literature and the set of guidelines issued to inspectors for the adjudication of such matters as copy-text and transcription had the effect (until the more flexible revisions of 1991) of restricting the very type of edition that could be considered for CSE sealing. It is no surprise that the committee, which formerly lacked representative nonanglophone editorial experience and a wider definition of editorial practice, awarded no seal to an edition of pre-Renaissance literature or to an edition in a language other than English in the first two decades of its existence. Thus, the ecumenical language (and hopes) of the CSE's 1977 *Introductory Statement* was not fulfilled during this period, but through the determined cross-disciplinary policies of its current chair, Jo Ann Boydston (who, as editor of the works of the philosopher Dewey, has successfully represented a discipline other than literature), the CSE will doubtless help construct new textual canons—of author, discipline, subject, genre, period, and editorial method.

Another textual control over the canon occurred, and occurs, during any major change in medium. Just as the move from roll to codex (the familiar folded, stitched book) during the early Christian Era determined the survival of ancient works into the medieval canon, so later the move from script to print and now the similar move from print to electronic publishing has determined, and will determine, what materials are preserved for later study. For example, when printing was introduced into England in the fifteenth century, William Caxton and his successors both reflected and created literary taste. They produced several editions of Chaucer, but William Langland's *Piers Plowman* had to wait a century more, to be published by Protestants because it was thought to be a precursor of the Tudor religious settlement. A third author, Thomas

Hoccleve, was ignored by the printers and thus by critics and most literary historians, even though (by manuscript count of his major work) he had been very popular in his time and in the earlier medium.

This bibliographical control of the canon is demonstrated throughout the early and middle history of textual scholarship, often at the most concrete level. The tenuous survival of the classical heritage is exemplified in the condition of Cicero's *De republica*, the "lower" text in a palimpsest, a manuscript in which a text is erased and another "upper" text, here a biblical commentary, is superscribed. The classical, pagan canon had to compete for the same physical space as the new biblical and patristic canon, and the latter usually won. The basic problem for medieval textual scholarship was thus the preservation of the classical inheritance; and despite the efforts of such figures as Lupus of Ferrières (c. 805–62), who tried to use the Alexandrian principle of collation on classical texts, in general the best the Middle Ages could hope for was the accurate transcription, and thus survival, of texts rather than an informed reconstruction. (On canonicity, see also Scholes in this volume.)

Renaissance to Nineteenth Century

A recognizable system of textual scholarship did not begin again until the early Renaissance. This renewed activity is shown in several ways: the success of the Florentine Coluccio Salutati (1331–1406) in bringing manuscripts from the Greek East to the Latin West in the fifteenth century; the book-collecting activities of his compatriot Poggio Bracciolini (1380–1459); the exposure of forgery by Lorenzo Valla (1407–57), most famously his philological demonstration that the Donation of Constantine, which purportedly gave secular power to the Church, was spurious and his *Adnotationes in Novum Testamentum*, emending the Vulgate Bible on philological principles; the early formation of a theory of manuscript genealogy by Politian (Angelo Poliziano, 1454–94) in his work on Cicero; and the controversial edition of the New Testament by Erasmus (c. 1466–1536) in 1516, in which he advocated that both biblical and secular texts should be subjected to the same objective editorial treatment. The cumulative contributions of these scholars led eventually to the so-called higher criticism, the study of biblical—and, by extension, vernacular—texts according to the science of philology (derived from the textual research of the lower criticism) rather than the dogmas of theology, codified in the nineteenth century under the term *Altertumswissenschaft*, the "science of ancient times." The work of Mabillon, Montfaucon, and other seventeenth-century Benedictine paleographers (Kenney 94–95) on the historical progression of scripts helped foster the assumption that texts could be arranged chronologically, on the basis of their linguistic and physical features, and that the manuscript or print transmission of a work could be shown as a genealogy, a family tree of correspondences, whereby shared errors in two or more "witnesses" (surviving documents) of a text would show them to be descended from the same "common ancestor." These correspondences could eventually enable scholars to reconstruct the "archetype," often an inferential, nonexistent document rather than a surviving witness. The archetype was the earliest stage of the family tree recoverable from this comparison of errors, but it was not necessarily identifiable with the author's fair copy, which for early texts usually lay in the realms of conjecture. This arrangement of extant and inferred witnesses into a stemma, traditionally associated with the work of Karl Lachmann on Lucretius, was to prove one of the most successful—yet contentious—of the textual ramifications of historical criticism (see Maas). The success of this technique was perhaps one of its problems: because it was based on the transmission of classical texts, its importation into vernacular editing (e.g., in Italian, Vandelli's edition of *I reali di Francia*, 1892–1900, and Barbi's edition of Dante's *La vita nuova*, 1907) became too often only a mechanical imposition of supposedly scientific principles. The technique was later questioned by, for example, Giorgio Pasquali's *Storia della tradizione e critica del testo* (1934), where the Lachmannian insistence on the archetype is repudiated and the rule of vertical (and downwardly corrupt) transmission is disputed. Giovanni Vandelli's abandonment of the possibilities of drawing up a single stemma in his edition of Dante's *Divine Comedy* (1921) exemplifies the theoretical problems discussed by Pasquali. Such questioning was necessary, for the science, or pseudoscience, of stemmatics depends on two assumptions: first, that an error can be recognized as such by the philologist and, second, that errors increase as one moves down the family tree from archetype to later copies. Both these assumptions rest on an underlying conviction that copyists make mistakes but that, in general, authors do not, and they both reinforce a textual article of faith that it is the business of textual scholarship to reconstruct authorial intention.

Twentieth Century

These assumptions about authors and copyists may initially seem unassailable, but the history of twentieth-century textual scholarship has called both into question in various ways. First, as A. E. Housman noted in his typically acerbic style, Germans like Lachmann seemed to have mistaken textual criticism for mathematics in their reliance on supposedly objective principles (132); he charged that they had frequently given up on criticism in the interests of science and that, despite their aim of restoring the archetype, they had put all their faith on a single extant document, once it could be shown to occupy a relatively high position in the family tree. In other words, the Lachmannians had become Pergamanians—subscribers to a best-text theory—despite themselves. Such a theory was later formally endorsed by Joseph Bédier, the founder of twentieth-century best-text editing in Old French, who was frankly suspicious of the way that stemmatic trees always seemed to resolve themselves into two neat branches and who decided to give up reconstruction of the ideal in favor of strict documentary fidelity or "anomaly."

Second, by using error in its mapping of variants and witnesses, stemmatics gave prominence to the content (or "substantives") of a text rather than to the surface features of its orthography (or "accidentals"). Therefore, until the mid–twentieth century most editors selected their copy-text (the authoritative version used as a standard for comparison with others and the one generally followed unless emendations were introduced) on the basis of its substantives. This practice was challenged in a famous article by W. W. Greg ("Rationale"), who suggested that authorial intention could best be embodied by selecting a copy-text for its accidentals—spelling, punctuation, capitalization, and so on—since subsequent copyings or reprintings would be more likely to change these features than they would the substantives. Later changes in substantives, which the editor could show were made by the author, could be read back into the copy-text to create an "eclectic" text, composed of features of several extant witnesses plus conjectures made by the editor. This method of responding to the claims of intentionality has been the dominant form of Anglo-American editing theory and practice in the last thirty or forty years, in part through the extensive scholarly editing of texts from the Renaissance to the twentieth century (e.g., Dekker, Dryden, Hawthorne, Crane) by its leading proponent Fredson Bowers and the vigorous defense of its principles by both Bowers and Tanselle. While not directly related to the Gregian issue and not motivated by the substantives-accidentals distinction, other efforts indicate that nonanglophone editing is confronting the question of early versus late states of text as copy-text. For example, the monumental editions of nineteenth-century scholars such as Louis Moland (Voltaire) and Charles Marty-Laveaux (Corneille, Ronsard), in which the last edition produced during the author's lifetime was taken as copy-text, can be set against more recent editing by, for example, Milorad R. Margitic (*Le Cid*) and R. C. Knight and H. T. Barnwell (*Andromaque*), who select early editions as copy-text.

As already observed, eclecticism is, in its mixing of early and late, thus another form of Alexandrian analogy. It is often associated with the New Bibliography, a conscious reaction against the old aesthetic, nontechnical, or belletristic editing of English and American literature. New Bibliography emphasized the importance of the technical history of a book, its physical makeup, and the creation and transmission of the text contained therein. For example, Charlton Hinman showed that in the Shakespeare First Folio certain verse passages were set as prose to save space and some prose passages were set as verse to waste space (xvi–xviii), on the basis of how accurately the compositor had estimated the amount of print a given page of manuscript copy would produce—called "casting off of copy"—in a folio "in sixes" (i.e., with each gathering made up of three sheets folded in half, to produce six leaves). The technical emphasis of the New Bibliography produced two subcategories of textual scholarship: analytical bibliography, or the study of the technical history of the printed book (how it was manufactured as an artifact), and descriptive bibliography, the formulaic listing of the technical attributes of each "ideal copy" of a book. This combination of technical sophistication and critical reconstruction of authorial intention gave eclectic editing an understandably forceful role in early- and mid-twentieth-century textual scholarship.

Third, Lachmannian stemmatics, by giving special privilege to the author beyond the archetype (since all extant manuscripts were ultimately derived therefrom), inevitably confirmed the principles of intentionalism, whether eclectic or otherwise. This approach has been challenged on two fronts. On the one hand, the influence of structuralism has favored the production of "genetic" editions in which all variants are listed in a continuous display of variation, rather than in the eclectic or stemmatic privileging of one, originary moment. This genetic tendency can be seen in a primitive state in the chronological ordering of Paul Laumonier, Raymond Lebègue, and Isidore Silver's Ronsard edition (1914–59), which shows the compositional process, and in the work of N. K. Piksanov (editor of Griboedov), who promoted the textual history of the "teleogenetic" approach, as a corrective to the dominant early-twentieth-century Russian reliance on editorial authority in the work of G. Vinokur, B. V. Tomasševskij, and B. Ejxenbaum. The genetic method has since then become virtually the norm in Franco-German editing (e.g., of Flaubert, Proust, Hölderlin, Klopstock and Kafka), beginning with the very influential work of Friedrich Beissner on Friedrich Hölderlin. As Gabler points out, Beissner's premise of "organic growth" does assume "an authorial intention toward perfection" ("Textual Studies" 163), and one could argue that Beissner's problematic assertion has prompted the retreat of some Germanists (e.g., Martens in "Textdynamik und Edition") into the apparent objectivity of simply recording in a synthetic (or synoptic) apparatus the variants of a work rather than then creating a separate reading text supposedly embodying the author's final intentions—as occurs on the recto pages of the famous Gabler edition of Joyce's *Ulysses*. If intention is present at all in Gunter Martens's model of genetic editing, it is in the changes between texts rather than in any finality to this process, and it is Marten's concern to exploit the theoretical implications of such internal variance (see "Texte ohne Varianten?").

On the other hand, Jerome J. McGann (e.g., in *Critique*) has challenged the peculiar status given to intention by the eclecticists when he suggests that the author and the originary moment favored by eclecticism should be regarded as only one stage in the text's transmission. McGann's position is thus very similar to that of the enormously influential Soviet textologist Dmitrij Lixačev, for whom the literary text is primarily "a history of its compilers and early readers," although Lixačev does defend the Platonic ideal of text against the imposition of a purely materialist, dialectical view associated with the more pragmatic Aristotelianism of B. Ja. Buxštab (qtd. in Kasinec and Whittaker, in Greetham, *Scholarly Editing*). McGann's "social textual criticism" (attacked by Howard-Hill and judiciously discussed in Shillingsburg's "Inquiry") therefore insists that all public appearances of a text—as revised and changed by authors, editors, readers, publishers, friends, and relations—have potentially equal textual significance and that the "bibliographical code" (the various physical forms in which a text appears publicly) is just as much a part of its social meaning as is the "linguistic code" of its verbal content ("Critical Editing" 23). D. F. McKenzie has advanced a similar position, one that treats all remains of a culture as "text" and therefore withdraws some of the privilege traditionally accorded "literature."

Other influences, too, shape the climate of current texual scholarship: The French school of "l'histoire du livre" associated with Lucien Febvre and Henri-Jean Martin, emphasizing the cultural rather than the technical history of the book, has been seen in the works of Elizabeth Eisenstein and G. Thomas Tanselle (*History of Books*). As already noted, the influence of the Russian textological school of remaniements (Fennell) and reception theory, and its collateral mid-European branches (see Hay; Zeller), can be observed indirectly in several recent textual propositions and practices: Derek Pearsall's call for a loose-leaf edition of Chaucer ("Editing Medieval Texts"); Gary Taylor's insistence on Shakespeare as inveterate reviser ("Revising Shakespeare"); Steven Urkowitz's promotion of multiple-text interpretations of, for example, *Lear* and *Hamlet* and Michael Warren's edition of the "complete" (i.e., multiple-text) *Lear*; Peter L. Shillingsburg's vision of multiple computer-created texts of nineteenth-century novels ("Limits"); Donald H. Reiman's emphasis on "versioning" rather than final intentions in the editing of the Romantics; Louis Lafuma's and Philippe Sellier's separate editing of the two states (*La première copie* and *La seconde copie*) of Pascal's *Pensées* to overcome the false sense of unity and organicism given in earlier editions by Pascal's nephew Etienne Périer; Aldo Rossi's insistence that there are three authorial versions, not one, of Boccaccio's *Decameron*; Domenico De Robertis's experimental apparatus for recording multiple authorial variants in Ungaretti's poetry; John Miles Foley's computer program HEURO for the continual construction and reconstruction of Yugoslav oral epic poetry, a medium that would otherwise be arrested by editing; Hershel Parker's designation of a "new scholarship," which promises a "full intentionality" drawn from the multiple, and frequently contradictory, states of many nineteenth- and twentieth-century American authors; and Philip Gaskell and Clive Hart's publication of a reader's kit for "repairing the major faults" of *Ulysses* editions, including Gabler's. What all these textual scholars have in common is a reaction against any simplistic imposition of the final-intentions principles of Greg-Bowers eclecticism. Instead of postulating a single, consistent, authorially sponsored text as the purpose of the editorial enterprise, they suggest multiform, fragmentary, even contradictory, texts as the aim of editing, sometimes to be constructed ad hoc by the reader. In general, then, the characteristic feature of textual scholarship in the closing years of this century is its democratic pluralism: there is no longer, in Anglo-American editing at least, any single orthodoxy among textual scholars, although eclectic, intentionalist editions are still being produced more often than any other form, perhaps because it takes some time for practice to catch up with theory.

COMPONENTS AND PRACTICE

Criticism of Texts

As Tanselle has quite properly insisted, all those involved in the "great enterprise" of textual transmission and preservation are textual critics (*Rationale* 47), and this category therefore includes archivists, librarians, rare-book dealers, and even literary critics. But the fullest embodiment of textual scholarship is usually considered to be the scholarly edition, which involves several important components and can be of several types.

Noncritical Editing

Editing has often been conventionally divided between nontextual or noncritical editing, in which an editor reproduces an established text rather than establishes a new one, and textual or critical editing, in which the scholar creates a text in a form not hitherto available. The first type includes anthologies of previously published materials collected by an "editor," variorum editions using a previously constructed text as the basis for the commentary, representations of single documents (often called diplomatic editions), and, of course, photographic facsimiles.

Obviously, noncritical editions can have a serious purpose behind them: they may provide basic materials for a study of paleography or typography; they may preserve the *textus receptus*, or received text, of an important cultural artifact (the *Beowulf* manuscript or the Shakespeare Quartos or T. S. Eliot's *Waste Land* manuscript); or they may be a device for charting the history of critical responses and annotation (the Chaucer, Shakespeare, or Milton variorums), in the tradition of the "commentaries" in classical or biblical scholarship. But problems, often of definition, do arise: in 1978, A. L. Rowse used a noncritical text of the 1864 Globe edition as the vehicle for his *Annotated Shakespeare*, representing this old text as the most authoritative version of Shakespeare, as if nothing had happened in Shakespearean scholarship in more than a century. But when the terms and distinctions are kept clear, noncritical editions take on important textual value, largely in their claims of fidelity to a document not otherwise easily accessible.

This fidelity is apparently at its greatest in the photographic facsimile, although even here there are noteworthy distinctions. Film often fails to preserve hairline flourishes or textually significant abbreviation marks in manuscripts (especially if these marks are in different inks or different colors), and it cannot, of course, transmit important information about bibliographical materials—parchment, paper, ink, binding, and so on. Following the photographic facsimile in fidelity is the type facsimile, which attempts to reproduce the physical appearance of the original in a different typesetting, by observing such features as the original lineation, typesize, and type family (e.g., roman, italic, gothic). A diplomatic transcript, however, dispenses with such scrupulous fidelity to appearance and concentrates on the textual context, reproducing the exact spelling, punctuation, and capitalization but not necessarily observing the lineation (except in verse) or the typesizes of the original. Both type facsimiles and diplomatic transcripts have been used by historical series such as the Malone Society Reprints in making available to modern scholars the primary texts of Renaissance drama. It is also possible to regard even modernized-spelling, or internally normalized spelling, editions of original documents as noncritical, in the sense that they are not concerned with establishing a new, critically independent text, although the number and type of decisions move the edition away from the claims of pure fidelity.

Critical Editing

Textual or critical editions make such critical interposition the very raison d'être of editing, usually because it is felt that no single document or representation of a single document fully delineates either the author's intention or the historical and social context of the work as, or after, it leaves the author. This critical establishment of a new text may be simply a matter of removing perceived errors from an old one, or it may involve the construction of an eclectic text composed of features of various documents, plus emendations derived from no specific documentary source. The editor of such a critical edition has to decide how to present the textual evidence for reconstruction. The basic choice is between a clear, or reading, text (which gives the evidence for reconstruction in apparatus and notes but leaves the actual text unencumbered with variant readings or signals to the reader that something has been emended) and an inclusive text (which prominently displays editorial symbols and alternative readings on the textual page). A clear text is often most conveniently employed for eclectic editions of published works or works intended for publication, where the author's final intentions to arrive at a definitive, public statement of the text can often be plausibly demonstrated; an inclusive text is usually associated with genetic editing, often of private documents such as letters and journals or of uncompleted works, where no final intention—and certainly not an intention to publish—is involved. As indicated in the above brief discussion of the history of textual scholarship and in the account of the narrative of editing that follows, most contentions in textual scholarship reside in the ideology and practice of critical editing, even though noncritical editions, especially in such matters as transcription, have their embedded ideological problems and involve some critical decisions. Thus, even though all editions are therefore critical and implicitly contentious to some extent and even though they all offer critical decisions of interpretation, the traditional "critical edition," in establishing a text for a scholarly audience from the evidence of multiple witnesses, still presents the widest range of textual operations and demonstrates to the full the logical narrative of textual scholarship.

Narrative of Editing

Access to the text through research and enumerative bibliography is the first part of this narrative. The editor must find out which primary witnesses to the text are extant. Under intentionalist auspices, *primary* meant any version of the text in which the author's intentions, direct or indirect, might be observed. Under the newer forms of social textual criticism and other remaniement schools, however, virtually all versions, even those constructed long after the author's death, become primary, since they are part of the text's social transmission. Enumerative bibliography arranges these witnesses according to some "systematic bibliography," which can be as obvious as chronological order or as arcane as the taxonomy of typeforms, used, for example, in the bibliography of incunabula, or books printed up till 31 December 1500.

The editor also works to describe the witness technically, using what may appear to the amateur a highly complex system of formulas that reflects the book's physical makeup. This descriptive bibliography involves a consideration of printing techniques, especially of the way a page of type is set up to be inked, and of imposition, the arranging of those pages on sheets to be folded and printed. This technical emphasis forms the backbone of the related disciplines of analytical bibliography (for printed books) and codicology (for manuscripts), which provide the empirical information on which the formulas appearing in descriptive bibliography are based.

Another stage in the editing of works with multiple, often contradictory, texts is the selection of a witness to be used as copy-text. A copy-text is followed whenever there is no convincing reason to cite a rival reading from another text or to construct a reading speculatively if all extant variants are unsatisfactory. Certain famous editions (e.g., the Robinson *Chaucer* and the Gabler *Ulysses*) do not employ any copy-text in the traditional sense but weave a seamless text out of the various extant witnesses, with no recourse to the "indifferent authority" of a specific or consistent copy-text. In such editions, the editor constructs the text word by word (even syllable by syllable), basing each choice on a variety of documents (plus the editor's own ingenuity where all documents appear to be deficient), instead of choosing the single document most likely to preserve authorial intention and then comparing all others with this "control." But most editions of verbal multiple-text works do still use copy-text theory, and most editions of Anglo-American literature appearing in the 1990s will probably still employ a version of Greg's rationale of copy-text described above. In fields relatively untouched by Gregian principles (e.g., medieval studies), the term *base text* may be used instead of *copy-text*. This difference in terminology may also reflect a different ideology of editing, since a base text is typically selected not for its accidentals but for its substantives, its provenance, or its relative completeness.

To evaluate the likely authority of the witnesses in multiple-text works, editors usually trace the transmission of the text through a genealogy of witnesses. Such genealogies may be very complex in cultures encouraging scribal participation in the construction of texts (e.g., the non-Vedic Sanskrit texts or the Wycliffite sermon industry of the late Middle Ages) or where sectarian strife is represented by the multiplicity of variant readings (e.g., the proliferation of manuscripts of the New Testament) but relatively consistent in other religious traditions (e.g., the early Masoretic "fixing" of the Hebrew Bible). Again, tracing the filiation of witnesses has often become extremely technical, as attested to by the algebraic formulas employed in Greg's *Calculus of Variants*, the "positive concordance apparatus" of Dom Henri Quentin's distributional analysis, and the symbolic logic of Vinton Dearing's "rings" and "rules of parsimony" (*Principles*). In representing readings discovered in the copy-text or other witnesses, the editor must have a consistent theory of transcription—especially for the reading of ancient manuscript texts—involving the skills of paleography. Transcription practices can also be very contentious, as the continuing conflict between old-spelling and modern-spelling factions demonstrates: the publishers of the Oxford Shakespeare, recognizing the contention, simply brought out two editions (plus an electronic version), one for each camp, but most publishers are not as understanding and are likely to demand that the editor make up his or her mind. The decision of most editors of current American historical editions to favor some form of modernization has led to the significant ideological rift between editors of literature (see Tanselle, "Editing"), who support the orthographic intentions of authors, and historians (see R. Taylor), whose views have been institutionalized by the Association for Documentary Editing. Since the historians, with the Jefferson edition as paradigmatic, conceive of the text primarily as a vehicle for meaning rather than form (regarding such meaning as inherent in "words" rather than "spellings") and since they consciously produce their editions with modern readers in mind, they are concerned more about ensuring the reader's convenience than about seeing the edited text as a representation of the document's original orthographic features. Thus, a historical edition typically expands contractions and abbreviations, normalizes or modernizes punctuation and capitalization, and avoids importing readings from other texts of the same work in the eclectic fashion. The historians' concern is with readability for the modern researcher, the literary editors' with the intention of the author. A related contention is the frequent attempt to restore a putative "classical" orthographic form to a text surviving only in other dialectal versions: the classical West Saxon constructed in some Old English editions is an example, as is the classical Middle High German in Lachmann's edition of the *Nibelungenlied* or the accepted normalization of Arabic texts to classical Arabic usage—as compared with M. Mahdi's edition of the Arabian Nights, which unusually preserves colloquial features (see Carter, in Greetham, *Scholarly Editing*).

Furthermore, the editor must know under what circumstances a dissatisfaction with the copy-text or other witnesses necessitates emendation: Is the edition to be generally conservative (whereby, say, the copy-text must be manifestly wrong to justify emendation), or will it be highly conjectural (whereby readings from other witnesses or from the editor's own conception of authorial intention are introduced more willingly and speculatively)? The editor must also decide whether to signal to the reader when an emendation has been made—by a different typeface or some symbol or other—or to adopt a clear text, as mentioned above, listing emendations in a separate apparatus appended to the clear text.

What happens to these other variants of the text, those not regarded as embodying final intention—or whatever other principle the edition supposedly reflects—is another highly contentious issue. In typical electic editions, where final intention is, indeed, the basic rationale, these other readings are usually cited in the textual apparatus, in reduced typeface, at the bottom of the page, at the end of the book, or even in a separate volume. The full "historical collation," which in CEAA/CSE editions is limited to postauthorial textual deterioration but in other editing traditions may include rejected readings arguably made by the author, is similarly excluded from the textual page in the typical eclectic edition. However, genetic editing depends on this variance for its very form, and so it normally includes authorial variants, and sometimes nonauthorial as well, on the textual page. Inevitably, this practice requires a series of special symbols or differing typefaces or other arrangements to distinguish one type of reading from another, and the resulting "barbed wire" has often been attacked by critics such as Lewis Mumford and Edmund Wilson for distancing readers from the text. One way round the problem is to publish both a genetic text and a final-intentions text, although this solution is theoretically a contradiction in terms; Gabler's 1984 *Synoptic Edition* of *Ulysses* gives both types of texts, on facing pages, but the reading text of the 1986 *Corrected Text* does not.

Finally, editors must have some notion of how to mediate between text and audience, as in the question of transcription. They need to have a sense of the threshold of information that the audience possesses, and they sometimes end up making rather arbitrary decisions. For example, a recent edition of Yeats glosses "all specific allusions" (e.g., proper names) but offers no "interpretative commentary" because "firm evidence for many . . . identifications is lacking" and "it is arguable that Yeats did not wish to narrow the meanings" (Finneran 613). Although this distinction might seem logical, it has unfortunate results: Readers learn that the Virgin Mary is the "mother of Christ," that Shakespeare is an "English playwright," and that Hamlet and Ophelia are "characters in William Shakespeare's *Hamlet*" (654, 669), but the edition withholds information on poems addressed to, but not naming, Maud Gonne or Olivia Shakespear. Logic may thus have to yield to common sense, and the editor must ask, What do my readers already know, and what therefore can I tell them without seeming to patronize them or to leave them mystified? This problem is confronted at one level by the "hard words" issue: at the one extreme, the editor can assume that the audience is as learned as both the author and the editor and needs no glosses; at the other, the editor can gloss everything to produce a lexicon, or concordance, of the work—not an unusual practice in the editing of medieval texts. The problem is the in-between, where the editor must decide, for example, whether to define words still familiar in contemporary usage but bearing a different meaning in the text—say, the Middle English and early modern English use of *sad* to mean "compact" or "dense" or of *wood* to mean "mad," for without an awareness of the double meaning, a reader would find Shakespeare's pun "And here am I wood within this wood" strange indeed (*Midsummer Night's Dream* 2.1.192). The linguistic (as opposed to the allusive) issue is well stated in Edmund Campion's study of the editing of early modern French and the principles of annotation used by Marty-Laveaux: "The premise which Marty-Laveaux and many later textual scholars accepted is that notes in a critical edition are needed whenever a well-educated modern reader would have difficulty understanding a word, an expression, or a structure because of grammatical or semantic differences between modern French and French usage in the works of French writers from earlier centuries" (in Greetham, *Scholarly Editing*). But in some types of work and in the editions representing them, the linguistic is only one of several components requiring separate levels of annotation. Sacred texts often produce such multilayering, as the long traditions of Talmudic commentary and its analogous, patristic commentary on the Bible demonstrate. The Sezgin edition of Qur'anic material, together with interpolated commentary of the patristic type and poetic quotations and other scholarly allusions that have become part of the tradition, illustrates the practical problem of presentation: Sezgin divides each page, placing Qur'anic materials at the top (with serial numbers identifying poetic citations) and two similar tiers of explanatory footnotes at the bottom. As Michael Carter notes, this complexity of levels of annotation is necessary to construct links between reader and text(s), and it is not dissimilar to the multilevel annotation in, for example, the Chaucer and Shakespeare variorum editions.

Editing and Technology

Because the skills textual scholars use to train a text for its public appearance appear highly technical, many literary critics assume that textual scholarship is merely a mechanical production of texts and thus only a preliminary to the real business of criticism. Textual scholars do need an array of technical skills, especially since the entry of the computer into textual editing, and there has always been a seductive appeal in the power of machines or formulas to confer objectivity on textual scholarship and so render it immune from editorial idiosyncrasy. Although the various technical developments that have been used in editing are too numerous to record here, computers have proved most useful in the early stages of editing, especially collation and filiation, and at the very end, in the preparation of concordances and indexes, with comparatively limited electronic influence on the middle stages of textual criticism or emendation.

For example, no complete record of the fundamental units of a verbal text—its words—will ever again be made without computer assistance. This fact does not disparage the heroic efforts of such preelectronic pioneers as Marty-Laveaux and his *Lexique de la langue de Pierre Corneille* (volumes 11 and 12 of his Corneille edition), a work still employed as a source for seventeenth-century French usage, but acknowledges that electronic production and access have made the construction and manipulation of concordances much more efficient. For such concordances to be of textual value, they should not merely list the words in a work or oeuvre but show a selection from the text in which the words appear. There are basically two ways of making such selections—with KWIC (keyword in context) and KWOC (keyword out of context) concordances. In a KWIC concordance, the keyword (the main entry) is recorded as it appears in a particular lexical position, say, in the middle of a word block with five or ten words on each side—with no reference to how the word appears on the textual page (e.g., at the beginning or end of a line). A KWIC concordance can be instructed to sort the keyword to the left or right of such a block, but a central position is generally more useful for observing how the word is used in its context. The KWIC system is widely used in fluid texts like prose or verse with much enjambment. The KWOC concordance, however, positions the keyword not in a particular lexical context but, rather, as it appears in a specific textual unit (e.g., a metrical line); in such concordances, an editor is more interested in how a word is used in a line than in how it is used in a word block. Thus, a KWIC concordance for the word *impediment* in Shakespeare's sonnets (with the keyword in a central context of five words on either side) would yield an entry "marriage of true minds / Admit *impediment*. Love is not love / Which." A KWOC concordance using the metrical line as its unit would record "Admit *impediment*. Love is not love." Despite the iambic pentameter of the sonnet structure, the KWIC system shows the enjambment better (in part because the sample is larger). Each method has its advantages, and the concordance maker will have to decide which better suits the textual conditions.

Other problems in concordances include homographs (e.g., How does the computer distinguish between *does*, the third-person singular form of the verb *to do*, and *does*, the plural of the female deer?) and lemmatization (How does the computer recognize a word temporarily disguised by, e.g., prefixes or variant spelling: should the computer regard the word *pressure* as having the prefix *pre-*?). Through morphological segmentation subprograms, it may be possible to make these distinctions, especially in texts with typically small lexicons, like Old English, but often the entire text may need to be presorted syntactically and morphemically. On a wider lexical scale—entire languages—a scholar may now do semantic, morphological, or syntactic searches through the parsing facilities of such dictionaries as the second edition of the *Oxford English Dictionary*, the *Dictionary of American Regional English*, the *Dictionary of Old English*,

Trésor de la langue française, and the *Dictionary of the Old Spanish Language*. The forthcoming *New Oxford English Dictionary*, conceived from the beginning as an electronic edition, will be published primarily in electronic form, although there will be periodic publications in conventional print format (see Stubbs and Tompa; Amos). An editor working on a Shakespeare text may determine not only whether a particularly word is ever used by Shakespeare—from the Spevack concordances to the Riverside edition—but also whether this word occurs in any other headnote citations collected in the *New Oxford*. An editor may also discover, say, all words entering the English language from Italian in the sixteenth century or all quotations from Shakespeare, Milton, Keats, or Melville cited in the *New Oxford*.

Another related form of computer assistance is in vocabulary or stylistic studies, which are usually concerned with forming a view of the author's idiolect, the personal imprint on the language choices available. However, one must be both careful to construct this imprint from neutral terms and wary of context. For example, a recent stylometric study of the Pearl poet (qtd. in Pearsall and Cooper 371–72) came up with the surprising results that the author had a high incidence of *I, me, she*, and *her* but a very low incidence of *he, him, they*, and *them*, where a quick look at the context of *Pearl*—a dialogue between a narrator-dreamer and a vision of a young maiden—would immediately determine why this was so. Similarly, *þ* is obviously a common alliterative initial in *Pearl*, *c* a common alliterative initial in *Cleanness*, and so on. Thus, the context may predetermine the results of stylometric studies, which ought therefore to concentrate as much as possible on unconscious selections within the idiolect, not substantive ones.

In collation of witnesses, computers can remove much of the drudgery formally associated with textual scholarship, especially when used with optical scanners such as the Kurzweil machine. However, scanners can be used only on printed texts of the machine-print, post-1800 era that have a chartable degree of uniformity and variance in the physical appearance of typeforms. Such machines are of little help in directly converting manuscripts to machine-readable form, since manuscripts usually still have to be converted to print by keyboard, thereby introducing an additional stage into the textual transmission. The margin of error, often as high as five percent in certain typeforms, also makes scanners of limited usefulness. But once the various witnesses have been scanned or otherwise entered into the collation program, the charting of variants and the mapping of filiation can proceed electronically. The range of collation and filiation programs, already very wide, will no doubt expand in the 1990s. Some programs work line by line, some with blocks of a specific number of words; some can compare only two texts at a time, others up to fifty. The best known at present include R. L. Widmann's program for *A Midsummer Night's Dream*, project OCCULT (ordered computer collation of unprepared literary text), the Margaret Cabaniss program, and COLLATE (see Hockey; Oakman). Ted-Larry Pebworth and Gary Stringer's collation program, based on the Donne Variorum, is available for personal computers, as is Shillingsburg's CASE (computer-assisted scholarly editing) system, which is based on the Thackeray edition. CASE is particularly useful, since it combines nine interrelated programs that do much more than merely collate. For example, CASE can produce fair copy from a diplomatic transcription, merge variant files into a single comprehensive historical collation, sort lists of selected variants, and turn working lists of variants into files appropriate for producing a textual apparatus. For filiation, Dearing has written several useful programs, including PRELIMDI, ARCHETYP, and MSFAMTRE; he wrote MSFAMTRE using the data from PRELIMDI and then arranged the variants according to theory of probability (Hockey 158–59).

While computers have been used to research, edit, produce, and typeset printed critical editions, fully electronic texts, marketed in computer-readable form and even manipulated by the reader and used to create reader-designed critical editions, are still in the planning stage—although there is little doubt that they will come soon. The very notion of "hypertext," a cumulative electronic storage of all forms and states of text forming that text's history, will assuredly provide the raw and combinatory materials for the production of reader- or, more correctly, viewer-created editions in the near future, as suggested by Shillingsburg ("Limits") and others. In fact, Foley's HEURO I has already shown the way, allowing computer-terminal operators to experiment among the various available forms of motifs arranged in the "object text"—a hypertextual electronic method of letting the receiver handle text transmission, as has always been the method in oral literature (85–89).

Editing and Literary Criticism

Despite all this technical assistance, textual scholarship remains basically suspicious and therefore basically critical. When confronted with the accumulated evidence, the textual scholar must still cast a critical eye over its value and applicability, as in the example of the pronouns in *Pearl*. Even the apparently straightforward skill of transcription requires a judgment every time a letter form, or even a space, in the original document is re-presented in the transcript. Even a simple photographic facsimile of a document or documents necessitates critical decisions. For example, Hinman's facsimile of the Shakespeare First Folio cited earlier is a first edition of *the* First Folio, for until Hinman's 1968 edition no extant version of the Folio represented "ideal copy," and all versions contained uncorrected leaves. By selecting carefully from the extant copies, leaf by leaf, Hinman successfully constructed the First Folio three centuries after its appearance in corrupted form. As both Anne Middleton and Hans Gabler have recently noted, textual annotation and commentary should also be considered as part of an "integrate[d] critical discourse" (Gabler, "Textual Studies" 163). Gabler commends Stanley Wells and Gary Taylor's *Textual Companion* to the Oxford Shakespeare as a particularly fine example of extended "discursive reasoning" that qualifies as both literary criticism and textual criticism; he also quotes Gerhard Seidel's commentary on the variant texts of a multiform, highly versioned Brecht poem as a case of textual and critical "interpenetration" (164). Middleton, in assessing her role as annotator of George Kane and E. Talbot Donaldson's edition of *Piers Plowman*, discusses a wide range of critical and theoretical models for what she describes as the annotator's "life in the margins." For example, she observes that annotation can be seen as an allegorizing of the text in its "occlud[ing of] the horizontal coherence of the text [its narrative] for the vertical plenitude . . . of information [its referentiality to an outside world]" (170).

Such current speculations on the critical and aesthetic significance of textual work have a long history and range; indeed, textual scholars as diverse as Bowers (e.g., *Textual and Literary Criticism*), Tanselle (e.g., "Textual Scholarship"), Gary Taylor (e.g., "Rhetoric"), and McGann (e.g., "Monks") have frequently observed that textual scholarship and critical evaluation are inextricably linked, even at the most basic bibliographical level, and thus each act of textual scholarship becomes essentially an act of literary criticism. A brief example: When the eclectic editors Kane and Donaldson emend the text of Langland's *Piers Plowman* to produce perfect alliterative lines, even when the cumulative evidence of the surviving manuscripts does not support such perfection (see Fowler's review), and when they use the concept of the *lectio difficilior* 'more difficult reading' to support an unusual or idiosyncratic authorial reading, they are embodying textually several literary-critical principles. First, they suggest that great authors are more original than their copyists, who will either not recognize or not understand this originality and will seek to reduce it to a flat normalcy. Second, they assert that copies are, for this reason and others connected with human and material decay, inevitably corrupt and unreliable. Third, they believe that this unreliability empowers the critical editor to become the author through a phenomenological shift, or psychological "transference," and therefore to recompose the author's intention despite the documentary evidence. And fourth, they reason that great authors aspire to perfection, which their proxies, the critical editors, must therefore resuscitate. When Kane smilingly announced in conference some years ago that "Chaucer never wrote a nonmetrical line," he meant not only that all manuscript nonmetrical lines were written by Chaucer's scribes rather than by Chaucer but also that he knew what a perfect Chaucerian line was, just as the Alexandrians claimed to know what was the perfect Homeric line. This reasoning is inevitably circular, for the concept of perfection, the belief in the utility of "analogy," is itself based only on the avowedly corrupt remains, which by definition cannot be relied on. Yet, once the standard of perfection has been articulated, an adjudication can be made among these corrupt remains, and they can be arranged in a hierarchy insofar as they support the analogical paradigm. Then, in accordance with copy-text theory, the hierarchy can be invoked at moments of indifferent authority to construct or reflect a putative authorial reading where no adjudication is otherwise possible.

Logical problems do exist in several stages of this typical procedure, but they have not stood in the way of active and interrogative textual scholarship, nor should they. When Steven Mailloux—one of the few literary theorists to have written on textual scholarship—analyzes the rationale given by the editors of the Northwestern–Newberry Library Melville for having emended *nations* to *matrons* (114–15), he is relying on the reader-critic's mind having been subsumed into the consciousness of the author by phenomenological transference. Mailloux is thus using a literary-critical skill, or intuition, to challenge the literary-critical skills, or intuitions, of the Melville editors; this critical process is based, as was Kane's and Donaldson's for Langland, on *becoming* the author for that moment, in posthumously rewriting Melville's text. All the technical assistance and all the computers in the world finally leave the editor alone, at that moment, to face the task of creating anew the abstract form behind the concrete decay. Making use of both bibliographical and textual information and yet relying on speculative intuition, textual scholarship is thus neither science nor art. Housman came close to the problem when he suggested that textual work involves "the science of discovering errors in texts, and the art of removing them" (131), but today most practicing textual scholars would probably insist that art and science are equally mixed in both parts of Housman's equation.

This brief survey of the mechanics, the how of textual scholarship, assumes the importance of such procedures. But, although textual scholarship was at the center of the literary disciplines a century ago, it is now often regarded as merely introductory, or even subservient, to the real business of criticism—at least in its hermeneutic aspects (even though hermeneutics was itself a product of the higher criticism of biblical and classical texts, considered as textual artifacts). It may even come as a surprise to literary critics that textual scholars regard themselves as "interpreters" of texts (in the act of reconstructing them), but if one must indeed become Langland or Melville (or Shakespeare, Joyce, Woolf, Beethoven, or Michelangelo) in the phenomenology of reconstruction, then clearly textual scholars are making very large claims for themselves, and those claims extend beyond narrow, technical, philological aims. Two examples of the why of textual scholarship—from disciplines other than literature—clarify the significance of these claims.

In 1979, in the first (posthumous) performance of the complete three-act version of Alban Berg's opera *Lulu*, a version based on the textual reconstruction by Friedrich Cerha, the director Patrice Chéreau insisted that Yvonne Minton, playing the role of Countess Geschwitz, sing the word *Verflucht* ("cursed" or "damned") to the "wordless sigh" that Berg had notated in his unedited score in the final bars of the third act. Chéreau argued that since this was the last word in Berg's source, a play by Wedekind, it should thus be incorporated into the operatic as well as the theatrical tradition, even though Berg had not done so. Chéreau's addition of *Verflucht* has since 1979 become accepted into performance practice elsewhere, but without this "interpolation" from another medium and another author, Geschwitz's last word would be *Ewigkeit* ("eternity"—a dying promise to be faithful to her murdered lesbian lover Lulu forever). The two endings—"cursed" or "eternity"—clearly change the entire moral and psychological meaning of the lesbian affair for an audience (and arguably could even affect the genre of the work), but there is a further textual complexity: the additional final word *Verflucht* does not appear in the published score either in the complete three-act version or in the extract published separately in the *Lulu Suite*. It occurs only in the tradition of performance practice in the opera house since Chéreau's Paris production. Thus, a "reader" of the text of the libretto or score comes away with an impression of the work that is very different from that of a "hearer" of the performed opera, but only a textual scholar aware of both literary and oral transmissions is able to chart the difference and to know that the performance misrepresents the verbal text. One word changes everything (as it does in the variance at the end of D. H. Lawrence's *Sons and Lovers*, where the choice is between whether Paul Morel "whimpers" or "whispers" the talismanic word *Mother*!). To demonstrate the cultural, and legal, importance of textual opinions, we can turn to the recent Italian lawsuit in which James Beck, professor of art history at Columbia and one of the dissenting voices to the Sistine Chapel cleaning, has been charged with "malicious slander" by the inventor of a pellet gun used to clean Renaissance statues (see Simons). And the complaint? That by favoring, in somewhat forceful language, the McGannian textual concept of the work existing in its accumulated history (grime and all) rather than in a false "originary" moment that can never be recaptured, Beck is maligning the rival "textual" theory of the cleaners. That Beck could, under Italian law, go to jail for three or four years for his textual opinions, will no doubt be a caution to all textual scholars, and the case demonstrates that a culture may place very high value indeed on "states" of the text. In these two examples, only a full critical edition of both oral and literary transmissions of *Lulu* would make the options clear (and exemplify the value of recording multiple witnesses in such critical editions), but for the Renaissance statues, since "text" and "work" compete for the same space, no critical edition can preserve both textual choices.

TEXTUALITY

Practice and Theory

While the periodic attempts by the technicians, mathematicians, and logicians to make textual scholarship into a science have doubtless enriched the discipline, the inevitable critical component of textual scholarship means that there can be no immunity from the various debates about text and criticism that have characterized recent developments in literary criticism and theory. At one time the empirical emphases of textual scholarship might have led its practitioners to assume that editing a text did not involve theory and that the traditional practices of collation, emendation, and so on, which seemed natural to the successful production of critical editions, did not depend on ontological assumptions. But virtually all textual scholars now recognize that, since the textual scholarship of literature is a form of literary criticism or vice versa, textual assumptions and practices both influence and are influenced by the literary contentions. Thus, it was no accident that the critical hegemony of the New Criticism paralleled that of the New Bibliography, with its similar concentration on closed formalistic texts bearing the imprint of a single consciousness and uniform act of composition—a "well-wrought urn" (Greetham, "Textual and Literary Theory" 14–15n4). Nor is it any accident that during the late 1970s and into the 1990s, textual scholarship has moved away from this model toward genetic texts, fragmented texts, versioning texts, social texts, multiple and contradictory texts, even reader-generated texts, through the work of such scholars as Gabler, Pearsall, Reiman, McGann, Parker, and Foley.

Each of these new models can be seen to represent one or more of the current movements in phenomenological, structuralist, poststructuralist, reader-response, feminist, or Marxist criticism. For example, as I have already suggested, an ideological conflict occurs in Gabler's *Synoptic Edition* between the right-hand (reading) pages, which represent "intentionality," and the left-hand (genetic) pages, which embody a formal structuralist approach to recording the text. This conflict arises because each choice that the reader makes on the genetic page consists of an "on" reading (that selected at a given moment) and at least one implied "off" reading (that not selected), without any privilege being permanently accorded to any and with the existence of each dependent on its structuralist "difference" from the others. Similarly, McGann's social textual criticism has been seen both as an "unattributed gloss" on the Marxist Pierre Macherey's dictum that "the work is not *created* by an intention (objective or subjective); it is *produced* under determinate conditions" (Sutherland 581) and as an exemplification of Stanley Fish's "interpretive communities," whereby textual meaning is constructed by a social contract within which the transmitted text operates rather than by an appeal to the intentions of a now absent author (Greetham, "Textual and Literary Theory" 11–12). Another approach is to confront literary theory directly and to interrogate its principles or even co-opt them: these two alternatives can be seen in two deconstruction articles by Tanselle ("Textual Criticism") and D. C. Greetham ("[Textual] Criticism"). An example of co-option in a specific period is Robert S. Sturges's recent article, in the medieval studies journal *Exemplaria*, on textual scholarship as "ideology of literary production," which incidentally demonstrates that textual and literary theory are as much a part of criticism of the early periods as they are of twentieth-century studies. As Tanselle's deconstruction article suggests, even the more traditional intentionalists have taken part in the debate; discussions range from Tanselle's comprehensive study of intention ("Editorial Problem")—drawing mostly on the philosopher Michael Hancher and the literary theorist E. D. Hirsch, Jr.—to James McLaverty's investigation of the ontology of the intentionalist text ("Concept") and his citing of a familiar problem (after Bateson): if the *Mona Lisa* is in the Louvre, where are *Hamlet* or *Lycidas* ("Mode of Existence" 82)?

Future Texts

If current publication plans are fulfilled, it is likely that the 1990s will see further speculation on the interrelation of textual, cultural, and literary theory. For example, Gary Taylor is working on a study of the historical hermeneutics of editing, tentatively entitled *The Matter of Text*; W. Speed Hill on the humanist antecedents of editing in the vernacular and on the text as scripture; Joseph Grigely on textual criticism and the arts; James L. W. West III on a volume entitled *Creating American Authors: The Language of Editing*; and Greetham on the conceptual and ideological matrix of literary and textual theory (*Theories*). The collections of essays on this problem appearing in a special issue of the journal *Critical Exchange*, entitled *Textual Scholarship and Literary Theory*, and in the volume that Philip Cohen has edited (*Devils and Angels*) will doubtless fuel the debate, as will McGann's forthcoming book *The Textual Condition*, George Bornstein's two collections (*Representing Modernist Texts* and *Palimpsest*), Tim Machan's *Medieval Literature*, and Dave Oliphant and Robin Bradford's *New Directions in Textual Studies*, the proceedings of a 1989 Texas conference in which the sociological and materialist aspect of text and textuality is very prominent. Textual scholars are thus confronting many of the critical issues (e.g., race, class, gender, interpretation, textuality) that characterize other parts of the discipline and that this volume addresses elsewhere. Perhaps the most provocative issue to date has been the attempt by some feminist scholars to interrogate not only the patriarchal canon of received texts but also the ideologies embedded in editions—for example, the status of text and apparatus as "center" and "margins" (see Bennett; King; Silver; White). Certainly, more editions bearing a nonintentionalist stamp, following the examples of European geneticism and other schools, will appear in the next few years. Until recently, the technical constraints of letterpress editions lent themselves quite readily to the production of definitive, fixed, permanent editions, both on the page and in time, so that eclectic, final-intentions editions seemed almost natural for the technical medium. But textual scholars can now produce fragmented, spliced, mutilated, multiform, grafted, or deconstructed texts—doubtless embodying the worst nightmares of New Critic and New Bibliographer alike—and most textual scholars now recognize that a natural affinity exists between the computer and the variable discourses of contemporary textual scholarship, as the electronic editions of the Oxford Shakespeare and the *OED* have begun to demonstrate. But counterbalancing these new electronic riches is the realization that composition on word processors or computers may destroy layer after layer of an evolving work, unless hard copies of each stage are made and retained.

As already noted, the new technical sophistication has not yet produced completely electronic editions. Thus, McGann is right ("Contemporary Literary Theory") to be somewhat circumspect about the current possibilities, even with hypertext, for representing electronically the variable "bibliographical code" of a text as well as its equally variable "linguistic code." But this present limitation is simply the result of an inevitable initial technical concentration on verbal forms, and reproducing the visual and other bibliographical conditions of textual states will probably become possible as computer programs grow more sophisticated. Even now, CD-ROM disks can contain graphic representations of each edition, and desktop editing and publishing will no doubt take advantage of such facilities, with or without modem connecting the editor directly to the printer or publisher.

Interdisciplinary study is another important area of speculation on textuality. This field has been enhanced in two ways: First, cross-disciplinary textual discussion has become institutionalized through such organs as the Association for Documentary Editing and the Society for Textual Scholarship—although the Association for Documentary Editing has gradually become identified primarily with the interests of historians, and it is, to some extent, as concerned with the practical matters of securing funding and employment as it is with being a forum for scholarly debate. The two journals of these bodies, *Documentary Editing* and *Text*, have published much important interdisciplinary work in the last decade, a trend that has been paralleled by an increasing hospitality to theoretical and interdisciplinary study in more traditional journals such as *Studies in Bibliography*, *Papers of the Bibliographical Society of America*, and *The Library*. Second, several scholars (e.g., Shillingsburg, "Key Issues" and "Text as Matter"; Tanselle, *Rationale*; and McGann, "Critical Editing") have made significant attempts to define some of the basic concepts of textual scholarship (e.g., *text, work, critical editing*) and to apply these concepts beyond the familiar verbal texts of literature to the media of film, painting, music, sculpture, and so on. By far the most wide-ranging and convincing of these attempts to date has been Tanselle's *Rationale of Textual Criticism*, which brings the author's encyclopedic knowledge of all aspects of textual scholarship to bear on the primary ontological questions of textuality.

Case Study: The Gabler Ulysses

Inevitably, these interdisciplinary studies cannot avoid contention—nor do they seek to do so. Since textual scholarship has always been marked by philosophical as well as methodological disagreements, from the days of the Alexandrians and the Pergamanians, it should not be expected that theoretical and interdisciplinary discussion will achieve consensus. Textual scholars, the dryasdusts of the scholarly world, may seem immune from the personal animus and emotional investment that characterize other critical dispensations, but this immunity is illusory. A particularly pertinent example of the problem, one that exemplifies many of the issues dealt with in this essay (access to documents, copy-text theory, genetic versus eclectic editing, types of apparatus, etc.), occurs in the conflict over the Gabler *Ulysses*.

The text of *Ulysses* has always been problematic: the 1922 first edition includes a note apologizing for the many typographical errors; Random House set the first American edition (1934) from a corrupt pirated version; and the revised (1961) edition compounds many earlier errors. Because of the estimated four thousand errors in the text of the major novel of the twentieth century, it was inevitable that contemporary textual scholarship would turn to the task of constructing an authoritative edition. The responsibility fell to a team headed by Gabler, a former student of Bowers and a professor of English at the University of Munich. Gabler decided not to bring out a traditional critical edition based on a single copy-text with variants from other texts but instead to produce a genetic, or "synoptic," text showing all stages of the authorial composition of *Ulysses*, complemented by a facing-page reading text of Joyce's supposed final intentions, which were not otherwise embodied in any single document. This synoptic edition, whose principles were articulated in Gabler's "Synchrony" article, was published in 1984, to much acclaim, and it was followed in 1986 by withdrawal of the old Random House edition and the publication of the reading text alone, without the synoptic apparatus. The Gabler edition, in both synoptic and clear-text form, was thus the exclusive text of Joyce's *Ulysses*. In the meantime, however, the activities of Kidd, then a postdoctoral fellow at the University of Virginia, in questioning Gabler's methods and specific readings, led to a reevaluation of the Gabler edition—and to an increasingly contentious debate between Kidd and Gabler and their supporters in conferences, learned journals, and the popular press (see Wilkerson; Treglown). A James Joyce Research Center affiliated with Boston University (with Kidd as its director) was set up, and a special committee was appointed by Random House to adjudicate the matter. However, this committee did not reach a definitive decision before disbanding, and since Random House decided to republish the 1961 edition, readers of *Ulysses* were therefore left as active textual critics, having to judge the texts rather than passively consume them. This choice will be compounded by Kidd's recent appointment as editor of the "Dublin" edition of Joyce's works, to be published by Norton. The *Ulysses* "scandal" was simply a public debate over the critical issues faced by all textual scholars and all critical readers, and it forcefully demonstrated to the academic world and general reader alike, at a time when such truths were perhaps in need of resuscitation, just how crucial is the role of textual scholarship in critically evaluating and re-creating the texts of our culture.

Suggestions for Further Reading

Useful bibliographies for the field occur in G. Thomas Tanselle's "Textual Scholarship" in the first edition of this book, the accounts of research in the CSE and CEAA pamphlets, William Proctor Williams and Craig S. Abbott's *Introduction to Bibliographical and Textual Studies*, Graham Falconer and David H. Sanderson's "Bibliographie des études génétiques littéraires" (which covers much more than strict "genetic editing"), Beth Luey's *Editing Documents and Texts*, and the "Suggested Readings" in Mary-Jo Kline's *Guide to Documentary Editing*. The annual checklists of textual scholarship published in *Studies in Bibliography* have now been discontinued, but they are still useful for earlier years. See also the bibliographies in O M Brack, Jr., and Warner Barnes's *Bibliography*, Ronald Gottesman and Scott Bennett's *Art and Error*, and Barnes's "Selective Bibliography." Most of the Tanselle articles cited contain rich documentation in the notes. General surveys of the field of textual scholarship include Tanselle's "Textual Scholarship," Fredson Bowers's "Textual Criticism," and D. C. Greetham's *Textual Scholarship: An Introduction*. While textual articles occasionally appear in general critical journals, most of the important essays have been published in *The Library*, *Papers of the Bibliographical Society of America*, *Studies in Bibliography*, *Documentary Editing*, *Analytical and Enumerative Bibliography*, *Text*, or *Editio* (in German); these journals can be supplemented by reference to articles in the various volumes of the annual University of Toronto *Conferences on Editorial Problems*, now published by AMS Press. Textual editions and textual work are frequently reviewed in the journal *Review*. General manuals of editing include Kline's *Guide* and Williams and Abbott's *Introduction*, supplemented by manuals for editing in specific fields (e.g., Foulet and Speer on Old French; Moorman on Middle English). The best introduction to analytical and descriptive bibliography is Philip Gaskell's *New Introduction* (supplemented by Bowers's monumental *Principles*) and to codicology, Barbara Shailor's *Medieval Book* and Bernard Bischoff's *Latin Palaeography*, which (as its title suggests) is also useful for paleography. A practical approach to texts and editing is taken by Gaskell's *From Writer to Reader*, which provides several examples of multiple-witness texts from the Renaissance to modern literature and of various editorial methods to deal with them. General surveys of editing methods occur in Bowers's collection *Essays in Bibliography, Text, and Editing*; Tanselle's collection *Textual Criticism since Greg* (which supplements his earlier collection of essays, *Selected Studies in Bibliography*); Donald H. Reiman's "Four Ages"; Peter L. Shillingsburg's *Scholarly Editing*; John McClelland's "Critical Editing" (for Continental editing); Jerome J. McGann's *Critique*; James Thorpe's *Princples*; George L. Vogt and John Bush Jones's *Literary and Historical Editing*; Dave Oliphant and Robin Bradford's *New Directions* and (for all periods from biblical to modern) Greetham's forthcoming *Scholarly Editing: A Guide to Research*, especially for further information on nonanglophone references in this present essay (e.g., Mary B. Speer and Edmund Campion on French, Michael Carter on Arabic, Paolo Cherchi on Italian, John Miles Foley on folk literature, Edward Kasinec and Robert Whittaker on Slavic, Bodo Plachta on German, and Ludo Rocher on Sanskrit). Other useful essays for the beginner include R. C. Bald's "Editorial Problems," Bowers's "Method for a Critical Edition," Brack's "Introduction" to the Brack and Barnes *Bibliography*, Lester J. Cappon's "Historian as Editor," Vinton Dearing's "Methods of Textual Editing," Dan H. Laurence's "Bibliographical Novitiate," and John Y. Simon's "Editors and Critics."

City University of New York

Works Cited

Note: Where a particular style of editing, or the specific contributions of an editor, is the reason for citation, editions are listed under the names of their editors (e.g., Gabler, Robinson, Bowers); otherwise, editions are listed under their authors (e.g., Shakespeare, Milton, Melville, Emerson).

Amos, Ashley Crandell. "Computers and Lexicography: The *Dictionary of Old English.*" Butler and Stoneman 45–64.

Bald, R. C. "Editorial Problems: A Preliminary Survey." *Studies in Bibliography* 3 (1950–51): 3–17. Rpt. in Gottesman and Bennett 37–53.

Barbi, Michele, ed. *La vita nuova.* By Dante Alighieri. Florence: Soc. Dantesca Italiana, 1907.

Barnes, Warner. "Eighteenth- and Nineteenth-Century Editorial Problems: A Selective Bibliography." *Papers of the Bibliographical Society of America* 62 (1968): 59–67.

Bateson, F. W. "Modern Bibliography and the Literary Artifact." *English Studies Today: Second Series.* Ed. G. A Bonnard. 1961. 66–77.

Bédier, Joseph, "La tradition manuscrite du *Lai du l'ombre*: Réflexions sur l'art d'éditer les anciens textes." *Romania* 54 (1928): 161–96, 321–56. Rpt. as pamphlet, 1970.

Beissner, Friedrich, ed. *Sämtliche Werke.* By Friedrich Hölderlin. Stuttgart: Gr. Stuttgart Ausgabe, 1943.

Bennett, Betty. "Feminism and Editing: The Mary Shelley Letters." Bornstein, *Palimpsest.*

Beowulf: Facsimile. Ed. Norman Davis. 2nd. ed. EETS. London: Oxford UP, 1959.

Bischoff, Bernhard. *Latin Palaeography: Antiquity and the Middle Ages.* Trans. Dáibhí O Cróinín and David Ganz. Cambridge: Cambridge UP, 1990.

Bornstein, George, ed. *Palimpsest: Editorial Theory in the Humanities.* Ann Arbor: U of Michigan P, forthcoming.

———. *Representing Modernist Texts: Editing as Interpretation.* Ann Arbor: U of Michigan P, 1991.

Bowers, Fredson, ed. *The Centenary Edition of the Works of Nathaniel Hawthorne.* 11 vols. Columbus: Ohio State UP, 1962–75.

———, ed. *The Dramatic Works of Thomas Dekker.* 4 vols. Cambridge: Cambridge UP, 1953–61.

———. *Essays in Bibliography, Text, and Editing.* Charlottesville: UP of Virginia, 1975.

———. "The Method for a Critical Edition." *On Editing Shakespeare and the Elizabethan Dramatists.* Philadelphia: U of Pennsylvania Lib., 1955. 67–101.

———. *Principles of Bibliographical Description.* Princeton: Princeton UP, 1949. New York: Russell, 1962.

———. *Textual and Literary Criticism.* Cambridge: Cambridge UP, 1966.

———. "Textual Criticism." *The Aims and Methods of Scholarship in Modern Languages and Literatures.* Ed. James Thorpe. 2nd. ed. New York: MLA, 1970. 29–54.

———, ed. *The Works of Stephen Crane.* 10 vols. Charlottesville: UP of Virginia, 1969–75.

Bowers, Fredson, with L. A. Beaurline, eds. *John Dryden: Four Comedies.* Chicago: U of Chicago P, 1967.

———. *John Dryden: Four Tragedies.* Chicago: U of Chicago P, 1967.

Brack, O M, Jr., and Warner Barnes, eds. *Bibliography and Textual Criticism: English and American Literature, 1700 to the Present.* Chicago: U of Chicago P, 1969.

Butler, Sharon, and William P. Stoneman, eds. *Editing, Publishing, and Computer Technology.* New York: AMS, 1988.

Cappon, Lester J. "The Historian as Editor." *In Support of Clio: Essays in Memory of Herbert A. Kellar.* Ed. William B. Hesseltine and Donald R. McNeil. Madison: State Historical Soc. of Wisconsin, 1958. 173–93.

Cather, Willa. *O Pioneers!* Ed. Susan J. Rosowski. Lincoln: U of Nebraska P, 1992.

Center for Editions of American Authors. *Statement of Editorial Principles and Procedures.* Rev. ed. New York: MLA, 1972.

Center/Committee for Scholarly Editions. *An Introductory Statement.* New York: MLA, 1977.

Chaucer, Geoffrey. *The Variorum Chaucer.* Ed. Paul G. Ruggiers. 8 vols. to date. Norman: U of Oklahoma P; Folkestone: Dawson, 1979–.

Cohen, Philip, ed. *Devils and Angels: Textual Editing and Literary Theory.* Charlottesville: UP of Virginia, 1991.

Dearing, Vinton. "Methods of Textual Editing." *Williams Andrews Clark Memorial Library Seminar Papers* (1962): 1–34. Rpt. in Brack and Barnes 73–101.

———. *Principles and Practice of Textual Analysis.* Berkeley: U of California P, 1974.

De Robertis, Domenico. "Per l'edizione critica del 'Dolore' di Giuseppi Ungaretti." *Studi di Filologia Italiana* 38 (1980): 309–23.

Eisenstein, Elizabeth. *The Printing Press as an Agent of Change.* 2 vols. Cambridge: Cambridge UP, 1979.

Ejxenbaum, B. "O tekstax Lermontova." *Literaturnoe nasledstvo.* Vols. 19–21. Moscow: Zurnal'no-gazetnoe ob"edinenie, 1935. 485–501.

Eliot, T. S. The Waste Land: *A Facsimile and Transcript.* Ed. Valerie Eliot. New York: Harcourt, 1971.

Emerson, Ralph Waldo. *The Collected Works of Ralph Waldo Emerson.* 4 vols. to date. Ed. Alfred R. Ferguson. Cambridge: Belknap–Harvard UP, 1971–.

Falconer, Graham, and David H. Sanderson. "Bibliographie des études génétiques littéraires." *Texte* 7 (1988): 287–352.

Febvre, Lucien, and Henri-Jean Martin. *The Coming of the Book: The Impact of Printing, 1450–1800.* Trans. David Gerard. London: Verso, 1990.

Fennell, John L. I. "Textology as a Key to the Study of Old Russian Literature and History." *Text* 1 (1981): 157–66.

Finneran, Richard J., ed. *The Poems of W. B. Yeats.* New York: Macmillan, 1983.

Flaubert, Gustave. *Corpus flaubertianum.* Ed. Giovanni Bonnacorso, Maria Francesca Davi-Trimarchi, Simonetta Micale, and Eliane Contaz-Sframeli. Paris: Belles Lettres, 1983.

Foley, John Miles. "Editing Yugoslav Epics: Theory and Practice." *Text* 1 (1981): 75–96.

Foulet, Alfred, and Mary Blakeley Speer. *On Editing Old French Texts.* Lawrence: Regents P of Kansas, 1979.

Fowler, David C. "A New Edition of the B Text of *Piers Plowman.*" *Yearbook of English Studies* 7 (1977): 23–42.

Gabler, Hans Walter. "A Response to John Kidd, 'Errors of Execution in the 1984 *Ulysses*.' " Soc. for Textual Scholarship. New York, 26, Apr. 1985. *Studies in the Novel* 22 (1990): 250–56.

———. "The Synchrony and Diachrony of Texts: Practice and Theory of the Critical Edition of James Joyce's *Ulysses*." *Text* 1 (1981): 305–26.

———. "Textual Studies and Criticism." Oliphant and Bradford 151–66.

———, ed. Ulysses: *Corrected Text.* By James Joyce. New York: Random, 1986.

Gabler, Hans Walter, with Wolfhard Steppe and Claus Melchior, eds. Ulysses: *A Critical and Synoptic Edition.* By James Joyce. 3 vols. New York: Garland, 1984.

Gaskell, Philip. *From Writer to Reader: Studies in Editorial Method.* Oxford: Clarendon–Oxford UP, 1978.

———. *New Introduction to Bibliography.* Oxford: Oxford UP, 1972.

Gaskell, Philip, and Clive Hart, eds. Ulysses: *A Review of Three Texts.* New York: Barnes, 1989.

Gottesman, Ronald, and Scott Bennett, eds. *Art and Error: Modern Textual Editing.* Bloomington: Indiana UP, 1970.

Greetham, D. C., ed. *Scholarly Editing: A Guide to Research.* New York: MLA, forthcoming.

———. "Textual and Literary Theory: Redrawing the Matrix." *Studies in Bibliography* 42 (1989): 1–24.

———. "[Textual] Criticism and Deconstruction." *Studies in Bibliography* 44 (1991): 1–30.

———. *Textual Scholarship: An Introduction.* New York: Garland, 1991.

———. *Theories of the Text.* Oxford: Oxford UP, forthcoming.

Greg, W. W. *A Calculus of Variants: An Essay on Textual Criticism.* Oxford: Clarendon–Oxford UP, 1927.

———. "The Rationale of Copy-Text." *Studies in Bibliography* 3 (1950–51): 19–36.

Hancher, Michael. "Three Kinds of Intention." *MLN* 87 (1972): 827–51.

Hay, Louis. "Genetic Editing, Past and Present: A Few Reflections of a User." *Text* 3 (1987): 117–34.

Hinman, Charlton, ed. *The Norton Facsimile: The Shakespeare First Folio.* New York: Norton, 1968.

Hirsch, E. D., Jr. *Validity in Interpretation.* New Haven: Yale UP, 1967.

Hockey, Susan. *A Guide to Computer Applications in the Humanities.* Baltimore: Johns Hopkins UP, 1980.

Hölderlin, Friedrich. *Sämtliche Werke.* Ed. D. E. Sattler. Frankfurt: Roter Stern, 1975.

Housman, A. E. *Selected Prose.* Ed. John Carter. Cambridge: Cambridge UP, 1961.

Howard-Hill, T. H. "Theory and Praxis in the Social Approach to Editing." *Text* 5 (1991): 31–46.

Jefferson, Thomas. *The Papers of Thomas Jefferson.* Ed. Julian P. Boyd, Charles T. Cullen, et al. 24 vols. to date. Princeton: Princeton UP, 1950–.

Joyce, James. *Ulysses.* Rev. ed. New York: Random, 1961.

Kafka, Franz. *Schriften, Tagebücher, Briefe*. Ed. Jürgen Born, Gerhard Neumann, Malcolm Pasley, and Jost Schillemeit. 6 vols. to date. Frankfurt: Fischer, 1982–.

Kane, George. Discussion. New Chaucer Society Conference. Washington, Apr. 1979.

Kane, George, and E. Talbot Donaldson, eds. Piers Plowman*: The B Version*. London: Athlone, 1975.

Kenney, E. J. *The Classical Text: Aspects of Editing in the Age of the Printed Book*. Berkeley: U of California P, 1974.

Kidd, John, ed. *Dublin Edition of the Works of James Joyce*. New York: Norton, in preparation.

———. "Errors of Execution in the 1984 *Ulysses*." Soc. for Textual Scholarship. New York, 26 Apr. 1985. *Studies in the Novel* 22 (1990): 243–49.

———. "An Inquiry into Ulysses: *The Corrected Text*." *Papers of the Bibliographical Society of America* 82.4 (1988): 411–584.

———. "The Scandal of *Ulysses*." *New York Review of Books* 30 June 1988: 32–39.

King, Katie. "Bibliography and a Feminist Apparatus for Literary Production." *Text* 5 (1991): 91–104.

Kline, Mary-Jo. *A Guide to Documentary Editing*. Baltimore: Johns Hopkins UP, 1987.

Klopstock, Friedrich Gottlieb. *Werke und Briefe*. Ed. Adolf Beck, Karl-Ludwig Schneider, Hermann Tiemann, Horst Gronemeyer, Elisabeth Höpker-Herberg, Klaus Hurlebusch, and Rosa-Maria Hurlebusch. 19 vols. to date. Berlin: Gruyter, 1974–.

Knight, R. C., and H. T. Barnwell, eds. *Andromaque*. By Jean Racine. Geneva: Droz, 1977.

Lachmann, Karl. *Der Nibelunge Noth und die Klage*. 12th ed. Berlin: Reimer, 1901.

Lafuma, Louis, ed. *Œuvres complètes*. By Blaise Pascal. Paris: Seuil, 1963.

Laumonier, Paul, Raymond Lebègue, and Isidore Silver, eds. *Œuvres complètes*. By Pierre de Ronsard. 17 vols. Paris: Hachette, 1914–59.

Laurence, Dan H. "A Bibliographical Novitiate: In Search of Henry James." *Papers of the Bibliographical Society of America* 52 (1958): 23–33.

Lixačev, Dmitrij. *Tekstologija russkoj literatury X-XVII vekov*. Leningrad: Nauka, 1983.

Luey, Beth. *Editing Documents and Texts: An Annotated Bibliography*. Madison: Madison, 1990.

Maas, Paul. *Textual Criticism*. Trans. Barbara Flower. Oxford: Clarendon–Oxford UP, 1958.

Machan, Tim W., ed. *Medieval Literature: Texts and Interpretation*. Binghamton: Medieval and Renaissance Texts and Studies, 1990.

Mahdi, M., ed. *The Thousand and One Nights . . . from the Earliest Known Sources*. 2 vols. to date. Leiden: Brill, 1984–.

Mailloux, Steven. *Interpretive Conventions: The Reader in the Study of American Fiction*. Ithaca: Cornell UP, 1982.

Margitic, Milorad R., ed. *Le Cid*. By Pierre Corneille. Amsterdam: Benjamins, 1989.

Martens, Gunter. "Textdynamik und Edition." *Texte und Varianten: Probleme ihrer Edition und Interpretation*. Ed. Hans Zeller and Gunter Martens. Munich: Beck, 1971. 165–201.

———. "Texte ohne Varianten?" *Zeitschrift für Deutsche Philologie* 101 (1982): 43–64.

Marty-Laveaux, Charles, ed. *Œuvres complètes*. By Pierre Corneille. 12 vols. Paris: Hachette, 1862–93.

———, ed. *Œuvres complètes*. By Pierre de Ronsard. 6 vols. Paris: Lemerre, 1887–93.

McClelland, John. "Critical Editing in the Modern Languages." *Text* 1 (1981): 201–16.

McGann, Jerome J. "Contemporary Literary Theory and Textual Criticism." Soc. for Textual Scholarship. New York, 7 Apr. 1989.

———. *A Critique of Modern Textual Criticism*. Chicago: U of Chicago P, 1983.

———. "The Monks and the Giants: Textual and Bibliographical Studies and the Interpretation of Literary Works." McGann, *Textual Criticism* 180–99.

———. *The Textual Condition*. Princeton: Princeton UP, 1991.

———, ed. *Textual Criticism and Literary Interpretation*. Chicago: U of Chicago P, 1985.

———. "What Is Critical Editing?" *Text* 5 (1991): 15–30.

McKenzie, D. F. *Bibliography and the Sociology of Texts*. London: British Lib., 1986.

McLaverty, James. "The Concept of Authorial Intention in Textual Criticism." *Library* 6 (June 1984): 121–38.

———. "The Mode of Existence of Literary Works of Art: The Case of the *Dunciad* Variorum." *Studies in Bibliography* 37 (1984): 82–105.

Melville, Herman. *The Writings of Herman Melville*. Ed. Harrison Hayford, Hershel Parker, and G. Thomas Tanselle. 12 vols. to date. Evanston: Northwestern UP; Chicago: Newberry Lib., 1968–.

Middleton, Anne. "Life in the Margins; or, What's an Annotator to Do?" Oliphant and Bradford 167–83.

Milton, John. *A Variorum Commentary on the Poems of John Milton*. Ed. Merritt Y. Hughes et al. 6 vols. New York: Columbia UP, 1970–75.

Moland, Louis, ed. *Œuvres complètes*. By Voltaire. 52 vols. Paris: Garnier, 1877–85.

Moorman, Charles. *Editing the Middle English Manuscript*. Jackson: UP of Mississippi, 1975.

Mumford, Lewis. "Emerson behind Barbed Wire." *New York Review of Books* 18 Jan. 1968: 3–5.

Oakman, Robert. *Computer Methods for Literary Research*. Rev. ed. Athens: U of Georgia P, 1984.

Oliphant, Dave, and Robin Bradford, eds. *New Directions in Textual Studies*. Austin: Harry Ransom Humanities Research Center, U of Texas P, 1990.

Parker, Hershel. *Flawed Texts and Verbal Icons: Literary Authority in American Fiction*. Evanston: Northwestern UP, 1984.

———. " 'The New Scholarship': Textual Evidence and Its Implication for Criticism, Literary Theory, and Aesthetics." *Studies in American Fiction* 9 (1984): 181–97.

Pasquali, Giorgio. *Storia della tradizione e critica del testo*. Florence: Monnier, 1934.

Pearsall, Derek. "Editing Medieval Texts." McGann, *Textual Criticism* 92–106.

Pearsall, Derek, and R. A. Cooper. "The *Gawain* Poems: A Statistical Approach to the Question of Common Authorship." *Review of English Studies* 39 (1988): 365–85.

Pebworth, Ted-Larry, and Gary A. Stringer. *Scholarly Editing on the Microcomputer.* In preparation.

Piksanov, N. K. "Novyj put' literanoj nauki. Izučenie tvorcěskoj istoriii šedevra. (Principy i metody)." *Iskusstvo* (1923): 94–113.

Proust, Marcel. *Matinée chez la princesse de Guermantes, Cahiers du temps retrouvé.* Ed. Henri Bonnet and Bernard Brun. Paris: Gallimard, 1972.

Quentin, Dom Henri. *Essai de critique textuelle.* Paris: Picard, 1926.

Reiman, Donald H. "The Four Ages of Editing and the English Romantics." *Text* 1 (1984): 231–55. Rpt. in Reiman, *Romantic Texts* 17–32.

———. *Romantic Texts and Contexts.* Columbia: U of Missouri P, 1987.

———. " 'Versioning': The Presentation of Multiple Texts." Reiman, *Romantic Texts* 167–80.

Robinson, F. N., ed. *The Works of Geoffrey Chaucer.* 2nd ed. Boston: Houghton; London: Oxford UP, 1957.

Rossi, Aldo, ed. *Il Decameron.* By Giovanni Boccaccio. Bologna: Capelli, 1977.

Rossman, Charles. "The Critical Reception of the Gabler *Ulysses*; or, Gabler's *Ulysses* Kidd-Napped." *Studies in the Novel* 21 (1989): 154–81.

———. "The New *Ulysses*: The Hidden Controversy." *New York Review of Books* 8 Dec. 1988: 53–58.

Rowse, A. L., ed. *The Annotated Shakespeare.* New York: Potter, 1978.

Sandys, J. E. W. *A History of Classical Scholarship.* 1906–08. 3 vols. New York: Hafner, 1964.

Seidel, Gerhard. "Intentionswandel in der Entstehungsgeschichte. Ein Gedicht Bertolt Brechts über Karl Kraus historisch-kritisch ediert." *Zeitschrift für Deutsche Philologie* 101 (1982): 163–88.

Sellier, Philippe, ed. *Pensées.* By Blaise Pascal. Paris: Mercure, 1976.

Sezgin, F., ed. *Majāz al-Qur'ān.* 2 vols. Cairo: Maktabat al-Kheanji, 1954–62.

Shailor, Barbara. *The Medieval Book.* Toronto: U of Toronto P, 1991.

Shakespeare, William. *The Complete Works.* Ed. Stanley Wells and Gary Taylor. Oxford: Clarendon–Oxford UP, 1986.

———. *The Complete Works: Electronic Edition.* Oxford: Oxford UP, 1989.

———. *The Complete Works: Original-Spelling Edition.* Ed. Stanley Wells and Gary Taylor. Oxford: Clarendon–Oxford UP, 1986.

———. *A New Variorum Edition of Shakespeare.* Ed. H. H. Furness, et al. 1871–. New and rev. eds. Ed. Robert. K. Turner, Richard Knowles, et al. New York: MLA, 1977–.

———. *The Riverside Shakespeare.* Ed. Gwynne Blakemore Evans. Boston: Houghton, 1974.

———. *Shakespeare's Plays in Quarto.* Ed. Michael J. B. Allen and Kenneth Muir. Berkeley: U of California P, 1981.

———. *The Works: Globe Edition.* Ed. William G. Clark and W. Aldis Wright. London: Macmillan, 1864. Rev. ed. with John Glover. 9 vols. London: Macmillan, 1863–66; further rev. 1891–95.

Shillingsburg, Peter L. "An Inquiry into the Social Status of Texts and Modes of Textual Criticism." *Studies in Bibliography* 42 (1989): 55–79.

———. "Key Issues in Editorial Theory." *Analytical and Enumerative Bibliography* 6 (1982): 3–16.

———. "The Limits of the Editor's Responsibility." Soc. for Textual Scholarship. New York, 11 Apr. 1987.

———. *Scholarly Editing in the Computer Age: Lectures in Theory and Practice.* U of New South Wales Dept. of English Occasional Papers 3, 1984. Rev. ed. Athens: U of Georgia P, 1986.

———. "Text as Matter, Concept, and Action." *Studies in Bibliography* 44 (1991): 31–82.

Silver, Brenda R. "Textual Criticism as Feminist Practice; or, Who's Afraid of Virginia Woolf, Part II." Bornstein, *Representing Modernist Texts* 193–222.

Simon, John Y. "Editors and Critics." *Newsletter of the Association for Documentary Editing* 3 (Dec. 1981): 1–4.

Simons, Marlise. "A Restoration Becomes a Criminal Case in Italy." *New York Times* 25 May 1991: B13–14.

Spevack, Marvin. *Complete and Systematic Concordance to the Works of Shakespeare.* 6 vols. Hildesheim: Ohms, 1968–70.

———. *The Harvard Concordance to Shakespeare.* Cambridge: Belknap–Harvard UP, 1973.

Stubbs, John, and Frank W. Tompa. "Waterloo and the *New Oxford English Dictionary.*" Butler and Stoneman 19–44.

Sturges, Robert S. "Textual Scholarship: Ideologies of Literary Production." *Exemplaria* 3 (1991): 109–31.

Sutherland, John. "Publishing History: A Hole at the Centre of Literary Sociology." *Critical Inquiry* 14 (1988): 574–89.

Tanselle, G. Thomas. "The Editing of Historical Documents." *Studies in Bibliography* 31 (1978): 1–56.

———. "The Editorial Problem of Final Authorial Intention." *Studies in Bibliography* 29 (1976): 167–211.

———. *The History of Books as a Field of Study.* Second Hanes Lecture, Hanes Foundation. Chapel Hill: U of North Carolina, 1981.

———. *A Rationale of Textual Criticism.* Philadelphia: Pennsylvania UP, 1989.

———. *Selected Studies in Bibliography.* Charlottesville: UP of Virginia, 1979.

———. "Textual Criticism and Deconstruction." *Studies in Bibliography* 43 (1990): 1–33.

———. *Textual Criticism since Greg: A Chronicle, 1950–1985.* Charlottesville: UP of Virginia, 1988.

———. "Textual Scholarship." *Introduction to Scholarship in the Modern Languages and Literatures.* Ed. Joseph Gibaldi. New York: MLA, 1981. 29–52.

Taylor, Gary. "Revising Shakespeare." *Text* 3 (1987): 285–304.

———. "The Rhetoric of Textual Criticism." *Text* 4 (1988): 39–56.

Taylor, Gary, and Michael Warren, eds. *The Division of the Kingdoms: Shakespeare's Two Versions of* King Lear. Oxford: Clarendon–Oxford UP, 1983.

Taylor, Robert. "Editorial Practices: An Historian's View." *Newsletter of the Association for Documentary Editing* 3.1 (1981): 4–8.

Textual Scholarship and Literary Theory. Spec. issue of *Critical Exchange* 24 (Fall 1989).

Thackeray, William. *The Thackery Edition Project.* Ed. Peter L. Shillingsburg et al. 4 vols. to date. New York: Garland, 1989–.

Thoreau, Henry D. *The Writings of Henry D. Thoreau.* Ed. William L. Howarth et al. 10 vols. to date. Princeton: Princeton UP, 1969–.

Thorpe, James. *Principles of Textual Criticism.* San Marino: Huntington Lib., 1972.

Tomaševskij, B. V. "Novoe o Puškine." *Literaturnaja mysl'. Al'manax.* 1 (1922): 171–86.

Treglown, Jeremy. "Editors Vary." *Times Literary Supplement* 10 May 1985: 520.

Urkowitz, Steven. *Shakespeare's Revision of* King Lear. Princeton: Princeton UP, 1980.

———. " 'Well Said, Old Mole': Burying Three *Hamlets* in Modern Editions." *Shakespeare Study Today.* Ed. Georgiana Ziegler. New York: AMS, 1986. 37–70.

Vandelli, Giovanni, ed. *I reali di Francia.* By Andrea da Barberino. Bologna: Romagnoli, 1892–1900.

———, ed. *La divina commedia.* By Dante Alighieri. *Le opere di Dante: Testo critico della Società Dantesca Italiana.* Ed. M. Barbi et al. Florence: Bemporad, 1921.

Vinaver, Eugène. "Principles of Textual Emendation." *Studies in French Language and Medieval Literature Presented to Professor* M. K. *Pope.* Manchester: U of Manchester P, 1930. 351–69.

Vinokur, G. *Kritika poètičeskogo teksta.* Gos. Akad. xudož. nauk. Istorija i teorija iskusstv 10. Moscow, 1927.

Vogt, George L., and John Bush Jones, eds. *Literary and Historical Editing.* Lawrence: U of Kansas Libs., 1981.

Warren, Michael, ed. *The Complete* King Lear. Berkeley: U of California P, 1989.

Wells, Stanley, and Gary Taylor, with John Jowett and William Montgomery, eds. *William Shakespeare: A Textual Companion.* Oxford: Clarendon–Oxford UP, 1987.

West, James L. W., III. *Creating American Authors: The Language of Scholarly Editing.* Ann Arbor: U of Michigan P, forthcoming.

White, Patricia S. "Black and White and Read All Over: A Meditation On Footnotes." *Text* 5 (1991): 81–90.

Whitman, Walt. *The Collected Writings of Walt Whitman.* Ed. Gay Wilson Allen, Sculley Bradley, et al. 22 vols. to date. New York: New York UP, 1961–.

Wilkerson, Isabel. "Textual Scholars Make Points about Points." *New York Times* 29 Apr., 1985: B2.

Williams, William Proctor, and Craig S. Abbott. *An Introduction to Bibliographical and Textual Studies.* 2nd ed. New York: MLA, 1989.

Wilson, Edmund. *The Fruits of the MLA.* New York: New York Rev. of Books, 1968.

Woolf, Virginia. Melymbrosia: *An Early Version of* The Voyage Out. Ed. Louise DeSalvo. New York: New York Public Lib., 1982.

Zeller, Hans. "A New Approach to the Critical Constitution of Literary Texts." *Studies in Bibliography* 28 (1975): 231–63.

ROBERT SCHOLES

Canonicity and Textuality

> Nay here in these ages, such as they are, have we not two mere Poets, if not deified, yet we may say beatified? Shakespeare and Dante are Saints of Poetry: really, if we think of it, *canonized*, so that it is impiety to meddle with them. The unguided instinct of the world, working across all these perverse impediments, has arrived at such result. Dante and Shakespeare are a peculiar Two. They dwell apart, in a kind of royal solitude; none equal, none second to them: in the general feeling of the world, a certain transcendentalism, a glory as of complete perfection, invests these two. They *are* canonized, though no Pope or Cardinals took hand in doing it!
>
> —Thomas Carlyle

> Beaucoup trop d'héroïsme encore dans nos langages; dans les meilleurs—je pense à celui de Bataille—, éréthisme de certaines expressions et finalement une sorte d'*héroïsme insidieux*. Le plaisir du texte (la jouissance du texte) est au contraire comme un effacement brusque de la *valeur* guerrière, une desquamation passagère des ergots de l'écrivain, un arrêt de "coeur" (du courage).
>
> —Roland Barthes, *Le plaisir du texte*[1]

FOR Carlyle, lecturing in 1840, the greatest poets were heroic figures, canonized saints of literature, whose names could readily sustain such adjectives as "royal" and such nouns as "transcendentalism," "glory," and "perfection" (85). Indeed, his lecture itself was called "The Hero as Poet." But for Barthes, writing in the early 1970s, the pleasure of the text emerges only when the writer's impulse toward heroism is in abeyance, when valor and courage are overcome. A text is, he says, or should be, like a "flippant person who shows his bottom to the *Political Father*" (84). Nothing saintly or heroic about that. These two statements, I believe, reveal something of the depths beneath our present debate about canonicity and textuality—and something of what is at stake in this debate.

The debate itself is the occasion of the present essay. If the concepts of canonicity and textuality were not currently active in our critical discourse, there would have been no reason for a discussion of them to be included in this volume. It is important to note, then, that these concepts are not merely active in our discourse but active in an oppositional way. Despite some shared meanings and implications in their etymological past, the two terms now stand in opposition (an opposition embodied in my epigraphs), as names (however crude) for two different conceptions of our practice as scholars and teachers: the literary, structured according to the hierarchical concept of canon, and the textual, disseminated around the more egalitarian notion of text. I cannot pretend to impartiality in these debates. I am a textualist. But I shall try, nonetheless, to give a fair idea of what is at stake in this dispute and to avoid excesses of special pleading. Even so, the reader, as always, should be on guard.

Let us begin gently, judiciously, by considering the history of the words *canon* and *text* as they have moved through Western culture from ancient times, when they first appeared in Greek, to the present. My survey is partial, of course (perhaps in more than one way), but I believe that a more ample and detailed study would produce histories much like those I recount. In ancient Greek we find the two words from which the modern English word *canon* (in its two spellings, *canon* and *cannon*) has descended: κάννα (*kanna*) 'reed'; and κᾰνών (*kanōn*) 'straight rod, bar, ruler, reed (of a wind organ), rule, standard, model, severe critic, metrical scheme, astrological table, limit, boundary, assessment for taxation' (Liddell and Scott[2]). Like *canon*, our word *cane* is also clearly a descendant of the ancient *kanna*, but its history has been simpler and more straightforward than that of its cognate. However, the second of the two Greek words, *kanōn*, has from ancient times been the repository of a complex set of meanings, mainly acquired by metaphorical extensions of the properties of canes, which are hollow or tubular grasses, some of which are regularly jointed (like bamboo), and some of which have flat outside coverings. The tubular channel characteristic of reeds or canes leads to the associations of the word *canon* with functions that involve forcing liquids or gases through a channel or pipe, while the regularity and relative rigidity of canes lead toward those meanings that involve measuring and controlling (ruling—in both senses of that word). And it is likely that the ready applicability of canes as a weapon of punishment (as in our verb *to cane*, or beat with a stick) supported those dimensions of the meaning of *kanōn* that connote severity and the imposition of power.

In Latin we find the same sort of meanings for the word *canon* as were attached to the Greek *kanōn*, with two significant additions, both appearing in later Latin. These two additions are due to historical developments that generated a need for new terms. On the one hand, the rise of the Roman Catholic Church as an institution required a Latin term that could distinguish the accepted or sacred writings from all others, so that "works admitted by the rule or canon" came themselves to be called canonical or, in short, the Canon. In this connection we also find a new verb, *canonizo-are*, to canonize. On the other hand, with the importation of gun powder and the development of artillery, the tubular signification of the word led to its becoming the name, in late Latin, for large guns (Lewis and Short). A common theme, of course, in these extensions is power. It is worth noting here that when the Hebrews became the People of the Book, the word they adopted for their canonical texts was also a word that meant the Law: *Torah*. As Gerald Bruns argues, the establishment of the Torah as the written Law in Jewish history meant the victory of a priestly establishment over the independent voices of the Prophets. In particular, once the Law was fixed in written form, the spoken words of Prophets could not make headway against it, leading to the replacement of prophecy by commentary on the now canonical Book in which the Law was embodied.

For our purposes, the significant point is the way that *canon* in Latin also combined the meaning of rule or law with the designation of a body of received texts. In its Christian signification, however, *canon* came to mean not only a body of received texts, essentially fixed by institutional fiat, but also a body of individuals raised to heaven by the perfection of their lives. In the latter signification, the canon referred to an open, not closed, system, with new saints always admissible by approved institutional procedures. This distinction is important because in current literary disputes over the canon, both models are invoked, one on behalf of a relatively fixed canon and the other on behalf of a relatively open one. In any case, our current thinking about canonicity cannot afford to ignore the grounding of the modern term in a history explicitly influenced by Christian institutions. As the epigraph from Carlyle indicates, the conscious use of religious terminology in literary matters is at least a century and a half old.

We must now backtrack a bit to note that the word *canon* also has a more purely secular pedigree going back to Alexandrian Greek, in which the word *kanōn* was used by rhetoricians to refer to a body of superior texts: ὁι κάνονεσ (*hoi kanones*) "were the works which the Alexandrian critics considered as the most perfect models of style and composition, equivalent to our modern term 'The Classics' " (Donnegan). Exactly how the interplay between the rhetorical and the religious uses of the notion of *canon* functioned two millennia ago is a matter well beyond the scope of this inquiry. What we most need to learn from the ancient significations of *canon*, however, is that they ranged in meaning all the way from a text possessing stylistic virtues that make it a proper model to a text that is a repository of the Law and the Truth, being the word of God. We should also remember that the word, as a transitive verb, referred to a process of inclusion among the saints.

In the vernacular languages, the meanings of *canon* found in late Latin are simply extended. In French, for instance, we can find the following in a modern dictionary: *canon* 'gun, barrel of a gun, cannon; cylinder, pipe, tube; leg (of trousers)'; and *canon* 'canon. *Canon des écritures*, the sacred canon; *école de droit canon*, school of canon law' (Baker). The French is especially useful in reminding us that the word for gun and the word for the law and the sacred texts are simply branches of a single root rather than two totally different words. That in English we regularized separate spellings (*cannon* and *canon*) for the guns and the laws in the later eighteenth century has tended to obscure the common heritage of both these spellings in the ancient extensions of a word for reed or cane. In English the most relevant meanings of the word *canon* for our purposes are these: *canon* 'a rule, law, or decree of the Church; a general rule, a fundamental principle; the collection or list of the books of the Bible accepted by the Christian

Church as genuine and inspired; hence, any set of sacred books; a list of saints acknowledged and canonized by the Church' (*OED*).

The nature of the connection between the Christian canon and the literary canon is crucial to our understanding of the present disputes about canonization. This connection was made most forcibly and enduringly in English letters by Mathew Arnold, as Northrop Frye pointed out more than thirty years ago in an exemplary discussion of Arnold's touchstones that laid bare Arnold's motivation:

> When we examine the touchstone technique in Arnold, however, certain doubts arise about his motivation. The line from *The Tempest*, "In the dark backward and abysm of time," would do very well as a touchstone line. One feels that the line "Yet a tailor might scratch her where'er she did itch" somehow would not do, though it is equally Shakespearean and equally essential to the same play. (An extreme form of the same kind of criticism would, of course, deny this and insist that the line had been interpolated by a vulgar hack.) Some principle is clearly at work here which is much more highly selective than a purely critical experience of the play would be.

Here we should pause to notice that Frye's notion of a "purely critical experience" conserves much of the Arnoldian project—which remains at the center of our present critical debates. We shall return to this point. But first, let us continue with Frye's next paragraph:

> Arnold's "high seriousness" evidently is closely connected with the view that epic and tragedy, because they deal with ruling-class figures and require the high style of decorum, are the aristocrats of literary forms. All his Class One touchstones are from, or judged by the standards of, epic and tragedy. Hence his demotion of Chaucer and Burns to Class Two seems to be affected by a feeling that comedy and satire should be kept in their proper place, like the moral standards and the social classes which they symbolize. We begin to suspect that the literary value-judgments are projections of social ones. Why does Arnold *want* to rank poets? He says that we increase our admiration for those who manage to stay in Class One after we have made it very hard for them to do so. This being clearly nonsense, we must look further. When we read "in poetry the distinction between excellent and inferior . . . is of paramount importance . . . because of the high destinies of poetry," we begin to get a clue. We see that Arnold is trying to create a new scriptural canon out of poetry to serve as a guide for those social principles which he wants culture to take over from religion. (21–22)

Like so much in that extraordinary book of Frye's, these crucial paragraphs opened the way to all our subsequent discussions and disputes about the literary canon. In particular, Frye made literary scholars and critics aware of two things that had been overlooked or concealed during the academic hegemony of the New Criticism. First, that "literary value-judgments are projections of social ones" (though he tried to reserve for himself a field of "purely critical experience"). And, second, that the Arnoldian tradition in criticism involved "trying to create a new scriptural canon out of poetry." The way we currently use the word *canon* in literary studies is very much the way we learned to use it from Northrop Frye. And it was also Frye who—when very few students of literature thought of calling their enterprise "literary theory"—told us that "the theory of literature is as primary a humanistic and liberal pursuit as its practice" (20). When Frye wrote, the word *canon* was used in literary studies mainly to refer to the body of texts that could be properly attributed to this or that author (a significance that is acknowledged in the Supplement to the *OED*). The MLA annual bibliographies are full of articles with titles like "The Shakespeare Canon" or "The Defoe Canon." Since Frye, however, and especially in the last decade, literary scholars have come to use the word as the name for a set of texts that constitute our cultural heritage and, as such, are the sources from which the academic curriculum in literature should be drawn. This situation is full of complexities and perplexities. We shall return to the problems of literary canonicity after further complicating matters by considering the cultural history of the word *text*.

This word has a history that is perhaps even more interesting than that of *canon*, in that it has been susceptible to a greater range of fluctuations in meaning—a process still very much alive. The variability (or duplicity) of the word is apparent even in its Greek beginnings:

> τικ-τικόσ (*tik, tikos*) Of or for childbirth, a medicine used for women lying in, a φάρμακον (*pharmakon*).
>
> τικτω (*tiktō*) bring into the world, engender; of the father: beget; of the mother: bring forth; of the earth: bear, produce; metaphorical: generate, engender, produce.
>
> τέκτων (*tektōn*) worker in wood, carpenter, joiner; generally: any craftsman or workman; metaphorically: maker, author.
>
> τεχνη (*technē*) art, skill, cunning of hand; cunning in the bad sense: arts, wiles; an art or craft; a method, set of rules, or system of making or doing, whether in the useful arts or the fine arts; work of art, handiwork; treatise (on grammar or rhetoric). (adapted from Liddell and Scott)

The single theme that runs through all these words and their meanings is that of creation. In this, the word *tiktō* appears central, with its fundamental meaning of physical or natural production (of children and the fruits of the earth) and its metaphorical extension to cover all kinds of production. Around this central core of meaning some curious and interesting extensions play. First, *tik*, the *pharmakon*, or drug, used to make childbearing easier for women. And here, perhaps, we should note that the two opposed meanings of *pharmakon* are very similar to those of our modern English word *drug*, which refers to both harmful and beneficial kinds of ingestible substances. Jacques Derrida has made much of this in "Plato's Pharmacy," but the double meaning of the word was fully noted regularly in Greek lexicons before Derrida's influential essay. For our purposes it is important to note another play in the meanings of *tik* and *tiktō*: on the one hand, the natural—begetting, engendering, and bringing forth—and, on the other hand, the artificial: the drug that must mitigate the "unnatural" pains of the natural process, or come to the aid of nature in this instance.

The word *tektōn* extends the meanings of *tiktō* in the direction of artifice or craft, by pointing first toward carpentry and other physical (though not natural) acts of making and finally to mental creation, production, or authorship. One facet of this extension is that it tends to obliterate female production as it moves away from nature and toward art, craft, and authorship. In the earliest formulations the role of woman as child-bearer and the earth as feminine bearer of fruits (regularly portrayed as a goddess rather than a god) were dominant. But gradually the gender emphasis shifted. In Greek culture, carpentry—a male occupation—assumed a central position in the paradigmatic structure of this word and its meanings. In the word that named the maker's skill, *technē*, there was some room for female handicraft, but the general pattern of thought embodied in this language seems to have aligned women with nature as primitive producers and men with culture as producers of consciously constructed objects of daily use and art. The word *technē* itself was frequently used to refer to metal work, ship building and other trades associated with male workers. This word, like *pharmakon*, has its pejorative sense, too, referring to guile or cunning. Finally, and this is especially relevant to our concerns, the meanings of the word were extended to refer to the methods or systems of the developing verbal disciplines of grammar and rhetoric.

When we pick up the history of these terms as they appear in Latin, we find that the notion of joining as in carpentry, or constructing as in metalwork, has been replaced by weaving, as the guiding concept of textual fabrication. We can see also that the extension from material handicraft to verbal construction is reinstated and extended, taking on specific references to verbal composition or style (as opposed to weaving). In Latin we find *texo, texere* 'weave; to join or fit together any thing; to plait, braid, interweave, interlace, intertwine; to construct, make, fabricate, build; to compose' and *textum* 'that which is woven, a web; that which is plaited, braided, fitted together, a plait, texture, fabric'; figurative: 'of literary composition, tissue, texture, style' (Lewis and Short). The meanings related to weaving and woven fabric were to remain with these words and with many of their descendants (*texture, textile*, etc.), but the verbal extensions of meaning toward literary style and composition became more and more important in the history of the word *textum* itself. In particular, the masculine *textus*, which appears first in poetry and in post-Augustan prose, seems to have become the favored form for the verbal and stylistic meanings of the word; and in medieval Latin, in particular, we find the masculine *textus* carrying specific adaptations for Christian verbal functions, including, finally, specific reference to the New Testament as the Text: *textus* 'text, wording, contents of speech or writing; charter; Gospel-book' ("Dedit rex Serenissimus Augustus quattuor evangeliorum librum, qui textus dicitur" 'He gave his serene majesty Augustus the book of the four evangelists, which is called text'—from the *Annales Francorum Anianenses*, about AD 1000, qtd. in Niermeyer).

In English the meanings found in later Latin, and in particular the reference of *textus* to verbal matters, have predominated in our word *text*, with the weaving references specifically relegated to the cognate, *textile*, while another cognate, *texture*, usually refers both literally to fabric and figuratively to verbal compositions. But let us consider the range of meanings the *OED* offers for our English word *text*:

1. **a.** The wording of anything written or printed; the structure formed by the words in their order; the very words, phrases, or sentences as written [fourteenth century to present].
   b. Applied vaguely to an original or authority whose words are quoted. *Obs.*
   d. The wording adopted by an editor as (in his opinion) most nearly representing the author's original work; a book or edition containing this; also, with qualification, any form in which a writing exists or is current, as a *good, bad, corrupt, critical, received text*.
2. esp. The very words and sentences as originally written: **a.** in the original language, as opposed to a translation or rendering; **b.** in the original form or order, as distinguished from a commentary, marginal or other [fourteenth century to present].
3. **a.** spec. The very words and sentences of Holy Scripture; hence, the Scriptures themselves [fourteenth to seventeenth century].
4. **a.** A short passage from the Scriptures, esp. one quoted as authoritative, or illustrative of a point of belief or doctrine [fourteenth century to present].
   b. A short passage from some book or writer considered as authoritative; a received maxim or axiom; a proverb; an adage [fourteenth to nineteenth century, now rare].

In the fortunes of this word we can clearly see the influence of its passage through the system of Christian thought. Like the word *canon*, the word *text* has acquired a verbal emphasis through its association with Christian doctrine. When we speak of *canon* and *text* now, we are usually speaking of verbal, which is to say written or printed, matters. In their Christian significations, we should also note, they acquired strongly restrictive meanings. That is, both *canon* and *text* refer to things with an inside and an outside. Both words function in such a way as to build fences around the privileged material inside and to relegate whatever is outside to a status of less significance if not to absolute evil. In their Christian significations, both words indicate the verbal domains of Spirit and, in fact, both were used specifically to refer to the Christian Bible.

The adaptation of these two words to the study of literature, then, is part of the historical process by which the word *literature* took on a new and quasi-religious meaning toward the end of the eighteenth century. To understand this connection, we must therefore pause and consider the history of this crucial word itself. Here, again, the *OED* can assist us. In it we find the following definitions of *literature*:

1. Acquaintance with "letters" or books; polite or humane learning; literary culture. Now *rare* and *obsolescent*. (The only sense in Johnson and in Todd 1818).
2. Literary work or production; the activity or profession of a man of letters; the realm of letters.
3. **a.** Literary production as a whole; the body of writings produced in a particular country or period, or in the world in general. Now also in a more restricted sense, applied to writing which has claim to consideration on the ground of beauty of form or emotional effect.

We should be attentive to a number of things about this word that has been so important to the enterprise of the Modern Language Association and to the individuals and institutions connected with it. First, we should note that in Samuel Johnson's *Dictionary* and as late as Henry John Todd's version of it (1818), *literature* referred to a learning or culture possessed by an individual rather than to a set of lettered objects or written texts. That is, it was customary to say that a person *had* literature rather than that a person *read* literature. Second, the word also came to name whatever texts were produced by a person (clearly thought of as male) who possessed "literature" or book learning. Third, the word, when it did refer to the written or printed texts themselves, included everything, the whole body of writings of a time or place—or of the "world." Fourth, in a process that emerges fully only at the end of the eighteenth century, literature came to mean belles lettres, as opposed to other kinds of writing.

In 1762, in what became an enormously influential textbook in American colleges, Lord Kames proposed a science of criticism. His *Elements of Criticism* was meant to apply to all of what he called the "fine arts" but was focused mainly on the arts of language as they are displayed in poetry, drama, and some prose. So far as I can tell, in over a thousand pages, he found no occasion to use the word *literature*. It is also true, of course, that for him the whole art of language lay in finding the proper means for the expression of human sentiments and passions. For him, the imagination was no more than one human faculty, and by no means was it the most important faculty with respect to the fine arts:

> Such is the nature of man, that his powers and faculties are soon blunted by exercise. The returns of sleep, suspending all activity, are not alone sufficient to preserve him in vigor. During his waking hours, amusement by intervals is requisite to unbend his mind from serious occupation. The imagination, of all our faculties the most active, and not always at rest even in sleep, contributes more than any other cause to recruit the mind and restore its vigor, by amusing us with gay and ludicrous images; and when relaxation is necessary, such amusement is much relished. But there are other sources of amusment beside the imagination.
>
> (1: 337; typography modernized)

What Kames meant by imagination was simply the "singular power of fabricating images independent of real objects" (3: 386). He has neither our notion of literature nor our sense of imagination. The momentous linking of these two terms, which was necessary for our modern idea of a literary canon to be developed, is primarily if not exclusively the work of Romantic writers, especially the Jena Romantics and their followers (among whom we must still, with whatever mixture of emotions, consider ourselves). This Romantic notion of imagination as the primary quality of literature was, of course, given its special potency in English by Coleridge. Coleridge himself thought of literature in the pre-Romantic manner. When, in the *Biographia Literaria*, he sought to advise young men not to take up literature as a "trade" (129), his list of literary men who had other careers included Cicero, Xenophon, Thomas More, Richard Baxter (the Puritan divine), and Erasmus Darwin (the poet of evolution). In its fully Romantic usage, however, literature took over the meanings formerly assigned to poetry alone, with the added insistence on the transcendental powers of imagination. The crucial distinction thus fell not between poetry and prose but between imaginative writing and writing that lacked this divine spark. This distinction was already nascent in Kames's separation of the fine arts from the useful arts, but the addition of imagination as the decisive criterion made the distinction more invidious. Imaginative writing—and Coleridge made this especially clear with his description of primary and secondary forms of imagination—connected certain texts directly to Divinity or Absolute Spirit. Materially useless but spiritually precious texts: that is what literature had come to mean when Mathew Arnold conceived the project of replacing dogma with literature—the project criticized by Frye in the "Polemical Introduction" to his *Anatomy of Criticism*. We must be aware, however, that this Arnoldian project was extended by writers as diverse as T. S. Eliot and I. A. Richards, as well as by the New Critics teaching in American universities after World War II. And it was alive and well in the work of Northrop Frye himself, as Barbara Herrnstein Smith vigorously demonstrates in an essay in an important collection entitled *Canons* (ed. von Hallberg), to which we shall return shortly.

By the end of the nineteenth century two simultaneous processes (or two facets of the same process) had led to the establishment of a literary canon. One of these was the separate, superior status claimed for works of verbal imagination, which, thus empowered, constituted a literary canon. The other was the professionalization of teaching in the newly established (and in particular the American) universities and graduate schools. As the study of the modern literatures, especially English, replaced the classics and oratory at the center of the humanist curriculum at the end of the nineteenth century, authors such as John Locke and Francis Bacon, who had loomed large in our early college curricula, gave way to writers who were literary in the now accepted sense of that word. For a time, criticism struggled against philology for power within the new English departments, each with its own canon of proper texts for study. In this struggle philology, which was really an attempt to carry on classical studies without classical texts, was doomed because its canon was based on antiquity, privileging texts in Old and Middle English, while criticism could select its canon on the basis of "pure literary merit."

Actually, of course, this selection required an institution to debate and ratify canonical choices, and, at the proper moment, the institution came into being. It was called the Modern Language Association. In the professionalization of literary studies, the canon supported the profession and the profession supported the canon. Likewise, the canon supported the literary curriculum and the curriculum supported the canon. The curriculum, in literary studies, represented the point of application, where canonical choices were tested in the crucible of student response. Works that proved highly teachable (like Shakespeare) remained central in the canon as well as in the curriculum. The revival of John Donne may have been begun by Herbert Grierson and T. S. Eliot, but it continued with such notable success because the New Critics found Donne perfectly suited to their pedagogy, their curriculum, and, hence, their canon. Authors who proved less amenable to critical exegesis (Oliver Goldsmith, for instance, who once bulked large in the American curriculum) were quietly allowed to drift out of that curriculum and, hence, out of the canon.

The most important thing about these processes is not that they went on but that they went on unnoticed. Until the last few decades they were seen as "natural"—or even as not occurring at all. What has happened to literary studies in those decades is a part of larger cultural happenings that can be described (and deplored, if you like) as the politicization of American life. Once upon a time we believed that if the best men (yes) were appointed to the bench, we would get the best judicial decisions. Now, we know that one set of appointments to the Supreme Court will give us one set of laws and another set of appointments will give us others. What is happening is part of the evolution of a democratic society. With respect to the literary canon, Frye's statement about Arnold's touchstones was a political bombshell: "We begin to suspect that the literary judgments are projections of social ones." Which is to say that the literary canon is a social, and therefore a political, object, the result of a political process, like so much else in our world.

Thus the battle lines were drawn, and the battle is still in progress. On the one hand are those who defend a universal standard of literary quality (among whom we may find Frye himself), and on the other are those who argue that standards are always relative, local, and political. There are militant universalists and there are laissez-faire or pragmatic universalists, which complicates matters. And the relativists are divided, also, into champions of different excluded groups, seeking canonical status for their own class of texts, and anarchists or absolute relativists, who would undo all canons and standards if they could. At this point I suppose I should run up my own flag, since I cannot pretend to neutrality on these matters. I do not see how anyone can teach without standards, but I cannot find any single standard for determining the worth of a text. I do not, that is, believe in literature either as a body of spiritually informed texts or as a universal standard of textual value. I have lost my faith (and, yes, I once had it) in literature as an institution. It is not my intention here, however, to preach literary atheism or to make my position central to this discussion. I mention it merely as a bias the reader may wish to discount, as I move on to what I take to be the best single focus of current canonical disputes, Robert von Hallberg's collection of essays, made under the auspices of *Critical Inquiry* in 1984.

We have already had occasion to note Barbara Herrnstein Smith's rich and complex argument, in von Hallberg's volume, against the transcendental or universal valorizing of our canonical texts—an argument I must summarize rather brutally here as suggesting that what supports canonical texts is not so much their own merits or relevance to our purposes as it is the way they have already been inscribed into an intertextual network of reference. That is, they are culturally important because they have been culturally important, a situation from which both the inevitability of change and its equally inevitable slowness may be inferred. Smith's essay has been positioned first in the volume, with the result that many of the others can be read as amplifications, qualifications, or counterstatements to it, though most of them were written quite independently. The most direct counterstatement is that made by Charles Altieri in an essay called "An Idea and Ideal of a Literary Canon."

Altieri argues that only an appeal to "a general high canon" can provide the "authority" we need to resist local and specific abuses of power. In making this case, he suggests that "if we want to measure up to a certain kind of judgment" we must turn to "those models from the past that have survived such judgments" (57, 55, 56). Drastically simplified, the argument is that we cannot have ideals such as justice unless we ground them in texts that have been judged ideal. Whether literary judgments and ethical or political justice have enough in common to support this necessary connection is a problem that the essay never quite resolves. Altieri argues that works in the high literary canon are there because they have three qualities: the forceful and complex presentation of moral categories, semantic scope and intensity, and either technical innovation or wisdom and ethical significance. He further argues that the submissive study of such texts is necessary for us to develop our ability as readers and judges of our own culture. He does not quite complete the argument by concluding that study of the canonical texts is the only path to an ethical and effective life, but he certainly implies this.

It would be possible to criticize this essay by probing into its internal contradictions and terminological slippages, as exemplified by the lumping together of technical innovation and wisdom in the same category. I prefer, however, to make two, more general observations. One is that it leaves us wondering how writers and thinkers who had a very limited canon themselves ever became canonical. How did Homer, Aeschylus, and Plato, for instance, acquire the qualities that Altieri would attribute to them, since they had scarcely any access to the canon now held to be so indispensable. Socrates apparently knew his Homer but most of what he had learned he seems to have learned from the Sophists. My second point is that I see little evidence that prolonged study of canonical literary texts has made professors of literature either wiser or more virtuous than anthropologists, say, or carpenters. A more complex counterposition to Altieri's, however, is to be found within the volume of *Canons* itself. I refer to John Guillory's discussion "The Ideology of Canon-Formation: T. S. Eliot and Cleanth Brooks."

Just as Altieri is not responding directly to Smith, Guillory is responding not directly to Altieri but to the general position that Altieri represents. His discussion traces the path from Eliot's reconstruction of the canon of English literature in his early essays to the institutional underwriting of that very canon by the New Critics through such books as Cleanth Brooks's *Modern Poetry and the Tradition* (1939) and *The Well-Wrought Urn* (1947). Guillory shows how this process functioned as a subtle and more attractive alternative to Mathew Arnold's attempt to replace dogma with literature. He does this by reminding us that what Eliot's essays suggested and the New Critics instituted was the replacement of doxa with paradox. Under this regime, canonical texts were seen not as repositories of truth and beauty but as embodiments of a discourse so ambiguous that it could not be debased and applied to any practical or dogmatic end. The study and teaching of the new canon of specifically noncognitive texts would of necessity fall to those trained to show that they are canonical precisely because they resist reduction to doxa or dogma. Those who understood this, either as teachers or students, became members of what Guillory calls a "marginal elite," an elite based on a canon of texts that aspired neither to scientific nor didactic status but to a literary purity defined explicitly as the absence of such ambitions:

> Nevertheless, literary culture has aspired to canonical consensus, an illusion reinforced by the cognitive silence of the literary work, the silencing of difference. Very simply, canonical authors are made to *agree* with one another; the ambiguity of literary language means nothing less than the *univocity* of the canon. I now want to examine this rule of canonical self-identity as it governs the institutional dissemination of literature. Eliot's fantasy of orthodoxy passes into the university both as an ideology of the marginal elite and as an instruction in the marginal relation of the poem to truth. (350)

To document his case, Guillory looks at Brooks's crucial treatment of Donne's poem "The Canonization"—a truly overdetermined choice by all concerned, including myself. Guillory sees Brooks as basing the poem's canonical status as poetry on its ability to offer and to inhabit a realm removed from and "above" the world of power and cognitive assertion:

> [T]he ideological function of Brooks' reading concerns the demarcation of a spiritual realm between the crudities of power and the crudities of fact. The spiritual realm is *defined* by the audience the essay addresses: the auditors are conceived at a moment of apostolic succession, at just the moment of transition between Eliot and Brooks, as representative figures of literary culture. The *incognito* clergy is

> relocated within a *visible* social structure: the pedagogical institution. The idealized reading of the lovers' withdrawal must be understood as symptomatic of the professional commitment to the preservation of value: just as the lovers institute love in their act of renunciation, so it is the marginality of value which is both deplored and established by the idealization of literature. (356)

As he has observed earlier in the essay, "in teaching the canon, we are not only investing a set of texts with authority; we are equally instituting the authority of the teaching profession" (351). Guillory's point is partly that we should strive for a certain critical distance in determining our own stake in maintaining a canon, but he also means to suggest a possible direction out of New Critical orthodoxy into a "state of heterodoxy where the *doxa* of literature is not a paralyzed allusion to a hidden god but a teaching that will enact discursively the struggle of difference" (359–60).

This is a brave conclusion to an elegant essay, but it seems to me dangerously close to simply replacing the New Critical canon with a new set of texts privileged by their heterodoxy or their enactment of the "struggle of difference." The problem, I believe, is that "difference" is itself a notion that has gained its privileged position in recent American theory partly because it allowed an easy transition from New Critical paradoxes. Believing, for instance, that the best texts are those "that deconstruct themselves" is just a step from equating paradox with literary value. It is a useful step, to be sure, but my own feeling is that something simpler is necessary: not texts that embody difference but just different texts. Perhaps this is what Guillory means, but I am wary of the tendency of American literary deconstruction to lead back to a canon more traditional than even that of the New Critics. Certainly the compatibility of a certain sort of deconstruction with traditional literary values is writ large in J. Hillis Miller's much quoted statement, "I believe in the established canon of English and American literature and in the validity of the concept of privileged texts. I think it is more important to read Spenser, Shakespeare, or Milton than to read Borges in translation, or even, to say the truth, to read Virginia Woolf" (qtd. by Froula in von Hallberg 152).

The issue of canonicity turns finally on the notion of literature itself, as, for instance, Arnold Krupat suggests in his discussion "Native American Literature and the Canon," in which he makes the following point:

> In our own time, the canon is established primarily by the professoriate, by teacher-critics who variously—passively or actively but for the most part—support the existing order. As Leslie Fiedler has remarked, "Literature is effectively what we teach in departments of English; or, conversely, what we teach in departments of English is literature" ([Fiedler and Baker] 73). Roland Barthes has offered a similar observation. "The 'teaching of literature,' " Barthes said, "is for me almost tautological. Literature is what is taught, that's all" (Doubrovsky 170). What the pedagogical canon includes from the past and from current production generally

> and substantially works to ratify the present and to legitimate an established hegemony. (310)

Krupat's position is necessary to his argument that by attending to Native American works in the curriculum, we will also establish them in the canon. Others in the volume who would not deny the connection of the curriculum to the canon would see the mechanisms of canonization as being more complicated. Alan C. Golding, for instance, brings to our attention the way that over the past century and a half American poetry anthologies have played a vital role in shaping the canon, but he, too, notices that over the decades curricular needs have become more influential even on the anthologies. Similarly, Richard M. Ohmann, examining contemporary mechanisms of canonization, describes a complicated process but suggests that the greatest power lies with a class that stretches from the marginal elite of the universities to a less marginal elite group in the magazines and publishing houses.

In another important essay in *Canons* ("When Eve Reads Milton: Undoing the Canonical Economy") Christine Froula, reminding us of how the canon has functioned as an instrument of domination, argues that the proper answer is both to add new textual voices to our curricula and to read the old texts in a different way:

> Few of us can free ourselves completely from the power ideologies inscribed in the idea of the canon and in many of its texts merely by not reading "canonical" texts, because we have been reading the partriarchal "archetext" all our lives. But we can, through strategies of rereading that expose the deeper structures of authority and through interplay with texts of a different stamp, pursue a kind of collective psychoanalysis, transforming "bogeys" that hide invisible power into investments both visible and alterable. In doing so, we approach traditional texts not as the mystifying (and self-limiting) "best" that has been thought and said in the world but as a *visible* past against which we can teach our students to imagine a different future. (171)

This volume on canons, which in turn points to other important discussions of the question, is certainly the place for later inquirers into canonical matters to begin. My own conclusion, however, after examining both this book and many of the texts cited therein, is that as long as we refrain from challenging the hegemony of literature itself, the essentially conservative and patriarchal processes of canonization will continue to function in much the same way. In a tendentious and vigorous essay in this volume, "The Making of the Modernist Canon," for instance, Hugh Kenner develops a literary standard that enables him to relegate Virginia Woolf and William Faulkner to secondary status as "provincials" and to largely ignore such writers as Gertrude Stein, Dorothy Richardson, Jean Rhys, and Djuna Barnes as beneath his notice. They are simply not high enough or modernist enough to be visible. As Guillory reminds us, and as Altieri implies, our present canonical situation is what it is precisely because of the passage of literature through modernism. What Kenner demonstrates, though it is not his explicit intention, is that Romanticism filtered through avant-gardism (which is the formula for modernism) yields a literary canon in which the oppressively absolutist and patriarchal tendencies of canonization are more visible than ever before.

Specifically, the modernist canon installed by Pound, Eliot and their followers in English departments in this country called for, on the one hand, an aggressively innovative approach to literary form and, on the other, a learned appropriation of mythology and poetical texts drawn from the ancient, medieval, and Renaissance canons. This modernist notion of literary excellence worked powerfully (and "naturally") against women who had no easy access to classical education and for whom the traditional verbal forms were in themselves experimental, in that they had never before been used to express the experience of women in a world of possibilities opening all too slowly but opening nevertheless at the end of the nineteenth century. A novel like May Sinclair's *Mary Olivier* (1919), for instance, shows us both how painfully difficult and how profoundly radical it was for a provincial woman to adapt to her situation the bildungsroman form recently energized by D. H. Lawrence and James Joyce. The result is a novel that is powerful and important but will never match the canonical works of the modernist masters by their own literary criteria. And this is just one example of countless texts in which marginal voices have found expression in forms too humble for canonization or already discarded in the relentless modernist search for innovation.

My point is not that modernism itself was some sort of error but that it represented the culmination of a process of literary canonization begun by the Romantics—a process that is now unworkable because it has become too visible and because we have at last become aware of its social costs. In response to this situation I (and it must be obvious that these are not the conclusions of the MLA itself) would argue that we need to scrutinize critically and if possible undo the privilege we have so long granted to the notion of literature itself. This is why the opposition of text to work and of textuality to literature is so important. As we have seen, the history of the word *text* and its cognates is not so different from that of *canon*. Both sets of signifiers passed through alliances with the significations offered by history; both took on Christian significance in the Middle Ages; and both have some specifically verbal significations in our own world. But where *canon* has persisted in its exclusionary and hierarchical functions, allowing only such qualifications as Alastair Fowler's potential, accessible, and selective canons (all literature, literature currently in print, and approved literature—discussed by Golding, in von Hallberg 279), *text* has acquired, especially at the hands of French theoreticians like Roland Barthes and Jacques Derrida, some new significations that are programmatically subversive of canonical distinctions. The new meanings of *text* are usefully summarized in the introduction to Dominick LaCapra's *Rethinking Intellectual History*:

> "Text" derives from *texere*, to weave or compose, and in its expanded usage it designates a texture or network of relations interwoven with the problem of language. Its critical role is to problematize conventional distinctions and hierarchies, such as that which presents the text as a simple document or index of a more basic, if not absolute, ground, reality, or context. Yet the use of the notion of the text (or of textuality) to investigate a relational network inevitably raises the specter of "textual imperialism" or "pantextualism." When the notion of the text is itself absolutized, one confronts the paralyzing and truly abstract sort of interpretative bind that the appeal to the notion of textuality was intended to avoid or at least to defer. (19)

This statement is helpful in two ways. It directs our attention to some primary features of current notions of textuality, and it warns us about the abuse of such notions. The important primary features are (1) the way in which textuality insists on the connection or "network" linking any particular bit of language to other bits and to the whole network, and (2) the way that this particular linkage supersedes or forestalls any limitation of the meaning of a particular textual object to some nontextual referent, author, or situation that could entirely regulate the flow of meanings evoked by that object. The warning LaCapra offers is also important. He reminds us that textuality itself is a metaphor that can be used and abused. One abuse is a denial of referentiality so absolute as to become a mere formalism, a problem addressed by Terry Eagleton in *Literary Theory*. Eagelton objects to the way that deconstructive critics of the Yale school have "colonized" history itself, viewing "famines, revolutions, soccer matches, and sherry trifle as yet more undecidable 'text' " (146). Fredric Jameson has tried to mediate between these positions in an important passage of *The Political Unconscious*, arguing that "history is *not* a text, not a narrative, master or otherwise, but that, as an absent cause, it is inaccessible to us except in textual form" (35). In Jameson's language, textuality refers to a collaboration between language and the human unconscious that always distances us from reality without ever replacing that reality.

This poststructuralist notion of textuality is based on the semiotic and deconstructive projects of Charles Sanders Peirce, Ferdinand de Saussure, and Jacques Derrida, in which human interaction with the world is understood as always mediated by signs that can be interpreted only by connecting them to other signs, without ever leading to some final resting place of interpretation that might be called Reality or Truth. This we may think of as the strong sense of the word *textuality* as it is used in contemporary literary theory. It is this sense to which Derrida referred in his famous statement about there being no outside to textuality: "il n'y a pas de hors-texte" (*Of Grammatology* 158), which means that we can "make sense" of things only by establishing our own connections within the network of textuality that enables our thinking and perceiving in the first place—as I have just done by interpreting Derrida's phrase. As LaCapra warns us, however, it is a mistake to take this metaphor of textuality literally—a mistake that can only be made by ignoring the way that the idea of the "literal" is ruled out by the metaphor itself. The function of this sense of textuality, then, is to resituate the reading or interpreting of texts in a more creative or, as Derrida says, "exorbitant" mode. But what is a text?

Here, Roland Barthes is our liveliest guide—and within the metaphor of textuality, liveliness contends with reliability (some would say supersedes it—but not I) for the most important attribute of guidance. In one of his most influential essays, "From Work to Text," Barthes uses the opposition named in his title as a way of situating his new criticism in opposition to the old. His method of accomplishing this at first seems to align Barthes's *nouvelle critique* with the American New Criticism as John Guillory described it. Barthes tells us that

> the Text is that which goes to the limit of the rules of enunciation (rationality, readability, etc.). Nor is this a rhetorical idea, resorted to for some "heroic" effect: the Text tries to place itself very exactly *behind* the limit of the *doxa* (is not general opinion—constitutive of our democratic societies and powerfully aided by mass communications—defined by its limits, the energy with which it excludes, its *censorship*?). Taking the word literally, it may be said that the Text is always *paradoxical*. (*Image* 157–58)

What makes Barthes's formulation quite different and in certain respects opposed to American New Criticism, however, is his specific opposition of the text to the work:

> The difference is this: the work is a fragment of substance, occupying a part of the space of books (in a library for example), the Text is a methodological field. . . . [T]he work can be seen (in bookshops, in catalogues, in exam syllabuses), the text is a process of demonstration . . . ; the work can be held in the hand, the text is held in language, only exists in the movement of a discourse (or rather, it is Text for the very reason that it knows itself as text); the Text is not the decomposition of the work, it is the work that is the imaginary tail of the Text; or again, *the Text is experienced only in an activity of production.* It follows that the Text cannot stop (for example on a library shelf); its constitutive movement is that of cutting across (in particular, it can cut across the work, several works).
>
> . . . The author is reputed the father and the owner of his work: literary science therefore teaches *respect* for the manuscript and the author's declared intentions, while society asserts the legality of the relation of author to work. . . . As for the Text, it reads without the inscription of the Father. Here again, the metaphor of the Text separates from that of the work: the latter refers to the image of an *organism* which grows by vital expansion, by "development" (a word which is significantly ambiguous, at once biological and rhetorical); the metaphor of the Text is that of the *network*; if the Text extends itself, it is as a result of a combinatory systematic. . . . Hence no vital "respect" is due to the Text: it can be *broken* . . . ; it can be read without the guarantee of its father, the restitution of the intertext paradoxically abolishing any legacy. It is not that the Author may not "come back" in the Text, in his text, but he then does so as a "guest." . . . He becomes, as it

> were, a paper-author: his life is no longer the origin of his fictions but a fiction contributing to his work . . . ; it is the work of Proust, of Genet which allows their lives to be read as a text. (*Image* 157, 160–61)

In American New Criticism, the boundedness of the literary work, its organic unity, its status as a "verbal icon" supported the role of the literary critic (or teacher) as a quasi-priestly exegete, introducing outsiders into the hermetic mysteries of literature. The notion of textuality weakens the boundaries of the individual textual object and reduces the strength of its connection to an individual author or a specific situation, in order to emphasize the intertextuality of every such object and the freedom of the reader to establish connections among many texts at many levels. This notion also changes the critic or teacher from a figure of automatic authority to one reader among others, whose performance of the reading act will have to be its own justification. The criteria for judging such performances may well include (I would say, must include) such traditional interpretive virtues as learning, attention to detail, and intensity of thought, but they will now also include range, creativity, and even exorbitance along with the traditional virtues. With this extension of the reader's range comes also a new freedom to take with equal seriousness (and playfulness) texts outside the "selective canon" of literature and indeed outside "literature" itself.

Perhaps the simplest and most radical implication of the concept of textuality is that it breaks down the barriers between verbal objects and other kinds of signification. The word *text* is useful—and indeed necessary—if we are to discuss the common semiotic properties of pictures, films, plays, operas, jokes, graffiti, poems, songs, stories, speeches, advertisements, novels, essays, and other . . . other what? Well, other texts, of course. A text is a cluster of signs or potentially signifying entities that can be connected by an act of reading to other such clusters.

A few years ago when a consortium of teaching organizations (the English Coalition) sought foundation support for a conference on the future of English studies from kindergarten to graduate school, one powerful foundation refused to consider supporting the proposal until the word *text* in the proposal was replaced everywhere by the word *literature*. This, my friends, is a true story, and it suggests that these matters, which may seem like trivial questions of terminology that concern only scholars and teachers, really do have political and economic consequences. In this opposition, *text* is aligned with the extension of democratic social, economic, and political processes and *canon* with the maintenance or recovery of more hierarchical structures. At their extremes, these two positions may imply anarchy and absolutism. In the middle, where most of us work and struggle, they may only be Jeffersonianism and Federalism. In any case, we may be certain that concepts of canonicity and textuality are themselves imbedded in the larger processes of our social text.

One final word. While I still have some control over this collection of words—before, that is, they enter the web of textuality even further—I would like to make a disclaimer. The notion of text deployed here is no panacea. It should be, at best, a stimulus to rethinking our enterprise. There is, I suppose, a possible curriculum of textuality that many writers on these matters could specify. And what, you may well ask, prevents that set of authors and works from becoming a canon just as exclusive and oppressive as the old one? I have two tentative answers to this very pertinent question. One is that, insofar as what we are considering is a set of theoretical writings, they are bound to be largely subsumed (*Aufgehoben*) by later theoretical writings. The other is that to the extent that we have really made it legitimate to consider—and study in our courses—any kind of textual object from graffiti to *The Making of Americans*, we have gone beyond canonization, because a canon requires that there be much more outside of it than inside. Without a canon, of course, we shall have to live our academic lives on an ad hoc basis. Individually, we may all be governed by habit and inertia more than we should, but perhaps we won't think that our hobby horses are cast in the mold of some Platonic Pegasus.[3]

Brown University

Notes

[1]"Far too much heroism still in our languages; in the best—I think of Bataille's—erethism [excessive irritability] of certain expressions and finally a sort of *insidious heroism*. The pleasure of the text (the joy of the text) is on the contrary like an abrupt erasure of warlike valor, a momentary desquamation [scaling off] of the writer's spurs, a stoppage of 'heart' (of courage)" (Barthes, *Plaisir* 50; trans. mine).

[2]In citing dictionaries and lexicons, I do not give page numbers because the words serve as their own locators. I also abridge and omit freely, in the interests of controlling what still seems like an ungainly amount of philological matter, though I think it is necessary to the discussion and may be useful beyond the immediate context.

[3]In preparing this essay I have received any amount of useful advice from anonymous readers and some very specific and extremely helpful criticism from John Murchek of the University of Florida. While teaching a course in canonicity, he located and drew my attention to the quotation from Carlyle that serves as the first epigraph. He also pointed to a number of weaknesses in an earlier draft, which I have done my best to remedy. For all this assistance I am extremely grateful.

Works Cited and Suggestions for Further Reading

Altieri, Charles. "An Idea and Ideal of a Literary Canon." Von Hallberg 41–64.

Baker, Ernest A. *Cassell's New French Dictionary*. New York: Funk, 1930.

Barthes, Roland. *Image, Music, Text*. Trans. Stephen Heath. New York: Hill, 1977.

———. *Le plaisir du texte*. Paris: Seuil, 1973.

Brooks, Cleanth. *Modern Poetry and the Tradition.* Chapel Hill: U of North Carolina P, 1939.

———. *The Well-Wrought Urn: Studies in the Structure of Poetry.* New York: Harcourt, 1947.

Bruns, Gerald L. "Canon and Power in the Hebrew Scriptures." Von Hallberg 65–84.

Carlyle, Thomas. *On Heroes, Hero-Worship, and the Heroic in History.* Centenary Edition. London: Chapman, 1897.

Coleridge, Samuel Taylor. *Biographia Literaria.* Ed. George Watson. London: Dent, 1982.

Derrida, Jacques. *Of Grammatology.* Trans. Gayatri C. Spivak. Baltimore: Johns Hopkins UP, 1976.

———. "Plato's Pharmacy." *Dissemination.* Trans. Barbara Johnson. Chicago: U of Chicago P, 1981. 61–171.

Donnegan, James. *Greek and English Lexicon.* London: Bohn, 1896.

Doubrovsky, Serge. *The New Criticism in France.* Trans. Derek Coltman. Chicago: U of Chicago P, 1973.

Eagleton, Terry. *Literary Theory: An Introduction.* Oxford: Blackwell; Minneapolis: U of Minnesota P, 1983.

Fiedler, Leslie A., and Houston A. Baker, Jr., eds. *English Literature: Opening Up the Canon.* Baltimore: Johns Hopkins UP, 1981.

Froula, Christine. "When Eve Reads Milton: Undoing the Canonical Economy." Von Hallberg 149–76.

Frye, Northrop. *Anatomy of Criticism: Four Essays.* Princeton: Princeton UP, 1957.

Golding, Alan C. "A History of American Poetry Anthologies." Von Hallberg 279–308.

Guillory, John. "The Ideology of Canon-Formation: T. S. Eliot and Cleanth Brooks." Von Hallberg 337–62.

Jameson, Fredric. *The Political Unconscious: Narrative as a Socially Symbolic Act.* Ithaca: Cornell UP, 1981.

Kames, Lord [Henry Home]. *Elements of Criticism.* 1762. 3 vols. New York: Johnson, 1970.

Kenner, Hugh. "The Making of the Modernist Canon." Von Hallberg 363–76.

Krupat, Arnold. "Native American Literature and the Canon." Von Hallberg 309–36.

LaCapra, Dominick. *Rethinking Intellectual History.* Ithaca: Cornell UP, 1983.

Lewis, Charlton T., and Charles Short. *A Latin Dictionary.* Oxford: Clarendon–Oxford UP, 1980.

Liddell, Henry George, and Robert Scott. *Greek-English Lexicon.* Oxford: Clarendon–Oxford UP, 1961.

Niermeyer, Jan Frederik. *Mediae Latinatis lexicon minus: A Medieval Latin-French/English Dictionary.* 2 vols. 1954. Leiden: Brill, 1976.

Ohmann, Richard M. "The Shaping of a Canon: U.S. Fiction 1960–1975." Von Hallberg 377–401.

Oxford English Dictionary. New York: Oxford UP, 1971.

Peirce, Charles Sanders. *Philosophical Writings of Peirce.* Ed. Justus Buchler. New York: Dover, 1955.

Saussure, Ferdinand de. *Course in General Linguistics.* Trans. Wade Baskin. New York: McGraw, 1966.

Smith, Barbara Herrnstein. "Contingencies of Value." Von Hallberg 5–40.

———. *Contingencies of Value: Alternative Perspectives for Critical Theory.* Cambridge: Harvard UP, 1988.

von Hallberg, Robert. *Canons.* Chicago: U of Chicago P, 1984.

DONALD G. MARSHALL

Literary Interpretation

HEGEL characterizes a profession as an institution that mediates between the individual's work and an encompassing social structure. One way it does so is by offering models that exemplify the practices of competent professionals. The scholar and the critic are two traditional models for literary professionals, and the theorist is a recent addition. Yet the salience of these figures obscures a professional practice that pervades all three and gives literary study its special character: the practice of interpretation. Few literary academics would identify themselves as "interpreters," yet most spend much of their careers training students in the practice of interpreting, presenting interpretations of literary works to students and to one another, and trying to make their own practices as interpreters subtle and penetrating enough to respond to the capacity of serious writing to provoke endless thought.

What is interpretation? The term's use outside literary study may furnish some guiding hints. *Interpreter* is the ordinary name for someone who translates, particularly in face-to-face situations.[1] Similarly, an interpreter is one who translates spoken words into sign language for the hearing impaired. In the performing arts, critics and audiences want to hear how a performer interprets a well-known musical composition or play. At parks or restored historic sites, an interpreter explains the sights or exhibitions to visitors. Despite variations, we find here a basic structure. An interpreter is someone who helps another understand the meaning of something. What is to be understood is already there, but it is unable to speak for itself. Its message needs mediation through the interpreter's special knowledge and skill. In Latin, the word *interpres* refers to a negotiator, mediator, or messenger, as well as to an expounder or explainer. The name for reflection on interpretation, *hermeneutics*, comes from a Greek word meaning variously to translate, to put into words, or to explain.

Literary interpretation is another specification of this basic structure. The literary interpreter helps someone understand the meaning of a text. Knowledge of a text's language and of relevant historical contexts and references is presupposed or must be supplied before interpreting can begin. But alienness is also presupposed: something in the text or in our distance from it in time and place makes it obscure. The interpreter's task is to make the text speak again. This task is accomplished by "reading" the text and by helping students learn to read it. Interpreting is reading; what makes professional literary study distinctive among the academic disciplines is its deployment of extremely complex skills of reading. What then is "reading," and where does it go wrong or fall short so that it needs the disciplined help interpreting gives it?

Before we can answer, we need to notice that this description—that the literary interpreter helps someone understand the meaning of a text—is not a definition in the classic sense of stating a genus and differentia or pointing to essential qualities of a thing. Instead, this description tells a story, inviting us to think about interpreting as an activity and to ask when and where it takes place and under what circumstances; who participates in it and with what commitments, interests, and purposes; and what practices it involves, how they came to be devised, and what their relations are to the whole of our ethical and political, that is, practical and active, lives. These are far-reaching questions, showing us the importance and scope of the topic.

Since the early nineteenth century, philosophers of interpretation have pointed to three closely related "hermeneutic disciplines," each centered on the problem of interpreting texts: law, religion, and literary study. Each of these has a long and complex history, and the nature of legal and religious interpretation continues to be vigorously debated. More recently, the importance of interpretation in anthropology, sociology, history, and other disciplines has been recognized. But comparing the fields of law, religion, and literary study may serve to bring out some key features of literary interpretation that are less evident when literature is seen only in the context of the arts and general aesthetics or of historical and cultural study.

A law is a general formulation. Its meaning becomes concrete only when it is applied in a particular set of circumstances—a "case"—by those who regard themselves as under its jurisdiction. Cases often involve a potential or actual dispute over this application, and a social institution exists for deciding these disputes: courts of law. The decision has to be rendered by particular persons, the judges. They are not free simply to decide what seems just without reference to the law. But the law cannot speak for itself, nor can those who originally made it be summoned. The judge's fundamental responsibility is to see that justice is done, but the specific task is to make justice speak through the law to the particular dispute. A judicial interpretation is not a statement of fact but a decision, an act that can have grave consequences for many more people than those engaged in the case under consideration. Judges are supposed to set aside personal interests and biases, yet human decisions always implicate values and beliefs. Consequently, controversies arise not only about particular decisions and understandings of the law but about these implicit values and beliefs. For a literary interpreter, what seems especially relevant is the judge's double responsibility to adhere to an existing text and yet also to make that text speak actively in a present situation that ordinarily involves deeply rooted disagreement.

In religion, the universal idea seems to be that a divine will can be expressed in signs, whether omens and oracles or sacred scriptures. A religious interpeter's task is to enable that will to reach its intended audience. Here, too, meaning is an act to be performed rather than a mere idea to be disclosed. The message may be good news, but it often imposes unwelcome demands, so that interpreter and audience may be in an antagonistic relation. Since religious signs are usually ambiguous and enigmatic yet also demand a strong response from believers, intense controversy often arises over how to interpret them, sometimes with dire historical consequences. As in law, religious interpreters claim to be reading sacred signs, not stating personal opinion.[2] Even more than in law, religious interpretation raises problematic questions about what community is addressed by a divine message. A tribal religion generally asserts authority only within the specific group that acknowledges it, so that unresolved disagreements over interpretation can produce schisms in the community. A few religions claim to address all humankind, and they proselytize among nonbelievers, that is, other communities who may refuse to accept that claim or even find it highly offensive. Religious interpretation thus forcefully raises issues about the source and authority of its signs and messages, about the authority of an interpreter and an interpretation, and about the claim of that authority on communities of believers and nonbelievers.

In both law and religion, a number of paradoxes emerge. Understanding the meaning of a legal or religious text is vital to right action, yet the text is unable to speak for itself. Understanding comes about through the interpreter's agency, yet the meaning conveyed is asserted to belong to the text, not the interpreter. The meaning is something to be done as well as to be known, yet the audience may not welcome this demand to turn meaning into responsive action. Meaning is addressed to a community, but specifying the community may be controversial, and those addressed may refuse to acknowledge the authority of either the message or the interpreter. While literary interpretation has neither the law's power to enforce decisions nor religion's claim of divine sanction, it contains its own versions of these paradoxes.

In thinking about literary interpretation, one may be tempted to move immediately to a practical concern with the contemporary variety of interpretive methods or approaches, such as deconstruction, formalism, new historicism, and so on. But it may be more useful in the long run to begin by reflecting on the basic components of interpretation so as to bring out what belongs to all interpretive practices. In the description I propose, these components are text, interpreter, the audience to whom interpretation is directed, meaning, and the resources that help achieve understanding. Whatever the approach or the debate about approaches, interpreting remains a complex social practice situated within a historical moment.

Let me begin with *text*. The word itself is somewhat strange and of recent vintage. Its increasing use in literary study reflects a sizable theoretical debate over how we should think of literature (see Barthes; Foucault). Until recently, literary interpretation focused on so-called great imaginative works, most often within a single country and language. The term *work* suggests that a poem or novel is an object that already has a determinate and permanent form crafted to express its maker's original idea. It implies that interpreters should direct themselves to single poems, novels, or plays; should relate parts of a single work to the work as a structured whole; and should understand a work as an expression of an author's or creator's originating idea. This conception may seem the obviously reasonable one, but the term *text* challenges it. As Robert Scholes's chapter "Canonicity and Textuality" in this book makes clear, literary interpreters increasingly question the designation of only a few works as "great" and therefore deserving of special attention or a special kind of attention. They want to read "noncanonical" literary works from American, European, and all other cultures, and, indeed, they want to read "texts" of all kinds, from philosophical works to psychological case histories; from legal cases to ethnographic reports of other cultures and other works of reportage; from sacred scriptures to song lyrics, bumper stickers, graffiti, music videos, and soap operas. They often connect "literary" texts with historical documents or with descriptions of historical events, and they do not feel obliged to read "whole" works or to keep different works separate.

The term *text* thus deliberately permits the interpreter wide scope. It encompasses the continuous substance of all human signifying activities and allows us to point to something very general, namely, to whatever seems to invite interpretation or to whatever the interpreter sets up as an object for interpreting. Academics speak of "reading" films, paintings, buildings, the urban landscape, or items from mass or material culture. Indeed, the philosopher Paul Ricoeur argues that all social action is "text" insofar as it contains and conveys a meaning ("Model of the Text"), and some literary academics treat current affairs, such as issues of nuclear policy, as texts to be interpreted. Perhaps the furthest extension is expressed in a now famous phrase of the philosopher Jacques Derrida: "Il n'y a pas de hors-texte," a rather carefully worded maxim that has been translated as "There is nothing outside the text" (*Of Grammatology* 158). The term *text* thus reminds us that interpreters decide, on the basis of their own interests and questions, what materials to interpret and what practices will satisfy the need or desire to interpret them. It lessens the implied gap between what interpreters write and what they write about—both are "texts." It reminds us that we focus our attention on a text for some purpose, to ask some question of it, and that these questions are as much ours as the text's. We must become active and decide where or even whether a text begins and ends, what questions we want to ask, how we will go about answering them, and so on.

D. C. Greetham's chapter "Textual Scholarship" in this book shows that texts are not simply there, waiting for us to find and interpret them. Every text emerges from a complicated historical process of creation and transmission. Its author may be anonymous or multiple. If "Homer" was a single poet, he assembled material that emerged in an oral bardic tradition. In Elizabethan and Jacobean plays, as in Renaissance and baroque painting, collaboration was common. Ezra Pound's editing and revision of T. S. Eliot's *Waste Land* made it a very different poem. Chaucer's *Troilus and Criseyde* translates, adapts, and expands a poem by Boccaccio. Jean Rhys's *Wide Sargasso Sea* rewrites Charlotte Brontë's *Jane Eyre* from the perspective of the mad Mrs. Rochester. Texts are constituted and reconstituted in a series of copies and editions that may vary significantly. William Wordsworth's *Prelude* exists in several manuscript revisions, one of which became the basis of the posthumous 1850 edition, but modern commentators often prefer to base their interpretations on an earlier version copied out in 1805. They sometimes print materials Wordsworth never worked into the *Prelude* or even assemble poems out of several drafts Wordsworth never brought to a fair copy. Moreover, a text reaches us already saturated with the purposes and estimates of those who transmitted it. Some biblical writings became the official canon of Jewish and Christian scriptures; others are apocryphal, accepted by some sects, rejected by others; yet another mass of writing is granted authority by no modern sect. Some texts or writers (Shakespeare, Homer, Plato) are already acclaimed; others (*Lady Chatterly's Lover*, Marx, Freud) are surrounded by controversy. The way a text is printed or bound, the scholarly apparatus of notes and commentary that may accompany it, the circumstances under which we first encounter it—whether we see it in a bookstore, library, or classroom or hear of it through a comment by a newspaper reviewer, a friend, a teacher, or in another book—all shape our initial orientation to it. Interpreters are therefore necessarily interested in how a text got put together and how and why it comes to us.

Yet if we cannot take for granted the text we interpret, neither do we set it up arbitrarily, willfully, or by individual fiat. A text is constituted and transmitted to us in a complicated social and historical process of which our act of interpretive attention becomes a part. This process and our participation in it presuppose interests that likewise have their own history (and consequently their own future as well). But even if it is not merely a given, the text does take the form of "signs," usually words but always some material bearer of meaning. What instigates interpreting is an interest in eliciting and appropriating this meaning.

The next components of interpretation are the interpreter and the audience. Some readers who find academic interpretations excessive or wrongheaded and who think such interpretations spoil direct enjoyment of the work may question the need for an interpreter. Students and even teachers may make sharp distinctions between texts to study and books to read for pleasure, that is, between texts whose interpretation is perhaps a duty but certainly a labor and texts where interpreting seems minimal and invisible. Pedagogy gives the interpreter an unusual authority: it is the teacher who grades the student's paper, not Sophocles, Jane Austen, or Wole Soyinka. Students learn the methods and approach of the teacher, not "literature" directly. It is rarely immediately clear to students why these particular texts are chosen for interpreting, what the purposes and results of interpreting them will be, or what the origin and justification of the teacher's basic interpretive questions and practices are.

The relations of interpreters to their audiences are various. Sometimes readers care so deeply about a particular text or book that they are eager to hear it discussed and to offer their own views. Christianity, for instance, begins as an interpretation of prophecies in Hebrew scripture and then of texts that record oral traditions of the life and teaching of Jesus. Christians ostensibly are a community constituted by a shared interpretation of texts regarded as sacred. Yet the development of interpretive practices and the debate over them has been central to Christianity, and these debates still offer important lessons for contemporary interpretive theory. Similarly, a student may be eager to know about Shakespeare but find his words, cultural context, and presuppositions alien. The history of interpretive commentary on Shakespeare tells us a great deal not only about Shakespeare but about the ideas and concerns of successive generations of interpreters and their audiences. Much modern poetry and fiction present a different kind of challenge to understanding, but, again, students may eagerly seek an interpreter's help. When a student reads a text and does not find it particularly puzzling, however, the teacher's interpretations may seem obvious or artificially manufactured. The interpretation may seem too detailed or picky or focused on questions tangential to the work, or it may seem to originate in a completely different agenda.

Academics who share their interpretations with other academics through publication or presentation at professional meetings find themselves in a context quite different from that of the classroom. The profession takes the form of an ongoing conversation or debate over what to interpret and how, and a professional must become aware of the current state of this conversation and of what will be seen by other professionals as a contribution to it. As students advance in literary study, they join more fully in this conversation. Good teachers always try to discern and respond to the questions students at any stage actually have. But teachers also lead students to ask other questions and to find other ways of answering those questions—ways closer to those regarded as important in current professional work. Students may find this transition awkward and may at first feel as if they are learning to play a highly artificial game. This view has some validity: students' skepticism encourages even expert interpreters to ask whether the enterprise makes sense and why. But ideally, as students learn the varied interpretive practices within the profession, they come to see the genuine insights and issues that underlie those practices and that characterize the professional debate.

Because this professional conversation has its own history and logic, it is not always immediately intelligible to outside observers. Nonparticipants can easily mock it by picking out bits of jargon or strange-sounding titles of essays presented at meetings or published in journals. Such mockery is sometimes ill-informed and unreasonable, as the hilarious but disheartening third book of Jonathan Swift's *Gulliver's Travels* demonstrates. In describing the absurd projects of the Academy of Lagado, Swift mocks modern science at its birth. But the subsequent achievements of science mock the mockery. Interpretation, too, may seem strange to nonprofessional readers, even those generally knowledgeable about literature. Like students, though in a different way, such readers may need an explanation of why a particular question or interpretation is significant and why expressing it may require a specialized vocabulary. Thus interpreters, whose aim is to help an audience understand, must take account of that audience's knowledge, interests, ways of talking, and membership—whether students, generally educated nonprofessionals, or other professional interpreters. But because interpreters are also responsible to the text and what they think it means, they often want to lead the audience to different questions and language. Interpreters not infrequently find themselves in the ethically perilous position of arguing or implying that their audience *ought* to care about this particular text, *ought* to feel the presence of these particular questions and problems, and *ought* to try to respond in this particular way.

Both the audience's trouble with specific parts of a text and the interpreter's choice of words to make the text understandable are historically situated responses. The relation of interpreter to audience can be problematic: to say an interpreter helps another reader understand a text does not exclude divergent or even antagonistic elements in the relationship. Professional interpreters are part of a professional interpretive community (or a network of communities) within which some interpretations and interpretive practices have become widely accepted while others are the subject of intense debate. If we focus on an isolated person reading a single text fixed in print, we can easily lose sight of the social and dialogic character of interpreting. But its full nature emerges only in that context.

Perhaps no topic in the theory of interpretation has been more debated in our century than the nature of the meaning that emerges in the complex social process called interpreting and the relation of meaning to the various and variegated texts that occasion it. Meaning in these cases has a paradoxical character: it is not simply there and waiting for us; and yet, though it cannot come into being without our activity, it is not a product simply of that activity. This paradox emerges in Plato's dialogue the *Protagoras*, when Socrates and Protagoras discuss the meaning of a poem by Simonides in order to focus their inquiry into whether virtue can be taught. Commenting on texts was a staple of the Greek Sophists' pedagogy, and Socrates shows he can interpret the poem as subtly as they do, if need be. But in the end, he objects to the way the argument becomes inconclusive when it becomes a matter of puzzling over what a text means, and he compares interpreters to vulgar people who bring in "flute-girls" to entertain at a party, whereas properly educated people know how to entertain one another with their own conversation (347b–348a). Why not just examine our own ideas to see which are true or false? If a text's meaning is so obscure that it needs interpreting, why bother with it?

In fact, the word *meaning* is somewhat misleading. Interpretation does not just aim to state a "theme" in the form of a proposition about the human condition or general social issues, a proposition that could be formulated separately from the text and with which we could agree or disagree on the basis of a quite different kind of evidence. Our comparison with law and religion suggests that "what the text says" has something of the character of a command, a word spoken to us whose consequences in and for our lives we feel obliged to consider, even if we decide to reject it. To say that an interpreter helps a text speak again underscores the complexity of interpretation's aim. In speaking, meaning has the form of an event in an intricate and historically situated social process with manifold ramifications that neither the speaker nor the hearer controls fully. A literary text is an instrument we can use to understand human experience, which means that it enables us to take up a complex, detailed, and nuanced orientation toward our lives. In a well-known formulation, Cleanth Brooks has argued that interpretation aims not at paraphrase but at making the experience of the text available to the reader ("Heresy of Paraphrase").

In the *Poetics*, Aristotle already grasps the philosophical depth of this kind of meaning. Tragedy, he says, aims to arouse and "purge" certain emotions (ch. 6). But later, speaking in terms of knowledge, he remarks that poetry is more philosophical and serious than history; this somewhat cryptic phrase asserts that, far better than records of fact, stories repay an attention aimed at gaining applicable insight into human experience. Stories, he adds, express the "universal," by which he means not some abstract proposition but the coherence of events in the story's plot (ch. 9). Aristotle does not explicitly coordinate the twin ideas of purging and the universal, but he seems to mean that the coherence of plot that gives tragedy its self-subsistence as a thing also gives to the flow of our feelings an exemplary formulation, an identifiable character we can call on in our ordinary lives.[3] From this perspective, interpretation neither states a proposition as the meaning of a text nor anatomizes a fixed textual structure. It aims to trace the weave of thoughts, feelings, words, figures, sounds, and representations in a text, a weaving taken up into the thinking and feeling that constitute readers' diverse responses.

This difficult idea has been repeatedly lost and recovered in the history of interpretation, but unless we grasp it, we miss the aim of interpretation. What characteristically instigates interpretation is that the interpreter anticipates more meaning than a text appears to deliver. This anticipation may be due to a text's cultural reputation or standing. It may arise from a conviction that a text is symptomatic of larger cultural forces or that it embodies or illustrates some psychological or philosophical insight. But in any case, interpretation begins when a text appears to stand out from a background and invite commentary. Consequently, the enigmatic poetic text is exemplary for interpretation. But what makes a text both poetic and enigmatic?

A student once told me he found, on the kitchen table in his apartment, an envelope on which his roommate had scribbled the following words: "Investigate the death of bears." As it happened, his roommate was a zoologist noting a possible dissertation topic. Yet the words are resonantly enigmatic. Encountered by chance, stripped of discursive context, they are bound together by an internal rhythm: a four-syllable latinate imperative verb balances four Anglo-Saxon monosyllables forming a noun phrase, the whole sentence in iambic meter. Such a sentence attracts the mind to linger over it, but it does not determine exactly what one might say. Anything we may feel stimulated to say aims not to dispel this attraction but to preserve it, along with the words to which it is a response.

This effect is even clearer with the far richer structures of poetry, as the following stanza by Emily Dickinson may illustrate:

> Safe in their Alabaster Chambers—
> Untouched by Morning
> And untouched by Noon—
> Sleep the meek members of the Resurrection—
> Rafter of satin,
> And Roof of stone. (*Poems* 100; no. 216)

She sent this stanza in a note to her sister-in-law Sue Dickinson, along with a second stanza that Sue did not like. Emily replied with a different second stanza, but Sue again demurred and added:

> It just occurs to me that the first verse is complete in itself it needs no other, and can't be coupled—Strange things always go alone—as there is only one Gabriel and one Sun—you never made a peer for that verse, and I *guess* your kingdom doesn't hold one—I always go to the fire and get warm after thinking of it, but I never *can* again—. . . . (*Letters* 162; no. 238)

Emily tried a third time, sending another second stanza to Sue with the question, "Is *this frostier?*" (162). The poem is usually published with this first stanza and at least one of the attempts at a second. But Sue heard the complex rhythms that make the first stanza virtually self-sufficient. Likewise, using her own image, she interprets for Emily the atmospheric "frostiness" of the stanza. In this private exchange between two close friends, poet and interpreter are virtually collaborating in the creation of the text. In fact, it is written for just such an intelligent reading, but because she rarely encountered that response, Dickinson left virtually all her poems unpublished.

The nature of textual meaning and its implications for interpretive practice have been at the heart of debates in contemporary literary study. Earlier in this century, the Russian formalist and Prague structuralist schools, as well as English and American New Criticism, sought an interpretive language adequate to their conviction that literary meaning was located at the intersection of a poem's linguistic structure and its imagistic rendering of experience. For the New Critics, interpretation meant revealing the coherence of the structure and the experience, both separately and together in the poem. Dissent from this conception fueled the important contemporary movement of deconstruction. Deconstruction calls into question the New Critical belief that a literary work synthesizes "experience" (that is, the themes and values literary works express) with the work's linguistic structures. In the deconstructive critic Paul de Man's terms, a text's "grammar"—the syntactic structures of its language—contradicts its "rhetoric," its figurality and the metaphoricity it aims to project. De Man once condensed this view into the elliptical formula, "every text is an allegory of its own unreadability." Literary theory, he argued, is the "resistance to theory," that is, a rigorous philosophical reflection on the way careful reading shows how every text's language undermines any attempt to articulate a meaning autonomous from that language that could be put to some further intellectual or practical use. De Man himself explicitly recognized that his ideas stood paradoxically close to those of Reuben Brower and other New Critics ("Return to Philology" 23–24). He shared their belief that literary study should focus on the reading of texts. But the New Critics went on to argue that interpretive reading, by demonstrating the inseparable unity between meaning and the way meaning is conveyed in language, would reveal both the defining nature of literature and the unique identity of each literary text. De Man tried to show instead the impossibility of precisely that unity.

De Man returns us, though with an opposed inflection, to the peculiarity of interpretive meaning Plato disclosed in the *Protagoras* and in his objections to writing at the end of the *Phaedrus*. Texts produce endless meaning, according to de Man, because they yield no definite meaning. This fact does not destroy the concept of text or of literature but defines a literary text as one that both evokes an anticipation of meaning and undercuts every meaning the interpreter proposes for it. De Man argued that this process was the essence of all language but that texts we call "literary" are distinguished by their knowledge of this unsettling state of affairs and their failure to disguise it ("Resistance to Theory" 9–11). His view forcibly captures the nonpropositional, undecidable, or indeterminable character of interpretive meaning, which is rather a way of lingering thoughtfully in the presence of a text. But deconstruction is also too negatively therapeutic. Phrased as a solecism, it asks the interpreter to not say, to unsay, meaning.

More recent developments in interpretive practice have not refuted deconstruction but attempted to displace it by situating interpretation in relation to political, ethical, and social issues (see Culler in this volume). Insofar as these developments do not turn into a kind of historiography or an intervention in current affairs that simply uses texts as a disposable launching pad for social commentary, they overlap with and yet also diverge from the twist deconstruction gave to New Criticism's central idea. I have already noted that the word *text* paves the way for regarding every kind of cultural or social phenomenon as an object of reading. This extension, by no means arbitrary, brings out the all-pervasiveness of meaning in human life. It follows that interpreters may read social life as a text and, by reading texts, bring social issues to the surface. Such interpretations diverge from de Man's kind of deconstruction insofar as they wish to harness interpretive practices to a particular agenda of social reform. De Man would question not the merits of that agenda but the subordination of reading texts to other sorts of aims. Deconstruction suggests that it is impossible to confine interpretive practices to literary study, and yet the consequences of those practices cannot be controlled or guaranteed in advance.

This issue, however, is inescapable, and it is already apparent in ancient interpretive practice. As social conditions changed, the text of Homer or Vergil came to seem alien, though it remained highly respected and its study was the core of childhood education. In response to this alienation, "allegorical" interpretation emerged as a way of talking about the text to reconnect it with current ideas about human life and thus reinforce its relevance. Because of the wide gap between our understanding of the text and what its late antique interpreters say about it, the older allegorical way of talking can seem to us very strained. For instance, Vergil's *Aeneid* opens with a storm and shipwreck. Aeneas is crossing the ocean with a band of exiles after the fall of Troy, and the oracles of the gods have revealed that he will found a new and even greater city. For various reasons, Juno hates him and instigates the storm to destroy the Trojans or at least delay their new beginning. A modern interpreter might say various things about this opening. In generic terms, it follows Horace's advice to start an epic "in the midst of things," and the exciting event gives Vergil an opportunity for much vivid description. Thematically, it shows the cosmic scale of the story, in which human beings live out their fates subject both to natural forces beyond their control and to inscrutable purposes of sometimes hostile gods who may or may not reward human virtue. Intertextually, by echoing a storm in Homer's *Odyssey*, it defines a tradition within which Vergil wishes to appear as a competitor for high rank.

An obscure grammarian named Fulgentius, writing more than five hundred years after Vergil died, offered a quite different interpretation, suited to a cultural context that had changed greatly since Vergil. As a schoolteacher, he used the poem to teach young boys Latin and induct them into Roman culture, which retained its prestige even though the Italian peninsula had fallen to the Ostrogoths and had to be reconquered in the seventh century. As a Christian, Fulgentius had to reconcile the values implicit in pagan culture with the values of a still alien religion (Christianity was adopted by the emperor Constantine early in the fourth century, repudiated by Julian the Apostate, and reconfirmed only after his death in 363). Adopting a self-conscious and sophisticated form that maneuvers neatly through this tangled cultural situation, he stages his interpretive work as a schoolroom dialogue between himself and the ghost of Vergil, which he calls up for the occasion. Vergil can thus authoritatively explain his moral meaning, and Fulgentius can agree with it where it is consistent with Christianity. Where it is not, Vergil can graciously concede that Christianity's insights are superior. Instead of an epic beginning in medias res, Fulgentius decides the poem is an encomium of a virtuous man, an oratorical form that was supposed to begin at birth. Therefore, Fulgentius contends, the storm and shipwreck symbolize the birth of the soul. Juno, Fulgentius points out, is the goddess of childbirth. The god who directly releases the storm is Aeolus, and Fulgentius connects his name to the Greek word *eonolus* (*aion* + *oloos*), which he translates as "the destructiveness of time," citing as authority a verse from Homer's *Iliad* (though the verse makes no mention of Aeolus).[4] By such devices, Fulgentius transforms the epic from the story of Rome's founding into a general allegory of moral development, preserving cultural continuity while rendering Vergil usable within a changed cultural context.

I do not suggest that we could endorse, still less adopt, Fulgentius's interpretive practice, though it was commonplace in interpretation from Plato to the Renaissance—and, indeed, this kind of symbiotic reconciliation of old and new through interpretation kept Vergil central to Western culture from Dante to T. S. Eliot and Hermann Broch's novel *The Death of Vergil.* The point is that interpreters do not just freely elicit meanings from texts; rather, they make interpretation the means of synthesizing and carrying on a whole culture. Interpretation always functions this way. If we ask, with Socrates, why we should bother "discovering" our own ideas by reading them out of past texts, the apparent answer is that in cultural and moral life humans have felt a need for traditional ideas, that is, ideas that they see as continuous with time-tested experience and not unprecedented insights with uncertain consequences.

It does not follow that interpretation is always conservative. Indeed, just the opposite is true. Interpretation, we recall, presupposes that a text does not speak its meaning for itself. It holds itself back from us in some ways. Even when the meaning of a text seems self-evident to most readers, interpretation may aim to reveal the acquired practices on which that self-evidence is grounded. In any case, the interpreter must talk in a way that reorients readers—by supplying background information, descriptions of the text and its structure, or explicit statements of its thematic, cultural, or artistic presuppositions—thus leading them into a situation (what phenomenologists call a "horizon") within which they can understand and respond to what the text says. But this process has a paradoxical consequence, for the need to make meaning explicit and conscious makes it apparent that what is said could at every point be otherwise. By reflectively recovering meaning from its embeddedness in the text and in social processes, interpretation makes it something that can be chosen or rejected.

This paradox has been posed as the tension between a "hermeneutics of recovery," which aims to bring the reader to sympathy with the text and what it says, and a "hermeneutics of suspicion," which lays bare the presuppositions and processes of signification of a text and renders them questionable.[5] Naomi Schor's essay "Feminist and Gender Studies" in this book shows some of the ways contemporary interpreters may unmask a text's refusal to question its own presuppositions and may dissolve its authority over its readers. But, in fact, both kinds of interpretation deploy the art of grasping what is questionable, in a text and also in the reader. The hermeneutics of recovery, directed to making the text speak again and speak to us, also presupposes a distance or alienation between text and reader. This kind of interpretation speaks on behalf of the text to people who have misunderstood it or who have understood it too reductively and failed to grasp it in its fullness. The hermeneutics of recovery brings the text into the present, but as a force contrary to the presumed self-sufficiency of present opinion, and in this way brings into question the reader's presuppositions and whatever in a reader blocks responsiveness to the text's meaning.

Suspicious interpreters, however, do not aim simply to destroy an interest in the text and consign it to the trash heap of history. They assume that some important present concern needs to be addressed at least in part by grappling with past texts.[6] Moreover, literary interpreters who wish to bring into question deeply rooted assumptions in our personal and social lives—assumptions whose depth lies precisely in the processes of language where we make meanings without being aware of doing so—have found a powerful inspiration and a powerful tool in the interpretive reading that has been the central achievement of literary study in our century. Accordingly, all interpretation has a doubly "critical" power: on the one hand, against readers who take their presuppositions and predilections for granted and, on the other hand, against the text, whose presuppositions and processes of signification lose self-evidence when brought to explicit consciousness. The specific nature of interpretation is still its commitment to bringing out a kind of meaning that remains indissociable from the structure of a particular text.

I have so far spoken of interpreting as a practice in which one person says something that aims to help another grasp the meaning and force of a text. But there are many interpreters, not just one. Interpretations accumulate over time and are not merely diverse but sometimes conflicting. If interpreting responds to a need to understand a text in our present situation, why attend to past interpretations, which may have become so alien as to need interpreting themselves? Is there some unity behind the various interpretations of a single text or behind the variety of interpretive practices? If interpretations contradict each other, how can we decide which interpretation is valid?

Since interpreters speak within a specific cultural situation, diversity is to some degree a function of varying contexts. Interpreting these interpretations may help us see the cultural situation within which an interpretive remark or practice had a local validity—and that interpretation may still seem valid to us, either because the situation has not changed or because we find something analogous in our own moment. The history of interpretation often reveals ideas about literature that authors shared or ways they anticipated their works would be read. In the famous letter to Can Grande della Scala (95–111; authorship is disputed), Dante applied to the *Divine Comedy* the complex allegorical interpretive methods that had been developed throughout the Middle Ages for reading the Bible. We may infer that he felt able to write a poem with such richly layered meanings in part because he knew at least some readers would be trained to read it this way. Studying past interpretations may thus help us understand how to approach past works. For example, when John Dryden in his "Essay of Dramatic Poesy" praises Ben Jonson's play *Epicoene* for observing the unities of time, place, and action, we can see that he is speaking within the context of a

Renaissance quest for the "rules" of poetry. Since few modern critics speak this way, a passion to find *the* rules may strike us as misguided. We have to remember that the Renaissance brought profound changes in the audience for drama and in taste. Dryden observes that although critics attributed the "unities" to Aristotle, the concept was invented by Italian and French critics, who then interpreted classical authors so as to assert a legitimating precedent. More generally, writers always need some social contract with their audience to specify what good poetry looks like. The Renaissance quest for rules is an unusually explicit renegotiation of that contract. Contemporary arguments among black American writers over which poetic and fictional forms are best suited to express their experience and to combat racism serve a similar need (see Gates in this volume). Requiring that plays observe the unities expresses a demand that literary works render experience in a concentrated, intensified form. To that extent, T. S. Eliot argues, the doctrine of the unities may claim a universal validity (37–39).

Quite different issues are raised by the multiplicity of contemporary interpretations. The New Critics insisted that interpretive reading was the core of literary study, and they created a reading practice that could be easily learned. The result—not achieved without a struggle—was that, for literary academics, publishing readings of literary works became as legitimate as publishing philological and historical investigations. With the steady increase in the number of college teachers after World War II and the requirement in many universities that faculty members publish in order to gain tenure and advance their careers, published interpretations proliferated rapidly. By now, so much has been published about some famous works that reading it all and keeping up with recent additions would be a full-time job.

The sheer bulk of interpretation creates a problem for a reader, particularly one who wants to learn from it how to become a professional interpreter and join in the professional conversation. Reading it all is impossible, but sifting out what is most valuable is difficult. Since most of it must perforce remain unread, one may be tempted to read none of it or as little as possible. The whole business of interpretation may come to seem pointless, as interpreters drown in the flood they have themselves created. Interpreters may cease to feel guided by a genuine need for understanding and may instead feel they are merely contending among themselves for professional recognition with no wider cultural significance.

Such discouraging conclusions seem to me unjustified. It is important to avoid misleading conceptions about both the production and the consumption of interpretive writing. Like all scholars, interpreters have a primary responsibility to the historical record. They need to know as much as possible about the author's life and other writings; the genesis and publication history of the text; the historical milieu, including contemporary writing; and the state of the language and relevant conventions and traditions of discourse. This kind of information does not render interpretation unnecessary, but situating the text in these various contexts opens interpretive possibilities.

The proliferation of interpretations usefully forces us to surrender the idea that we can master a literary work or its interpretation. Within the humanities, we carry on a conversation that is partial and endlessly open; we do not speak from a position of authority based on total knowledge. It would be equally mistaken either to ignore what has already been written or to think one must read it all before saying anything. As in all modern social experience, we are members to a greater or lesser degree in an overlapping network of variously constituted groups. Interpretation is the practical activity, the concrete substance, of the social group or groups for whom the meaning of a text or a body of texts is a matter of concern. Professional interpreters are simply those who have given their working lives to that concern, and within the profession we find a further overlapping network of specialties. Some interpreters, of course, may misunderstand their profession and speak as though interpretations are new discoveries that contribute to collective progress toward a unified and final understanding of a text. And there is some justice to the fear that such a large and dispersed profession will lose its sense of common purposes, its mutually intelligible ways of working, and its shared standards for estimating which professional work is valuable. But if we see professional interpretation as a set of collective practices for holding in mind texts worth the effort of understanding, then joining in that profession requires only that we read widely enough to develop a sense for when our own interpretations may justifiably claim other professionals' attention. Above all, we should seek out interpretations that stretch and challenge our own understanding, because the more varied and diverse the contexts within which the text has been enabled to speak, the deeper that understanding will become.

To be sure, interpretations do not just coexist peaceably, as the following, much debated poem by Wordsworth illustrates:

> A slumber did my spirit seal;
>   I had no human fears:
> She seemed a thing that could not feel
>   The touch of earthly years.
>
> No motion has she now, no force;
>   She neither hears nor sees;
> Rolled round in earth's diurnal course,
>   With rocks, and stones, and trees.
>
> (216)

This short lyric may seem too obvious to invite much interpretation, but dozens of comments, often in sharp disagreement with one another, have been directed to it. A first-time reader might simply wonder who "she" is. An interpreter might point out that this poem is one of a series that Wordsworth wrote about a young girl he named "Lucy," who died young. Historical investigation has identified no actual "Lucy," and she appears to have been a fictional creation.

In saying these things, the interpreter has taken for granted that a reader feels it is explanatory to set a poem in the context of its author's other writings and to supply documented historical context. The historical approach is not just a method but a way of making sense that is deeply embedded in our individual and social life. That way could in theory be challenged: this particular text does not say how old "she" is, nor does it explicitly instruct a reader to group this text with any others. To refuse historical explanations, therefore, is not indefensible in theory, though it may seem quixotic or perverse. The important point is that the force of even so "self-evident" an interpretive remark rests implicitly on practices that make sense to a social group.

The tone of the second stanza and the relation of the second stanza to the first stanza have evoked disagreement between interpreters. Some hold that the second stanza expresses the speaker's horror as he moves from illusion to the harsh reality that the girl has been reduced to a motionless, dead thing. This interpretation also rests on cultural presuppositions. Dying occasions grief, and the shattering of illusion is painful. But the text does not use the word *death*, nor does the second stanza name the speaker's feelings. Are other attitudes toward death possible? A well-attested alternative is to see a dead person as reassimilated into the endless cycles of nature. It would follow that the tone of the second stanza is resigned, perhaps to some degree celebratory. Some interpreters have tried to document that Wordsworth held such beliefs in the period when he wrote this poem. They are using a biographical and historical approach to support their side in a dispute over a psychological approach to the poem.

It would be easy to add other examples of this interaction between detailed readings of a text and a more or less explicit, more or less systematically stated, body of orienting presuppositions. A feminist reading might attend to the silence of Lucy throughout these poems, to the male poet's particular variant on the traditional theme of the female muse, or to the association of the female figure with nature. Annabel Patterson's essay "Historical Scholarship" in this book discusses new historicism. Representatives of that approach might be struck by the poet's passivity or by his strong investment in rural nature as a locus of value, and they might seek to understand the political, social, and economic forces that influence the development of an individual writer who sees experience in these terms. Proponents of any of these readings might deploy several such approaches or draw on elements of them. In actual critical practice, however, we encounter not just disagreement within a single framework of assumptions but both a mix of approaches used to support or contradict interpretations and potential disagreement over the legitimacy of different approaches and of mixing them.

How can we settle these various disagreements? If the text's own words were decisive, the dispute would not have arisen in the first place. We seem to have no choice but to go "outside" the text. The author and the author's intentions seem temptingly close at hand. The New Critics argued that a poem is a public utterance, so that the author's intentions are irrelevant because private (Wimsatt and Beardsley). Their critics have argued that only the author's intention establishes meaning and provides a basis for validating interpretation (see Hirsch; Juhl; Harris). In our ordinary social experience, when we do not understand what others say, we ask them to explain their meaning. Wordsworth is long dead, but we might hope that documents in which he stated his opinions survive and could provide a substitute. But obviously those documents, too, need interpretation, as does their relation to the particular poem. We quickly find ourselves in a circle. To discover Wordsworth's intention, we have to interpret texts; but that intention was supposed to tell us how to interpret those very texts. In fact, what we are doing is not moving from texts to the author's intention but widening the circle of interpretation to include more and more texts and using those we find most clear to interpret those we find most obscure. We have not discovered facts that settle the dispute; we have widened its arena.

The idea that a text must have a single, clear meaning and that interpretation should aim to state it is highly questionable, but it has deep roots in our culture. When interpreters discover that what some other interpreters say either fails to capture their own understanding or even conflicts with it, they enter into disputes and eventually ask how to resolve those disputes. But the supposition that interpretive controversies should be or need to be "settled" ought itself to be examined. Ever since its origins in the seventeenth century, science has provided some modern intellectuals with an attractive model of a discipline that seems to have an effective method for settling disputes among its practitioners. It is tempting to suppose that if we could find the right method, we could be sure of our interpretive results. Yet many contemporary philosophers of science have argued that scientific inquiry is far more complex than the traditional model allows. It seems even more evident that our understanding of literary texts is open to the whole texture and activity of our lives.

In the materials collected in *Lectures and Conversations on Aesthetics, Psychology, and Religious Belief*, the philosopher Ludwig Wittgenstein observes, "In order to get clear about aesthetic words you have to describe ways of living" (11). What we call "science," he argues, consists not just of statements of presumed fact but also of elaborated ways of disputing facts and theories and resolving disputes. To try to subject matters of religious belief or aesthetics to scientific ways of talking would be to misunderstand and distort both them and science (53–59). But, Wittgenstein suggests, science is so pervasive a force in modern life that people succumb to this temptation over and over (19–20, 24–28). He argues that both artworks and what we take to be our immediate experience of them are rooted in "forms of life," that is, in an indeterminate background of theories, convictions, commitments, practices, and experiences. Controlled experiments or tests against numerically precise predictions are not possible here, and, consequently, disagreements in these matters cannot be brought to a narrow focus that could decide between competing hypotheses.

For instance, Wordsworth wrote his poem about "Lucy" during one of the coldest winters on record in the German village where he and his sister Dorothy were living in dire poverty and studying the German language. He sent the poem in a letter to Samuel Coleridge, who speculated to another correspondent that "in some gloomier moment [Wordsworth] had fancied the moment in which his sister might die" (qtd. in Wordsworth 506–07n). Like the first-time reader I postulated, Coleridge asks who "she" is and then pursues a characteristic interest in the poet's creative process, which he locates in Wordsworth's emotional and imaginative life. Some recent interpreters take a psychoanalytic approach and say that by imagining that death has put Lucy, a symbolic substitute for his sister, beyond his touch, Wordsworth has defended himself against an incestuous wish. We might find this interpretation convincing if it seems consistent with how we make sense of human experience and thus helps us understand what the text is saying. If we reject a psychoanalytic interpretation, we do so because the Freudian way of talking no longer seems plausible—perhaps because Freud's biologism seems reductive, perhaps because we find recent criticisms of psychoanalysis by feminists cogent, or perhaps for other reasons.

Rejecting the psychoanalytic interpretation is not quite the same as saying that psychoanalysis has been "refuted." Knowing how to interpret a text means knowing what to say about it to enhance a particular audience's understanding of it against the background of that audience's whole form of life. To understand a text is to find in our own form of life points of contact with the form of life of which the text is a witness. Where no such points of contact exist, we are simply at a loss for words, and ordinary modes of arguing will not fill the gap. We can understand how believing that the dead are reabsorbed into nature could console someone, but a person who felt no grief at the death of a loved child would be unintelligible to us. Wittgenstein put it aphoristically: "If a lion could talk, we could not understand him" (*Philosophical Investigations* 223e). Because understanding is rooted in the form of our life together as human beings, differences of understanding cannot be resolved by merely applying the correct method to determine the facts. Interpreters will certainly argue and cite evidence, and no clear line separates localized argumentation within shared assumptions from the tacit background of our individual and shared ways of life. Consequently, interpretive disputes rapidly lay bare the far-reaching contrasts among interpreters' orientations to the deepest realities of human experience.

Reflecting on these issues—the variety of interpretations and interpretive disputes—reveals that in interpretation, as Hans-Georg Gadamer argues, "the knower's own being comes into play" (*Truth and Method* 491). The need for interpreting arises when a text with which we find ourselves concerned resists immediate absorption into the ongoing stream of our practical life. In this moment of our incomprehension, understanding cannot be coerced by argument or manufactured by method or technique. It occurs when an interpreter finds a responsive word through which the text speaks to us again, so that the varied meanings and force of the text are activated in new and diverse contexts. What word will accomplish this reactivation cannot be predicted or guaranteed. But our capacity to find that word is interpretation's humane significance and the reason it remains at the heart of literary study.

Suggestions for Further Reading

Hermeneutics is the term increasingly used for theoretical reflections on making, understanding, and interpreting meaning. Two philosophers, Hans-Georg Gadamer and Paul Ricoeur, provide the most comprehensive and penetrating accounts of hermeneutics available. Among their many books, Gadamer's *Truth and Method* is long, difficult, learned, and immensely rewarding, while Ricoeur's *Interpretation Theory* is a concise but comprehensive summary. Richard E. Palmer's book remains a useful introductory survey. Among recent works on literary interpretation, those by Gerald L. Bruns, Christopher Butler, Walter A. Davis, Wendell V. Harris, Susan R. Horton, Hans Robert Jauss, and Joseph A. Mazzeo grapple with the full range of issues. Davis classifies the leading concerns of various interpretive practices, gives a particularly useful demonstration of the different ways each practice would read William Faulkner's short novel *The Bear*, and then tries to integrate them within an encompassing approach to interpretation. Butler addresses the challenge to established interpretive practices from structuralism and deconstruction, as well as interpretation's relation to beliefs or ideologies, such as Marxism, that the interpreter may wish to promote. Anthologies by Gayle L. Ormiston and Alan D. Schrift and by Kurt Mueller-Vollmer provide key selections on the theory of interpretation since the Enlightenment.

Interpretive practice is as old as culture, and the history of reflections on interpretation is nearly as old. In Western antiquity, three interpretive practices dominate. Allegorical interpretation arose among the Greeks as a way of forging anew the relation between current cultural realities and the poetic and mythological tradition recorded in Homer, Hesiod, and other poets. Plato was skeptical of allegory, and yet he also practiced it in his own way. As a result, philosophical schools after Plato elaborated various techniques for making an examination of traditional poetic texts the occasion for leading students into the philosophical life. A different strand of interpretive practice arose among the Jews, whose religious life was largely conducted by the elaboration and interpretation of received religious texts. Gradually, what is called "midrash" emerged as a means of meditating on, elaborating, and debating the meaning and implications of Scripture. A third strand, which emerged among the librarians of Hellenistic Alexandria in Egypt, was carried on among teachers of grammar and rhetoric. They worked to establish texts and developed techniques for analyzing and expounding them, usually line by line, in a school setting. Good introductions to the allegorical tradition include those by Jon Whitman and James A. Coulter. Michael Fishbane is a leading scholar of Jewish interpretation. Several recent books, including those by Geoffrey H. Hartman and Sanford Budick, Susan A. Handelman, and José Faur, have discussed midrash in its historical context and in relation to contemporary theory. *The Cambridge History of the Bible* provides excellent introductory essays on Jewish and Christian interpretation and interpreters. The philological or pedagogical tradition is only beginning to be studied in depth. Medieval Christian culture absorbed all three strands and added its own complications. Robert M. Grant's survey is brief and excellent. The headnotes in A. J. Minnis and A. B. Scott's anthology provide a comprehensive short survey of medieval commentary.

The Renaissance and Reformation led to important developments in interpretive theory and practice. The scholarly resources developed for editing and expounding rediscovered ancient texts are the source of modern scholarship. The same techniques were applied to Scripture and other religious texts, with predictably controversial results. But even more important, Martin Luther rejected the practices of the Catholic church and insisted that religious doctrines be based on the Bible alone and that obscurities in the Bible be interpreted solely by reference to other biblical texts. As a result, the Reformation in its intellectual dimension largely took the form of a debate over how to understand the Bible. In the course of that debate, several interpreters came to stress the importance of the writers' original historical context. Hans Frei provides an overview of the rise of historical interpretation.

The post-Renaissance context of interpretation is defined by the emergence of a richly varied secular culture fully aware of non-Christian antiquity and of the historical diversity of cultures, by disagreements among sects that dissolved Christianity's power to provide an apparent common ground of understanding, and by the rise of a scientific and antihistorical model of knowledge. The German theologian Friedrich Schleiermacher responded most fully to this situation, and his work is decisive for modern hermeneutics through Wilhelm Dilthey, Martin Heidegger, Gadamer, and Ricoeur. Mueller-Vollmer's anthology includes key selections and has a good bibliography.

Interpretive theory was transformed, however, by the recognition that interpreters' personal and cultural interests decisively influence their understanding. Friedrich Nietzsche stressed interpreters' will to dominate texts and extract from them what served their own lives and creativity. Karl Marx unmasked the ideological distortions rooted in class and economic relations. Fredric Jameson has most fully developed a Marxist model of interpretation. Sigmund Freud analyzed the force of instinctual and repressed impulses in all thought processes. In a number of his writings, Jacques Lacan synthesizes Freud with other currents of modern thought and exhibits the results in analyses of literary works. Probably the richest synthesis of these various hermeneutics of suspicion, with a strongly Nietzschean accent, is the movement known as deconstruction. The complex and sophisticated works of its founders, Paul de Man and Jacques Derrida, offer no easy points of entry, but de Man's *Allegories of Reading* and Derrida's *Dissemination* and *Writing and Difference* contain extended examples of deconstruction in action on texts. General introductions include those by Jonathan Culler, Vincent B. Leitch, and Christopher Norris. For a contrast between hermeneutics and deconstruction, see Diane P. Michelfelder and Richard E. Palmer's *Dialogue and Deconstruction: The Gadamer-Derrida Encounter.*

University of Illinois, Chicago

Notes

[1]Translation offers particularly suggestive parallels to interpretation. See Gadamer's discussion in *Truth and Method* 384–89.

[2]Of course, critics of religion treat this claim as self-serving mystification. See Ricoeur, "The Critique of Religion" (esp. 213). Religious communities themselves frequently warn against false prophets who let personal factors distort their reading of the divine message. Moreover, since different religions take different signs to be sacred, questions arise about how a sign's authority gets established. But in the narrower sense, controversy over a religious interpretation presupposes an agreement that some particular signs do indeed express a binding divine will and therefore that the task is to grasp the message expressed in them.

[3]The richest explanation of Aristotle's insight has been given by Wesley Trimpi, who shows how the plot of tragedy stands between and mediates the abstract principles articulated in philosophy and the contingent particulars of actual life (see esp. ch. 2, "The Hypothesis of Literary Discourse").

[4]The punning etymology and the Homeric citation run afoul of modern scholarly canons, but they enable Fulgentius to synthesize Greek and Roman culture. Moreover, he relies on a Stoic view that similarities between the sounds of two words reveal connections in their meaning that are obscured by their thoughtless and merely practical use in everyday speech (see de Lacy).

[5]The distinction is already present in Ricoeur, *Freud and Philosophy* 32–36 and 506–24. The terminology had become commonplace by the time of Gadamer's "Hermeneutics of Suspicion."

[6]Thus, Fredric Jameson argues that "a Marxist negative hermeneutic" must be "exercised *simultaneously* with a Marxist positive hermeneutic" (296). He also argues that Marxism provides the "absolute horizon" within which other current interpretive methods should be situated (17). He defends interpretation and the construction of a hermeneutic against recent theories, including deconstruction, which have been critical of such aims (see 21 and 21n5).

Works Cited

Aristotle. Poetics: *A Translation and Commentary for Students of Literature.* Trans. Leon Golden. Commentary by O. B. Hardison, Jr. Englewood Cliffs: Prentice, 1968.

Barthes, Roland. "From Work to Text." Davis and Finke 712–18.

Brooks, Cleanth. "The Heresy of Paraphrase." *The Well-Wrought Urn: Studies in the Structure of Poetry.* New York: Harcourt-Harvest, 1947. 192–214.

Bruns, Gerald L. *Inventions: Writing, Textuality, and Understanding in Literary History.* New Haven: Yale UP, 1982.

Butler, Christopher. *Interpretation, Deconstruction, and Ideology: An Introduction to Some Current Issues in Literary Theory.* Oxford: Clarendon–Oxford UP, 1984.

Cambridge History of the Bible. Vol. 1: *From the Beginnings to Jerome.* Ed. P. R. Ackroyd and C. F. Evans. Vol. 2: *The West from the Fathers to the Reformation.* Ed. G. W. H. Lampe. Vol. 3: *The West from the Reformation to the Present Day.* Ed. S. L. Greenslee. Cambridge: Cambridge UP, 1963–70.

Coulter, James A. *The Literary Microcosm: Theories of Interpretation of the Later Neoplatonists.* Leiden: Brill, 1976.

Culler, Jonathan. *On Deconstruction: Theory and Criticism after Structuralism.* Ithaca: Cornell UP, 1982.

Dante Alighieri. *Literary Criticism.* Trans. Robert S. Haller. Lincoln: U of Nebraska P, 1973.

Davis, Robert Con, and Laurie Finke, eds. *Literary Criticism and Theory: The Greeks to the Present.* New York: Longman, 1989.

Davis, Walter A. *The Act of Interpretation: A Critique of Literary Reason.* Chicago: U of Chicago P, 1978.

de Lacy, Phillip. "Stoic Views of Poetry." *American Journal of Philology* 69 (1948): 241–71.

de Man, Paul. *Allegories of Reading: Figural Language in Rousseau, Nietzsche, Rilke, and Proust.* New Haven: Yale UP, 1979.

———. "The Resistance to Theory." De Man, *Resistance* 3–20.

———. *The Resistance to Theory.* Minneapolis: U of Minnesota P, 1986.

———. "The Return to Philology." De Man, *Resistance* 21–26.

Derrida, Jacques. *Dissemination.* Trans. Barbara Johnson. Chicago: U of Chicago P, 1981.

———. *Of Grammatology.* Trans. Gayatri C. Spivak. Baltimore: Johns Hopkins UP, 1976.

———. *Writing and Difference.* Trans. Alan Bass. Chicago: U of Chicago P, 1978.

Dickinson, Emily. *Complete Poems.* Ed. Thomas H. Johnson. Boston: Little, 1960.

———. *Selected Letters.* Ed. Thomas H. Johnson. Cambridge: Belknap–Harvard UP, 1971.

Dryden, John. "Essay of Dramatic Poesy." *Of Dramatic Poesy and Other Critical Essays.* Ed. George Watson. Vol. 1. London: Everyman-Dent, 1962. 10–92. 2 vols.

Eliot, T. S. *The Use of Poetry and the Use of Criticism.* Cambridge: Harvard UP, 1933.

Faur, José. *Golden Doves with Silver Dots: Semiotics and Textuality in Rabbinic Tradition.* Bloomington: Indiana UP, 1986.

Fishbane, Michael. *Biblical Interpretation in Ancient Israel.* Oxford: Clarendon–Oxford UP, 1985.

———. *The Garments of Torah: Essays in Biblical Hermeneutics.* Bloomington: Indiana UP, 1989.

Foucault, Michel. "What Is an Author?" Davis and Finke 718–32.

Frei, Hans. *The Eclipse of Biblical Narrative: A Study in Eighteenth- and Nineteenth-Century Hermeneutics.* New Haven: Yale UP, 1974.

Fulgentius. "The Exposition of the Content of Virgil." *Fulgentius the Mythographer.* Trans. Leslie George Whitbread. Athens: Ohio State UP, 1971. 119–35.

Gadamer, Hans-Georg. "The Hermeneutics of Suspicion." *Hermeneutics: Questions and Prospects.* Ed. Gary Shapiro and Alan Sica. Amherst: U of Massachusetts P, 1984. 54–65.

———. *Truth and Method.* Trans. rev. Joel Weinsheimer and Donald G. Marshall. 2nd ed. New York: Crossroad, 1989.

Grant, Robert M., with David Tracy. *A Short History of the Interpretation of the Bible.* 2nd ed. Philadelphia: Fortress, 1984.

Handelman, Susan A. *The Slayers of Moses: The Emergence of Rabbinic Interpretation in Modern Literary Theory.* Albany: State U of New York P, 1982.

Harris, Wendell V. *Interpretive Acts: In Search of Meaning.* Oxford: Clarendon–Oxford UP, 1988.

Hartman, Geoffrey H., and Sanford Budick, eds. *Midrash and Literature.* New Haven: Yale UP, 1986.

Hirsch, E. D., Jr. *Validity in Interpretation.* New Haven: Yale UP, 1967.

Horton, Susan R. *Interpreting Interpreting: Interpreting Dickens'* Dombey. Baltimore: Johns Hopkins UP, 1979.

Jameson, Fredric. *The Political Unconscious: Narrative as a Socially Symbolic Act.* Ithaca: Cornell UP, 1981.

Jauss, Hans Robert. *Aesthetic Experience and Literary Hermeneutics.* Trans. Michael Shaw. Minneapolis: U of Minnesota P, 1982.

Juhl, Peter D. *Interpretation: An Essay in the Philosophy of Literary Criticism.* Princeton: Princeton UP, 1980.

Leitch, Vincent B. *Deconstructive Criticism: An Advanced Introduction.* New York: Columbia UP, 1983.

Mazzeo, Joseph A. *Varieties of Interpretation.* Notre Dame: U of Notre Dame P, 1978.

Michelfelder, Diane P., and Richard E. Palmer, eds. *Dialogue and Deconstruction: The Gadamer-Derrida Encounter.* Albany: State U of New York P, 1989.

Minnis, A. J., and A. B. Scott, with David Wallace. *Medieval Literary Theory and Criticism, c. 1100–c. 1375: The Commentary-Tradition.* Oxford: Oxford UP, 1988.

Mueller-Vollmer, Kurt, ed. *The Hermeneutics Reader: Texts of the German Tradition from the Enlightenment to the Present.* New York: Continuum, 1985.

Norris, Christopher. *Deconstruction: Theory and Practice.* London: Methuen, 1982.

Ormiston, Gayle L., and Alan D. Schrift, eds. *The Hermeneutic Tradition: From Ast to Ricoeur.* Albany: State U of New York P, 1989.

———. *Transforming the Hermeneutic Context: From Nietzsche to Nancy.* Albany: State U of New York P, 1989.

Palmer, Richard E. *Hermenutics: Interpretation Theory in Schleiermacher, Dilthey, Heidegger, and Gadamer.* Evanston: Northwestern UP, 1969.

Plato. *Protagoras.* Trans. W. K. C. Guthrie. *Collected Dialogues.* Ed. Edith Hamilton and Huntington Cairns. New York: Pantheon, 1961. 309–52.

Ricoeur, Paul. "The Critique of Religion." *The Philosophy of Paul Ricoeur: An Anthology of His Work.* Ed. Charles E. Reagan and David Stewart. Boston: Beacon, 1978. 213–22.

———. *Freud and Philosophy: An Essay on Interpretation.* Trans. Denis Savage. New Haven: Yale UP, 1970.

———. *Interpretation Theory: Discourse and the Surplus of Meaning.* Fort Worth: Texas Christian UP, 1976.

———. "The Model of the Text: Meaningful Action Considered as a Text." *Hermeneutics and the Human Sciences: Essays on Language, Action, and Interpretation.* Trans. John B. Thompson. Cambridge: Cambridge UP, 1981. 197–221.

Trimpi, Wesley. *Muses of One Mind: The Literary Analysis of Experience and Its Continuity.* Princeton: Princeton UP, 1983.

Whitman, Jon. *Allegory: The Dynamics of an Ancient and Medieval Technique.* Oxford: Clarendon–Oxford UP, 1987.

Wimsatt, W. K., and Monroe Beardsley. "The Intentional Fallacy." *The Verbal Icon: Studies in the Meaning of Poetry.* Lexington: U of Kentucky P, 1954. 4–18.

Wittgenstein, Ludwig. *Philosophical Investigations.* 3rd ed. Trans. G. E. M. Anscombe. New York: Macmillan, 1958.

———. *Wittgenstein: Lectures and Conversations on Aesthetics, Psychology, and Religious Beliefs.* Ed. Cyril Barrett. Berkeley: U of California P, 1967.

Wordsworth, William. *Poetical Works.* 2nd ed. Vol. 2. Ed. Ernest de Selincourt. Oxford: Clarendon–Oxford UP, 1952. 5 vols. 1940–54.

ANNABEL PATTERSON

Historical Scholarship

IN A powerful essay on the "three cultures" in Germany, defined as Old, New, and Popular, Karl Heinz Bohrer entered a salutary reprimand to those who regard themselves as heralds or even observers of the "new":

> The category of the "new," advanced primarily by way of formal innovation, has constituted, ever since the emergence of an aesthetic concept of modernism, the criterion by which contemporary art is to be comprehended. As a consequence it may well suffer the fate experienced by the hare in the fairy tale who imprudently entered into a race with the hedgehog only to discover that the latter was always at the finish line ahead of him. This, to be sure, was a deceptive maneuver: the cunning hedgehog had placed his wife there, who looked exactly like him. Yet the hare failed to notice this before he died of exhaustion. (133)

Although in its tragic form Bohrer's ancient fable applies only to those driven continuously to seek the cutting edge, to be members or discoverers of yet another avant-garde, it must also more gently ironize any project such as this collection of essays, which assumes that our disciplines (the academic approach to modern languages and literatures) change so much every decade that a new description is warranted of the shape of the profession, its necessary skills and dominant assumptions.

It is my task, therefore, to consider what has happened since Barbara K. Lewalski wrote the 1981 account of historical scholarship. I define this assignment neither as replacing her broad-ranging survey (an invaluable foundation that readers of this volume should also be sure to consult) nor precisely as following in her footsteps. Lewalski herself began by suggesting what had changed since *her* predecessor, Robert E. Spiller, wrote *his* account of literary-historical scholarship: "the high walls thrown up in the 1930s to safeguard the purity of literary criticism . . . from the supposed encroachments of literary history" had "been largely demolished," and it was no longer possible simply to do either one or the other (Lewalski 53). This relatively modest statement now sounds inadequate to describe the extraordinary explosion of literary criticism and scholarship that either is, or claims to be, "historicist"; my essay focuses primarily on this phenomenon and explores developments that were only in the air or peripheral to Lewalski but that can now be seen as dominant paradigms (at least until they, too, succumb to the built-in obsolescence of intellectual movements).

Lewalski's categories of historical inquiry were still predominantly "literary." They included literary biography; sources and influences; "contexts," subdivided into scientific thought, intellectual history, theology, contemporary politics, the social milieu, the other arts; the history of literary elements, forms, genres; literary history proper, by which she meant the great summative works from Hippolyte Taine's nineteenth-century *Histoire de la littérature anglaise* to Robert Spiller's *Literary History of the United States*, produced in the middle of our own century; and, in a final category, social and cultural history. It is fair to say that the new historical criticism of the 1990s will likely be situated mostly within the territory of social and cultural history, which will have expanded to include some of the subjects Lewalski listed under "contexts," especially the role of contemporary politics and the social milieu; although the latter term, with its connotations of circles and salons, already seems misleading in relation to work on economic status, literacy and readership, women's education, gynecology, the role of the police, incarceration and hospitalization, the relation between forms of recreation and class consciousness, dress as a social code, suicide, amnesia, war memorials—to name just a few of the topics that have altered the face of literary journals. The history of the literary marketplace has become a substantial topic in its own right, and we are beginning to see how such matters as the timing and pricing of editions, the way they are marketed and reviewed, instead of being merely the fine print in literary biographies, can actually construct literary reputations and control the social meaning of works, while censorship, of course, can entirely prohibit their appearance and circulation.

It is no longer clear, as it was earlier in this century, that intellectual history is the most appropriate context for literary studies or the form of inquiry that confers the most prestige on its investigators; and while literary biographies will certainly continue to be seen as one of the greatest challenges to the scholar-critic, it is a sign of what has happened to Lewalski's categories that we can now read an essay entitled "The Biography of a Memorial Icon." In this powerful account of Nathan Rapoport's monument to the Warsaw ghetto, a story that subsumes the biography of Rapoport himself, along with the chronicle of the Warsaw ghetto uprising and its afterlife in the struggles of the Solidarity trade union with the Polish government, James E. Young demonstrates what happens when both the humanist instinct of biography and the belief that the arts must have shared principles are recharged by a reverently historical mnemonics and an international politics. Indeed, Young's declaration of his biographical aims might well serve as this essay's thematics:

> In its fusion of public art and popular culture, historical memory and political consequences, this monument demands a critique that goes beyond questions of high and low art, tastefulness and vulgarity. We might ask not only how the monument reflects past history but, most important, what role it now plays in current history. . . . For there is a difference between avowedly public art—exemplified in public monuments like this—and art produced almost exclusively for the art world—its critics, other artists, and galleries—that has yet to be properly recognized. People do not come to a monument like Rapoport's because it is new, cutting edge, or fashionable. . . . Where contemporary art is produced as self- or medium-reflexive, public Holocaust monuments are produced specifically to be

historically referential, to lead viewers beyond themselves to an understanding or evocation of events. (69, 99)

The new interest in history seems newest, and has taken on the force of a polemic, in literary studies, a phenomenon that itself requires historical explanation. As a polemic, it derives its energy from a conviction that literary texts have always been, more or less, products of their historical, social, political, and economic environments and that they cannot be understood unless one attempts to resituate them within those conditions; but for several decades such an activity, as a premise of literary criticism, had been rendered professionally taboo. This outlawing occurred, it scarcely needs saying again, during the reign of New Criticism (whose very title underscores Bohrer's point and my opening gambit). In *After the New Criticism*, Frank Lentricchia dates the demise of this powerful critical movement, with its strong taboos against going "outside" the literary text for clues to its interpretation, as already visible in 1957, when Northrop Frye produced his monumental *Anatomy of Criticism*, a great system of texts interrelated by their cultural inheritance, by the shared stories they tell; but a structuralist mythology, however itself critical of New Critical assumptions, was not itself any encouragement to find the road back to history (3–26).

That impetus had to come from an entirely different direction—from France, from another branch of structuralism, and from another discipline (a blend of philosophy with social history, but self-described as "cultural archaeology"). I refer, of course, to the work of Michel Foucault, who turned from a first, unsuccessful attempt to describe cultural change as a series of language or thought shifts, or *epistemes (Order of Things)*, to a somewhat different theory of the "discursive formations" of earlier periods (*Archaeology of Knowledge*). The concept of discursive formations implied that "history" could be restructured; it need no longer be conceived vertically as a chronological list of dates, names, and events (a model that favors myths of continuity, tradition, primogeniture, progress) but, like the new medical technology that produces images of the body sliced like a loaf of bread, could be seen rather, at any given juncture, as a horizontal system of interrelated institutions and the "codes," or discourses, that made them work. Antagonist both to received ideas he saw as repressive—essentialist theories of the individual as derived from Enlightenment rationalism, of the Cartesian cogito, of the literary author and *his* chronological continuum in the oeuvre, of influence and development—and to the actual repressions that social systems and institutions contrive against their disorderly or incompetent members, Foucault created a form of historical inquiry that focused attention on what he called "statements" and the historically constituted relations among them that make up discursive formations. A discursive formation is "a body of anonymous, historical rules, always determined in the time and space that have defined a given period, and for a given social, economic, geographical, or linguistic area" (*Archaeology* 117). Cutting across conventional disciplinary boundaries and emphasizing disjuncture and dispersion, rather than unity and coherence, as the new historical ideals, Foucault also disposed of the speaking subject "who, in speaking, exercises his sovereign freedom, or who, without realizing it, subjects himself to constraints of which he is only dimly aware" and replaced both the Enlightenment and the Marxist writer, in effect, by the "it is said," "the totality of things said" at any historical juncture (122). One of Foucault's favorite metaphors was of discourse as a web of which individual writers are not the masters, implying that history is the invisible spider and ourselves the flies. This theory (still bearing, in its notion of rules, strong traces of linguistic structuralism) has, in the end, less liberating consequences than Foucault imagined; from many sides warnings are now being issued that Foucauldian impersonalism demotes and even derides the crucial category of human agency required for any theory of social change (A. Patterson 23–24; Lentricchia, "Foucault's Legacy" 236–37; Liu 732–36); but for a decade or more after *The Archaeology of Knowledge* was translated into English, it served to authorize a free-ranging historicism that encouraged intellectual miscegenation and deregulation. All texts were now equal.

In particular, Foucault's thought inspired enormous changes in English Renaissance studies, generating what is now widely (and ironically) known as the new historicism. Initiated by Stephen Greenblatt's *Renaissance Self-Fashioning* but more thoroughly characterized, perhaps, by Jonathan Goldberg's *James I and the Politics of Discourse*, this work stresses the construction of identity as a social function within the power system of the Renaissance court (Greenblatt) or within the discursive field of the monarch's own discourse (Goldberg). Its distinctive emphases have been Renaissance theater and spectacle and, in obvious deference to Foucault's *Discipline and Punish*, the more theatrical and punitive aspects of the legal system. Some gestures were made toward breaking down the boundary between "text" and "context"; documents relating to colonial entrepreneurialism have been read like plays and vice versa; royal portraits have their own stories to tell. But, as Edward Pechter complains, the larger social implications of Foucault's egalitarianism in the archives has not effected a corresponding shift in the new-historicist account of Renaissance literary history: "For despite their protests about being open, new historicists tend persistently to fix and close their attention on the dominant institutions of Renaissance society, especially the monarchy . . . the titled or monied classes, institutions of religious authority, or male power" (296).

An important part of new-historicist polemic has consisted too, in casual attacks on what they call the "old" historicism; the latter term, however, is really a shorthand for one or both of the following: first, a particularly idealized view of Elizabethan society and literature promoted by, among others, E. M. W. Tillyard; second, a particularly naive view of "history" as an unproblematic category of the factual that can be brought to bear, with positivistic force, on literary interpretation. Actually, a crude positivism (this historical "fact" produces this aspect of a text) was less common among "old" historicists than was a laborious and sometimes contentious focus on detail; but without the historical scholarship that preceded New Criticism and, for that matter, continued undeterred during its reign, none of us could proceed very far. We rely, continuously if not completely, on the work of nineteenth- and early-twentieth-century scholars, those who patiently deciphered manuscripts and edited them; wrote the history of the early drama; and retrieved from state papers and county records the biographical, legal, and political data that pertains to the writers in whom we are, perhaps for different reasons, now interested.

In fact, the influence of Foucault and the cachet of new historicism were themselves probably only signs, rather than causes, of a more widespread dissatisfaction with formalism in either its New Critical or deconstructive phase and of some still larger shift in the *episteme* itself, caused by social and political factors inside and outside the academy. Where the impulse to a new historically grounded criticism has spread beyond the English Renaissance, it appears that the object of study has been affected by the democratization of the American university, by the impact of feminism, and, in American literature, by the United States' history of race relations. In medieval studies, as Lee Patterson argues in *Negotiating the Past*, there had been an unbroken professional tradition of historical scholarship, exemplified by such monumental figures as F. J. Furnivall (creator of the Early English Text Series) and W. W. Skeat (editor of Chaucer and Langland), whose careers would themselves repay a biographer; and for several decades the field was dominated by that brand of intellectual history established by D. W. Robertson (L. Patterson 9–39). But the appearance of a volume entitled *Literary Practice and Social Change in Britain, 1380–1530* (ed. L. Patterson) initiates the turn to political and economic history as an interpretive tool, while Gail McMurray Gibson's scrupulous documentation of the social conditions in which medieval drama was created and performed in Suffolk and Norfolk sets new standards for the critical application of guild records, wills, stained-glass windows, and carvings.

Such work not only definitively bridges the old divide between historical scholarship and criticism-interpretation but requires the development of new research skills and courageous access to previously neglected archives. For example, as Susan Staves discovered, Restoration drama, a field that had been of relatively secondary importance in university curricula, acquired a whole new range of interest when approached by way of legal history and the economics of marriage (*Players' Scepters*). To master the legal history, however, required several years of retraining. Staves's book is exemplary, too, for solving the theoretical problem of what constitutes validity in the selection of a context by the bracing application of common sense.

> The selection of cultural evidence is to some extent arbitrary. . . . If we want to know what a culture thought about authority, then politics, philosophy, drama,

> and the law seem more obvious and likely places to look than, say, agriculture and music. (xvii)

Legal history is important for Staves's inquiry precisely because it is a conservative institution, "provid[ing] clear evidence of change when it occurs" (xvi–xvii). But by the same token, if one's project is Shakespeare's *Coriolanus*, which begins with a grain riot and was written in the aftermath of the Midlands Rising, one's "context" must indeed include the history of agriculture (for grain prices in the reign of James I) and the history of popular protest (A. Patterson).

Nineteenth-century British literature has always been partially immune from New Critical dogmas, which have never provided adequate criteria for the intelligent reading of novels. Nevertheless, a new historicism has now infiltrated the study of Romantic poetry. Jerome J. McGann has demonstrated that Byron's *Don Juan* is "fundamentally an autobiographical poem which comments upon and interprets the course of European history between 1787 and 1824" (280). James Chandler and Marjorie Levinson have rewritten the story of Wordsworth's withdrawal from politics to nature, finding not so much a false consciousness as a conspiracy of silence between the poet and his earlier revolutionary self (Chandler 3–30; Levinson 14–57). And Olivia Smith, in a study of English-language theory in the aftermath of Thomas Paine's *Rights of Man*, has situated the Preface to *Lyrical Ballads*, William Cobbett's *Grammar of the English Language*, and Coleridge's *Biographia Literaria* in a context of anti-Jacobin repression. In so doing, she continues into the nineteenth century the penetrating work of John Barrell on the ideologically fraught language theory of the eighteenth century, particularly as represented by Samuel Johnson and his *Dictionary* (Barrell 110–75).

In American literature, the move to a new historical criticism and scholarship has been more closely related to the ferment over the canon. What required only a sentence in Lewalski's essay—the expansion of the literary canon, and hence of the literary histories that describe it, to include especially the writings of women and black authors—has now expanded into a considerable industry; and more that is genuinely new, in the sense of discovering unregarded writers and underexplored contexts, has been accomplished here than in the more celebrated Renaissance new historicism. Henry Louis Gates, Jr., has initiated a major series of editions of black American authors. Studies of the literary marketplace, especially as it has affected women, include Jane Tompkins's work on sentimental fiction and its female readership; Susan Coultrap-McQuin's *Doing Literary Business*; and Nina Baym's analysis of reviewing, its powers and consequences, in the antebellum period. Also directed by an impulse to canonical justice are Hazel V. Carby's account of the emergence of the African American woman novelist; Elaine Showalter's essay "Women Writers between the Wars" in the *Columbia Literary History* (ed. Elliott); and Cary Nelson's "recovery" of poets like Langston Hughes.

But not all the new historical work in American literature has a feminist or African American agenda. Cathy N. Davidson's *Revolution and the Word* explores the reading audience in the revolutionary and postrevolutionary period and relates reading practices generally to socioeconomic status; Michael Rogin's biography of Melville shows what happens when a canonized writer's story is reinserted into the political history of the author's time; Larry J. Reynolds places the literature of the American renaissance in the context of the European revolutions of 1848, showing, for instance, that the image of the gallows in Hawthorne's *Scarlet Letter* derives directly from contemporary newspaper accounts; Eric Sundquist imbricates Twain's *Pudd'nhead Wilson* in the "climate" of Reconstruction and against the "legal backdrop" of *Homer Plessy* v. *Ferguson*; Amy Kaplan's *Social Construction of American Realism* establishes a discursive formation for the fiction of Howells, Wharton, and Dreiser; and Michael Denning's *Mechanic Accents* investigates dime fiction and working-class novels in terms of the theory of culture developed by the Birmingham school out of the work of Raymond Williams.

The same ferment is evident in American literary history proper; especially the projected *Cambridge History of American Literature*, a five-volume joint product of twenty-two authors under the general editorship of Sacvan Bercovitch, and the two collections of revisionist essays that have appeared under his aegis, *Reconstructing American Literary History* and *Ideology and Classic American Literature* (ed. Bercovitch and Jehlen). The *Cambridge History* has been marked by controversy well before its appearance and has generated in the process some useful definitions of its precedecessors, as well as of the theoretical issues. In a review of Lawrence Buell's *New England Literary Culture: From Revolution through Renaissance*, James Tuttleton explaines how, in effect, the procedural decisions literary historians make are themselves historically determined. The first *Cambridge History of American Literature* (ed. Trent et al.), completed in 1921, was self-defined as a reaction against turn-of-the-century aestheticism (which the editors described as "the current finical and transitory definition of literature"), and hence it privileged intellectual history and "the nonliterary context in which our works of the imagination had arisen" (Tuttleton 2). Likewise, when the *Literary History of the United States*, a corporate project of fifty-five persons with Robert E. Spiller as editor, appeared in 1948, its agenda was to show, in the immediate aftermath of World War II, that America had become a world power with a literature commensurate with its political status. Accordingly, the Spiller *History* focused on "two great movements in our literary history"—the era of Emerson, Melville, and Whitman and the then modern moment of 1948—and, in order "to follow our writers into the actualities of American life" and to explain the national experience, it put the literature firmly in context with accounts of "politics, theology, publishing history, oratory, immigration, folklore, bibliography, business practices, etc." (Tuttleton 3).

While proclaiming the Spiller generation's approach a "bankrupt older historical determinism" (4), Tuttleton was, if anything, more dismayed by what offered to replace it; namely, the new *Cambridge History*, with its explicitly ideological agenda of eschewing consensus in favor of "dissensus" and of demystifying the myths of "Americanness," including the selection of great writers believed, since F. O. Matthiessen's *American Renaissance* (1941), to best represent it. In a theoretical essay that must have directly inspired counterattack, Bercovitch had located his best-known predecessors as participating in a "process of legitimation," to accompany the "emergence of the United States, between World War I and World War II, as the major capitalist power or, in the Cold War terms of the late forties, the leader of the Free World" ("Problem" 632). Bercovitch wrote:

> It seems to me largely a matter of history that both Matthiessen and Spiller assumed that American literary history transcended ideology: *American* because it stood for the universal possibilities of democracy, *history* because it was an objective account of the facts, and *literary* because great art was to be judged in its own timeless terms. It seems to me equally a matter of history, a measure of the dissensus of our times, that all those concepts—history, literary, American, and transcendence—are now subjects of ideological debate. (637)

When we turn from British or American literature to some of the other modern languages and literatures for which the Modern Language Association speaks, the story of historical scholarship in this past decade varies, as one would expect, from one national literature to another. In France, literary studies have always maintained unbroken links with the other *sciences humaines*. In particular, the study of *mentalités* initiated by Lucien Febvre, who founded in 1929 the journal *Annales d'histoire sociale et économique*, provided a new model for cultural history that, by also interrogating developments in sociology and anthropology, mediated between the old historicism of Hegel and Herder (a belief in a somewhat mysterious spirit of the times) and the positivism of Condorcet or Comte (a belief in a more precise and determined relation between thought and material conditions of experience, especially technological change). In the 1960s, as Samuel Kinser observes, a new generation of historians, including such figures as Philippe Ariès and Le Roy Ladurie, "stimulated by the postwar development of economic and demographic research," developed the new cultural history in "a sharply quantitative direction" (964). Yet their work has acquired vast prestige among literary scholars, and the issues it raises are at the heart of the new literary historicism. As Kinser explains, the *Annales* historians gradually displaced the history of cultural elites with "the solid forms of mass culture":

> Such history offers no more total cultural history than the history of great men and their ideas, which Febvre wanted to displace. But it did take a step toward unraveling what Febvre in *Le problème de l'incroyance* called "the most important problem" for the historian, the relation of individuality . . . to what is socially, collectively composed. . . . More epochal, however, is what inspired the achievement: a vision of culture as composed of junctures between ideas and emotions, rituals and innovations, instruments and their applications, rather than of either the ineffable insights of some special class of nations or individuals or the automatic inventiveness of materially stimulated masses. (964–65)

The *Annales* paradigm has continuously shifted, sometimes in direct response to those short-term events devalued by the *longue durée*. In May 1968 Fernand Braudel cut short a visit to Chicago to return to Paris and redefine the project on a still more interdisciplinary basis, to include linguistics, semiotics, and comparative mythology (Stoianovich 59–60).

Which is not to say that French cultural history of the past decade has been solely in the *Annales* tradition; the monarchical focus of new historicism as practiced by Greenblatt and Goldberg also has certain parallels in studies of French culture under Louis XIV. Nicole Ferrier-Caverivière's *L'image de Louis XIV dans la littérature française de 1660 à 1715* deserves comparison with Goldberg's book on James I, although in this instance the monarch's image, a concentrated cultural icon, is seen as constructed by his writers instead of constructing them; Erica Harth's *Ideology and Culture in Seventeenth-Century France*, which cites Foucault in its bibliography, considers as aspects of a single cultural formation painted and literary "portraits" of the aristocracy, the tax structure, the evolution of fictional forms (pastoral, romance, *nouvelles, histoires*, voyage narratives), Descartes's *Discourse on Method*, and the economic and colonialist implications of Colbert's Académie des sciences.

In the history of the press, always a strong suit, there has been a considerable expansion in the field of eighteenth-century publishing, especially the periodical press, some of it sparked by the bicentenary of the French Revolution. A volume of essays entitled *Press and Politics in Pre-revolutionary France* (ed. Censer and Popkin) suggests that this motivation has retroactive effect. The new interest in readership is exemplified by Claude Labrosse's work on *La Nouvelle Héloïse*, and the interest in the literary marketplace by Robert Darnton's work on the publishing history of the *Encyclopédie*, which would previously have been conceived primarily as a document in the history of ideas, not as the "business" of Enlightenment. A highly eclectic consortium of scholars in various fields is working on a grand *Histoire du livre*; the same impulse appears in Pierre Rétat's critical bibliography of the 1789 periodicals. A particularly vigorous example of the new culturalism appears in the work of Roger Chartier, *The Cultural Uses of Print in Early Modern France*, which follows the development of a print culture from its beginning through the French Revolution and includes chapters on the arts of dying; the history of civilité; the *cahiers de doléances*, or lists of grievances drawn up for the convocation of the Estates General in 1789; literacy; the *bibliothèque bleue*; and the literature of roguery. In the *Annales* tradition, Chartier insists that "culture" does not exist in some domain "over and above economic and social relations" but is, rather, the sum of all social practices, which in turn "are articulated according to the representations by which individuals make sense of their existence." This stress on representation is, in effect, the meeting place between literary-historical and "real" historical scholarship (11).

An unintended long-term consequence of the move to social history has been the erosion of the political as a category of analysis; Chartier's highly quantified essay on the *cahiers de doléances* of 1789 constantly confirms Tocqueville's opinion that the estates were not divided against one another. The *cahiers* "show proof that the bourgeoisie of talent and service and an urbanized nobility met on common cultural grounds; and . . . give expression to a determination that the peasantry had already attained, translated into a style that was not yet its own" (144). In this context, the bicentennial struggle for interpretive control over the French Revolution should also be relevant, even if primarily conducted by historians. The three-volume project entitled *The French Revolution and the Creation of Modern Political Culture* was launched in 1987 by volume 1, Michael Baker's *Political Culture of the Old Regime*. At stake is the question of whether the events of 1789 and afterward significantly redirected the cultural history not only of France but of the rest of Europe. Also at stake is the importance, among other venerated cultural treasures, of the works of Voltaire and Rousseau, the second of whom has, of course, been the subject of a strong appropriation by deconstructive critics. According to Victor Hugo, all the thinkers of the nineteenth century, "the poets, the writers, the historians, the orators, the philosophers, all, all, all derive from the French Revolution" (qtd. in Petrey 567). In the aftermath of 1989, French studies will surely continue to evaluate this claim.

Finally, one must note the appearance of *A New History of French Literature* (ed. Hollier et al.), the source for the essays by Sandy Petrey and Samuel Kinser cited above. Making the claim to novelty in its title, this volume promotes a willfully nontraditional, yet event-centered, notion of the past; dates seemingly selected at random serve as the starting points for discussion and create new miniperiods, or *epistemes*. "The juxtaposition of these events," the editors declare, "is designed to produce an effect of heterogeneity and to disrupt the traditional orderliness of most histories of literature" (xix). And, echoing in a different key the polemical tone of Sacvan Bercovitch, Denis Hollier contributes an opening essay, "On Writing Literary History," that, as well as denying the "commonly held idea that literary historians ought to belong to the same linguistic background as their object," concludes with a Foucauldian attack on boundaries other than the national one:

> Today it is increasingly difficult to draw one solid line of demarcation between the inside and the outside of a work of art; sometimes it is even impossible to distinguish between form and background. Context itself has been "textualized." . . . Literature is engrossed by what takes its place. The possibility of a history of literature is thus dependent on both literature's resistance to history and literature's resistance to literature. . . . As a result, the question today is no longer, as it still was for Sartre, "What is literature?" but rather, "What is not?" (xxv)

Such fully fledged iconoclasm is not yet to be found in the other Romance languages and literatures. In Hispanic studies, for obvious geographic and historical reasons a larger institution in North America than Italian studies, the traditional preoccupation with Romance philology has remained longer in force, due in part to the calcification of Spanish intellectual life for the forty years under Franco and in part to the centrifugal effect of Latin American studies. This is a field of such vitality, and so historically driven, whether by an interest in the conquest or in the later troubled political history, that to do it justice is impossible here, even by naming names. Where innovation has reached traditional Spanish literature, both in Spain and in the United States, it has tended to come by the route of "theory" rather than of "history." There are, however, major exceptions. The court politics of Golden Age drama, particularly Calderón's, have been explored by Margaret Greer; the picaresque in relation to bourgeois *mentalité*, by Michel Cavillac; a volume entitled *Conflicts of Discourse: Spanish Literature of the Golden Age*, edited by Peter Evans, indicates a shift in the field similar to that beginning in medieval studies; while in 1986 José Antonio Maravall, a commanding figure in cultural history in the *Annales* tradition, published no less than three studies of exceptional importance for European literature of the early modern period, one of which, on the culture of the baroque, has been translated for Anglophone readers. As written by a lonely figure of intellectual resistance to the Franco regime, Maravall's work on monarchical absolutism; on the "baroque pedagogy of violence" and on the reconception of freedom, a perspective that "abandoned the soul's interiority to project itself into the world of external action" (*Culture* 163, 171); and on the picaresque as the voice "de resignacion, de resentimiento, de venganza sin claras posibilidades" (*La literatura picaresca* 12) may be seen, in analogy to Walter Benjamin's work on the German *Trauerspiel*, as an allegory of Spanish fascism.

Italian studies in North America have been since the nineteenth century largely preoccupied with the great canonical writers of the medieval and Renaissance periods: Dante, Petrarch, Boccaccio. After World War II certain obvious historical factors—the presence of Italian Americans on American campuses, the exodus from Europe of Italian scholars, the growing prestige of Italy in postwar culture—contributed to a great increase in the number of Italian departments and a corresponding broadening of the field. The influence of Italian theorists—Umberto Eco in semiotics, Antonio Gramsci on the social construction of the intellectual—probably helped to decenter the earlier tradition of philology and aesthetic appreciation; yet the first signs of such destabilization have pointed, as with Spanish literature, to "theory" rather than history. The work of E. H. Wilkins on Petrarch's obsession with chronology has had no heirs; the *Canzoniere* has become an exhibit of deconstruction; and "history" in Dante studies refers primarily to problems of citation and literary genealogy (Barolini; Schnapp). It seems symbolic that the Dartmouth Dante project brings a new technology to a traditional task, providing an online database giving access to six centuries of earlier commentary. Ariosto studies point (though somewhat equivocally) in a different direction. Albert Ascoli's book on the *Orlando Furioso* intends to promote in its readers "a troubled awareness of the interrelated crises of faith, of politics, and of culture which cry out in the principal documents and events of Italy in the early *Cincequento*," while at the same time alerting readers to the history of Italian studies and its effects on knowledge. It was Benedetto Croce, "whose enduring influence on the course of Ariosto criticism is coextensive with his dominance of much of Italian literary study for the last fifty years," who was responsible for the construction of an Ariosto "not anguished by doubts, not worried about human destiny"; while Francesco De Sanctis assumed "that the poem refers, *avant la lettre*, to an eighteenth-century theory of aesthetics, perhaps to Kant's definition of the work of art as a 'purposive object without purpose' " (Ascoli 3, 4, 22). Yet for all its commitment to the "poetry of crisis," Ascoli's book remains an extended exercise in textual exegesis, with a modernist or perhaps postmodernist twist—allegory and history deconstruct each other: "Reference 'takes place,' but its own place is soon taken by forgetfulness and deadly repetition" (229).

Elsewhere, in studies of late-nineteenth-century or early-twentieth-century authors, the fear of forgetfulness can itself generate new historical scholarship, revisionist in a way that affects the canon. The revaluation of figures rendered problematic by their politics, like D'Annunzio, has been urgent in *Italianistica*, in what Renzo De Felice calls "una sorta di purgatorio culturale" (viii). Its echoes in France are parallel studies of intellectuals of fascist leanings, as in Alice Kaplan's work on Céline, and of resistance literature. Work on the period of the great modern wars can scarcely be anything other than historical; yet the powerful motives for pursuing it are as theoretically troublesome for the idea of literature, aesthetics, and the history of ideas as any postmodern "theory." In a collection of intensely documentary essays, *Vichy France and the Resistance* (ed. Kedward and Austin)—executed by scholars from the United Kingdom and Ireland, conceived in the Archives départementales at Mende in the Lozere, and assisted by French archivists—we can see how collaboration between historians and scholars in the modern literatures can put clout behind the word *culture*, but we can also see the limitations of that collaboration. In a critique of Zeev Sternhell's *Ni droite ni gauche: L'idéologie fasciste en France*, Brian Darling writes:

> Sternhell works at another level, in which books count for more than actions in politics. It is for that reason that so much of his book is taken up with literary analysis, seeking the political message where a Leavis may distill the moral element. . . . The history of ideas, as with the analysis of discourse, becomes a very arid exercise when it is detached from history and from "le vécu des gens." It may give some satisfaction, that the inhumanities, the tragedies, the betrayals, of the twentieth century can be explained by the writings of a handful of not excessively gifted writers. But what really is the importance of a dozen books in shaping the political life of a society? How many fascists did they make, and were they really made by reading books? (Kedward and Austin 155–56)

One would think that a postwar consciousness would have similar consequences for *Germanistik*, which is where, with Bohrer's essay "The Three Cultures," we began. For Bohrer, writing as a disendowed heir of the Frankfurt school, everything has gone downhill since 1968, and the question to be answered is "whether Europe now finds itself in its *posthistoire*" (131). A more optimistic stance is taken by Anton Kaes, in an essay on the potential of

American new historicism for extension into German literature: "we have few such studies in German or American *Germanistik*," Kaes concludes, "although they are not hard to imagine" ("New Historicism" 213). Citing only Friedrich A. Kittler's *Aufschreibesysteme 1800/1900* and his own work on representations of the Third Reich in the New German cinema, both of them using Foucauldian principles, Kaes nevertheless looks forward to, or calls for, much more of the same, especially for the postwar period. Yet one of the most commanding figures of the German intellectual scene, Hans Ulrich Gumbrecht, also a theorist of the *posthistoire* mentality in Europe ("Posthistoire"), has himself focused on the Middle Ages, on French drama in the Enlightenment ("Französische Theater"), and, most recently, on Spanish social and literary history.

But if we attribute continental drift in the academic world to real historical events, a form of causality this essay assumes to be self-evident, the possibility for significant changes will surely be in Slavic studies in the coming decade, when a *glasnost* culture in the former Soviet Union not only makes possible the migration of peoples but offers up to the new cultural historian a body of texts and facts of which we have all been too long deprived.

If I return, at last, to the field I know most about, I can perhaps formulate, empirically, a few propositions for the aspiring historical-literary scholar. When I was a graduate student writing my dissertation on Thomas Wyatt in the British Library, I was told that the way to proceed was to identify everything that had been written on Wyatt in the past and from the bibliographical notes in those books to reconstruct (and read) what those authors had read, and so on. The result was that I was always going backward into what had been known and said before, so that any possible contribution had to take the form of disagreement. All the transactions were between literary or critical texts; and although I did make some discoveries about Wyatt's Italian sources, I spent far more time than was useful on the history of English prosody as conceived by George Saintsbury and his followers and virtually none on the history of the Reformation in England or on the reform policies of Thomas Cromwell. I knew that Wyatt had adapted Petrarch's sonnet on the death of Giovanni Colonna for his own sonnet on the fall of Cromwell but not what that choice meant in terms of political history. And although Wyatt's social milieu could indeed be understood through John Stevens's *Music and Poetry in the Early Tudor Court* and commonplace books provided a very strong surviving manuscript record of how poetry was circulated, nobody suggested to me that *public* records had anything to do with my subject of inquiry. If I were now supervising a dissertation on Wyatt, I would advise a student to read only as much of the criticism as would serve to indicate the state of the art; to begin with G. R. Elton's *Tudor Revolution in Government: Administrative Changes in the Reign of Henry VIII* and *Policy and Police*; to include among the basic research tools for the early modern period in England (which in Lewalski's list were the *New Cambridge Bibliography of English Literature, British Library Catalogue, National Union Catalog, Short-Title Catalogue, Oxford English Dictionary*, and *Dictionary of National Biography*) the appropriate calendars of state papers and the reports of the Historical Manuscripts Commission; to read some up-to-date social and economic history of the early Tudor period; and, for a model, to consider Greg Walker's *John Skelton and the Politics of the 1520s*. I would urge the student to believe that new knowledge really can be found in the interstices between conventional disciplines or subfields and not to consider the task as merely describing in a more fashionable vocabulary the already known. For early British literature and history, the chronological catalogs of the Folger Institute or the Huntington Library are invaluable as tools for slicing history against the grain of a vertical chronology; they permit one to investigate what Foucault might have called a discursive formation for a decade or a year at a time; something similar can be done for the 1640s by using the Thomason Tracts in the British Library, now also available (like the STC) on microfilm.

Such advice must be capable of translation for students in other fields, whose most valuable archives will also be in process of discovery and redefinition. I would encourage students who are, like many more advanced scholars, intimidated by the task of historical research to understand that one need not necessarily learn to do from scratch the basic archival research in original documents done by historians themselves, that for a first stage it is probably sufficient to rely on the historians or to use records that are printed and readily accessible. But I would also stress that, as one's knowledge and curiosity grows, someone whose primary training is in literature can certainly do, rather than merely to call on, historical research and even occasionally challenge the historians themselves, precisely in that area of *interpretation* that literary professionals are trained to manage.

Finally, it is important to stress that the old taboos against historical work must not now be replaced by a new tyranny, in which it becomes impossible to find an audience for intellectual history, say, or the history of literary forms and genres. For if the new, lower-case historicism described above is driven, internationally, by an up-to-date humanism whose natural enemies are constraints and intolerance, then it behooves its practitioners to rephrase Sartre's question yet again: not What is historical scholarship? but, rather, What is not?

It remains only to say that this essay could not have been written without the assistance of colleagues in many places, who generously passed on their knowledge about fields regrettably beyond mine. It is, therefore, truly a collaborative project, although I would not want them held responsible for the way I have pieced it together.

Duke University

Works Cited and Suggestions for Further Reading

Ascoli, Albert R. *Ariosto's Bitter Harmony: Crisis and Evasion in the Italian Renaissance.* Princeton: Princeton UP, 1987.

Baker, Michael, ed. *The Political Culture of the Old Regime.* Oxford: Pergamon, 1987.

Barolini, Teodolinda. *Dante's Poets: Textuality and Truth in the* Comedy. Princeton: Princeton UP, 1984.

Barrell, John. *English Literature in History, 1730–80: An Equal, Wide Survey.* London: Hutchinson, 1983.

Baym, Nina. *Novels, Readers, and Reviewers: Responses to Fiction in Antebellum America.* Ithaca: Cornell UP, 1984.

Bercovitch, Sacvan. "The Problem of Ideology in American Literary History." *Critical Inquiry* 12 (1986): 631–55.

———, ed. *Reconstructing American Literary History.* Cambridge: Harvard UP, 1986.

Bercovitch, Sacvan, and Myra Jehlen, eds. *Ideology and Classic American Literature.* New York: Cambridge UP, 1986.

Bohrer, Karl Heinz. "The Three Cultures." *Observations on "The Spiritual Situation of the Age": Contemporary German Perspectives.* Ed. Jürgen Habermas. Trans. Andrew Buchwalter. Cambridge: MIT P, 1984.

Buell, Lawrence. *New England Literary Culture: From Revolution through Renaissance.* Cambridge: Cambridge UP, 1986.

Carby, Hazel V. *Reconstructing Womanhood: The Emergence of the Afro-American Woman Novelist.* New York: Oxford UP, 1987.

Cavillac, Michel. *Geux et Marchands dans le* Guzmán de Alfarache *(1599–1604): Roman picaresque et mentalité bourgeoise dans l'Espagne du Siècle d'Or.* Bordeaux: Institute d'études iberiques et ibero-américaines de l'Université de Bordeaux, 1983.

Censer, Jack R., and Jeremy D. Popkin, eds. *Press and Politics in Pre-revolutionary France.* Berkeley: U of California P, 1987.

Chandler, James. *Wordsworth's Second Nature: A Study of the Poetry and the Politics.* Chicago: U of Chicago P, 1984.

Chartier, Roger. *The Cultural Uses of Print in Early Modern France.* Trans. Lydia G. Cochrane. Princeton: Princeton UP, 1987.

Coultrap-McQuin, Susan. *Doing Literary Business: American Women Writers in the Nineteenth Century.* Chapel Hill: U of North Carolina P, 1990.

Darnton, Robert. *The Business of Enlightenment: A Publishing History of the* Encyclopédie, *1775–1800.* Cambridge: Belknap–Harvard UP, 1979.

Darnton, Robert, and Daniel Roche, eds. *Revolution in Print: The Press in France.* Berkeley: U of California P, 1989.

Davidson, Cathy N. *Revolution and the Word: The Rise of the Novel in America.* New York: Oxford UP, 1986.

De Felice, Renzo. *D'Annunzio politico, 1918–1938.* Rome: Laterza, 1978.

Denning, Michael. *Mechanic Accents: Dime Novels and Working Class Culture in America.* London: Verso, 1987.

Elliott, Emory, ed. *Columbia Literary History of the United States.* New York: Columbia UP, 1988.

Elton, G. R. *Policy and Police: The Enforcement of the Reformation in the Age of Thomas Cromwell.* Cambridge: Cambridge UP, 1972.

———. *The Tudor Revolution in Government: Administrative Changes in the Reign of Henry VIII.* Cambridge: Cambridge UP, 1953.

Evans, Peter, ed. *Conflicts of Discourse: Spanish Literature of the Golden Age.* Manchester: Manchester UP, 1990.

Ferrier-Caverivière, Nicole. *L'image de Louis XIV dans la littérature française de 1660 à 1715.* Paris: Gamber, 1930.

Foucault, Michel. *The Archaeology of Knowledge.* Trans. A. M. Sheridan-Smith. New York: Harper, 1972.

———. *Discipline and Punish: The Birth of the Prison.* Trans. Alan Sheridan. New York: Vintage-Random, 1979.

———. *The Order of Things: An Archaeology of the Human Sciences.* Trans. Alan Sheridan. New York: Vintage-Random, 1973.

Frye, Northrop. *Anatomy of Criticism: Four Essays.* Princeton: Princeton UP, 1957.

Gibson, Gail McMurray. *The Theater of Devotion: East Anglian Drama and Society in the Late Middle Ages.* Chicago: U of Chicago P, 1989.

Goldberg, Jonathan. *James I and the Politics of Literature.* Baltimore: Johns Hopkins UP, 1983.

Greenblatt, Stephen. *Renaissance Self-Fashioning: From More to Shakespeare.* Chicago: U of Chicago P, 1980.

Greer, Margaret. *The Play of Power: Mythological Drama of Pedro Calderón de la Barca.* Princeton: Princeton UP, 1990.

Gumbrecht, Hans Ulrich. "Das französische Theater des 18. Jahrhunderts als Medium der Aufklärung." *Sozialgeschichte der Aufklärung in Frankreich.* Ed. Gumbrecht, Rolf Reichardt, and Thomas Schleich. Vol. 2. Munich: Oldenbourg, 1981. 64–88.

———. "For a History of Spanish Literature 'Against the Grain.' " *New Literary History* 11 (1980): 277–302.

———. "Posthistoire Now." *Epochenschwellen und Epochenstrukturen im Diskurs der Literatur und Sprachhistorie.* Ed. Gumbrecht and Ursula Link-Heer. Frankfurt am Main: Suhrkamp, 1985. 34–50.

———. *Zola im historischen Kontext: Für eine neue Lektüre des Rougon-Maquart Zyklus.* Munich: Fink, 1978.

Harth, Erica. *Ideology and Culture in Seventeenth-Century France.* Ithaca: Cornell UP, 1983.

Hollier, Denis, et al., eds. *A New History of French Literature.* Cambridge: Harvard UP, 1989.

Kaes, Anton. *Deutschlandbilder: Die Wiederkehr der Geschichte als Film.* Munich: Text und Kritik, 1987.

———. "New Historicism and the Study of German Literature." *German Quarterly* 62 (1989): 210–19.

Kaplan, Alice. *Reproductions of Banality: Fascism, Literature, and French Intellectual Life.* Minneapolis: U of Minneosta P, 1986.

Kaplan, Amy. *The Social Construction of American Realism.* Chicago: U of Chicago P, 1988.

Kedward, Roderick, and Roger Austin, eds. *Vichy France and the Resistance: Culture and Ideology.* London: Croom, 1985.

Kinser, Samuel. "1942: The Problem of Belief." Hollier et al. 958–66.

Kittler, Friedrich A. *Aufschreibesysteme 1800/1900.* Munich: Fink, 1985.

Labrosse, Claude. *Lire au XVIIIe siècle:* La Nouvelle Héloïse *et ses lecteurs.* Lyon: PU de Lyon, 1985.

Lentricchia, Frank. *After the New Criticism.* Chicago: U of Chicago P, 1980.

———. "Foucault's Legacy: A New Historicism." *The New Historicism.* Ed. H. Aram Veeser. New York: Routledge, 1989. 231–42.

Levinson, Marjorie. *Wordsworth's Great Period Poems: Four Essays.* Cambridge: Cambridge UP, 1986.

Lewalski, Barbara K. "Historical Scholarship." *Introduction to Scholarship in Modern Languages and Literatures.* Ed. Joseph Gibaldi. New York: MLA, 1981. 53–78.

Liu, Alan. "The Power of Formalism: The New Historicism." *ELH* 56 (1989): 721–71.

Maravall, José Antonio. *Culture of the Baroque: Analysis of a Historical Structure.* Trans. Terry Cochran. Minneapolis: U of Minnesota P, 1986.

———. *Estado moderno y mentalidad social: Siglos XV a XVII.* Madrid: Alianza, 1986.

———. *La literatura picaresca desde la historia social: Siglos XVI y XVII.* Madrid: Taurus, 1986.

Matthiessen, F. O. *American Renaissance: Art and Expression in the Age of Emerson and Whitman.* New York: Oxford UP, 1941.

McGann, Jerome J. "The Book of Byron and the Book of a World." *The Beauty of Inflections: Literary Investigations in Historical Method and Theory.* By McGann. Oxford: Clarendon–Oxford UP, 1985. 255–93.

Nelson, Cary. *Repression and Recovery: Modern American Poetry and the Politics of Cultural Memory, 1910–1945.* Madison: U of Wisconsin P, 1989.

Patterson, Annabel. *Shakespeare and the Popular Voice.* Oxford: Blackwell, 1989.

Patterson, Lee, ed. *Literary Practice and Social Change in Britain, 1380–1530.* Berkeley: U of California P, 1990.

———. *Negotiating the Past: The Historical Understanding of Medieval Literature.* Madison: U of Wisconsin P, 1987.

Pechter, Edward. "The New Historicism and Its Discontents: Politicizing Renaissance Drama." *PMLA* 102 (1987): 292–303.

Petrey, Sandy. "1789." Hollier et al. 566–72.

Rétat, Pierre. *Les journeaux de 1789: Bibliographie critique.* Paris: CNRS, 1988.

Reynolds, Larry J. *European Revolutions and the American Literary Renaissance.* New Haven: Yale UP, 1988.

Rogin, Michael. *Subversive Genealogy: The Politics and Art of Herman Melville.* Berkeley: U of California P, 1985.

Schnapp, Jeffrey T. *The Transfiguration of History at the Center of Dante's Paradise.* Princeton: Princeton UP, 1986.

Smith, Olivia. *The Politics of Language, 1791–1819.* Oxford: Clarendon–Oxford UP, 1984.

Spiller, Robert E. "Literary History." *The Aims and Methods of Scholarship in Modern Languages and Literatures.* Ed. James Thorpe. 2nd ed. New York: MLA, 1970.

Spiller, Robert E., et al., eds. *The Literary History of the United States.* 4th ed. 2 vols. New York: Macmillan, 1974.

Staves, Susan. *Players' Scepters: Fictions of Authority in the Restoration.* Lincoln: U of Nebraska P, 1979.

Stevens, John. *Music and Poetry in the Early Tudor Court.* London: Methuen, 1961.

Stoianovich, Trajan. *French Historical Method: The* Annales *Paradigm.* Ithaca: Cornell UP, 1976.

Sundquist, Eric. "Mark Twain and Homer Plessy." *Representations* 24 (1988): 102–28.

Tillyard, E. M. W. *The Elizabethan World Picture.* London: Chatto, 1943.

Tompkins, Jane. *Sensational Designs: The Cultural Work of American Fiction, 1790–1860.* New York: Oxford UP, 1985.

Trent, W. P., et al., eds. *The Cambridge History of American Literature.* 4 vols. New York: Putnam, 1917–21.

Tuttleton, James W. "Rewriting the History of American Literature." *New Criterion* 5.3 (1986): 1–12.

Walker, Greg. *John Skelton and the Politics of the 1520s.* Cambridge: Cambridge UP, 1988.

Wilkins, E. H. *The Making of the* Canzoniere *and Other Petrarchan Studies.* Rome: Edizioni di storia e letteratura, 1951.

Young, James E. "The Biography of a Memorial Icon: Nathan Rapoport's Warsaw Ghetto Monument." *Representations* 26 (1989): 69–106.

JONATHAN CULLER

Literary Theory

IN *Theory of Literature*, the classic manual for graduate education in literature in the United States from the 1950s until the 1970s, René Wellek and Austin Warren wrote that "literary theory, an *organon* of methods, is the great need of literary scholarship today" (19). Forty years later, few critics or scholars would subscribe to this statement. The proliferation of theoretical writings and the importance of theory in debates about literary study have, if anything, led critics to call for less rather than more theory (although they frequently call for more theory of one sort or another). Formerly a marginal activity of philosophically inclined critics, literary theory has become a general and variegated reflection about the relation of literature to other activities and about the stakes of different ways of thinking about literary and other discourses. Once spurned as obscurantist, rebarbative, and irrelevant, theory is now criticized for its complicity with structures of patriarchal authority and its contribution to a false universalism—criticisms that themselves emanate from theoretical reflection and debate.

Institutionally, literary studies in the United States have passed from a phase where theory was something unnecessary (except, perhaps, in a department's single graduate course on methods of literary study) to a phase where every department had to have one theorist (theory became a legitimate subfield of literary specialization), to a phase where theory seems pervasive, where its existence is largely taken for granted and arguments are mounted against the hegemony of theory. But the widespread notion that theory has "taken over" literary studies in the United States since the late 1970s comes not from the number of scholars or critics who consider themselves theorists or who "work in theory" but from the fact that, increasingly, for a piece of critical writing to appear generally significant, it has to seem theoretically significant.

If such a change has occurred, it is no doubt because the character of literary studies has been modified by work identified as "theory." Three modes whose impact seems greatest are the wide-ranging reflection on language, representation, and the categories of critical thought themselves undertaken by deconstruction; the analyses of the role of gender and sexuality in every aspect of literature and criticism by feminism and then gender studies; and the development of historically oriented cultural criticisms that study a variety of discursive practices, involving many objects (the body, the family, race, the medical gaze) not previously thought of as having a history.

What seems to have occurred in literary studies—a field where critical and scholarly writing usually focuses on individual authors and particular works—is the breakdown of an older framework that supported one notion of "generality" (i.e., a notion of how a piece of critical writing becomes of general interest) and its replacement by a notion of generality as theoretical significance. It is difficult to characterize earlier notions of generality, perhaps because such conceptions are the unspoken unifying factors of a disciplinary space. One might suggest, however, that in the field of English in the 1940s through the 1960s, for example, the general interest and import of a critical study was likely to come from some contribution to raising or lowering the estimation of a major literary figure or from claims about the shape of English literary history: what belongs to the "great tradition," whether Romantic poetry is central to English literature or a detour from the main line that connects the metaphysicals to the moderns, for instance. In the 1980s arguments of this sort were less likely to be the goal of studies aspiring to general significance than were theoretical points about the operation of language, the relation between text and reader, or the political complicities and resistances of literary discourses. As publishers and their blurbs tell us, a theoretical point or claim has come to be what you aim for when you are trying to reach a broad audience in literary studies. The influential journal *Critical Inquiry*, for example, has fostered the presumption that its articles, although they may focus on particular writers, artists, or works, always have some theoretical matter at stake, for this is what makes them of general interest. The payoff is not a new interpretation of a literary or nonliterary work but, even in interpretive articles, an engagement with some recognized theoretical issue. (As a result, points of general interest are taken to be theoretical positions even if they do not rely on anything like theoretical argument.) The success of theory lies not in the number of those who practice it but in its status as the stake of work presented as of general interest.

Theory of Literature, the title of Wellek and Warren's book, suggests an account of literature's defining and distinguishing characteristics and, perhaps, of its social, ethical, intellectual, and political dimensions and uses. A good deal of theoretical writing in the 1960s and earlier did focus specifically on the nature of literature. For Roman Jakobson and the Russian formalists, the "literariness" of literature involved the foregrounding of language itself, the dependence of a work's effect and significance on its relations to other works of the literary tradition, and its compositional unity—the integration of its levels of linguistic structure and the inseparability of form and meaning (see Erlich). Writings by such French structuralists as Roland Barthes and by various Anglo-American New Critics, emphasizing the central role of ambiguity in literary language (see Empson) or arguing that "the language of poetry is the language of paradox" (Brooks 3), identify literariness with certain linguistic structures or conventions. A second approach has taken the fictionality of literature as its defining feature: literature consists of fictional imitations of ordinary or "real-world" speech acts (Smith, *Margins*). But in both cases it seems that any feature taken to define literature can turn up in nonliterary works as well, and the variety of literary works is such that to find significant properties possessed by all is exceedingly difficult. A novel—*Jane Eyre* or *A la recherche du temps perdu*—may closely resemble an autobiography, and what distinguishes them may have little in common with what distinguishes a lyric poem from a song. Given the historical variations in what has counted as literature and the similarities between literary and closely related nonliterary forms, it is scarcely surprising that, as Northrop Frye concludes, "We have no real standards to distinguish a verbal structure that is literary from one that is not . . ." (13). Research in the theory of literature has analyzed many structures characteristic of literary works, but instead of uncovering defining qualities, it focuses attention on important aspects of literature and orients literary studies toward analysis of them.[1]

Wellek and Warren called literary theory "an *organon* of methods" for literary study, but even this broad definition has grown too narrow. Today the writings that the academic profession calls "literary theory" range far beyond questions of critical and interpretive method. Ferdinand de Saussure, Karl Marx, Sigmund Freud, Jacques Lacan, Michel Foucault, Luce Irigaray, Frantz Fanon, Jürgen Habermas, Clifford Geertz, Erving Goffman, Nancy Chodorow are none of them theorists of literature, though their writings assuredly belong to "theory," as it is called.

What, then, is theory? In literary studies people have come to speak of taking or teaching a "theory course," of being interested in or hostile to theory, or of working in theory, without further specification (theory of what?). Theory in this sense is not a set of methods for literary study but an unbounded corpus of writings about everything under the sun, from the most technical problems of academic philosophy to the body in its relations to medical and ethical discourses. Jacques Derrida calls the concept of theory a "purely North American *artefact*, which takes on sense only from its place of emergence in certain departments of literature" ("Statements" 71). The genre of theory includes works of anthropology, art history, gender studies, linguistics, philosophy, political theory, psychoanalysis, social and intellectual history, and sociology. Its works are tied to argument in these fields, but they become theory because their visions or arguments have been suggestive or productive for people not working primarily or professionally in those disciplines.

The philosopher Richard Rorty gives this protean genre an illustrious pedigree: "Beginning in the days of Goethe and Macaulay and Carlyle and Emerson, a new kind of writing has developed which is neither the evaluation of the relative merits of literary productions, nor intellectual history, nor moral philosophy, nor epistemology, nor social prophecy, but all these things mingled together into a new genre" (*Consequences* 66). The most convenient designation of this miscellaneous genre is simply the nickname *theory*, which has come to designate works that succeed in challenging and reorienting thinking in domains other than those to which they ostensibly belong because their analyses of language, mind, history, or culture offer novel and persuasive accounts of signification, make strange the familiar, and perhaps persuade readers to conceive of their own thinking and the institutions to which it relates in new ways. Though these writings may rely on familiar techniques of demonstration and argument, their force comes not from the accepted procedures of a particular discipline (whether Lacan's work commands the assent of psychoanalysts or Foucault's that of other historians is secondary here) but from the persuasive novelty of their redescriptions or reconceptions. When, for example, Foucault maintains that what has generally been interpreted as a nineteenth-century repression of sexuality is in fact part of an incitement to discourse that seems to make sexuality the secret of the individuality of the individual, this hypothesis does not just make possible new readings of nineteenth-century novels and other writings of the period; it stimulates a general reconsideration of the relation of sexuality, discourse, and social control. When Derrida's *Of Grammatology* argues that classic discussions of language set writing aside as a supplement (a representation of a representation) because it instantiates basic yet troubling features of language in general, which are relegated to the periphery in order to create a conception of language and its functioning based on an idealized model of speech, his argument not only refocuses thinking about speech and writing but provides a powerful general model of the relation between terms of the hierarchical oppositions that structure much of our thought. When Laura Mulvey's pioneering article of feminist film theory, "Visual Pleasure and Narrative Cinema," shows how the cinema reproduces male voyeurism, making woman an object observed rather than an observer, this provokes not only controversy about what sort of cinematic cases are described (a particular tradition of narrative cinema, a range of cinematic genres, or the cinematic apparatus itself?) but also a questioning of the nature and effects of representation in other media as well, including literature. Or, in a theoretical project that starts from literary representations, when Eve Kosofky Sedgwick in *Between Men* studies what she calls "male homosocial desire" in English literature, describing a continuum of male-male relationships or male bonding (male friendship, mentorship, rivalry, competition for women) ranging from the homosexual to the homophobic, she encourages both literary and nonliterary scholars to study the relations between attitudes they had not previously thought related and the role of the historically contingent forms of male homosocial desire in the power relations that organize the lives of men and women.

Theory is not theory of literature, but it relates to literature in several ways. Since literature takes as its province not just all human experience—the articulating, ordering, and interpreting of experience—but the incoherences and impossibilities of experience as well, any compelling theoretical discourse will have some potential relation either to literature as institution and practice (the making or unmaking of meaning) or to matters treated in literature. Since literature analyzes the relations between men and women; the most common and puzzling manifestations of the human psyche; the effects of material conditions, social organization, and political power on individual and collective experience; and the human and inhuman dimensions of the play of language and representation, the theoretical writings that most powerfully and insightfully explore such matters will have a bearing on the workings of literature. The very comprehensiveness of literature draws theoretical discourses from other fields into theory. Or, as Leslie Fiedler wrote in 1950, when theory in this sense was scarcely imagined, "Literary criticism is always becoming 'something else,' for the simple reason that literature is always 'something else' " (564).

Theory might, then, appear to mean philosophical, psychoanalytical, historical, political, or anthropological theory that provides frameworks for the interpretation of literature. In the *Anatomy of Criticism*, one of the first attempts in North America to give a theoretical account of the domain of literary studies, Frye cautioned against the use of theoretical frameworks and categories from other disciplines, fearing that literary works would be reduced to manifestations of something nonliterary. But, in fact, one of the features shared by many works treated as theory is their discovery of the "literariness" of nonliterary phenomena.

In psychoanalysis, for example, Lacan's argument that "the unconscious is structured like a language" (*Ecrits* 234) and the rereadings of Freud undertaken by Jacques Derrida, Shoshana Felman, Samuel Weber, and others, stressing the role of verbal connections and wordplay, show the importance, in the functioning of the psyche, of a logic of signification that is most clearly observed in literary discourse.[2] Philosophical inquiry has postulated the inescapability of figurative language and rhetorical structures thought to be especially characteristic of literature: even the philosophical attempt to separate the literal from the figurative depends on concepts, such as "clarity" and "directness," that are themselves scarcely free from metaphorical qualities.[3] In anthropology Claude Lévi-Strauss identified a "logic of the concrete" at work in myths as well as in forms of social organization: the totems of the totemic systems are selected not because of their economic significance but because they are "good to think with," lending themselves to the construction of the powerful thematic polarities through which literary works characteristically organize the world—inner versus outer, day versus night, terrestrial versus celestial, and so on. Or again, discussions of the character of historical understanding have profitably focused on what is involved in understanding a story, thus taking literary narrative as the model for historical intelligibility. Hayden White argues, for example, that to describe historical narratives we must consider them as verbal fictions, whose explanatory effects depend on operations of emplotment: "By emplotment I mean simply the encodation of facts contained in chronicle as components of specific kinds of plot structures, in precisely the way Northrop Frye has suggested is the case with fictions in general" (83). These discourses, in short, make literariness not simply a property of poems, plays, and novels but a set of semiotic mechanisms that can be studied by analysts from many different domains. Critics' interest in theoretical discourses drawn from other fields has not, as Frye and others feared, led to a takeover of literary studies by linguistics, philosophy, or psychoanalysis; instead, a loose interdisciplinarity has emerged that might be conceived as an expanded rhetoric: a study of signifying structures and strategies, in their relation to systems of signification and to human subjects.

The multifariousness of theory has another aspect as well. As scholars and critics trained in literary studies engaged with theoretical writings from other disciplines, they discovered that literary modes of interpretation could enrich and complicate the discourses on which they were drawing. Consequently, these scholars began to read philosophical texts, psychoanalytic case histories, and historical documents with the attention and resourcefulness hitherto reserved for fictional and poetic writing, and their work has even come to constitute interventions in these other fields. In fact, theory courses and research projects developed in literature departments may not have the elucidation of literature as their goal at all now but may aim to show, for instance, how conceptions of the body in the Renaissance support the discourse of state power, or how images of the machine affect the discourse of the caring professions, or how structures of imperialism and colonialism affect the ways in which the national identity of colonial powers is conceived. Students of law and anthropology, but also of art history, music, classics, and even occasionally history and psychoanalysis, have increasingly taken note of developments in what literary critics call theory and have sometimes turned to it for stimulation. Rorty claims that in England and the United States literary studies have come to play the central cultural role that philosophy once played but has lost because of "the Kantian and anti-historicist tenor of Anglo-Saxon philosophy" (*Philosophy* 168), but in fact theory in literary studies seems more concretely diverse in its concerns than philosophy has been, at least in modern times.

The very expansion and diversification of theory has, though, produced resistance. The most intimidating feature of theory in the 1980s and 1990s is that it is endless: an unbounded corpus of writings that is always being augmented as the young and the restless, in critiques of the guiding conceptions of their elders, promote and exploit the possible contributions to theory of new thinkers and rediscover the work of older, neglected ones. Theory can seem obscurantist, even terrorist, in its resources for endless upstagings: "What? You haven't read Lacan! How can you talk about the lyric without addressing the specular constitution of the speaking subject?" Or, "How can you write about the Victorian novel without using Foucault's account of the deployment of sexuality and the hysterization of women's bodies and Gayatri Spivak's demonstration of the role of colonialism in the construction of the metropolitan subject?" At times, theory presents itself as a diabolical sentence to hard reading in unfamiliar fields, where even the completion of one task brings not respite but further difficult assignments. ("But you have to read Benita Parry's critique of Spivak and her response.")

The unmasterability of theory is a major cause of resistance to it. No matter how well versed you may think yourself, you can never be sure whether you "have to read" Jean Baudrillard, Mikhail Bakhtin, Walter Benjamin, Wayne Booth, Hélène Cixous, C. L. R. James, Jürgen Habermas, Melanie Klein, Julia Kristeva, and I. A. Richards or whether you can "safely" forget them. (The answer, of course, depends on who "you" are and who you want to be.) A good deal of the hostility to theory no doubt comes from the fact that to admit the importance of theory is to make an open-ended commitment, to leave oneself in a position where there are always important things one doesn't know. But this is very much the condition of life itself, especially in the realm of literature—though one function of a literary canon is to conceal this. The principal virtue of a canon, one might say, is that you know what to feel guilty about not having read. You can then either flaunt or hide the fact that you have never actually read *The Magic Mountain* or didn't get past book 1 of the *Faerie Queene* or could never abide Balzac. Today, with the canon opening or expanding in all directions to include the literatures of historically marginalized groups, along with popular literature, film, world literature, and so on, it is no longer clear what a professor of Spanish or English, much less a teacher of comparative literature or cultural studies, is supposed to know. The reach of theory vastly compounds this problem for both teachers and students, creating possibilities of anxiety about one's ignorance of philosophy or psychoanalysis or the history of the body, for instance.

Theory is not a domain one could ever master, though it simultaneously presents mastery as a goal (you hope that theoretical reading will give you the concepts, the metalanguage, to order and understand the phenomena that concern you) and makes mastery impossible, not just because there is always more to know but more specifically and perhaps more painfully because theory is itself the questioning of presumed results and the assumptions on which they are based. The nature of theory, by this account, is to undo, through a contesting of premises and postulates, what you thought you knew, so that there may appear to be no real accumulation of knowledge or expertise.

Can we say anything at all, then, about the direction or general effect of this protean and self-reflective genre? The main thrust of recent theory, diverse though it is, has been the critique of whatever is taken as natural, the demonstration that what has been thought or declared natural is in fact a historical, cultural construction. This orientation is shared by Marxism, psychoanalysis, deconstruction, and to a certain extent by feminism, new historicism, and the theoretical dimensions of what this volume calls "ethnic and minority studies." For Marxism, apparently natural social arrangements and institutions, as well as the habits of thought of a society, are the products of underlying economic relations and an ongoing class struggle, the real conditions of existence, whose effects are to be mapped. Psychoanalysis explores the extent to which the phenomena of conscious life may be produced by unconscious forces whose logic requires analysis. Deconstruction characteristically shows that the hierarchical oppositions that structure our thinking and behavior are not natural and inevitable but are constructions, ideological impositions—demonstrating this in a work of de-construction that seeks to displace these oppositions. Feminism undertakes a critique of supposedly natural gender and sexual relations, which define woman in relation to man, and an exposure of the sexual assumptions and sexual codes that have played a role in organizing every domain of social and intellectual life; exposing nature as culture is the first step in attempting to change culture. The studies grouped under the rubric "new historicism" generally attempt both to demonstrate the historically contingent character of modern ways of thinking by displaying, through striking historical documents and discourses, the otherness of other ages, and to show the frequently unsuspected political valences of discursive practices of all sorts by analyzing the role of these discourses in processes of subversion and containment. A major task of ethnic studies is to reconstruct different versions of history and culture, exposing the limitations of "white" conceptions of the world, which take as natural the marginalization of other peoples—a conception of which the idea of ethnic studies itself, as the study of the cultures of only nonwhite or non-Anglo-Saxon peoples, is a primary example.

But if the critique of the natural is a common denominator of much recent theory, it can be neither its goal nor its achievement. In contexts where certain values or modes of thought or behavior are cited as natural, the exposure of their contingent, historical character can have a significant critical effect, but the thesis loses much of its point once it is accepted. What follows, after all, from the fact that the practices or concepts of a culture are cultural rather than natural? Nothing at all. Questions about their effects or implications, their desirability, the possibility of changing them, and the efficacy of particular ways of understanding or contesting them remain open and are variously addressed by different theoretical enterprises. Thus, feminist theory debates the advisability, within various political and intellectual contexts, of positing anything like woman's nature and considers the weight to put on women's "experience." New-historicist and cultural materialist studies explore the possibility of avoiding complicity with the hegemonic discourses of knowledge and power that they seek to analyze. Theoretical writings engaged with psychoanalysis, a discourse whose authority seems linked to its implicit concern with the "nature" of "man" and possibly woman, find themselves pressed to negotiate, for instance, the relation between the cultural construction of identity and the stubborn failure of those constructions (our failure to become happily, unproblematically, "men" and "women"), without appealing to nature as if it were a solution. In general, critiques of the natural raise questions about the relation between demystifying analyses of "false consciousness" and the appeal to the experience of individuals. Accounts of the constructedness or historical character of the social body, for instance, must be placed in some relation to invocations of bodily experience, such as those pervasive in literary works.

The diverse challenges to ideas of the natural are not literary theory, in the sense of a theory of literature, but they are certainly pertinent to literature, which serves as a major site for constructing and contesting the natural, for articulating the everyday world, for bringing that world into discourse, and for celebrating, criticizing, and, in principle, displaying it as a discursive construction. Since the most general subject of the novel, for instance, is how the world is given meaning and how these meanings are variously challenged and since the lyric characteristically explores both the positing of significance in personal experience and the powers of language to outstrip experience, literature is a space that offers special opportunities for observing the construction of the natural and its exposure as a construction and thus for reflecting on the significance of both the processes of construction and the act of critical analysis.

The expansion of theory and especially of its role as the site of generality—to have general significance is to be a theoretical proposition—entangles theory with the problem of universality. Theoretical writings characteristically address such questions as the nature of "the subject" and the relation of literature to power or of speech to writing or of gender, race, and class to modes of representation. Even though a critic or theorist may be working on an issue as it emerges in certain texts of a particular time and place, the theoretical imperative encourages a rhetoric of generality if not universality. This is nothing new in literary studies, of course. The very notion of the "human" and traditional conceptions of literature as investigations of the nature of "man" have steeped literary criticism in a rhetoric of universality, but as that sort of claim to universality has been questioned, especially by theoretical writings themselves, the discourse of theory has taken on much of the universalizing rhetoric, particularly as it has become the locus of generality for literary studies. As Barbara Johnson writes, "The problem with theory is that it is appropriated by dominant groups to underwrite their own particularity as if it stood for universality" ("Moses"). Until recently, theory has been a discourse deployed largely by white males, who characteristically take themselves as unmarked subjects, presuming the universality of the most comprehensive vision they can attain. The remarkably blatant combination, in Enlightenment thought, of the universalizing celebration of "man" and the denigration of blacks and other nonwhite races as fundamentally inferior, barely human, marks the propensity of even the most advanced and apparently self-critical members of a dominant group to take the features of their own race, sex, class, culture, and experience as normative.

Arguments about the status and value of theory have been especially charged in the debates of African American literary studies. Some critics see the rise of theory as an attempt by whites, especially white males, to retain the power to adjudicate other enterprises in literary and cultural studies, so that African Americans and others must reject "white" theory to escape domination. Barbara T. Christian writes:

> I see the language it creates as one which mystifies rather than clarifies our condition, making it possible for a few people who know that particular language to control the critical scene—that language surfaced, interestingly enough, just when the literatures of peoples of color, of Black women, of Latin Americans, of Africans began to move to "the center." (55)

Other critics assert the importance of the theoretical enterprise in developing the study of black writing, defining its distinctiveness, and articulating its relations to European traditions of writing, criticism, and thought generally. To the question, "From whence does a truly empowering and comprehensive criticism of Afro-American expressive culture develop?" Houston A. Baker, Jr., and Patricia

Redmond respond that theory is "a ground on which Afro-Americanists can meet. . . . [It is] an *active* site that gives birth to expanded notions of the nature and function of Afro-American expressive cultural criticism" (225, 227). Rather than reject theory as the white man's colonizing discourse, critics of black literature may find that theory helps them define their own differences—from one another as well as from the models and assumptions that have governed white criticism. In the process, they develop their own theoretical perspectives and initiatives, which also intervene in the world of white literary criticism. Adapting theoretical discourses to illuminate black writing and criticism may complicate or modify the original theoretical frameworks by showing how the workings of this double-voiced African American tradition bear on concepts used to discuss dominant European and American traditions and by thus contesting the hegemonic assumptions of Eurocentric conceptions of literature.

In *The Signifying Monkey*, Henry Louis Gates, Jr., links the problem of signification—a central issue in American and European theory of the past century—to the trickster figure of African American folklore. Gates writes that he hopes to have "located within the African and Afro-American traditions a system of rhetoric and interpretation that could be drawn on both as *figures* for a genuinely 'Black' criticism and as *frames* through which [he] could interpret, or 'read,' theories of contemporary literary criticism" (ix). The way texts of African American literature "signify upon" one another provides a general model of tropological relations among texts, of intertextuality, which can be tested on other literary traditions as well. The goal, as Gates explains, is both to analyze black writing as effectively as possible and "to create something that is validly 'African' in contemporary literary theory" ("*Race*" 405; see also Gates in this volume).

An analogous enterprise in Chicano studies, Ramón Saldívar's *Chicano Narrative: The Dialectics of Difference*, explores how Chicano narratives expose the world they represent as the product of figurative and ideological operations. Such analysis, Saldívar argues, does not describe a particular literary tradition but reveals what has been left unexamined in canonical American literature—what these canonical writings have taken for granted about the world they represent. Thus the dialectical strategies of Chicano narrative call for critics to reconceive and restructure the major theories of American literature and culture, which have been based on exclusion. Saldívar presents theory as a discourse that, though it comes from positions of dominance, can be a powerful arm against the unexamined conceptions of that dominant tradition. A more precise delimiting of universalizing claims is a project of current work in theory.

In fact, some criticism of theory for its universalizing claims might be more pertinently considered as a debate within theory about the particularity or generality of certain problems: Is there such a thing as "language in general," or are there only particular languages? What is the relation between transhistorical psychoanalytical claims about the subject and historicist or Marxist claims about the construction of the subject in particular historical conjunctures? Do not the historicist or Marxist claims also rely on some theory of the constitution of subjects in general? When feminist theorists criticize Marxism's failure to take oppression of women seriously or to explain why that oppression persists through a series of supposedly different historical stages, and when they look to psychoanalytic accounts of the constitution of the subject, they are not so much making a universalist claim as seeking an explanation of a persistent hierarchical structure, which has transcended particular economic configurations (Rose 83–99). Often the critique of some universalizing claims or concepts of a theory does not involve a struggle between theory and its other but concerns the appropriate extension and limits of certain theoretical concepts.

At least two further points need to be made about theory's relation to universality. First, the recognition, which theory has encouraged, that all discourses, including those of theory, emanate from particular subject positions (situated in a network of sexual, racial, national, class, and disciplinary structures) does not by any means solve the problem of false universality or unjustified presumption of universality. To assert that one speaks from a partial position rather than a position of mastery and neutrality may be strategically important, but it is not a solution, for rationality itself is scarcely separable from the attempt to universalize. For a proposition to be true, it must be deemed to hold whoever is the observer. If the cat is truly on the mat, it will be so whether the observer is male or female, white, black, or brown; and if we discover that what we imagined true for all is only true for some, then the appropriate reaction is to attempt to take account of these other perspectives or conceptions by modifying our claim: acknowledging, for instance, that our description presumes the priority of the cat and that, from another point of view, the mat is under the cat. To try to correct biases, exclusions, and unwarranted presumptions is, of course, precisely the attempt to put oneself in the position of universal subject, but it seems both the necessary and the appropriate course for thought. When white bourgeois liberal feminists are told that their account of women ignores women of the Third World, it seems preferable for them to seek to correct such exclusions in future talk about women rather than to carry on as before; and feminist theory has generally sought to take this course. To try to rectify limitations of vision, sympathy, and understanding when they are exposed is fundamental to attempts to think about the world; what is oppressive is a group's belief that it has done this and its members' presumption that they function as unmarked, universal subjects.

Second, although the complaint about the universalizing propensities of theory is presented as a charge against theory, the critiques of false universality mostly derive from theoretical analyses and rely heavily on concepts developed in theoretical debates. The most far-reaching critiques of the assumptions male theoretical discourses make, for example, have often drawn on the work of male theorists. Rather than a division between hegemonic male theory and oppressed female practices, we have a division or self-division within theory itself, where theory provides the strategies and concepts for a critique of the false universalism of theory, a critique that exposes the fiction of universality as a fictional construction.

The complaint—heard more often outside the academy than within—that critiques of the presumed universality of the white male Western subject, along with other presumed universals such as absolute value and objective truth, leave us in a world of relativism where "anything goes" is frequently accompanied by calls for a return to notions of absolute value, objectivity, and the neutral philosophical subject, as though these were the alternatives to chaos. But, as Barbara Herrnstein Smith writes in a scrupulous study of these matters, the assumption that nonobjectivist thought or discourse is ineffective and leads to chaos is highly dubious:

> [T]he power, richness, subtlety, flexibility, and communicative effectiveness of a *nonobjectivist idiom*—for example, forceful recommendations that do *not* cite intrinsic value, or justifications, accepted as such, that *do* cite contingent conditions and likely outcomes rather than fundamental rights and objective facts—are characteristically underestimated by those who have never learned to speak it or tried to use it in interactions with, among others, real policemen, peasants, and politicians. (*Contingencies* 158)

Moreover, it is not that there are *new* dangers to which critiques of universality supposedly make us vulnerable; what we are said to be threatened with are precisely the sorts of things that have occurred in a world that purportedly believes in transcendent values and objective truths (and that often have occurred, indeed, as a *consequence* of some single-minded vision of the true or the good). As Smith notes, "the theoretical dominance and widespread affirmation of objectivist thought" have obviously not prevented the death camps, the Gulag, and all the other evils it is supposed to defend against (154). We do appear to live in a world where "anything goes," in the specific sense that no transcendent principles prevent it, and any attempt to persuade or dissuade others by analyzing or describing must offer reasons relevant to the particular circumstances in which participants find themselves. Even when argument and analysis do involve the invocation of fundamental rights or transcendent values, this can work only if the interlocutors see its pertinence. Attacks on relativism, frequent in popular condemnations of theory, invoke the sort of imaginary argument we used to call "straw men," such as the supposed belief that all thoughts, ideas, and texts are of equal value—missing the point that value is, specifically, *relative* to purposes and circumstances, which may be very general and widespread as well as local and particular. These attacks also fail to describe how justification, correction, and argumentation actually work in the world of discourse.

The success of theory has spawned, predictably, "antitheory theory," which has sometimes been called the "new pragmatism," an argument about the impossibility and irrelevance of theory. Theory, the argument goes in Steven Knapp and Walter Benn Michaels's "Against Theory," is based on the mistaken belief in a distinction between theory and practice. Theory is impossible because one can never get outside of practice to produce a discourse that would be something other than practice. Theory is in fact more practice. Of course the critique of a rigorous distinction between theory and practice is scarcely a conclusion at odds with recent theory. One of the continuing contentions of the sorts of theory styled "poststructuralist"—possibly the only claim by which poststructuralism can be identified and distinguished—has been that theories are caught up in and affected by the phenomena they claim to theorize. A theoretical account of political forces is itself also part of that field of forces, a political event or intervention; a philosophical theory of metaphor does not escape metaphoricity. According to Lacan, "there is no metalanguage," in that any metalinguistic statement is also language, structured by the very unconscious processes and signifying mechanisms it seeks to describe. For Lacan, the transference and repression at work in Freud's theories of transference and repression, far from invalidating the theoretical activity, are a confirmation that Freud is on the right track. In any event, the fact that theoretical reflection is a form of practice is scarcely an argument against it.

Although Knapp and Michaels maintain that their own theoretical argument against theory has no consequences, in fact it would substitute what they call "beliefs" for what is now considered theoretical argument. We have beliefs, they declare, that help us determine what is relevant, what to look for, how to proceed, and there is nothing "deeper" than belief. Beliefs, they insist, do not have grounds, do not have to be justified. A belief is just what we believe, and when we change our beliefs, it is just because we have come to believe something different: "Beliefs cannot be grounded in some deeper condition of knowledge" (738).

This might be true for such things as religious beliefs, but the various beliefs that function as principles, criteria, and premises in people's work on literature most probably belong to a structure of knowledge and argumentation. The "beliefs," for instance, that unity is a principal criterion for excellence in a work of art, that the history of the work's reception is a key to its significance, and that we should attend to the representation or nonrepresentation of gender in any discourse we are studying are not grounded in demonstrable truths, but they are not groundless either; they are connected with a history of knowledge and reflection, which is the realm we have come to call theory.

Antitheory theory starts from the recognition, promoted by recent theoretical argument, that in reflecting on our assumptions, interests or purposes, language, mental operations, or subject position, we cannot render these things transparent or get outside them; but that is no reason to abandon attempts at theoretical reflection and argument, since the world of theoretical discussion is above all one in which the writings and arguments of others enable us to perceive and to modify aspects of our own position and procedures that we could not grasp through self-reflection. The necessary incompleteness of self-reflexivity does not mean that theoretical reflection and discussion should cease.[4]

If theory is the domain of questions about how people study texts and why they proceed as they do, of reflections on the assumptions, categories, methodological frameworks, and procedures employed in analyses of discourse of various sorts, then it is difficult to oppose it, except by claiming that there is in some places a disproportion between theoretical reflection and analyses of particular texts or discourses. But, in fact, what makes criticism seem so theoretical these days is precisely the difficulty of separating theory from practice so as to expand one and reduce the other. Theoretical categories are not simply tools that, when established, can be put to practical use. On the contrary, those who study literature and the other discourses with which it is engaged find the categories put into question or modified by the operation of the discourses they are being used to analyze. To call for a greater proportion of practice to theory, then, may be a matter of insisting on the importance of allowing theoretical implications or reflections to emerge from the effects of analysis.

Literary theory is often presented, especially in introductory theory courses, as a series of schools or movements, each with some founding texts that articulate theoretical principles and then a body of criticism applying these principles to literary and other works. Thus, anthologies and surveys speak of phenomenological criticism, reader-response criticism, the aesthetics of reception, and structuralist criticism, in addition to the kinds that have already been mentioned. Such labels have some usefulness, especially in describing work of the past and in identifying sources of theoretical vocabularies, but they generally seem restrictive rather than enabling. The fact that critics do not announce, "I am a structuralist/deconstructionist/new historicist/cultural materialist," does not prove anything but does indicate that "fidelity" to a school or movement is not required. Most thinkers associated with structuralism denied at one point or another that they were structuralists, and in the first avowedly new-historicist reader (Veeser), many of those identified with the movement wrote critiques of it. A resistance to labels (spurred by the academic system's irresistible need for labels) animates contemporary theoretical discourse, which seems driven by the desire to analyze and question any apparently settled assumptions or theoretical commitments.

The more significant the movement, one might hypothesize, the more it is a site of debate, not a unified school with established principles that could be simply applied. The power and resiliency of a critical mode, one might say, is connected to the internal divisions generated by debate. Thus feminism is particularly important on the critical and theoretical scene as a space of argument about relations between gender and sexuality; about identity and essence; about relations among biological, psychic, social, and cultural forces and structures; about tradition, political strategies, and techniques of reading and writing; about the relation of film and popular culture to the construction of subjects and these subjects' use of them. The theoretically engaged historical criticism of recent years, discussed in Annabel Patterson's essay in this volume, is a particularly lively area of debate because of the clash and intersection of aggressive forms of contextualism: British "cultural materialism," defined by Raymond Williams as "the analysis of all forms of signification, including quite centrally writing, within the actual means and conditions of their production" (210); other versions of Marxism, which insist on a distinction between culture as superstructure on the one hand and the social and economic forces of the material base on the other; American new historicism, which is less inclined, as Catherine Gallagher explains, to posit a "fixed hierarchy of cause and effect" as it traces "connections among texts, discourses, power, and the constitution of subjectivity" (Veeser 37); "thick description," in the phrase of the anthropologist Clifford Geertz, which sees the culture of a period and place as a semiotic system that must be reconstructed in anthropological fashion; Foucauldian "archaeology" of discursive practices, which studies the way discourses of knowledge and the institutional practices associated with them create the objects they describe and restructure the network of power relations in a society; the study of the discourses of colonialism and decolonization or postcoloniality, which takes up issues familiar to students of Western literature and criticism but in new contexts that cast a different light on the construction of subjects, their relations to languages—local and metropolitan—and the effect of those relations on possibilities of thought and action, on the complicities of any discourse with the power that supports it, and on problems of the incommensurability of languages and cultures.[5]

A list of this sort should not be taken to suggest that there are delimited and defined "schools" here or that a piece of criticism or theory could be assigned to one category rather than another. Such a list is better seen as a way of naming positions that are constructed or adopted in argument and of indicating some of the influences that produce the questions and disagreements that animate the field.[6] What these contextualizing discourses share is an investment in references to "concrete," "particular," "specific," "material" historical circumstances, configurations, and practices—a rhetoric of particularity that they deploy in arguments about various topics: whether one can or should attempt to grasp the historical processes of a society as a whole, in a "totalizing" vision, from a single analytical standpoint; whether works of art can exercise subversive force or whether they are always co-opted by systems of power and perspectives of order; whether sites of marginality are exemplary and strategic or whether the celebration of these positions by authors engaged in critical and theoretical discourse is an imperialistic power play in the game of criticism; and whether it is appropriate to distinguish cultural and institutional superstructure from economic base and set them in a relation of causation or reflection.[7]

Anything worthy of being called a school will no doubt prove, on inspection, to be, rather, a contested intersection of diverging projects and practices. Moreover, people engaged in literary studies generally do not want to "do" Marxist or deconstructive or psychoanalytic criticism to the exclusion of other modes but characteristically attempt to find ways of synthesizing, negotiating relations, drawing on diverse insights. Considering the "state of theory," Derrida notes that "each *species* . . . constitutes its own identity only by incorporating other identities—by contamination, parasitism, grafts, organ transplants, incorporation, etc." ("Statements" 66). Seeking to deal with aspects or elements of texts (such as figure, rhetoric, gender, race, class, history, the unconscious) emphasized by other theoretical orientations, critics are led to take on and transform concepts from apparently competing discourses. Since the general theoretical imperative seems to be, Do not leave some aspect of the problem unthought or your flank unguarded, critics have a powerful incentive to find ways to deal with or at least to situate the questions that psychoanalysis or feminism or deconstruction or historicism raises. Thus, the best way to describe the scene of contemporary theory may be not as a set of competing schools or methods but as discussions of problems or issues that people are striving to cope with or resolve. This has the disadvantage of making criticism seem less quarrelsome than it is, but we too easily assume that theorists disagree because one is a "Marxist" and the other a "psychoanalytic critic." Bypassing these labels forces us to look more closely at the extent to which critics are saying similar things in different vocabularies and the extent to which they genuinely disagree. I take up six issues that seem particularly important.

RELATIONS BETWEEN ANALYTICAL CATEGORIES

The first general problem is the relation between psychic (or psychoanalytical), linguistic, and sociohistorical categories. Can one set of terms be mapped onto another, and if so, how? Is one set reducible to another? Which is "more basic"? Or is the language of depth and foundation part of the problem? Much of the appeal of psychoanalysis may lie in the presumption that it goes "deeper" than other theories, uncovering the most fundamental, hidden structures, relations constitutive of sexual identity. Historicizing and contextualizing theories frequently stake a good deal on their appeal to history as the ultimate reality. "History is what hurts," writes Fredric Jameson (*Political Unconscious* 102), although it is only fair to point out that history is also what does not hurt; what hurts (like those who have power) just has a better chance of making it into a historical narrative than what doesn't hurt. The most self-reflective contextualizing approaches demonstrate, however, that context is more text, which requires interpretation in the same way as the text one hopes to interpret by contextualizing it, so that reference to history does not escape or get "below" signifying mechanisms. Moreover, the historicizing concentration on the "local," the "particular," or the "concrete" or on "specific" practices or logics relies on a figurative operation, a logic of synecdoche, by which the particular in its most concrete particularity is charged with the greatest significance.[8]

The result of the arguments so far, it seems, has been to confirm the difficulty of sustaining the priority of one or another set of terms. On the one hand, language, gender, class, race, and the subject seem to be historical entities, susceptible to historical analysis. On the other, the faculties of the mind are the transcendental condition of possibility of any history we could conceive, and any particular history that analysis might appeal to or treat as basic proves to be a narrative and rhetorical construction. Of course, one might say that language, mind, gender, race, and history are not alternatives; we are ineluctably both in language and in history. Nor, it appears, can we escape being identified as gendered subjects or placed in some race, however defined. These are not alternatives among which one can choose, even if a process of analysis must seem to assign priority in configurations that prove unstable and contestable.

Hopes for synthesis, or at least for the discovery of meeting ground, do frequently arise here, and recently rhetoric has been the terrain of choice, since it is both the analysis of linguistic and discursive resources and the study of social uses and effects of language, contextually embedded possibilities of persuasion. Theories of history, from Giambattista Vico to W. B. Gallie, Hayden White, and Hans Kellner, have found in rhetorical and narrative structures the resources for understanding what history is; and psychoanalysis, in Freud, Lacan, and their successors, uses a rhetorical vocabulary to characterize the operations of the psyche, so rhetoric seems a possible medium of encounter. When two theorists such as Paul de Man and Terry Eagleton place literary studies within a general rhetoric, this may be a sign of a possible convergence—or else of possibilities for gross misunderstanding.[9]

"PROGRESSIVE" CRITICISM

A second major focus has been the desire of many critics and theorists to make literary and cultural criticism politically progressive. This desire has stimulated work on noncanonical writings, especially those by members of groups that have been oppressed by or within Western cultures, but it does not stop with discussion of writings whose elucidation might contribute to movements of liberation. Since the wish to make criticism politically progressive accompanies a growing sophistication about the ways in which any supposedly oppositional practice becomes part of the system it purports to oppose and may thus work to reinforce that system, the task of finding a way to be politically radical in criticism is not easy. By far the most popular way to make one's critical activity politically "correct" is by attacking other critics for failing to be politically progressive. Evaluating the progressiveness of critical and theoretical projects is, of course, a matter of considerable difficulty, even with the most celebrated works of the past where we seem to have the benefit of hindsight. Was Kant or Freud progressive or regressive? One can frequently identify certain disciplinary or conceptual levels at which innovative writings challenge received ideas and transform discursive practices, but just as surely, one can find other levels at which the transformation of a discursive practice might amount to an evasion of radical political activity.

One virtue of Ernesto Laclau and Chantal Mouffe's *Hegemony and Socialist Strategy*, which has energized this region of theoretical debate, is that it addresses the issue of a radical politics in terms that avoid presumptions of what is or is not radical. No set of concepts has a fixed political valency, but each is open to appropriation and redefinition in the process of constructing linkages and alliances that constitutes political life. Politics is the realm where there are no guarantees. And the freedom and responsibility of the subject as agent lie in the possibilities of construction created by the indeterminacies of institutional and signifying structures. It is precisely because political values and political consequences are not predictable that politics is a space of action.

The desire for a theory that guarantees political radicalism and, ideally, political effectiveness has been strong in recent years—it is among the most powerful forces driving theoretical argument. The pursuit of this goal creates a danger that criteria of political correctness which—and here is the point to emphasize—are often only tenuously linked to the actual political effects of different ways of writing and thinking about literature and culture may sometimes play a dominant role in debate, as the standard by which any analysis is to be judged. Whatever directions the radical new criticism and theory of the 1990s take, it is likely that their political effects will be characteristically unpredictable, not determined by their relation to some standard of political correctness.

REPRESENTATION

A third major issue in critical and theoretical discussions has been the nature of representation. Since Aristotle, literature has been seen as a mode of representation, an imitation of persons and actions, and theories of literature have sought to describe the relation of these representations to what they represent and the effects of the difference between them. Even explicitly "antirepresentational" accounts of literature, which deny that literature imitates action and which regard literature as a reflection on itself or on language and signification, have focused on a relation of representation—namely, self-representation.

Recently two significant developments have occurred. First, argument has increasingly focused on the constitutive power or performative nature of discursive representation (including literary representation), which often produces what it describes, as when the priest's or minister's words "I now pronounce you man and wife" bring into being the married couple those words refer to (see Austin) or when a nation, in a declaration of independence, declares itself to be the independent nation it has previously suffered from not being. What deconstructive analysis calls the relation between the performative and constative dimensions of language (de Man, *Allegories* 119–31, 246–77) appears in

Marxist and new-historicist argument as a question about the efficacy of literary and nonliterary representations: To what extent do representations simply reflect the working of other, "real" forces in society? To what extent do discursive practices create the world they represent, including, particularly, the subjects who are brought to see themselves as men and women engaged in the gendered scenarios of a culture? And if representation is performative, what effects can representations have? Debates about the effects of pornography and mass culture focus on issues such as whether representations reflect, create, or possibly deflect desires and whether and how the "artistic or literary merit" of representations is relevant to whatever efficacy they do have.

Second, there has been increasing interest in the relation between the political and literary or linguistic senses of *representation*, which come together at points such as Foucault's argument in *The History of Sexuality* that juridical systems of power produce the subjects they come to represent and regulate. Indication that the two aspects of representation may have a good deal in common emerges in questions that may be asked just as pertinently about political representatives as about literary representations. For instance, to what extent can representations or representatives be subversive of, or resistant to, the systems of power and representation in which they function? Is subversion or resistance even possible? Are representations and representatives necessarily co-opted by, and therefore reflective of, the system itself? Can they expose and subvert ideology, or do they only and inevitably produce and embody it?

IDENTITY AND THE SUBJECT

The fourth topic of debate, noted above in the discussion of universality, involves a number of questions: What is the relation between critiques of essentialist conceptions of identity (of a person or group) and the psychic and political demands for identity? How do the urgencies of emancipatory politics conflict with or engage psychoanalytic and poststructuralist critiques of the subject's identity? In what terms should critics and theorists seek to define women's writing or Chicano literature, for example? The question of identity of the subject becomes a major theoretical as well as practical issue because the problems encountered seem rather similar, whether the groups involved are defined by nationality, race, gender, sexual preference, language, class, or religion. On the one hand, critical investigations of issues of identity demonstrate the illegitimacy of taking certain traits, such as sexual orientation, gender, or visible morphological characteristics, as essentially defining features of group identity, and these investigations refute the imputation of essential identity to all members of a group characterized by gender, class, race, religion, or nationality. On the other hand, identities imposed on marginalized groups may, in turn, become resources for that group. Foucault notes that the development of medical and psychiatric discourses defining homosexuals as an essentially deviant class in the nineteenth century, while facilitating the imposition of social controls, also made possible "the formation of a 'reverse' discourse: homosexuality began to speak in its own behalf, to demand that its legitimacy or 'naturality' be acknowledged, often in the same vocabulary, using the same categories by which it was medically disqualified" (*History* 101).

These two operations—the critique of essentializing definitions and the celebration of the distinctiveness and identity of the group—frequently coexist, though not without considerable tension. The strategic and theoretical situation becomes complicated, however, when the ascription of identity that is supposed to energize a group seems, to some who are supposed to be included, to neglect or deny many of their own characteristics or most urgent problems. Black feminists have noted that feminist discussions of women may bear little relation to the concerns of black women, and Third World women have objected to conceptions of women constructed by middle-class white Western intellectuals. Christian maintains that the Black Arts movement, in asserting a black identity, in effect legislated one way to be black: "Writers were told," for instance, "that writing love poems was not being Black" (58).

But is it a coincidence that just when women, blacks, Chicanos, gays, lesbians, and members of other groups marginalized in American and Western European societies began to assert an identity, to present themselves as subjects, white male theory argues that there is no subject, or rather that the subject is a discursive effect and product of a misrecognition? Having denigrated other races for years, whites realize—just when other races are developing racial identity and racial pride—that race is a delusive trope, a dangerous fiction. Baker observes, "Hence 'race,' as a recently emergent, unifying, and forceful sign of difference *in the service* of the 'Other,' is held up to scientific ridicule as, ironically, 'unscientific.' A proudly emergent sense of ethnic diversity in the service of new world arrangements is disparaged by whitemale science as the most foolish sort of anachronism" (385). It may also be true, however, that reflection on the imperfect constructedness of identity does not so much counter the claim to identity by historically oppressed groups as encourage the postulation of identities by emphasizing that the identities hitherto foisted on groups were not natural and inevitable. If so, then the critique of identity may be less a ploy of domination than a contribution to the politicization of identity and a contribution also to possibilities of resistance to the identities leaders construct for those they would lead. Certainly the continuing argument about the power and dangers of essentializing conceptions of racial, sexual, gender, and national identity promises to influence the various shapes theory takes in the foreseeable future.

It seems increasingly unlikely that any simple solution to this problem will emerge, for work in a number of different fields—Marxism, psychoanalysis, film theory, cultural studies, feminism, gay and lesbian studies, the study of colonial and postcolonial discourse, for instance—has revealed difficulties that seem structurally similar. We find something like a common mechanism whether, with Louis Althusser, we say that a person is "culturally interpellated" or hailed as a subject, made a subject by being addressed as the occupant of a certain position or role; whether we stress, with psychoanalysis, the role of a "mirror stage" in which subjects acquire identity by misrecognizing themselves in an image; whether, with Stuart Hall, we define identities as "the names we give to the different ways we are positioned by, and position ourselves within, the narratives of the past" (70); whether we follow film theory in analyzing the way in which a subject position—that of the viewer—is produced by the "suturing" of gaps between what is represented so as to enable us to imagine a position and condition that can never be shown by the camera; or whether we stress, as in studies of colonial and postcolonial subjectivity, the construction of a divided subject through the clash of contradictory discourses and demands. The process of identity formation involves not only foregrounding some differences and neglecting others but taking an internal difference or division and projecting it as a difference between individuals or groups, as when the construction of "male" identity treats some traits shared by men and women as constitutive differences *between* men and women. Work in a range of fields seems to be converging in its investigation of the ways in which subjects are produced by unwarranted, though perhaps inevitable, positings of unity and identity—positings that may be strategically empowering but that also create gaps between the identity or role attributed to individuals and the varied events and positionings of their lives.

One source of confusion here is an assumption that often seems to structure debate: that challenges to the identity of the subject somehow foreclose the possibility of agency, of responsible action. A simple answer might be that critics who demand more stress on agency want theories to say that deliberate actions will change the world, and these critics are frustrated by the very conditions that theories are attempting to describe: a world where acts are more likely to have unintended than intended consequences and where intentions themselves are products to be analyzed. But this simple answer should be supplemented by two others. First, as Judith Butler explains, "the reconceptualization of identity as an *effect*, that is, as *produced* or *generated*, opens up possibilities of 'agency' that are insidiously foreclosed by positions that take identity categories as foundational and fixed" (147). If identity is an effect, of subject positions and of actions, then to act is to take on a role, to take up a relation to it. Butler, writing of gender identities that are constructed and of gender as a performance or an act, locates agency in the variations of action, the possibilities of variation in repetition that carry meaning and create identity.

Moreover, various traditional constructions of the subject work to limit responsibility and thus agency, to make it possible to disclaim responsibility. For example, equating the subject with consciousness (and excluding from the realm of the subject both the unconscious and the positions the subject occupies) would make it possible for agents to claim innocence, to deny responsibility whenever they had not consciously chosen or intended the consequences of actions they had committed—a dubious and self-interested limitation of responsibility. Emphasis on the structures of the unconscious or on positions ("subject positions") one occupies without choosing them or being aware of them (emphasis produced by the critique of notions of a self-possessed or self-identical subject) calls one to responsibility for events and structures—of racism, sexism, and oppression, for instance—that one did not explicitly intend. The critique of the subject thus combats the restriction of agency and responsibility derived from particular conceptions of the subject.

Kwame Anthony Appiah notes that "the whole debate over structure and agency has tended to suppose an opposition between them" but that they represent different levels of theory, which compete not for causal but for narrative space (74). A discourse of agency flows from our concern to live intelligible lives among other people, to whom we ascribe beliefs and intentions. A discourse of structure, of subject positions, comes from our interest in understanding social and historical processes, in which individuals figure as socially determined. Some of the fiercest conflicts in contemporary theory arise when narratives about individuals as agents and narratives about the power of social and discursive structures are seen as competing causal explanations. In studies of colonial discourse there has been heated debate about the agency of the "subaltern" or native (Spivak, "Subaltern"). Some critics, seeking the voice or agency of the native, have stressed acts of resistance to, or compliance with, colonialism, but they are accused of ignoring the most insidious effect of colonialism, its definition of the field of thought and action, which constitutes the native as "native." Others, describing the power of colonial discourse, are accused of denying agency to the subaltern subject. According to Appiah's argument, these different accounts are not in conflict: the natives are still agents, and a language of agency is still appropriate, no matter how much the possibilities of action are defined by the discourse of colonialism, no matter how convincing this narrative of structure and subject positions may be. The accounts belong to different registers, just as do an account of the decisions that led a consumer to buy a new Mazda, on the one hand, and a description of the marketing of Japanese cars in America and of the workings of international capitalism, on the other. Appiah's point that "there is much to be gained by disconnecting these concepts [subject-position and agency] from each other analytically" (83), by recognizing that they belong to different sorts of narratives, could do much to redirect the energy from these theoretical disputes to questions about how identities are constructed and about the oppressive as well as energizing effects of essentializing tropes of identity.

THE LITERARY AND THE NONLITERARY

Fifth, a good deal of the most interesting work in theory has focused on structures common to literary and nonliterary discourses. Theoretical writings that may be associated with different movements, such as Marxism, psychoanalysis, feminism, symbolic anthropology, linguistics, deconstruction, and so on, in fact share a concern with the problem of how far literary and nonliterary discursive practices can be described in similar terms. Mary Louise Pratt's *Toward a Speech Act Theory of Literary Discourse*, for example, undertakes to show that "ordinary language" possesses many of the features of literary discourse and that both literary and nonliterary narratives can be treated by the same models. René Girard's *Deceit, Desire, and the Novel* identifies a fundamental structure of novels that he calls "mimetic desire"—triangular desire, in which what is desired is the image produced by another desire—a structure that his later works claim is the basis of civilization itself. Edward Said's *Orientalism* studies the interaction of literary and nonliterary materials in the invention of "the Orient" and "Orientals." Moving between Rousseau's literary and nonliterary writing, de Man's *Allegories of Reading* focuses on relations between tropological structures and rhetorical force and on the political import of the relations between the performative and constative dimensions of language in these texts. Jacqueline Rose's *Sexuality in the Field of Vision* explores the relations between psychoanalytic theory and the representation of feminine sexuality in literature, political and psychoanalytic debate, and mainstream and avant-garde cinema and film theory. Above all, the examples of film theory and the growing field of cultural studies, where similar structures are discovered in a range of media and discourses, suggest that theoretical work has found its place when focused on theoretically defined problems that encompass both literary and nonliterary discourses. Those who think of contemporary criticism as a battlefield of conflicting methods miss this shared interest in connecting the literary and the nonliterary. What remains relatively undeveloped here is reflection on the implications of those differences between literary and nonliterary discourses that resist the imposition of common models.

LITERATURE AND THE AESTHETIC

Finally, an issue in recent theory is the nature and function of the aesthetic: aesthetic objects, aesthetic experience, aesthetic value. Whereas previously the value of literature had been linked to its embodiment of aesthetic values, which themselves were generally taken for granted, now not only the values themselves but literature's relation to them are subjects of debate. The first argument questions whether the aesthetic is, as both hostile and sympathetic twentieth-century discussions often assume, a realm of special objects and experiences divorced from the rest of the world or whether, as in the conception established by Kant, the aesthetic is not, on the contrary, precisely the name of the attempt to find a bridge between the phenomenal and the intelligible, the sensuous and the conceptual (Lacoue-Labarthe and Nancy). Aesthetic objects, with their union of sensuous form and spiritual content, serve, in this perspective, as potential guarantors of the general possibility of articulating the material and the spiritual, a world of forces and magnitudes with a world of value. The study of literature has frequently been enlisted in this project, as the interpretation and celebration of these special objects that will make us whole again, restore an organic society, overcome alienation of the material from the spiritual, or give us, in direct concrete experience, a special kind of knowledge.

The second argument, articulated in de Man's *Aesthetic Ideology*, concerns the extent to which literature promotes or puts in question the aesthetic values attributed to it when it is treated as a major embodiment of the aesthetic. De Man argues that literature, in the sense of the rhetorical character of language revealed by close reading, "involves the voiding rather than the affirmation of aesthetic categories" (*Resistance* 10). For example, the convergence of sound and meaning in literature—a fusion of form and content taken to exemplifly aesthetic value—is an effect that language can achieve "but which bears no relationship by analogy or by ontologically grounded imitation, to anything beyond that particular effect. It is . . . an identifiable trope that operates on the level of the signifier and contains no responsible pronouncement on the nature of the world—despite its powerful potential to create the opposite illusion" (*Resistance* 10). Literature itself raises the question of its relation to aesthetic value in various ways: on the one hand, it articulates aesthetic themes and foregrounds relations of form and content; on the other, it offers evidence of the autonomous, mechanical functioning of language, of the uncontrollable figural basis of forms, suggesting that formal structures cannot serve as the basis of reliable cognition and, in some texts, allegorically exposing the violence that lies hidden behind the aesthetic as condition of its realization.

The stakes of this discussion of the aesthetic and its relation to literature are considerable, because, as Eagleton notes, the aesthetic has

> figured in a varied span of preoccupations: freedom and legality, spontaneity and necessity, self-determination, autonomy, particularity and universality. . . . The aesthetic is at once . . . the very secret prototype of human subjectivity in early capitalist society, and a vision of human energies as radical ends in themselves which is the implacable enemy of all dominative or instrumentalist thought.
>
> (*Ideology* 3, 9)

Benjamin writes of fascism's effort "to render politics aesthetic" (241), and indeed, the leader's attempt to shape human society to a vision as the artist shapes clay, violently imposing form on matter or the intelligible on the material, takes the aesthetic as its model. Exploring the relations between the aesthetic as the model of unity and the aesthetic as disarticulation of presumed unity—and of the relation of literary works to both conceptions—is a continuing project for various sorts of theory.

But what can we say about the monstrous theoretical enterprise to a student who seeks to become seriously engaged in literary and cultural studies today?

The description of "schools" in the "marketplace of ideas" that is the American university may seem to leave the student in the position of a shopper confronted with shelves of detergents and hyperbolic claims about the superior power of each (Goes deeper! Handles the toughest jobs! Nontoxic! Brings out all the dirt of the past! Leaves no residue! Harmful or fatal if swallowed!). Perhaps, then, one chooses randomly and develops brand loyalty, or perhaps, playing the knowing consumer, buys several and tries to pick the right one for the task at hand.

The view that competing discourses are methods of interpretation or ways of approaching literary works takes each as a partial vision, more appropriate to some books than to others. To simplify: Marxism suits novels about the impact of social and economic organization on personal experience; psychoanalysis, novels whose protagonists or narrators or authors behave strangely; deconstruction, those concerned with the intricacies and instabilities of language and representation; feminism, those about relations between the sexes or about the condition of women. Such a conception of theory is more widespread than might be imagined from theoretical debates, where it is seldom mentioned. But, in fact, each theoretical discourse claims to have things to say about those works that do not thematically address its explicit preoccupations. One might even maintain that feminist criticism, for example, is especially important for works that ignore feminist issues and that the value of the theoretical orientation is its bringing to light of what is unsaid or unthought in a particular work.

We might ask, though, whether choice is not something of an illusion here, since wherever you start, if you work seriously in the field of theory, you will have to encounter the questions raised by supposedly different models and reflect on their premises as well as your own. What does this imply for students who might have hoped to choose a theory? And if you do not choose a theory, how do you enter the field, then, since it is vast and impossible to master? Not by trying to "cover" it—though such a remark may appear disingenuous in an essay purporting to present the field, in a volume that seeks, precisely, to cover the major activities in the study of language and literature. First of all, there is no "one" here, no universal, unmarked student or reader or subject, confronting an array of theories from a position of neutrality and exteriority. Anyone likely to be reading this essay already has some relation to the discourse of literature and theory, with particular interests and investments—whether as an undergraduate in Asian studies who is thinking about graduate school and wants to find out about the "professional" study of literature; as a student of literature from a small liberal arts college who has come to a university French department rife with "theory" and who feels a need to understand it; or as a graduate student in English who knows about some "approaches" but not about others. Anyone who asks how to enter the field has most probably already entered it in some way—has already been engaged by some kind of thinking about literature and culture. There are innumerable entries, and you always begin where you are.

Either of two general strategies may help you discover where you are. The first is to plunge into a theoretical discourse that seems exceedingly foreign to your prior concerns, a technique of estrangement that may both raise a host of questions not previously entertained and delimit, from a position of exteriority, your previous assumptions and concerns. The second strategy, by contrast, is to attempt to learn more about those aspects of literature and criticism that attracted you in the first place and to investigate the premises of the modes of study in which you have some experience. Since theory is initially a reflection on whatever is taken as natural, a questioning of the assumptions on which one proceeds, the way further into theory is a more critical interrogation of those conceptions of literature and discourse with which you are already involved. This may come, in particular, from a practice of reading attentive to ways in which texts fail to do what they are said to do, ways in which they resist the imposition of meanings they have been previously given. Close reading that notes resistance to meaning and observes the ways language generates thought will bring encounters with the sort of questions that are debated in theoretical texts.

With its open horizon of questioning, theory can lead you anywhere, so it is perhaps all the more important to ask where you are and what theoretical questions organize the particular region of discourses you are principally engaged with. Useless advice, no doubt, for if you ask, "What is happening in my area of literary or cultural studies today?" the answer in this age of theory may well be a contesting of divisions, the positing of new boundaries, the unearthing of new questions, and the investigation of new configurations of texts.[10]

Suggestions for Further Reading

For general reading in literary theory, William Ray's fine *Literary Meaning: From Phenomenology to Deconstruction* focuses on major theorists' treatment of meaning, producing a coherent story of the shifting relations between meaning conceived as an intentional act (of author or reader) and meaning as a textual fact, or property, of the language of the work. Kaja Silverman's *The Subject of Semiotics*, is an impressive synthesis of semiotics, psychoanalytic theory, and film theory that describes the mechanisms of signification and the production of the subject (with special emphasis on sexual difference); it also contains many brief and vivid literary and cinematic examples and can serve as an excellent advanced introduction to poststructuralist theory. Barbara Johnson's succinct, lucid essays in *The Critical Difference* and *A World of Difference*, which draw on linguistic, philosophical, and psychoanalytical theory to explore relations among literature, criticism, sexual difference, and race, provide exemplary encounters with many issues in contemporary theory. Terry Eagleton's *Literary Theory: An Introduction* is a lively overview that, interestingly, omits discussion of the Marxist theory it espouses.

Among the many anthologies of modern theory now available, two of the most judicious and comprehensive selections are Dan Latimer's *Contemporary*

Literary Theory and Hazard Adams and Leroy Searle's *Critical Theory since 1965*, which despite its title contains eighteen essays from earlier in the century. Other important collections with more particular focus are Elaine Showalter, *The New Feminist Criticism*; Henry Louis Gates, Jr., *"Race", Writing, and Difference*; Houston Baker and Patricia Redmond, *Afro-American Literary Study in the 1990s*; Gloria T. Hull et al., *All the Women Are White . . . : Black Women's Studies*; Shoshana Felman, *Literature and Psychoanalysis*; Andrew Parker et al., *Nationalisms and Sexualities*; Philip Rosen, *Narrative, Apparatus, Ideology: A Film Theory Reader*; Tony Bennett et al., *Culture, Ideology, and Social Process*, a reader in cultural studies; Jonathan Dollimore and Alan Sinfield, *Political Shakespeare*, which includes a range of examples from British cultural materialism as well as American new historicism; H. Aram Veeser, *The New Historicism*; and Cary Nelson and Lawrence Grossberg, *Marxism and the Interpretation of Culture*, the most wide-ranging collection of contemporary Marxist work.

Valuable books on particular theoretical issues include Judith Butler's *Gender Trouble: Feminism and the Subversion of Identity*, the most sustained investigation of the problem of identity and the misconceptions that surround it; Eve Kosofsky Sedgwick's *Between Men: English Literature and Male Homosocial Desire*, a study of the varieties of male bonding and their bearing on women that has stimulated work in gay studies and extended the bounds of feminist theory (see also her subsequent *Epistemology of the Closet*); Gates's *Signifying Monkey: A Theory of Afro-American Literary Criticism*; Barbara Herrnstein Smith's *Contingencies of Value*, the most thorough study of the production of value, evaluation, and relativism; Gerald Graff's *Professing Literature*, an engaging history of the organization of and rationales for the teaching of English literature in universities in the United States; and Vincent B. Leitch's *American Literary Criticism from the Thirties to the Eighties*.

Recommended readings and bibliographies for some topics are provided by other essays in this volume: for feminist theory, see Naomi Schor; for ethnic studies, see Henry Louis Gates, Jr.; for the intersection of ethnic and women's studies, see Paula Gunn Allen; for interdisciplinary studies, see Giles Gunn; for film and cultural studies, see David Bathrick; for canonicity, see Robert Scholes; for historical criticism, see Annabel Patterson.

Reflections on language have been central to contemporary theory. Roy Harris, *The Language Makers*, while not concerned with literary theory, is a smart, highly original account of the history of thinking about language. Jonathan Culler's *Ferdinand de Saussure* offers an introductory account of the work of Saussure, the founder of modern linguistics, and its relation to modern theory, and his *Structuralist Poetics* gives an overview of the structuralist movement. Roland Barthes's *S/Z* contains wide-ranging speculations on literature, especially its dependency on codes. Shlomith Rimmon-Kenan's *Narrative Fiction: Contemporary Poetics* is a synthesis of modern accounts; Wallace Martin's *Recent Theories of Narrative* surveys particular theories. Stanley Fish's *Is There a Text in This Class?* is a collection of lively essays that, taken together, narrate the rise of reader-response criticism and its fall into the new pragmatism. Robert Holub's *Reception Theory* focuses on Hans Robert Jauss's aesthetics of reception and Wolfgang Iser's work on implied readers.

In addition to Silverman, *The Subject of Semiotics*, which describes the relevance of Freud's and Lacan's theories to the analysis of discourse and the subject, Jean Laplanche, *Life and Death in Psychoanalysis*, is arguably the best initiation to Lacanian thought, perhaps because it is written as a discussion of Freud rather than of Lacan. Malcolm Bowie's *Lacan* is a fine introduction. Despite its misleading title, Samuel Weber, *The Legend of Freud*, is an acute investigation of Freud's writings as insightful examples of the mechanisms they analyze. Neil Hertz, *The End of the Line: Essays on Psychoanalysis and the Sublime*, which combines psychoanalytic and deconstructive insights with the attention to tone and attitude of the New Criticism, shows that a critic can achieve great theoretical power with only modest references to theory. Jane Gallop, *The Daughter's Seduction*, energetically explores the feminist attraction to and use of Lacan.

Derrida's *Positions*, a series of interviews, is the easiest of his works; *Limited Inc* focuses on problems of meaning and speech-act theory and contains a very useful "Afterword" that answers common questions. *Derrida on Literature* is a collection of his writings that examine literature's potential resistance to the aesthetic and social considerations by which it is usually defined. De Man's "Semiology and Rhetoric" and "Return to Philology" are useful approaches to his work. Gregory Ulmer's *Applied Grammatology* treats poststructuralism as a form of postmodern writing. Culler's *On Deconstruction: Theory and Criticism after Structuralism* takes deconstruction, rather, as a critical and philosophical orientation and seeks to explicate it as such.

The study of Third World literature and colonial and postcolonial discourse has become a major area of theoretical debate. A useful guide, with an extensive bibliography, is *The Empire Writes Back: Theory and Practice in Post-colonial Literatures*, edited by Bill Ashcroft et al. Edward Said's *Orientalism*, on the construction of the "East" by Western "orientalism" and its impact on the thinking of Eastern and Near Eastern peoples themselves, has energized this field and stimulated further studies, such as Gauri Viswanathan's *Masks of Conquest*, which argues that the canon of English literature was, to a considerable extent, devised for the education and "civilization" of colonial peoples. See, in addition, the works listed in note 5.

William Dowling's *Jameson, Althusser, Marx* situates and explicates Fredric Jameson's influential *Political Unconscious* but not Jameson's important later work, *Postmodernism; or, The Cultural Logic of Late Capitalism*. The other Marxist theorist who has been crucial to contemporary theory is Louis Althusser, whose "Ideology and Ideological State Apparatuses" is collected in *Lenin and Philosophy*. Two studies of special interest are John Frow's *Marxism and Literary History*, which puts forward a sophisticated program, and Michael Sprinker's *Imaginary Relations*, which develops an Althusserian perspective on aesthetic activity.

For new historicism, in addition to the works of Stephen J. Greenblatt (*Renaissance Self-Fashioning, Shakespearean Negotiations*, and *Learning to Curse*) and the anthologies edited by Veeser and by Dollimore and Sinfield listed above, see Marjorie Levinson's contributions to *Rethinking Historicism*, which are among the most penetrating reflections on the mode. Michel Foucault's *L'ordre du discours*, an excellent introduction to his work, has been incompetently translated as "The Discourse on Language"; it should be read in the version by Ian McLeod ("The Order of Discourse") in Robert Young's *Untying the Text*. *The History of Sexuality* has been the most influential of Foucault's late works.

Among the important journals in literary theory are *Critical Inquiry, Diacritics, Genders, New Literary History, Representations*, and *Textual Practice*.

Cornell University

Notes

[1]For the attempt to define literariness in linguistic terms, see Jakobson 62–94 and Culler, *Structuralist Poetics* 55–74, 89–90, 113–37, 161–88. For advantages and disadvantages of this approach and the approach through fictionality, see Angenot 31–43; Pratt; and Smith, *Margins*.

[2]See Lacan's "Seminar," which has been reprinted with many supplementary discussions in Muller and Richardson. In addition to Derrida's commentary therein, see his "To Speculate—On Freud" and Felman's classic "Turning the Screw of Interpretation".

[3]See, for example, Derrida, "White Mythology," and, for discussion of some philosophical attempts at purification, de Man, "Epistemology."

[4]Distinguishing "theoretical arguments of the purest sort, deriving from a reflection on . . . concepts" from a posteriori explorations of how concepts function in discursive, psychological, and institutional situations, Appiah notes that, paradoxically, "it is the anti-theory Michaels who is, along with Stanley Fish, most clearly committed to the most theoretical line of argument" (72).

[5]For work in this growing field, see Anderson, Bhabha, Brantlinger, Chinweizu, Fernández Retamar, JanMohammed, JanMohammed and Lloyd, Miller, Mudimbe, Ngugi, Said, Spivak, Viswanathan, and the guide by Ashcroft et al.

[6]Important works and collections in this area include those by Dollimore and Sinfield, Foucault (*History*), Geertz, Greenblatt, and Nelson and Grossberg; for debate on the issues mentioned, see, for example, Cohen, Gallagher, Levinson et al., Porter, and the essays in Veeser. For further references, consult Patterson's essay in this volume.

[7]There is a certain historical irony in the fact that contextualizing theories have become popular just at the moment when the globalization of electronic media has made it normal and predictable that many cultural products, films and television programs especially, are being consumed outside of their original context.

[8]For reflections on the problem of the particular or the detail, see Liu and Schor. Schor writes, "The truth value of the detail is anything but assured. As the guarantor of meaning, the detail is for that very reason constantly threatened by falsification" (7). For the developing investigation of the problem of the exemplarity of the "example," see Caruth; Derrida, "Parergon"; Lloyd; and Warminski 95–111, 150–62, 174–79.

[9]See de Man, "Semiology and Rhetoric," and Eagleton, *Literary Theory* 205–10.

[10]I am much indebted to friends and colleagues—Ellen Burt, Cathy Caruth, Cynthia Chase, Walter Cohen, Henry Louis Gates, Jr., Gerald Graff, Barbara Johnson, Andrew Parker, Shirley Samuels, Mark Seltzer, and Hortense Spillers—as well as to several anonymous readers, who commented on this essay at various stages in its production.

Works Cited

Adams, Hazard, and Leroy Searle, eds. *Critical Theory since 1965.* Tallahassee: Florida State UP, 1986.

Althusser, Louis. "Ideology and Ideological State Apparatuses." *Lenin and Philosophy.* Trans. Ben Brewster. London: New Left, 1971. 127–86.

Anderson, Benedict. *Imagined Communities: Reflections on the Origin and Spread of Nationalism.* London: Verso, 1983.

Angenot, Marc, et al., eds. *Théorie littéraire.* Paris: PUF, 1989.

Appiah, Kwame Anthony. "Tolerable Falsehoods: Agency and the Interests of Theory." *The Consequences of Theory.* Ed. Jonathan Arac and Barbara Johnson. Baltimore: Johns Hopkins UP, 1991. 63–90.

Ashcroft, Bill, et al., eds. *The Empire Writes Back: Theory and Practice in Post-colonial Literatures.* London: Routledge, 1989.

Austin, J. L. *How to Do Things with Words.* Ed. J. O. Urmsson and Marina Sbisa. Cambridge: Harvard UP, 1975.

Baker, Houston A., Jr. "Caliban's Triple Play." Gates, *"Race," Writing, and Difference* 381–95.

Baker, Houston A., Jr., and Patricia Redmond, eds. *Afro-American Literary Study in the 1990s.* Chicago: U of Chicago P, 1989.

Barthes, Roland. *S/Z.* Trans. Richard Miller. New York: Hill, 1974.

Benjamin, Walter. *Illuminations: Essays and Reflections.* Ed. Hannah Arendt. Trans. Harry Zohn. New York: Schocken, 1968.

Bennett, Tony, et al., eds. *Culture, Ideology, and Social Process.* London: Batsford, 1981.

Bhabha, Homi, ed. *Nation and Narration.* New York: Routledge, 1990.

Bowie, Malcolm. *Lacan.* Cambridge: Harvard UP, 1991.

Brantlinger, Patrick. *Rule of Darkness: British Literature and Imperialism, 1830–1914.* Ithaca: Cornell UP, 1988.

Brooks, Cleanth. *The Well Wrought Urn: Studies in the Structure of Poetry.* New York: Harcourt, 1947.

Butler, Judith. *Gender Trouble: Feminism and the Subversion of Identity.* New York: Routledge, 1990.

Caruth, Cathy. "The Force of Example: Kant's Symbols." *Yale French Studies* 74 (1988): 17–38.

Chinweizu et al. *Towards the Decolonization of African Literature.* London: KPI, 1985.

Christian, Barbara T. "The Race for Theory." *Cultural Critique* 6 (1987): 51–63.

Cohen, Walter. "Political Criticism of Shakespeare." *Shakespeare Reproduced: The Text in History and Ideology.* Ed. Jean Howard and Maureen O'Connor. New York: Methuen, 1987. 18–46.

Culler, Jonathan. *Ferdinand de Saussure.* Rev. ed. Ithaca: Cornell UP, 1986.

———. *On Deconstruction: Theory and Criticism after Structuralism.* Ithaca: Cornell UP, 1982.

———. *Structuralist Poetics: Structuralism, Linguistics, and the Study of Literature.* Ithaca: Cornell UP, 1976.

de Man, Paul. *Aesthetic Ideology.* Ed. Andrzej Warminski. Minneapolis: U of Minnesota P, 1992.

———. *Allegories of Reading: Figural Language in Rousseau, Nietzsche, Rilke, and Proust.* New Haven: Yale UP, 1979.

———. "The Epistemology of Metaphor." *Critical Inquiry* 5 (1978): 13–30.

———. *The Resistance to Theory.* Minneapolis: U of Minnesota P, 1986.

———. "The Return to Philology." de Man, *Resistance* 21–26.

———. "Semiology and Rhetoric." de Man, *Allegories* 3–19.

Derrida, Jacques. *Derrida on Literature: Selected Writings of Jacques Derrida on Literary Texts.* Ed. Derek Attridge. New York: Routledge, 1991.

———. *Limited Inc.* Trans. Samuel Weber and Alan Bass. Rev. ed. Evanston: Northwestern UP, 1988.

———. *Of Grammatology.* Trans. Gayatri C. Spivak. Baltimore: Johns Hopkins UP, 1976.

———. "Parergon." *The Truth in Painting.* Trans. Geoffrey Bennington and Ian McLeod. Chicago: U of Chicago P, 1987. 52–110.

———. *Positions.* Trans. Alan Bass. Chicago: U of Chicago P, 1982.

———. "Some Statements and Truisms about Neologisms, Newisms, Postisms, Parasitisms, and Other Small Seismisms." *The States of "Theory": History, Art, and Critical Discourse.* Ed. David Carroll. New York: Columbia UP, 1990. 62–94.

———. "To Speculate—On Freud." *The Post Card: From Socrates to Freud and Beyond.* Trans. Alan Bass. Chicago: U of Chicago P, 1987. 257–409.

———. "White Mythology." *Margins of Philosophy.* Trans. Alan Bass. Chicago: U of Chicago P, 1983. 207–72.

Dollimore, Jonathan, and Alan Sinfield, eds. *Political Shakespeare: New Essays in Cultural Materialism.* Manchester: Manchester UP, 1985.

Dowling, William. *Jameson, Althusser, Marx: An Introduction to* The Political Unconscious. Ithaca: Cornell UP, 1984.

Eagleton, Terry. *The Ideology of the Aesthetic.* Oxford: Blackwell, 1990.

———. *Literary Theory: An Introduction.* Minneapolis: U of Minnesota P, 1983.

Empson, William. *Seven Types of Ambiguity.* 1930. Harmondsworth, Eng.: Penguin, 1961.

Erlich, Victor. *Russian Formalism: History-Doctrine.* 3rd ed. New Haven: Yale UP, 1981.

Felman, Shoshana, ed. *Literature and Psychoanalysis: The Question of Reading Otherwise.* Baltimore: Johns Hopkins UP, 1982.

———. "Turning the Screw of Interpretation." Felman, *Literature* 94–207.

Fernández Retamar, Roberto. *Caliban and Other Essays.* Trans. Edward Baker. Minneapolis: U of Minnesota P, 1989.

Fiedler, Leslie. "Towards an Amateur Criticism." *Kenyon Review* 12 (1950): 560–71.

Fish, Stanley. *Is There a Text in This Class? The Authority of Interpretive Communities.* Cambridge: Harvard UP, 1980.

Foucault, Michel. *The History of Sexuality.* Trans. Robert Hurley. Vol. 1. New York: Pantheon, 1980.

———. "The Order of Discourse." Trans. Ian McLeod. *Untying the Text: A Post-structuralist Reader.* Ed. Robert Young. London: Routledge, 1981. 48–77.

Frow, John. *Marxism and Literary History.* Cambridge: Harvard UP, 1986.

Frye, Northrop. *Anatomy of Criticism: Four Essays.* Princeton: Princeton UP, 1957.

Gallagher, Catherine. "Marxism and the New Historicism." Veeser 37–48.

Gallie, W. B. *Philosophy and Historical Understanding.* London: Chatto, 1964.

Gallop, Jane. *The Daughter's Seduction: Feminism and Psychoanalysis.* Ithaca: Cornell UP, 1982.

Gates, Henry Louis, Jr., ed. *"Race," Writing, and Difference.* Chicago: U of Chicago P, 1986.

———. *The Signifying Monkey: A Theory of Afro-American Literary Criticism.* New York: Oxford UP, 1988.

Geertz, Clifford. *Local Knowledge: Further Essays in Interpretive Anthropology.* New York: Basic, 1983.

Girard, René. *Deceit, Desire, and the Novel: Self and Other in Literary Structure.* Trans. Yvonne Freccero. Baltimore: Johns Hopkins UP, 1965.

Graff, Gerald. *Professing Literature: An Institutional History.* Chicago: U of Chicago P, 1987.

Greenblatt, Stephen J. *Learning to Curse: Essays on Early Modern Culture.* New York: Routledge, 1990.

———. *Renaissance Self-Fashioning: From More to Shakespeare.* Chicago: U of Chicago P, 1980.

———. *Shakespearean Negotiations: The Circulation of Social Energy in Renaissance England.* Berkeley: U of California P, 1988.

Hall, Stuart. "Cultural Identity and Cinematic Representation." *Framework* 36 (1987): 68–81.

Harris, Roy. *The Language Makers.* Ithaca: Cornell UP, 1980.

Hertz, Neil. *The End of the Line: Essays on Psychoanalysis and the Sublime.* New York: Columbia UP, 1985.

Holub, Robert. *Reception Theory: A Critical Introduction.* London: Methuen, 1984.

Hull, Gloria T., et al. *All the Women Are White, All the Blacks Are Men, but Some of Us Are Brave: Black Women's Studies.* Old Westbury: Feminist, 1982.

Jakobson, Roman. *Language in Literature.* Ed. Krystyna Pomorska and Stephen Rudy. Cambridge: Harvard UP, 1987.

Jameson, Fredric. *The Political Unconscious: Narrative as a Socially Symbolic Act.* Ithaca: Cornell UP, 1981.

———. *Postmodernism; or, The Cultural Logic of Late Capitalism.* Durham: Duke UP, 1990.

JanMohammed, Abdul. *Manichean Aesthetics: The Politics of Literature in Colonial Africa.* Amherst: U of Massachussets P, 1983.

JanMohammed, Abdul, and David Lloyd, eds. *The Nature and Context of Minority Discourse.* New York: Oxford UP, 1990.

Johnson, Barbara. *The Critical Difference: Essays in the Contemporary Rhetoric of Reading.* Baltimore: Johns Hopkins UP, 1980.

———. "Moses and Intertextuality: Sigmund Freud, Zora Neale Hurston, and the Bible." *Psychoanalysis and Afro-American Literature.* Chicago: U of Chicago P, forthcoming.

———. *A World of Difference.* Baltimore: Johns Hopkins UP, 1987.

Kellner, Hans. *Language and Historical Representation: Getting the Story Crooked.* Madison: U of Wisconsin P, 1989.

Knapp, Steven, and Walter Benn Michaels. "Against Theory." *Critical Inquiry* 8 (1982): 723–42.

Lacan, Jacques. *Ecrits: A Selection.* Trans. Alan Sheridan. London: Tavistock, 1977.

———."Seminar on 'The Purlioned Letter.' " *The Purloined Poe: Lacan, Derrida, and Psychoanalytic Reading.* Ed. John Muller and William Richardson. Baltimore: Johns Hopkins UP, 1988. 28–54.

Laclau, Ernesto, and Chantal Mouffe. *Hegemony and Socialist Strategy: Towards a Radical Democratic Politics.* Trans. Winston Moore and Paul Cammack. London: Verso, 1985.

Lacoue-Labarthe, Philippe, and Jean-Luc Nancy. *The Literary Absolute: The Theory of Literature in German Romanticism.* Trans. Philip Barnard and Cheryl Lester. Albany: State U of New York P, 1988.

Laplanche, Jean. *Life and Death in Psychoanalysis.* Baltimore: Johns Hopkins UP, 1976.

Latimer, Dan, ed. *Contemporary Critical Theory.* New York: Harcourt, 1989.

Leitch, Vincent B. *American Literary Criticism from the Thirties to the Eighties.* New York: Columbia UP, 1988.

Levinson, Marjorie, et al. *Rethinking Historicism.* Oxford: Blackwell, 1989.

Lévi-Strauss, Claude. *Totemism.* Boston: Beacon, 1963.

Liu, Alan. "Local Transcendence: Cultural Criticism, Postmodernism, and the Romanticism of Detail." *Representations* 32 (1990): 75–113.

Lloyd, David. "Kant's Examples." *Representations* 28 (1989): 34–54.

Martin, Wallace. *Recent Theories of Narrative.* Ithaca: Cornell UP, 1985.

Miller, Christopher. *Theories of Africans.* Chicago: U of Chicago P, 1991.

Mudimbe, Valentin. *The Invention of Africa: Gnosis, Philosophy, and the Order of Knowledge.* Bloomington: Indiana UP, 1988.

Mulvey, Laura. "Visual Pleasure and Narrative Cinema." *Screen* 16.3 (1975): 6–18. Rpt. in *Visual and Other Pleasures.* Bloomington: Indiana UP, 1989. 14–26.

Nelson, Cary, and Lawrence Grossberg, eds. *Marxism and the Interpretation of Culture.* Urbana: U of Illinois P, 1988.

Ngugi wa Thiong'o. *Decolonizing the Mind: The Politics of Language in African Literature.* London: Currey, 1986.

Parker, Andrew, et al., eds. *Nationalisms and Sexualities.* New York: Routledge, 1991.

Porter, Carolyn. "Are We Being Historical Yet?" *The States of "Theory."* Ed. David Carroll. New York: Columbia UP, 1990. 27–62.

Pratt, Mary Louise. *Toward a Speech Act Theory of Literary Discourse.* Bloomington: Indiana UP, 1977.

Ray, William. *Literary Meaning: From Phenomenology to Deconstruction.* Oxford: Blackwell, 1984.

Rimmon-Kenan, Shlomith. *Narrative Fiction: Contemporary Poetics.* London: Methuen, 1983.

Rorty, Richard. *The Consequences of Pragmatism.* Minneapolis: U of Minnesota P, 1982.

———. *Philosophy and the Mirror of Nature.* Princeton: Princeton UP, 1980.

Rose, Jacqueline. *Sexuality in the Field of Vision.* London: Verso, 1986.

Rosen, Philip, ed. *Narrative, Apparatus, Ideology: A Film Theory Reader.* New York: Columbia UP, 1986.

Said, Edward. *Orientalism.* New York: Pantheon, 1978.

Saldívar, Ramón. *Chicano Narrative: The Dialectics of Difference.* Madison: U of Wisconsin P, 1990.

Schor, Naomi. *Reading in Detail: Aesthetics and the Feminine.* New York: Columbia UP, 1987.

Sedgwick, Eve Kosofsky. *Between Men: English Literature and Male Homosocial Desire.* New York: Columbia UP, 1985.

———. *Epistemology of the Closet.* Berkeley: U of California P, 1991.

Showalter, Elaine, ed. *The New Feminist Criticism: Essays on Women, Literature, and Theory.* New York: Pantheon, 1985.

Silverman, Kaja. *The Subject of Semiotics.* New York: Oxford UP, 1983.

Smith, Barbara Herrnstein. *Contingencies of Value: Alternative Perspectives for Critical Theory.* Cambridge: Harvard UP, 1988.

———. *On the Margins of Discourse: The Relation of Literature to Language.* Chicago: U of Chicago P, 1978.

Spivak, Gayatri Chakravorty. "Can the Subaltern Speak?" Nelson and Grossberg 271–313.

———. *In Other Worlds: Essays in Cultural Politics.* New York: Routledge, 1988.

Sprinker, Michael. *Imaginary Relations: Aesthetics and Ideology in the Theory of Historical Materialism.* London: Verso, 1987.

Ulmer, Gregory. *Applied Grammatology.* Baltimore: Johns Hopkins UP, 1985.

Veeser, H. Aram., ed. *The New Historicism.* New York: Routledge, 1989.

Viswanathan, Gauri. *Masks of Conquest: Literary Study and British Rule in India.* New York: Columbia UP, 1989.

Warminski, Andrzej. *Readings in Interpretation: Hölderlin, Hegel, Heidegger.* Minneapolis: U of Minnesota P, 1987.

Weber, Samuel. *The Legend of Freud.* Minneapolis: U of Minnesota P, 1982.

Wellek, René, and Austin Warren. *Theory of Literature.* New York: Harcourt, 1949.

White, Hayden. *Tropics of Discourse: Essays in Cultural Criticism.* Baltimore: Johns Hopkins UP, 1978.

Williams, Raymond. *Writing in Society.* London: Verso, 1984.

Cross-Disciplinary and Cultural Studies

GILES GUNN

Interdisciplinary Studies

IN THE strict sense of the term, *interdisciplinary studies* is not a "field." Even if many scholars and critics think of themselves as participating in interdisciplinary studies, they do not, by virtue of this understanding, share anything like a set of interests, methods, or problems. What they share, instead—for want of a better term—is a predisposition to pursue their questions into areas of critical inquiry that cannot be mapped at all by the cartographic practices of contemporary disciplines or that can be mapped only when one redraws the critical coordinates supplied by those disciplines. Either way, students of interdisciplinary studies are marked by their willingness not simply to challenge, but also to cross, traditional disciplinary boundaries. Their hope, or at any rate their assumption, is that important dimensions of human experience and understanding lie unexplored in the spaces between those boundaries or the places where they cross, overlap, divide, or dissolve.

These practices involve risks of several kinds. The first relate to the disciplinary structure of the university system itself, at least in the United States, and the possibility that attempts to question its territorial boundaries and experiment with changing them may look like subversive activities. These risks are particularly high for junior scholars who lack the protection of tenure but possess the creative impatience necessary to the continuing development not only of the university but also of any particular field. Youthfulness—or, rather, inexperience—often entails a second kind of liability for interdisciplinary study. To bring two or more disciplines into significant interaction with one another requires considerable mastery of the subtleties and particularities of each, together with sufficient imagination and tact, ingenuity and persuasiveness, to convince others of the utility of their linkage. Such mastery, and the finesse that must accompany it, is not often acquired quickly or without extensive research and reflection. In rapidly changing fields such as the natural and physical sciences, where the bulk of graduate education is devoted to the state of the art of particular discipline or subdiscipline, interdisciplinary reconfigurations of methods and subject areas can—and often must—occur quite swiftly, but in the humanities, where one can scarcely learn the state of the art of any discipline without acquiring considerable knowledge of its history, they occur more slowly. It would be a mistake, however, to suppose that boundary-crossing is either an infrequent practice in humanistic studies or a recent one.

The humanistic practice of interdisciplinary excursions into foreign territories goes all the way back in the West to classical antiquity, when Greek historians and dramatists drew on medical and philosophical knowledge, respectively, for clues to the reconception of their own material. It has continued down to our own time, where much social thinking has been "refigured," to use the coinage of the cultural anthropologist Clifford Geertz, by encouraging social thinkers from a variety of disciplines to explore analogies between their own material and such aesthetic activities as play, ritual, drama, symbolic action, narrative, speech acts, games, and writing ("Blurred Genres"). In the Middle Ages, literary study put itself in the debt of systematic theology for its theories of interpretation and language. In the Renaissance, or early modern period as it is now called, the theologians, philosophers, and scholars known as the "humanists" differentiated themselves as a semiprofessional class by adopting, over against the medieval schoolmen, the theories and practices of the classical Greek and Roman philosophers. The movement known as the Enlightenment, in the eighteenth century, could easily be described as a raid by the philosophes on the conceptions and methods of the physical sciences, and what we call nineteenth-century Romanticism is only another term for what might be thought of as the intellectual appropriation, by fields such as theology, philosophy, literature, and the fine arts, of biologic and organic metaphors drawn from the natural sciences.

But if there is nothing unusual about humanists conducting sorties into alien "disciplinary" territory (students of comparative literature have made a virtue of such necessities), there is nonetheless something distinctive and exciting about the modern interest in such cross-field and cross-disciplinary peregrinations. This has to do with the reasons why, and the ways in which, contemporary literary scholars and critics have permitted such sallies to redefine both their subject matter and the kinds of questions they put to it. That is to say, the interdisciplinary move to explore the alien terrain of nonliterary genres and fields has amounted to considerably more than an attempt to draw different disciplines into conversation with one another, or to broaden the horizons of one discipline by borrowing some of the insights and techniques of another. Even where the interdisciplinary impulse has been prompted by motives no more suspect than the desire to improve communication across territorial boundaries or to expand the parameters that define them, it rarely ends there. What may have begun as the simple promotion of a kind of good neighbor policy, or as an innocent exploration of the exotic material of some foreign field, often results in something less benign than boundary-crossing and more unsettling than boundary-changing. What is at stake, to return to Geertz, is not just another redrawing of the disciplinary map but the principles of mapping as such. In this more contemporary sense, then, interdisciplinarity is not achieved through simple confrontations between specialized fields of knowledge—literature with history, chemistry with engineering, art history with the history of ideas—or through the placement of the insights and techniques of one discipline on loan to another—textual study borrowing the methods of computer science, history utilizing the techniques of demographers. The effect, if not the purpose, of interdisciplinarity is often nothing less than to alter the way we think about thinking ("Blurred Genres" 165–66).

CONTEMPORARY INTERDISCIPLINARY PRACTICE

The process of interdisciplinary revisionism usually begins with a period of courtship between two distinct and often diverse disciplines that suddenly discover spheres of mutual interest and complementary resources, then proceeds to a kind of marriage based on the belief that there are significant areas of compatibility between their respective methods and intellectual focus, and culminates in the production of offspring who share the parental genes and some of their dispositional features but possess a character all their own. Hence interdisciplinary exchanges depend on something more than ratcheting up the level of sophistication with which one explores the relations between literature and another endeavor—myth, psychology, religion, film, the visual arts—by utilizing methods appropriate to the study of each in a close, perhaps even symbiotic, cooperation. Interdisciplinarity requires, instead, an alteration of the constitutive question that generates such inquiry in the first place. Thus where relational studies proceed from the question of what literature (in its traditions, its formal conventions, and its thematic concerns) has to do with some other material (like music or social behavior) or some other field (such as history, political science, or sociolinguistics), interdisciplinary inquiries proceed from the double-sided question about how the insights or methods of some other field or structure can remodel our understanding of the nature of literature and the "literary" and, conversely, about how literary conceptions and approaches can remodel our conception of the allied field and its subject material.

An excellent example can be found in the emerging field of ethical criticism, first explored by moral philosophers like Iris Murdoch, Mikel Dufrenne, Bernard Williams, and Hilary Putnam, and now being developed by, among others, Wayne Booth and Martha Nussbaum. An outgrowth of an ancient interest in the relations between literature and philosophy that has been maintained for moderns by writers such as Friedrich Schiller, Samuel Taylor Coleridge, Friedrich Nietzsche, Martin Heidegger, John Dewey, Stuart Hampshire, Isaiah Berlin, Stanley Cavell, and Nelson Goodman, the interdisciplinary challenge of ethical criticism is conceived to be the transcendence of two related views. The first is that literature possesses moral dimensions even though it is not a form of moral experience. The second is that philosophical conceptions of morality can be illustrated by literary forms despite the fact that such forms are incapable of reflecting systematically on moral questions.

In *The Fragility of Goodness* and *Love's Knowledge*, Nussbaum in particular is concerned to revise both nostrums by arguing, first, against most academic moral philosophers, that certain conceptions of the good life, both individual and social, are not fully or adequately represented in forms of writing as abstract and affectless as traditional philosophical disputation; and, second, against many literary critics and theorists, that the conventional aesthetic prejudice against the ethically heuristic value of forms of writing like prose narrative or lyric poetry derives in part from a false assumption (widely shared by most moral and other philosophers as well) that the emotions lack cognitive content even where they convey felt quality.

Nussbaum's argument against both fallacies turns on their traditional resistance to the view that aesthetic forms play an educative as well as illustrative role in practical reflection on ethical issues, and it expresses itself in the assertion that while works of art often represent and express emotional effects, their deeper significance stems from the fact that their forms "are themselves the sources of emotional structure, the paradigms of what, for us, feeling is" ("Narrative Emotions" 236). Nussbaum is therefore interested in developing a new structure of interdisciplinary inquiry that will demonstrate, at the same time, the extent to which certain kinds of moral reflection and insight are dependent on narrative and other aesthetic structures and the extent to which practical ethical reasoning is in many instances a concomitant result of literary interpretation.

However, it must be added immediately that ethical criticism is by no means confined to Nussbaum's adroit and compelling practice of it. The term—which has been the source of opprobrium by critics as various as Northrop Frye and Fredric Jameson, and of praise by the likes of F. R. Leavis, Lionel Trilling, and David Bromwich—can be applied more widely to various kinds of interdisciplinary study that go by different names—feminist criticism, African American criticism, postcolonial criticism, ideological criticism, cultural studies—that also seek to submit literary forms to moral scrutiny or to challenge ethical reflection with metaphoric restructuring (see the essays by Schor, Allen, Gates, and Bathrick in this volume).

The interdisciplinary field of American studies provides another example of how such inquiry reconfigures the constituent disciplines that compose it. Beginning in the 1930s as an attempt to link literary and historical studies—when literature was viewed by historians as little more than a set of illustrations of themes, ideas, and events from beyond the world of literature, and history was seen by critics as merely the background of literature—American studies quickly turned into a more complicated attempt to examine the interactions between forms of collective mentality such as myths and archetypes, products of individual consciousness such as works of art and intellect, and social structures such as institutions and practices. In this interdisciplinary reformulation, accomplished by the "myth and symbol" school, as it is now called, a loose grouping of critics that included Henry Nash Smith, John William Ward, and Leo Marx, literature was reconceived both as a repository of historical value and as an example of historical practice; history, as a perceptual as well as material field significantly defined by large imaginative constructs such as myths and other metanarratives that can fuse concept and emotion in an image. In more recent years, with the help of conceptual and methodological insights borrowed from Marxist criticism, social history, feminist criticism, and other areas, the notions of literature and history operative in American studies have been revised even further as studies like Myra Jehlen's *American Incarnation* and Alan Trachtenberg's *Reading American Photographs* have shown how figurative representations become a historical force in their own right and operate like any other material factor in the public world.

It has lately been claimed that the American studies movement failed because it never led to the creation of separate departments of American literature, but this claim amounts to measuring the success of an interdisciplinary field of inquiry in terms of whether it achieves full institutional recognition by various fields it succeeds in at least partially redefining (Culler 8; Graff 211). The success of the American studies movement derives, rather, from the number of separate undergraduate programs and majors it has generated throughout the United States and the world, the kinds and quality of graduate programs it has produced, the new areas of research it has opened up, the professional associations it has sponsored, and, most important, the creativity, integrity, and resilience of the scholarship produced in its name. Judging by these standards, American studies has been as efficacious an interdisciplinary initiative as any undertaken in American higher education in the postwar period.

But this only indicates how difficult it is to demarcate precisely where, and how, to draw the boundaries not only *between* different kinds of interdisciplinary study but also *within* them. For example, feminist criticism, like cultural critique or African American or postcolonial criticism, is more of a composite methodological site where other interdisciplinary modes cross and recross—reader-response criticism, semiotic analysis, psychoanalytic inquiry, ethnic studies, cultural anthropology, gender studies—than a unitary mode of interdisciplinary study all its own. Furthermore, there are sharp and sometimes seemingly incommensurable differences between and among, say, feminist critics over whether to organize their research around biological, psychological, cultural, or linguistic models. What this suggests, to repeat, is that interdisciplinary studies may not refer to anything as specific or unified as a "field" in itself so much as to a predisposition to view all fields as potentially vulnerable to re-creation in the partial image of some other or others. This, in turn, renders the fields in question what Roland Barthes calls "transversals," whose reconfiguration seeks to produce or recover meanings that their formerly configured relations tended to blur, camouflage, or efface ("From Work to Text" 75).

THE THEORY OF INTERDISCIPLINARY STUDIES

As numerous students of interdisciplinarity in all fields can attest, the process of converting disciplines into transversals can be not only discomfiting but also potentially violent. When the parameters of traditional fields grow permeable or suspect under the pressure of questions that, as presently constituted, they cannot address, such fields grow ripe for infiltration, subversion, or outright assault. Such military metaphors may seem excessive, but they are apt. When the academic field now called anthropology first attempted to carve out a space for itself between history and sociology, it was described by one of its proponents, and not altogether inaccurately, as "a disciplinary poaching license." Thus images of encroachment, trespass, offense are inescapable: interdisciplinary studies risk disciplinary transgression in the name of interdisciplinary independence, disciplinary revisionism in the name of interdisciplinary emancipation and creativity (Fish, "Being Interdisciplinary" 15–21).

But the ideology of interdisciplinary freedom captures only those aspects of interdisciplinary activity that are potentially invasive and disruptive. There is another side to interdisciplinary practice that, according to some, is by contrast peremptory, juridical, prescriptive, and imperialistic. This threat derives from the fact that the redescriptive impulses of interdisciplinary studies almost of necessity place one discipline in a position of subordination to another. As a result, the subordinated discipline is not only destabilized but threatened with subsumption in an anomalous, substitutionary structure that on the pretext of situating itself, as the prefix *inter* implies, between the two more traditionally constituted matrices, actually manages to incorporate them both in some larger hegemonic framework. Whether one construes the new interdisciplinary formation as merely a product of the merger of the other two, or as itself a metadiscipline beyond them, seemingly matters scarcely at all. A new field has been produced, the imperiousness of whose procedures often runs counter to the redemptive heuristics used to justify it. Thus if interdisciplinarity is most often legitimated in the name of greater intellectual autonomy and openness, the transdisciplinary exploration it sanctions possesses the capability of masking another form of metadisciplinary despotism. Barthes writes:

> Interdisciplinary work is not a peaceful operation: it begins *effectively* when the solidarity of the old discipline breaks down—a process made more violent, perhaps, by the jolts of fashion—to the benefit of a new object and a new language, neither of which is in the domain of those branches of knowledge that one calmly sought to confront. . . . [T]here now arises a need for a new object, one attained by the displacement or overturning of previous categories.
>
> ("From Work to Text" 73–74)

Barthes defines this new mutational object as the *text*, arguing that it displaces or overturns the old "Newtonian" concept of the "work." By "text" Barthes means to refer less to a specifiable entity than to a site or intersection of productive activity—that is, to processes of signification rather than to forms of the signified. But whether the metadiscipline Barthes invokes is described as textual studies, or intertextuality, or—as certain contemporary critics now argue—cultural studies, his view that interdisciplinarity always supplants one set of structures with another, still more encompassing and dominant is by no means shared by all scholars. What looks to Barthes like a monolithic metadiscipline rising from the imperialistic subversion and partial fusion of two others appears to another group of scholars and critics rather more like the integration of strategies, methods, and queries that acquire their particular sense of authority from what the two disciplines on which heretofore they have traditionally drawn have customarily dismissed, repressed, or occluded. I cite but two examples. Feminist studies, as the chapter by Naomi Schor in this volume suggests, arose initially as a protest against the stereotypes created about women in the literature written by men and sought to recuperate the very different representations that women had furnished of their experience in their own writing. In like fashion, the successive stages of African American criticism—from its inception in the Black Arts movement of the 1960s to its attempt, in the late 1980s and early 1990s, to retheorize social and textual boundaries in all American cultural contexts and thus turn black studies into a critique of American studies generally—demonstrate, as the essay by Henry Louis Gates, Jr., in this book reveals, that African American criticism arose in part out of discoveries of what more conventional inquiries had typically omitted.

MAPPING THE INTERDISCIPLINARY TERRAIN

For purposes of this discussion, it is perhaps enough to say, then, that there is a loose historical connection between the various associations that literature has for some time, and in some instances for many centuries, enjoyed with other fields or structured forms—forms like painting, film, sculpture, architecture, discursive argument, dogmatic and speculative theology, social thought, music, and, now, photography and the law; fields like jurisprudence, linguistics, anthropology, sociology, musicology, philosophy, religion, science, history, and politics—and the development of at least some interdisciplinary approaches to such relations. But this assertion needs to be qualified to the bone. These developments have not followed an orderly pattern; they are by no means fully descriptive of all the fields with which literature has possessed important conceptual and methodological filiations; and they are related closely, as might be expected, to developments in literary and critical theory as well as to the emergence of new notions of textuality and intertextuality, particularly as they apply to the concept of culture itself. More exactly, genuinely interdisciplinary modes of study have usually developed through the crossing, displacement, or alteration of the boundaries between forms of relational study, or have otherwise constituted themselves in the spaces between those forms as attempts to understand the asymmetric relations between the protocols and perspective that divide them.

As a case in point, deconstruction arose as a joining of the philosophical interest in the critique of Western metaphysics and the new science of linguistics that in Ferdinand de Saussure's version stressed that language is composed of signs that can be differentiated as to function: the material means of transmission or acoustic image of any sign is known as the signifier, the conceptual image or intellectual referrent of any sign as the signified. The relation between signifier and signified is what becomes problematic for the deconstructionist by virtue of his or her perception of the irreducible *differance*—as in the words *differing* and *deferring*—between them, and the inevitable suppression, repression, and dissemination of meaning to which it leads. Often misdescribed as a method or critical theory, its chief aim, according to its founder and most famous exponent, Jacques Derrida, is to deconstruct all the classical oppositions on which literary criticism (like theology and philosophy) is based—between word and referent, language and being, structure and process, text and context—in order to see what such oppositions have traditionally veiled or disguised. By contrast, the new historicism, discussed in detail by Annabel Patterson in this book, has taken up methodological residence somewhere between deconstruction's preoccupation with the conflicting, if not self-canceling, forces of signification in any text and the neo-Marxist fascination with how processes of textualization not only reflect material circumstances and institutional patterns but frequently, and often simultaneously, generate them.

But if interdisciplinary studies is sometimes formed by traversing inherited disciplinary boundaries, sometimes by transfiguring them, and sometimes by exploring the spaces between them, how is one to go about mapping the studies' own permutations and forms? The simplest answer is probably to be found by reverting to the set of critical coordinates that have conventionally been employed to model literary texts—the author, the reader, the material or linguistic components of the text itself, and the world to which the text refers. This model, first delineated by M. H. Abrams in *The Mirror and the Lamp*, has been vastly complicated in recent years as our sense of each one of its coordinates has been extended, but its use can nonetheless be instructive (Hernadi). Such a model helps clarify immediately, for example, that much of the activity in interdisciplinary studies in recent years has been selectively focused. Because of suspicions about the status of the author in contemporary criticism and the whole question of authorial intention, and the no less grave theoretical misgivings about the mimetic properties of art and the role of representation generally, interdisciplinary work has placed far less emphasis on the first and last coordinates of this literary model, the author and the world, than on the middle two, the reader and the work.

This selectivity is apparent everywhere. It is as visible in all the contemporary variants of psychological criticism, which tend to be preoccupied with the mental and emotional states of individuals, even when such states are taken to represent real-life psychological processes in the world, as it is in social and political criticism that is typically concerned with the way the material environment serves either as a source of literary production, as an object of literary representation, or as a determinant of literary reception and influence. Thus Freudian criticism has for some time been less interested in the psyches of individual authors, or the capacity of literary texts to mirror the psychological processes of persons and groups, than in the way psychological structures, such as the unconscious, can be viewed as analogues to literary structures like language, or in the way strategies of literary typification and signification, such as metonymy, synecdoche, and irony, can be read psychoanalytically both as representing and as enabling processes of repression, displacement, transference, and countertransference. Similarly, much of the most influential interdisciplinary criticism promoted by the newer Marxist theories has abandoned careful examination of the class background of writers, or the sociopolitical verisimilitude of the world they create, in favor of exploring the manner in which works of literature and other art forms not only reflect discursive traces of the class struggle and resolve social conflicts symbolically but also inscribe stylistically the modes of production by which they were first legitimated.

The map of interdisciplinary studies would look rather different, however, if only one of these critical coordinates were used as the cartographic axis. Take, for example, the focus in recent criticism on the reader, which links the phenomenological criticism that Wolfgang Iser practices in *The Implied Reader* and *The Act of Reading* with the *Receptionsästhetik* of Hans Robert Jauss that examines, in studies like *Toward an Aesthetic of Reception* and *Aesthetic Experience and Literary Hermeneutics*, the changing responses of entire peoples or communities over time. Nevertheless, under the same heading one could make room for the parallel, and much more empirical, emphasis of critics like Nina Baym, in *Novels, Readers, and Reviewers*, and Cathy N. Davidson, in *Revolution and the Word*, who seek to rehistoricize the reading experience itself by examining the recorded responses of the readers of any text or the history of the use of particular books, and align such criticism with the stress that Frank Kermode, in *The Classic*, and Stanley Fish, in *Is There a Text in This Class?*, have placed on the roles, respectively, of interpretive institutions and interpretive communities. Such a map would reveal that much recent interdisciplinary criticism focusing on the experience of the reader has been propelled by a grammar of feminist, ethnic, or class-oriented ideological motives, but it would also disclose that some of this criticism—Norman Holland's *Dynamics of Literary Response*, Barthes's *Pleasure of the Text*, Gilles Deleuze and Félix Guattari's *Anti-Oedipus*, Julia Kristeva's *Powers of Horror*, Peter Brooks's *Reading for the Plot*, Robert Scholes's *Textual Power*, and Mary Jacobus's *Reading Women*—has reflected interests that were psychoanalytic, structuralist, feminist, deconstructionist, semiotic, or a combination of all five.

Were one to redraw the map of contemporary interdisciplinary studies in relation to the critical coordinate of the text itself, however, one could similarly highlight, as well as link, a variety of still other kinds of interdisciplinary studies. One point of departure for such a cartographic exercise might be the extraordinary developments that followed on the emergence of modern linguistics, a field that grew out of the convergence of work by Russian formalists, like Viktor Shklovsky and Yuri Tynyanov, and Czech linguists associated with Jan Mukarovsky and the Prague school, with, again, the language theory of Saussure and the semiotics theory of Charles Sanders Peirce, all of which conspired to produce methods that applied linguistic insights to the study of culture conceived as a system of signs. A key figure in these developments was Roman Jakobson, who, in emigrating first from Moscow to Prague and then from Prague to the United States, helped bridge the gap between linguistics and semiotics and thus encouraged interdisciplinary activities as widely varied as the stylistics criticism of Michael Riffaterre, the poetics analysis of Juri Lotman, and the narratological studies of scholars like A. J. Greimas, Tzvetan Todorov, Gérard Genette, Claude Bremond, and, now, Paul Ricoeur (see also the essay by Finegan in this volume).

But the emergent field of linguistics also promoted interdisciplinary work in areas quite distant from the study of the structure and properties of language. In one direction, it influenced the structuralist orientation that Claude Lévi-Strauss, and later Edmund Leach, brought to ethnographic studies and the development of social anthropology in general (see the essay by Baron in this volume). In another, it helped shape formalistic and generic interests that run from the conservative, archetypal criticism represented by Northrop Frye's *Anatomy of Criticism* to the radical dialogic criticism associated with Mikhail Bakhtin's *Rabelais and His World* and *The Dialogic Imagination.*

But the field of linguistics and its many affiliations (indeed, far more than can be enumerated here) is only one of the interdisciplinary modes of study promoted by (even as it promoted) the study of the literary coordinate known as the text. To draw out the lines of interdisciplinary relation that emanate from the textual coordinate, one would have to take into account everything from the development of hermeneutics (or interpretation theory), starting with the work of Wilhelm Dilthey and Martin Heidegger and continuing through that of Hans-Georg Gadamer and Paul Ricoeur, to the new criticism of what Fredric Jameson calls "the political unconscious." The latter has its roots in the work of Walter Benjamin and other members of the Frankfurt school (Max Horkheimer and Theodor Adorno), as well as in the writings of Antonio Gramsci, and its expression in the writings of critics as various as Lucien Goldmann, Louis Althusser, Raymond Williams, Pierre Macherey, and Robert Weimann (see also the essay by Marshall in this volume).

Still another way to map the varieties of interdisciplinary study would be to start with some of the new subjects it has helped make available for critical analysis—the history of the book; the materialism of body; the psychoanalysis of the reader and the reading process; the sociology of conventions; the semiotics of signification; the historization of representation; the ideology of gender, race, and class; intertextuality; power; otherness; and undecidability—but it would be necessary to add that each of these topics, as currently, though variously, construed, has also served both to attract and to project still further lines of interdisciplinary investigation. Studies like *The Body in Pain* by Elaine Scarry, for example, have woven psychoanalytic, cultural, materialistic, neo-Marxist, and new-historicist strands of disciplinary interrogation; studies of representation such as Stephen J. Greenblatt's *Shakespearean Negotiations* have drawn into new combinations historicist, reader-response, cultural materialist, hermeneutic, semiotic, and often deconstructionist inter- and cross-disciplinary modes. But in much of the newer interdisciplinary scholarship, studies of the body become studies of representation. Thus the threading of disciplinary principles and procedures is frequently doubled, tripled, and quadrupled, in ways that are not only mixed but, from a conventional disciplinary perspective, somewhat off center.

So described, the overlapping, underlayered, interlaced, crosshatched affiliations, coalitions, and alliances toward which these cartographic operations lead can become truly baffling. Furthermore, insofar as they imply that disciplinary traditions of descent or influence always flow in one direction and in continuously visible and hence traceable channels, such mapmaking exercises can also become misleading, since the inevitable result of much interdisciplinary study, if not its ostensible purpose, is to dispute and disorder conventional understandings of the relations between such things as origin and terminus, center and periphery, focus and margin, inside and outside.

These observations raise an obvious question about whether the simplest, or at least the most coherent, way to conceptualize the kinds of interdisciplinary studies that have emerged from relational or interrelational studies might not be to focus directly on the associations that literature, or rather literary study, has developed with other recognized, institutionalized fields of academic inquiry. On this basis one could simply describe the interdisciplinary endeavors that have grown out of the study of, say, literature and philosophy (phenomenological criticism, hermeneutics, deconstruction, neopragmatism, ethical criticism, the new rhetorical criticism), literature and anthropology (structuralism, ethnography, or "thick description," folklore and folklife studies, myth criticism), literature and psychology (psychoanalytic criticism, reader-response criticism, anxiety-of-influence criticism, cultural psychology), literature and politics (sociological criticism, cultural studies, ideological criticism, materialist studies), literature and religion (theological apologetics, recuperative hermeneutics, generic and historical criticism, rhetoric studies), and literature and linguistics (Russian formalism, stylistics, narratology, semiotics). However, what has to be borne in mind is that these correlate fields (anthropology, philosophy, religious studies, psychology, etc.) have themselves changed—and sometimes dramatically—during the last quarter century, and among a variety of factors generating that instability and revisionary ferment has been the success of the particular interdisciplinary initiatives they have either stimulated or helped sustain. It is also worth noting that fewer than half the academic fields with which literature has historically enjoyed or established important ties are even mentioned here (some of the others cited in specific chapters of Barricelli and Gibaldi's *Interrelations of Literature* include myth, folklore, sociology, law, science, music, the visual arts, and film). Among those omitted, several, like law and science, are tethered to literature's earliest beginnings, and at least one—film studies—is intimately connected to literature's future fortunes.

But if relational and interrelational studies have precipitated and promoted the creation of certain kinds of interdisciplinary studies, they have clearly discouraged the development of others. Consider, for example, the relations between literature and music. Study of the relations between literature and music goes back to the prehistory of literature itself, when verbal forms were first emancipated from their sedimentation in sound and song. This interest has taken a variety of forms over the ages, from the study of such musical elements as rhythm, rhyme, alliteration, tone, voice, variation, balance, repetition, contrast, and counterpoint, to the vast and complex historical ties between particular musical types, like the rondeau or the symphony, and the verse forms of Alfred de Musset and Algernon Swinburne or Thomas Mann's *Doctor Faustus* and Herman Broch's *Sleepwalkers*. The musicality of literature and the literariness of music are synonymous with works like Giuseppe Verdi's *Macbeth* and *Otello*, Alban Berg's *Wozzeck*, Benjamin Britten's *Billy Budd*, Franz Liszt's *Dante* and *Faust* symphonies, Richard Strauss's *Don Juan*, Claude Debussy's *Prélude à l'àpres-midi d'un faune*. Writers such as Jean-Jacques Rousseau, Denis Diderot, Novalis, Heinrich Heine, E. T. A. Hoffmann, Giuseppe Mazzini, Friedrich Nietzsche, André Gide, Bertholt Brecht, Aldous Huxley, James Joyce, and T. S. Eliot have all sought to translate musical technique into literary practice. Yet despite the eloquent arguments of critics like George Steiner that the quintessential form of art in literature is its music, or the testimony of distinguished musicologists like Leonard B. Meyers that music can never rid itself completely of the element of story, the venerable association of music with literature and literature with music—so intelligently interpreted in texts like T. S. Eliot's *Music of Poetry*, Calvin S. Brown's *Music and Literature*, Carl Dahlhaus's *Musikästhetik*, Steven Paul Scher's *Literatur und Musik*, John Hollander's *Untuning of the Sky*, or even the chapter "Literature and the Other Arts" in *Theory of Literature*, edited by René Wellek and Austin Warren—has rarely led to the programmatic development of interdisciplinary approaches to the study of either the musicality of literary forms and meanings or of the literary dimensions of music. In musical studies itself, however, the case is different, as the interdisciplinary fields of opera studies, ethnomusicology, and even the aesthetics of music amply attest.

Similarly, despite countless distinguished examples, the long record of informed study of the relations between the visual and the verbal arts has only rarely resulted in the creation of interdisciplinary, as opposed to cross- or transdisciplinary, modes of study, in which disciplinary boundaries, instead of merely being bridged, are actually redrawn. While there have been numerous disciplinary exchanges between the literary and the plastic arts, there has been surprisingly little reconception of each in the image of the other. This is the more to be marveled at both because of the existence of academic programs organized to examine this relationship and because of the brilliant interdisciplinary research in which it has issued in the work of Rudolf Arnheim, E. H. Gombrich, Erwin Panofsky, Meyer Schapiro, Richard Wollheim, Ronald Paulson, Arthur C. Danto, Barbara Novak, and Michael Fried. There are countless literary texts that treat works of visual art or the things they delineate, that employ visual techniques, that are linked to historical movements and manifestos associated with the visual arts, that call on interpretive skills they have helped develop, or that otherwise inscribe visual modes of conception and assessment; but none has proved capable of overcoming either one of two kinds of resistance—the first to interpretation itself on the part of many art historians, the second to the intellectual power and percipience of the visual on the part of many literary scholars and critics. If art historians routinely eschew criticism for cataloging, evaluation for description, literary historians and critics have typically treated all the fine arts as mere complements, adjuncts, illustrations of the verbal arts.

Striking evidence of this latter phenomenon can be found in Thomas Bender's *New York Intellect*, a study of the intellectual life of New York City from the middle of the eighteenth century to the middle of the twentieth. By the end of this period, the culture of the city was recognized throughout the world for its eminence in at least three of the fine arts—painting, dance, and music. By mid-century it had also nurtured an extraordinary group of critics, known as the New York intellectuals, who were associated with the *Partisan Review* and other magazines. Yet despite the cosmopolitanism of figures like Lionel Trilling, Philip Rahv, Alfred Kazin, Irving Howe, and Sidney Hook, virtually none of the New York intellectuals, with the occasional exception of a Harold Rosenberg and a Clement Greenberg, paid any attention to the artistic areas in which New York culture had achieved international recognition.

This is not to suggest, then, that there have been no interfield or transfield studies of literature and art or literature and music, much less that these initiatives have failed to produce work of enormous and lasting value. Nor is it to claim that in the future such initiatives may not generate still more systematic and more institutionalized modes of interdisciplinary inquiry that reconstitute the materials and methods that currently compose those modes. It is merely to assert that a new confederation of practices, however salutary, is not a new configuration of methods, however experimental; and until a new configuration of methods produces a refiguration of material, one does not have what can be called a genuinely interdisciplinary form of study. Interdisciplinarity involves a rethinking not just of conceptual frames but of their perceptual ground, as Alan Liu has argued in an as yet unpublished paper entitled "Indiscipline, Interdiscipline, and Liberty: The Revolutionary Paradigm." What gets reconceived, as Liu notes, are not only the paradigms by which one discipline makes sense of itself to itself with the help of another but the way such processes of reconception provide both disciplines with new ways of representing their own knowledge to themselves.

FACTORS CONTRIBUTING TO INTERDISCIPLINARITY

Where did this new interest in interdisciplinarity come from? Was it the result of factors confined to the institutional culture of academic literary studies or the product of wider educational and social forces? Did it emerge all at once or in successive historical stages? What forms of resistance has the development of interdisciplinarity met? How is one to assess its benefits, and what sorts of problems is interdisciplinary study likely to confront in the future?

These difficult and important questions are being vigorously contested. In addition to admitting of different and frequently conflicting answers, they are questions whose very form can be challenged as prejudicial. What they presume is that interdisciplinarity can be treated as a unified or coherent movement whose progress has typically been forward and uninterrupted, when its development seems more often to have described a course of successive, tentative, often uncoordinated forays and retreats whose progress was more crabwise than linear. Another way to put this would be to say that just as intelligent theory always holds out the possibility of unintelligent practice, as Gilbert Ryle once observed, so it is equally possible that intelligent practice can sometimes be performed in the name of unintelligent, or at least unconscious or only half-conscious, theory. If this notion tells us anything, it should confirm the fact that forms of interdisciplinary study often emerge by accident. When not driven simply by the vagaries of fashion or the metaphysics of theory, they are usually occasioned by critical conundrums and simply offer themselves as workable solutions to practical problems. In other words, interdisciplinarity is the pragmatist's response to the dilemma of disciplinary essentialism.

Yet this is not to say that interdisciplinary study can flourish in an unfavorable environment. After World War II, for example, when the pedagogy known in the United States as the New Criticism was in full sway, interdisciplinary literary studies were in a state of noticeable arrest and, where not arrested, were seriously eclipsed by other, more formalistic and inward-looking methodologies. But the ideology of interpretive refinement then epitomized by the New Criticism, or rather epitomized by its pedagogic practitioners in the schools—among its various proponents, like John Crowe Ransom, Allen Tate, R. P. Blackmur, Kenneth Burke, Cleanth Brooks, and Robert Penn Warren, there were sharp and sometimes irreconcilable differences in poetics and procedure—had a much more deleterious effect (and still does) in England than in the United States; and even where similar prejudices were at work on the Continent, Europeans have always been more responsive to interdisciplinary initiatives than either the British or the Americans. Part of this difference stems, no doubt, from the looser departmental structure of the European university system, and part, as well, from the role that philosophical discourse and ideas generally have traditionally played in European intellectual culture.

But generalizations like this are notoriously porous. The American university in the twentieth century has been surprisingly hospitable to a variety of interdisciplinary experiments without altering the way it organizes the structure of knowledge. With respect to literary study, this paradox has been explained by Gerald Graff as the result of the "field-coverage principle" (6–9). According to Graff, the principle enables departments of English to retain their power and organization by welcoming new fields and methods to the fold without permitting them to challenge their established hierarchies concerning the nature and teaching of literature.

The trouble with this explanation is that it may concede too much to the leftist view that identifies the American university with other institutions of the corporate state and postulates that its expansion, like that of capitalism generally, derives from its ability to absorb the elements of conflict it produces. While academic institutions certainly exhibit something of the "repressive tolerance," as Herbert Marcuse called it, of late capitalism, it would be more accurate to say that the movement toward interdisciplinary studies has no doubt resulted from many factors, both institutional and conceptual. If the field-coverage principle has proved influential in determining the way the field's intentions and achievements have been perceived and assimilated, the seismic theoretical shift that Roland Barthes first noticed from *work* to *text* has influenced the way interdisciplinary studies has, insofar as it can be said to possess an integrated vision at all, construed itself.

The discovery of the new world of textuality and intertextuality has served to question a number of interpretive shibboleths that controlled literary study for many decades. Among them are the following: that there is one "definitive" meaning of any text that is to be associated with the intentions of some transcendent Author; that there is any such thing as an Author, transcendent or otherwise, who is alone, or even chiefly, responsible for what a text means; that texts must be read independent of their relations, anxious or imperialistic, to other texts; that reading can be viewed only as a process of reception and absorption but not of production and intervention; and that when reading, interpretation, criticism are seen as creative and not merely reflective activities, their operations must still be restricted to individual works and cannot be expanded to apply "literary" modes of analysis to the entire spectrum of cultural phenomena (Macksey).

Recent exploration of the new world of the text and the intertext has brought with it a new diversification of our sense of the relations not only between one text and another but also between any text and its putative "context." Not only has the notion of "context" been broadened to encompass things that had never been construed as "literary" before—the experiences of women, of people of color, of members of so-called underclasses like the poor, the illiterate, and the homeless, of ethnic minorities, of regions like the South, the West, or the Northeast, and of marginalized groups like gays, the aged, and, now, thanks to the hospice movement and the awareness of AIDS, the terminally ill—it has also been reconstrued as a concept no less "artificial," "constructed," or "fictive" than that of "text" itself.

In modern literary study, the notion of "context" has been most closely associated with the notion of "culture," but in recent years "culture" has itself been radically historicized. As the concept of culture has been viewed against the background of its appearance in the eighteenth century and its transformation in the nineteenth century in response to such complex social and political developments as the rise of nationalism, the emergence of the middle class, the industrialization and urbanization of commerce, the democratization of social life, and the professionalization of the arts, it has become clear that cultures function in different ways in different historic communities, and even in various ways at different times in the same community. Like canons, cultures are always in the process of revision as their constituent elements are challenged, refashioned, and replaced. This same process of historicization has also raised important questions about whether the culture concept has not outlived its usefulness. As the anthropologist James Clifford has proposed (21–54), cultures are not only unstable, selective, contingent, strategic, and incompletely integrated; in actual historical experience, they tend to function less as enduring forms than as, in Wallace Stevens's phrase, "Supreme Fictions": ways of creating collective identity in the face of forces that threaten it.

The problematization of the concept of culture has in turn contributed to skepticism about the idea of the "West." This skepticism has naturally been aroused by discoveries by social and cultural anthropologists, but it has also been generated by the results of postcolonial criticism (in the work of, to name only a few, Octavio Paz, Nadine Gordimer, Homi Bhabha, Edward Said, Stuart Hall, and Carlos Fuentes) and the new interest now beginning to be displayed by departments of English and comparative literature in writers from Central and South America, the Caribbean world, Africa, Asia, the Middle East, the Indian subcontinent, and Eastern Europe. Causing further erosion of the boundaries between cultures and contexts, these interdisciplinary undertakings have revealed how, when used comparatively, the idea of the "West" has been employed repeatedly to the disadvantage of its discursive opposites (the "Orient," the "Third World," "newly liberated peoples"), and how, when used normatively, as a broadly monocentric cultural entity, it has served to cloak many of the tensions, confusions, conflicts, and divisions that characterize it.

Taken together, these factors have created a more pluralistic and, in some ways, more adversarial, or at least more disputatious, climate in criticism, a climate that has opened the way for what Paul Ricoeur once called "the conflict of interpretations." Aside from the fact that some critics take this conflict of interpretations to be a cacophony, what really has occurred is not an increase in the level of discord so much as a realization that dialogue, contestation, diversity of opinion may be all that interpretation shall ever finally attain. But if the achievement of interpretive consensus, or agreement, or uniformity has come to be recognized as quite possibly an illusory ideal in the human sciences—just as, earlier, Thomas Jefferson perceived it to be an illusory ideal in political affairs—then one can begin to appreciate how essential, how really crucial, interdisciplinary studies are to that "refinement of debate," in Clifford Geertz's phrasing, that can be achieved in its place (*Interpretation* 29).

THE PROSPECTS OF INTERDISCIPLINARY STUDIES

Interdisciplinarity will remain integral to this deepening of the debate in the human sciences only so long as it remains suspicious of its own grounds, only so long as it refuses to hypostatize or totalize its methodological fascination with discrepancies, divergences, disjunctions, and difference. The threat of hypostatization or totalization in interdisciplinary studies comes from one of two temptations. The first is disciplinary reductionism, or the temptation to think that the methods of one field are sufficient to interpret the materials of many. The second is the appetite for metaphorical transfer, or the temptation to treat the materials of one field as mere epiphenomena of the subjects of another. The future of interdisciplinary studies depends, of course, on avoiding such temptations. But it also depends on a number of other, more institutional and material factors, such as the availability of funds to support the development of graduate programs, centers for study, summer institutes, visiting and permanent professorships, outlets for publication, interdepartmental colloquia, and scholarships.

Chief among these more objective elements is the ongoing controversy within the humanities (and beyond them) about whether universities are to be defined as institutions devoted principally to the reproduction and transmission of culture or, rather, to the critique and re-creation of culture (Culler 33–36). While this is not a distinction anyone would have thought of making, at least in American higher education, twenty or thirty years ago, it now shapes much of the debate about the reorganization of knowledge and the politics of the academy. Within the humanities the debate centers on the nature and effect of cultural representations, and within interdisciplinary studies (if not also outside) the division takes place between those who see the study of cultural representations as a political struggle over the sources and symptomatics of power and those who view that study, instead, as a hermeneutic struggle over the hierarchies and heuristics of value. In studying cultural texts, what are we trying to do: determine how and by whom the world should be governed, or decide which values should organize our experience of it?

While these purposes are by no means unrelated, neither are they the same. The long-term challenge for interdisciplinary studies is to remain undaunted by the tension between them without being seduced into thinking that this tension can be easily reduced or overcome. What is most productive intellectually in the current practice of interdisciplinary studies is neither the utopian hope that the tension can ultimately be erased nor the complacent belief that it finally doesn't matter; what has been most productive is the inescapable fact of the tension itself and the deepened, pragmatic appreciation to which it has given rise: of how knowledge is always open to further interpretation and criticism, of how understanding is always susceptible to further correction and realization.

Suggestions for Further Reading

It is well to remember that reflection on interdisciplinary studies possesses a long and illustrious genealogy. In the West it begins with such texts as Plato's *Republic* and Aristotle's *Nichomachean Ethics* and proceeds through Francis Bacon's *Novum*

Organum and Giambattista Vico's *New Science* to Georg Wilhelm Friedrich Hegel's *Phenomenology of Spirit*, Charles Sanders Peirce's pioneering essays on the theory of signs, and Wilhelm Dilthey's *Gesammelte Schriften*. As we move closer to the present and confine ourselves to works that have developed general models for the reorganization of disciplinary inquiry with particular bearing on literary studies, we must make special mention of Northrop Frye's compendium of myth and archetypal criticism, *Anatomy of Criticism*; Hans-Georg Gadamer's magisterial study of the theory of interpretation, *Truth and Method*; Michel Foucault's highly influential attempt to create an archaeology of the human sciences, *The Order of Things*; Umberto Eco's elaboration of a theory of signs, *A Theory of Semiotics*; Jacques Derrida's development of the theory of deconstruction, *Of Grammatology*; and Pierre Bourdieu's attempt to reground the social sciences in a theory of symbolic capital and authority, *Outline of a Theory of Practice*.

In American literary study, interdisciplinary thinking in a number of fields has been been broadly influenced by a variety of important late-twentieth-century texts. Among the most important are Roland Barthes's *Writing Degree Zero*, Raymond Williams's *Culture and Society, 1780–1950*, Claude Lévi-Strauss's *Structural Anthropology*, E. D. Hirsch's *Validity in Interpretation*, Georg Lukács's *Realism in Our Time*, Clifford Geertz's *Interpretation of Cultures*, Hayden White's *Metahistory*, Walter Benjamin's *Illuminations*, Harold Bloom's *Anxiety of Influence*, Jacques Lacan's *Ecrits*, Sandra M. Gilbert and Susan Gubar's *Madwoman in the Attic*, John Searle's *Speech Acts*, Mikhail Bakhtin's *Rabelais and His World* and *Dialogic Imagination*, Paul Ricoeur's *Freud and Philosophy*, Edward Said's *Orientalism*, Stephen J. Greenblatt's *Renaissance Self-Fashioning*, and Roger Chartier's *Cultural History*.

The most readable history of interdisciplinary initiatives, and the resistances they have encountered, in the formation of American literary study is Gerald Graff's *Professing Literature*. The most accessible summary of the ideology of interdisciplinarity in contemporary literary studies appears in Stanley Fish's "Being Interdisciplinary Is So Very Hard to Do." But the most impressive demonstrations of the efficacy of interdisciplinary inquiry are still to be found in the way it has helped redefine and extend research in every period of literary study, from the Age of Pericles to postmodernism, and in every methodological orientation, from philology to phenomenology and from history to hermeneutics.

University of California, Santa Barbara

Works Cited and Recommended

Abrams, M. H. *The Mirror and the Lamp: Romantic Theory and the Critical Tradition.* New York: Oxford UP, 1953.

Althusser, Louis. *For Marx.* Trans. Ben Brewster. New York: Pantheon, 1969.

Aristotle. *Nichomachean Ethics.* Trans. L. H. G. Greenwood. Cambridge: Cambridge UP, 1909.

Bacon, Francis. *Bacon's* Novum Organum. Ed. Thomas Fowler. Oxford: Clarendon P, 1878.

Bakhtin, Mikhail. *The Dialogic Imagination.* Ed. Michael Holquist. Trans. Caryl Emerson and Michael Holquist. Austin: U of Texas P, 1981.

———. *Rabelais and His World.* Trans. Helene Iswolsky. Cambridge: MIT P, 1968.

Barricelli, Jean-Paul, and Joseph Gibaldi, eds. *Interrelations of Literature.* New York: MLA, 1982.

Barthes, Roland. "From Work to Text." *Textual Strategies: Perspectives in Post-structuralist Criticism.* Ed. Josue V. Harari. Ithaca: Cornell UP, 1979. 73–81.

———. *The Pleasure of the Text.* Trans. Richard Miller. New York: Hill, 1975.

———. *Writing Degree Zero.* Trans. Annette Lavers and Colin Smith. New York: Hill, 1967.

Baym, Nina. *Novels, Readers, and Reviewers: Responses to Fiction in Antebellum America.* Ithaca: Cornell UP, 1984.

Bender, Thomas. *New York Intellect: A History of Intellectual Life in New York City from 1750 to the Beginnings of Our Time.* New York: Knopf, 1987.

Benjamin, Walter. *Illuminations: Essays and Reflections.* Ed. Hannah Arendt. Trans. Harry Zohn. New York: Schocken, 1968.

———. *The Origin of German Tragic Drama.* Trans. John Osborne. London: New Left, 1977.

Bhabha, Homi, ed. *Nation and Narration.* New York: Routledge, 1989.

Bloom, Harold. *The Anxiety of Influence: A Theory of Poetry.* New York: Oxford UP, 1975.

Booth, Wayne C. *The Company We Keep: An Ethics of Fiction.* Berkeley: U of California P, 1988.

Bourdieu, Pierre. *Outline of a Theory of Practice.* Trans. Richard Nice. Cambridge: Cambridge UP, 1977.

Bremond, Claude. *Logique du recit.* Paris: Seuil, 1973.

Bromwich, David. *A Choice of Inheritance: Self and Community from Edmund Burke to Robert Frost.* Cambridge: Harvard UP, 1989.

Brooks, Peter. *Reading for the Plot.* New York: Knopf, 1984.

Brown, Calvin S. *Music and Literature: A Comparison of the Arts.* Athens: U of Georgia P, 1948.

Cavell, Stanley. *The Senses of Walden.* New York: Viking, 1972.

Chartier, Roger. *Cultural History: Between Practices and Representations.* Trans. Lydia G. Cochrane. Ithaca: Cornell UP, 1988.

Chodorow, Nancy. *The Reproduction of Mothering: Psychoanalysis and the Sociology of Gender.* Berkeley: U of California P, 1978.

Clifford, James. *The Predicament of Culture: Twentieth-Century Ethnography.* Cambridge: Harvard UP, 1988.

Coleridge, Samuel Taylor. *Biographia Literaria.* Oxford: Clarendon, 1907.

Culler, Jonathan. *Framing the Sign: Criticism and Its Institutions.* New York: Blackwell, 1988.

Dahlhaus, Carl. *Musikästhetik.* Köln: Gerig, 1967.

Danto, Arthur C. *The Philosophical Disenfranchisement of Art.* New York: Columbia UP, 1986.

Davidson, Cathy N. *Revolution and the Word: The Rise of the Novel in America.* New York: Oxford UP, 1986.

Deleuze, Gilles, and Félix Guattari. *Anti-Oedipus: Capitalism and Schizophrenia.* Trans. Robert Hurley et al. New York: Viking, 1977.

Derrida, Jacques. *Of Grammatology.* Trans. Gayatri C. Spivak. Baltimore: Johns Hopkins UP, 1976.

Dewey, John. *Art as Experience.* New York: Capricorn, 1959.

Dilthey, Wilhelm. *Gesammelte Schriften.* 14 vols. Leipzig: Tuebner, 1921–90.

Dufrenne, Mikel. *The Phenomenology of Aesthetic Experience.* Trans. Edward S. Casey and Albert Anderson. Evanston: Northwestern UP, 1973.

Eco, Umberto. *A Theory of Semiotics.* Bloomington: Indiana UP, 1976.

Eliot, T. S. *The Music of Poetry.* Glasgow: Glasgow UP, 1942.

Fish, Stanley. "Being Interdisciplinary Is So Very Hard to Do." *Profession 89.* New York: MLA, 1989. 15–22.

———. *Is There a Text in This Class? The Authority of Interpretive Communities.* Cambridge: Harvard UP, 1980.

Foucault, Michel. *The Order of Things: An Archaeology of the Human Sciences.* Trans. Allan Sheridan. New York: Vintage-Random, 1973.

Fried, Michael. *Realism, Writing, Disfiguration: On Thomas Eakin and Stephen Crane.* Chicago: U of Chicago P, 1987.

Frye, Northrop. *Anatomy of Criticism: Four Essays.* Princeton: Princeton UP, 1957.

Fuentes, Carlos. *Myself with Others: Selected Essays.* New York: Farrar, 1988.

Gadamer, Hans-Georg. *Truth and Method.* Trans. Garrett Barden and John Cumming. New York: Seabury, 1975.

Geertz, Clifford. "Blurred Genres: The Refiguration of Social Thought." *The American Scholar* 49.2 (1980): 165–79.

———. *The Interpretation of Cultures.* New York: Basic, 1973.

Genette, Gérard. *Narrative Discourse: An Essay in Method.* Trans. Jane E. Lewin. Ithaca: Cornell UP, 1980.

Gilbert, Sandra M., and Susan Gubar. *The Madwoman in the Attic: The Woman Writer and the Nineteenth-Century Literary Imagination.* New Haven: Yale UP, 1979.

Goldmann, Lucien. *The Hidden God: A Study of Tragic Vision in the* Pensées *of Pascal and the Tragedies of Racine.* Trans. Philip Thody. London: Routledge, 1964.

Gombrich, E. H. *Art and Illusion: A Study in the Psychology of Pictorial Representation.* New York: Pantheon, 1960.

Goodman, Nelson. *Languages of Art: An Approach to a Theory of Symbols.* Indianapolis: Bobbs, 1968.

Gordimer, Nadine. *The Essential Gesture: Writing, Politics, and Places.* Ed. Stephen Clingman. London: Cape, 1988.

Graff, Gerald. *Professing Literature: An Institutional History.* Chicago: U of Chicago P, 1987.

Gramsci, Antonio. *Letters from Prison.* Trans. Lynne Lawner. New York: Farrar, 1989.

Greenberg, Clement. *Art and Culture: Critical Essays.* Boston: Beacon, 1961.

Greenblatt, Stephen J. *Renaissance Self-Fashioning: From More to Shakespeare.* Chicago: U of Chicago P, 1980.

———. *Shakespearean Negotiations: The Circulation of Social Energy in Renaissance England.* Berkeley: U of California P, 1988.

Greimas, A. J. *Structural Semantics: An Attempt at a Method.* Trans. Daniele McDowell, Ronald Schleifer, and Alan Velie. Lincoln: U of Nebraska P, 1983.

Hall, Stuart, et al., eds. *Culture, Media, Language.* London: Hutchinson, 1983.

Hegel, Georg Wilhelm Friedrich. *The Phenomenology of Spirit.* Trans. A. V. Miller. Oxford: Clarendon–Oxford UP, 1977.

Heidegger, Martin. *The End of Philosophy.* Trans. Joan Stambaugh. New York: Harper, 1973.

———. *Poetry, Language, and Thought.* Trans. Albert Hofstadter. New York: Harper, 1971.

Hernadi, Paul, "Literary Theory: A Compass." *Critical Inquiry* 3 (1976): 369–86.

Hirsch, E. D., Jr. *Validity in Interpretation.* New Haven: Yale UP, 1967.

Holland, Norman. *The Dynamics of Literary Response.* New York: Oxford UP, 1968.

Hollander, John. *The Untuning of the Sky: Ideas of Music in English Poetry, 1500–1700.* Princeton: Princeton UP, 1961.

Horkheimer, Max, and Theodor Adorno. *Dialectic of Enlightenment.* Trans. John Cumming. New York: Seabury, 1972.

Iser, Wolfgang. *The Act of Reading: A Theory of Aesthetic Response.* Baltimore: Johns Hopkins UP, 1978.

———. *The Implied Reader.* Baltimore: Johns Hopkins UP, 1974.

Jacobus, Mary. *Reading Women: Essays in Feminist Criticism.* New York: Columbia UP, 1986.

Jakobson, Roman. *Selected Writings.* 2nd ed. The Hague: Mouton, 1972–85.

Jameson, Fredric. *The Political Unconscious: Narrative as a Socially Symbolic Act.* Ithaca: Cornell UP, 1981.

Jauss, Hans Robert. *Aesthetic Experience and Literary Hermeneutics.* Trans. Michael Shaw. Minneapolis: U of Minnesota P, 1982.

———. *Toward an Aesthetic of Reception.* Trans. Timothy Bahti. Minneapolis: U of Minnesota P, 1982.

Jehlen, Myra. *American Incarnation.* Cambridge: Harvard UP, 1986.

Kermode, Frank. *The Classic: Literary Images of Permanence and Change.* New York: Viking, 1975.

Kristeva, Julia. *Powers of Horror: An Essay on Abjection.* Trans. Leon Roudiez. New York: Columbia UP, 1982.

Lacan, Jacques. *Ecrits: A Selection.* Trans. Alan Sheridan. New York: Norton, 1977.

Leach, Edmund. *Genesis as Myth and Other Essays.* London: Cape, 1969.

Leavis, F. R. *The Great Tradition.* Garden City: Anchor-Doubleday, 1954.

Lévi-Strauss, Claude. *Structural Anthropology.* Vol. 1. Trans. C. Jacobson and B. G. Shoepf. London: Allen, 1968.

———. *Tristes Tropique.* Trans. John Weightman and Doreen Weightman. New York: Pocket, 1977.

Lotman, Juri. *Analysis of the Poetic Text.* Trans. D. Barton Johnson. Ann Arbor: Ardis, 1976.

Lukács, Georg. *Realism in Our Time: Literature and the Class Struggle.* Trans. John Mander and Necke Mander. New York: Harper, 1964.

Macherey, Pierre. *A Theory of Literary Production.* Trans. Geoffrey Wall. London: Routledge, 1978.

Macksey, Richard. "A New Text of the World." *Genre* 16 (1983): 307–16.

Macksey, Richard, and Eugenio Donato, eds. *The Structuralist Controversy: The Languages of Criticism and the Sciences of Man.* Baltimore: Johns Hopkins UP, 1970.

Marcuse, Herbert. *Eros and Civilization: A Philosophical Inquiry into Freud.* Boston: Beacon, 1974.

Mukarovsky, Jan. *Aesthetic Function: Norm and Value as Social Facts.* Trans. Mark E. Suino. Ann Arbor: U of Michigan P, 1970.

Nietzsche, Friedrich. *The Will to Power.* Trans. Walter Kaufmann. New York: Vintage, 1968.

Novak, Barbara. *Nature and Culture: American Landscape and Painting, 1825–1875.* New York: Oxford UP, 1980.

Nussbaum, Martha C. *The Fragility of Goodness: Luck and Ethics in Greek Tragedy and Philosophy.* New York: Cambridge UP, 1986.

———. *Love's Knowledge.* New York: Oxford UP, 1990.

———. "Narrative Emotions: Beckett's Genealogy of Love." *Ethics* 98 (1988): 225–54.

Panofsky, Erwin. *Studies in Iconology: Humanistic Themes in the Art of the Renaissance.* New York: Harper, 1972.

Paulson, Ronald. *Emblem and Expression: Meaning in English Art of the Eighteenth Century.* Cambridge: Harvard UP, 1975.

Paz, Octavio. *The Labyrinth of Solitude.* Trans. Lysander Kemp. New York: Grove, 1962.

Peirce, Charles Sanders. *Collected Papers.* Ed. Charles Hartshorne and Paul Weiss. 6 vols. Cambridge: Harvard UP, 1931–35.

Plato. *Republic.* Trans. Paul Shorey. Cambridge: Harvard UP, 1935.

Ricoeur, Paul. *The Conflict of Interpretations: Essays on Hermeneutics.* Ed. Don Ihde. Evanston: Northwestern UP, 1969.

———. *Freud and Philosophy: An Essay on Interpretation.* Trans. Denis Savage. New Haven: Yale UP, 1970.

———. *Time and Narrative.* Trans. Kathleen McLaughlin and David Pellauer. 3 vols. Chicago: U of Chicago P, 1984–88.

Riffaterre, Michael. *Text Production.* Trans. Therese Lyons. New York: Columbia UP, 1983.

Rosenberg, Harold. *The Tradition of the New.* New York: Horizon, 1959.

Said, Edward. *Orientalism.* New York: Pantheon, 1978.

Saussure, Ferdinand de. *Course in General Linguistics.* Trans. Wade Baskin. New York: McGraw, 1966.

Scarry, Elaine. *The Body in Pain: The Making and Unmaking of the World.* New York: Oxford UP, 1986.

Schapiro, Meyer. *Modern Art, Nineteenth and Twentieth Centuries: Selected Papers.* New York: Brazillir, 1979.

Scher, Steven Paul, ed. *Literatur und Musik: Ein Handbuch zur Theoric und Praxis eines komparatistischen Grenzgebietes.* Berlin: Schmidt, 1982.

Scholes, Robert. *Textual Power: Literary Theory and the Teaching of English.* New Haven: Yale UP, 1985.

Searle, John. *Speech Acts: An Essay in the Philosophy of Language.* Cambridge: Cambridge UP, 1969.

Shklovsky, Viktor. *Works.* Moscow: Khudozh' Lit'ra, 1973–74.

Todorov, Tzvetan. *The Poetics of Prose.* Trans. Richard Howard. Ithaca: Cornell UP, 1977.

Trachtenberg, Alan. *Reading American Photographs: Images as History from Matthew Brady to Walker Evans.* New York: Hill, 1989.

Trilling, Lionel. *The Liberal Imagination: Essays on Literature and Society.* Garden City: Anchor-Doubleday, 1950.

Tynyanov, Yuri. *The Problem of Verse Language.* Trans. Michael Susa and Brent Harvey. Ann Arbor: Ardis, 1981.

Vico, Giambattista. The New Science *of Giambattista Vico.* Rev. trans. of 3rd ed. (1774) by Thomas Bergin and Max Fisch. Ithaca: Cornell UP, 1968.

Weimann, Robert. *Structure and Society in Literary History: Studies in the History and Theory of Historical Studies.* Rev. ed. Baltimore: Johns Hopkins UP, 1984.

Wellek, René, and Austin Warren. "Literature and the Other Arts." *Theory of Literature.* New York: Harcourt, 1949. 124–35.

White, Hayden. *Metahistory: The Historical Imagination in Nineteenth-Century Europe.* Baltimore: Johns Hopkins UP, 1974.

Williams, Raymond. *Culture and Society, 1780–1950.* New York: Harper, 1966.

———. *Marxism and Literature.* London: Oxford UP, 1977.

Wollheim, Richard. *Painting as an Art.* Princeton: Princeton UP, 1987.

NAOMI SCHOR

Feminist and Gender Studies

BEFORE the 1970s, readers and teachers of literature were assumed to be neutered beings who left their multiple subjectivities at the door of the academy. As students during that immediately prefeminist era, we learned the impersonal rhetoric of both New Criticism and structuralism. We were taught to speak from the position of the universal, sometimes at the cost of painful mutilations and self-denials, though our professors of the universal were, with insignificantly few exceptions, white, male university professors of European ancestry who were either straight or closeted. Today, in this last decade of the twentieth century, a first-year graduate student, whether male, female, black, Hispanic, young, old, gay, lesbian, bisexual, Jewish or Arabic, postcolonial or metropolitan, or any combination of these "identities"—and the list of possibilities is constantly being updated and nuanced—enters a radically reconfigured institution, where various and complex subjectivities are accommodated on all sides of the seminar table in the "house of difference" many American institutions are becoming (Lorde, *Zami* 226). But this house was not built in a day or by a single hand; the process of construction is collective and at times contentious. Of all the forces that have participated in this ongoing enterprise, none has had a more profound impact than feminism.

And yet the 1980 edition of the MLA's *Introduction to Scholarship* contained no essay on feminist criticism, a revolutionary new approach to literary analysis and theory that emerged in the late 1960s and stood on the verge of academic respectability at the close of the 1970s. In 1989, when this edition of that volume was being planned, I was invited to provide an introduction to gender studies, a rubric meant to encompass feminist criticism and theory but also to account for more recent studies of the effects of gender on literary analysis (studies of masculinity, sexuality, and lesbian and gay issues). While these new areas of study are clearly political, they are less closely linked to women's liberation, the political movement with which feminist criticism in its most vital form has been identified and intertwined from the outset. It was only after some negotiation—an expected part of the complex process of assembling this volume—that the term *feminist* was added to my title.

This brief history of the respective places of feminist criticism and gender studies immediately suggests the approach I take in presenting feminist and gender studies in the 1990s. Although gender studies has evolved from feminist criticism and although feminist studies has always been in the most literal sense a form of gender studies, the two cannot be simply collapsed onto each other. Such a move risks erasing the specificity either of feminist criticism and its radical challenge to earlier gender-blind studies of literature or of gender studies and their elaboration, questioning, and, ultimately, reconfiguration of the insights of feminist criticism. At a moment when many institutions are debating whether to opt for a program in women's studies or for one in gender studies, it is important to understand that such decisions can be made only in terms of local contexts and situations. For instance, had the 1980 edition of *Introduction to Scholarship* contained an essay on feminist criticism, then I would now have less of a problem folding feminism into gender. But in an institutional context where feminism has not been foregrounded, it is strategically important to feature it.

By identifying my own position—I speak as an American teacher of French whose postgraduate professional career developed along with feminist criticism and for whom gender studies is an intriguing yet problematic notion—I am already performing a feminist critical act, namely, refusing to speak from a position of supposed neutrality and pseudoscientific objectivity. Two chief axioms of feminist criticism state that all acts of language are grounded in the dense network of partial positions (e.g., sexual, class, racial) occupied by speaking subjects and that to claim to speak for all (women, feminists, literary critics) is to speak from a position of assumed mastery and false universality. This position is precisely the one we as feminists seek to interrogate and dismantle, even though, as many of us have discovered, assumed mastery and false universality constantly reassert themselves.

Because gender has proved to be the central and thus, simultaneously, the most powerful and most vulnerable category of analysis elaborated by feminism, I have chosen to organize my account of feminist and gender studies around the category of gender and its vicissitudes, with all the consequences such a choice entails. One result is that I violate precedence, not to say precedent, by placing Simone de Beauvoir ahead of Virginia Woolf as a tutelary figure of feminism. Among the other consequences, I single out two.

First, obviously and inevitably, making gender the focus means subsuming the other categories of difference that currently organize feminist analysis, notably race and class, under the privileged category of gender. The current yoking of race, class, and gender can have the unfortunate effect of suggesting that these terms function as a harmonious, monolithic unit, that the articulation of these levels of analysis is nothing if not dauntingly delicate.

Of course, from the perspective of black or working-class women who are caught up in "a simultaneity of discourses" (Henderson 17), the very notion that such a choice exists at all is illusory, an indelible mark of privilege. As socialist and black feminists have argued, blindness and invisibility threaten those critics who fail to attend to the ways in which gender, race, and to a lesser extent class overdetermine the subjectivities of the unprivileged in our racist, sexist, and classist society. Certainly the possible interweavings and tensions among the stories of race, class, and gender are far more complex than current well-meaning calls for pluralism allow, and each critic working in the field of gender studies must constantly negotiate conflicting and coordinate claims (see also the essays by Allen and Gates in this volume).

Second, because gender, at least in its emergent phase, was not the operative concept informing gay-male studies, privileging the category of gender means presenting a skewed and partial view of a field initially less concerned with issues of sexual difference and the social construction of sexual roles than with undoing centuries of persecution, pathologizing, and erasure (Crew and Norton). Misogyny and homophobia share—alas—many features, but they cannot simply be mapped onto each other. In phallocentric societies, however much gay males may suffer from the myths of masculinity, they do share in the privilege of the phallus, just as in heterosexual societies, women, however disabled by the myths of femininity, can benefit from the hegemony of the heterosexual norm if they are straight. Making gender the focus, then, means privileging the more recent work in gay-male studies that collaborates in feminism's unveiling of the phallus and the hierarchies it underwrites.

If, borrowing from Joan Scott, we define gender as "a social category imposed on a sexed body" (32), then we can state unequivocally that the distinction between the "facts" of biology or anatomy and the constructs of culture constitutes the very foundation of feminist theory and criticism and continues to inform gender studies today. Yet gender studies has come under penetrating criticism from extreme constructionists (e.g., Butler), who argue that while seeming to accord primacy to the sociocultural, the notion of gender covertly preserves the myth of an unmediated access to nature, to the body. Because the distinction between gender and sex is a relatively recent one, feminist and especially gender studies—unlike several of the other approaches discussed in this volume that trace their origins back to classical antiquity—are newly constituted disciplines with short histories and still evolving problematics. Women figure prominently as writers, characters, and readers throughout the Western literary tradition, but feminist criticism is a strictly modern phenomenon born of the Enlightenment philosophies of individual rights, which enabled the fight for women's emancipation and franchise. Feminist criticism is further intimately bound up with deep transformations of the humanistic curriculum within nineteenth- and twentieth-century institutions of higher learning.

BEAUVOIR AND WOOLF

When Beauvoir stated boldly in *The Second Sex*, "One is not born a woman, one becomes one," she performed a radical gesture whose far-reaching consequences even she did not foresee (301). For reasons as much linguistic as epistemological—French has no strict equivalent for *gender* (one says, "la différence sexuelle"), and in 1949 the category of gender had not yet been elaborated by scientists and social scientists (Bock; Haraway)—Beauvoir, the most ardent of constructionists, never spoke of gender as such in *The Second Sex*.

Determined to liberate women from the disempowering constructs of patriarchy, Beauvoir studied an array of symbolic systems and cultural artifacts to deconstruct the "womanizing" of the female of the species, the process whereby a human infant born female is transformed into the embodiment of femininity, is made to function as man's other. Beauvoir demonstrated, in several studies of the way five modern male authors (André Breton, Stendhal, Henri de Montherlant, D. H. Lawrence, Paul Claudel) represented woman, that the most prevalent form of "othering" in literature is the doublet misogyny/idealization, the reduction of female characters to variants of two types, the angel-mother and the monster-whore. Following in the tradition inaugurated by Beauvoir, pioneering feminist critics such as Katharine Rogers, Mary Ellmann, and Kate Millett used what Gayle Rubin was to dub the "sex/gender" distinction to denaturalize the representation of women chiefly in male-authored fictions. Portrayals of female protagonists that had long claimed to be realistic were revealed through careful and often scathing analyses to be largely stereotypical projections of the patriarchal psyche, a psyche ruled by linguistic and cultural codes and legitimated by the unequal distribution of power between men and women in the society at large. What was quickly dubbed "images of women criticism" (Cornillon) and then "feminist critique" (Showalter, "Feminist Poetics") was in fact part of a larger and very powerful critical trend of the early 1970s, the structuralist-poststructuralist critiques of mimetic representation. Though much of the work on representation by theorists such as Roland Barthes and Michel Foucault did not take gender into account and certainly did not adopt a feminist perspective, it did intersect with the early feminist project in laying bare the sexual politics at work in seemingly innocent and authoritative imitations of social reality. The primacy of the phallus is as much the target of Barthes's playful reading of Balzac's *Sarrasine* in *S/Z* as it is of Kate Millett's scornful accounts of Norman Mailer's *American Dream* in *Sexual Politics*.

Most pioneering work in feminist criticism was produced by academically based American critics working on a predominantly white, Anglo-American corpus of nineteenth- and twentieth-century fictional texts and espousing a liberal humanist politics of individualism and experience. With the twenty-twenty vision of hindsight, we can now see American feminists as sharing many features of an essentially Continental body of male-authored theory and its feminist counterparts. Yet the initial encounters between so-called French feminism, a shorthand covering both French feminist theory and the broader conceptual framework on which it relies (the writings of Freud, Marx, Nietzsche, Saussure, Lacan, Derrida, Foucault, et al.), and so-called Anglo-American feminism were marked in the United States by suspicion and hostility, some of it justified, some not. One casualty of these initial encounters was the work on women and representation in male-authored fiction. Despite the extraordinary productivity and political efficacy of this form of critical inquiry, this first stage of gender study was quickly overtaken by what was deemed the more proper study of feminist critics, the interpretation of women's writings influentially termed "gynocriticism" by Elaine Showalter ("Feminist Poetics"). Implicitly and in practice, the exemplary gynocritic was a female feminist.

Throughout the 1970s, many feminist critics continued to work on male-authored texts from a feminist perspective and to engage theories produced by male (and often French) philosophers, psychoanalysts, anthropologists, and semioticians. Similarly, feminist film criticism, because of film's emphasis on the visual and because of the industry's dearth of female-authored or female-"auteured" films, notably continued to pursue questions of representation in highly sophisticated terms even into the 1990s (E. A. Kaplan; Doane; Bathrick in this volume). But the cutting edge of feminist criticism and theory in the United States shifted from re-visioning the cultural productions of patriarchy (Rich, "Awaken") to recovering a generally discredited, underread, and often even forgotten corpus of writing by women and to elaborating a new literary history and poetics specifically adapted to women's writing (Moers; Spacks; Gilbert and Gubar; Showalter, *Literature*). Throughout the 1970s and into the 1980s, a woman-centered feminist criticism bent on reclaiming a lost legacy of women's writing undertook to revalorize less prestigious genres associated with the feminine, such as the sentimental novel (Tompkins), and reputedly minor forms of nonfiction prose, such as diaries and letters in which women were acknowledged to excel. The canon and its often subtly gendered mechanisms of inclusion and exclusion became and remain, necessarily, a central concern of feminism (see Scholes in this volume).

What *The Second Sex* was to "images of women criticism," Woolf's *Room of One's Own* was to gynocriticism. Confronted in the reading room of the British Museum, as Beauvoir was some years later under the cupola of the Bibliothèque Nationale, with the overwhelming record of patriarchal objectification of woman, Woolf, like Beauvoir, set out to ground a subjectivity for women. However, unlike Beauvoir, for whom subjectivity is ideally and necessarily universal, Woolf undertook through an archaeology of women's writing to theorize and valorize a specifically female subjectivity and textuality, and that specificity was bound up with the maternal. Woolf writes, "We think back through our mothers if we are women" (79). Gynocriticism in its most productive form was an attempt to (re)constitute a female literary tradition by exploring the complex and hitherto hidden workings of the literary reproduction of mothering. The reigning metaphor of gynocriticism was maternal, although there were others, many of them spatial (e.g., the attic, the pavillion).

THE MATERNAL METAPHOR

One of the first works by a woman author to be included in Columbia University's famed Humanities Course syllabus, which claims to account for the best thinking and writing in the entire Western humanist tradition, was Marie-Madeleine LaFayette's *La Princesse de Clèves*. The work gradually emerged as a central

French text in the feminist rewriting of the canon, although it has not always held a privileged position in French literary history. Written in the seventeenth century by an aristocratic author close to the center of literary power, *La Princesse* has long been considered the inaugural work in the great French tradition of psychological fiction. From its anonymous publication in 1678, the controversial work has been the object of a large body of criticism, most of which focuses on its transgressions of the laws of verisimilitude and the conventions of closure: the Princess's implausible confession to her husband of her love for another man and her enigmatic final renunciation.

In a well-known essay entitled "Emphasis Added: Plots and Plausibilities in Women's Fiction," Nancy K. Miller boldly brought the question of gender to bear on the traditional debate over plausibility, by hypothesizing a link between the text's alleged implausibilities and the specificity of women's writing. Now to posit a sexual-textual specificity is to take as one's guiding assumption the basic tenet of gynocriticism: that the sex-signature of an author matters, that to be born female—and especially to be socialized as a woman in a society where education, money, and control over cultural production accrues disproportionately to those born male and socialized as men—is to write with a difference, to write otherwise. The status of the signature has been at the center of one of the longest-running debates within the Franco-American feminist community, beginning with Peggy Kamuf's "Writing like a Woman," which has since become the privileged intertext both in the debate between Kamuf and Miller and in a series of pieces concerned with the place of men in feminism (Kamuf and Miller; Culler; Modleski; Scholes; Fuss). Indeed, the debate over female signatures quickly slides into a debate over male readers, a move supporting the argument that as soon as one attacks the biological foundation of women's writing, writing by women tends to drop out of the discussion and the emphasis shifts instead to the sex of the reader. Biology is not really eliminated, merely displaced.

Even for those theorists willing to grant the premise of a sexually differentiated textuality, the question of just what form this difference might take has proved both endlessly stimulating and frustratingly elusive; it has largely centered on violent but unresolved (and perhaps unresolvable) debates within feminism over the interplay of social constructionism and essentialism. For critics who hold the view of sexual difference as socially constructed, the specificity of women's writing up to the present has been tied to cultural factors that are largely historical and thus, at least in theory, amenable to change. There is no immutable, biological reason why women writers should write the double-voiced discourse to which they, like many dominated members of society (especially racial and sexual minorities), have traditionally resorted to gain critical recognition from the establishment while at the same time resisting and subverting it. They have simply been constrained to do so by bourgeois patriarchy. Those theorists who subscribe to a view somewhat loosely labeled essentialism argue that a complex but presumably transhistorical and cross-cultural relation exists between women's language and women's bodies. Because women's pleasure is polymorphous, because women are multiorgasmic, because women's bodies are somehow bound up with the fluid (blood, milk, amniotic waters), women's writing is (or should be) essentially different: more fluid and multivoiced, less centered and hierarchized, than men's writing.

This belief in the bodily grounding of linguistic difference is referred to as *écriture féminine*, and it is somewhat misleadingly associated with the early writings of the French feminists, notably Hélène Cixous and Luce Irigaray. Not that Cixous, Irigaray, and others did not at times posit such unmediated relations between bodies and texts, for, of course, they did (Cixous; Irigaray, *This Sex*). But, as is all too often forgotten, their speculations were fraught with significant contradictions and were, furthermore, utopian poetic manifestos rather than the somewhat crude hard-line positions they have been cast into by their critics. The specters of biological determinism these French feminists raised did have the virtue of reminding more empirically oriented American feminist thinkers that language was neither transparent nor purely instrumental and that to go beyond the sexual indifference of patriarchy (Irigaray, *Speculum*), it might be necessary to challenge prevailing symbolic and representational systems, such as realism, by exploring alternative experimental uses of language by no means restricted to *écriture féminine*.

By 1981, when Miller first published "Emphasis Added," serious doubt had already been cast on the early assumption that female specificity might be located in a bodily grounded language, that what Woolf called a "woman's sentence" might be marked by specific tropes, such as metaphor or metonymy, that were somehow connected to aspects of the female body or sexual economy. Instead, Miller proposed that the elusive specificity lay in the way women writers inflected the maxims that Gérard Genette had shown to ground plausibility: this was the "emphasis added." Women's writing manipulated the cultural rather than the linguistic code. From this perspective what seemed aberrant about *La Princesse de Clèves*—the ways in which it confounds readerly expectations based on masculine cultural paradigms—became suddenly intelligible, plausible. The Princess's famed renunciation, her refusal to enter into a heterosexual marriage contract with the Duke, stemmed not from some sexual dysfunction (i.e., frigidity) but rather from a uniquely feminine economy of desire that privileged fantasy over consummation.

How, then, was one to account for this specifically feminine form of desire, a desire not oriented by the inevitable rush toward closure but one that, in Rachel Blau DuPlessis's words, strained to go "beyond the ending"? The answer to this question inevitably entailed another explanatory model, one based in psychoanalysis. Like other feminist readers working in a psychoanalytic rather than a formalist framework, some students of *La Princesse de Clèves* sought to locate that specificity in the psychological relationship between mother and daughter. Marianne Hirsch proposed a reading of *La Princesse* that located the text's feminine specificity in the representation of the intense pre-Oedipal bonds between mother and daughter that Freud had belatedly discovered to specify female sexual development.

In *The Pleasure of the Text*, Barthes made explicit a long-unspoken assumption that all narrative is Oedipal. Calling this idea into question, feminist critics working in a psychoanalytic perspective on texts ranging from the high classical *La Princesse de Clèves* to contemporary mass-market romances (Radway) have challenged the claims to universality of a theory of narrative based on a normative Oedipal model congenial to male sexual development and entirely oriented by the quest for closure. Rejecting the dominant Oedipal grid as an explanatory model unsuited to women's writing, feminist psychoanalytic critics have sought to uncover or recover the operations of a pre-Oedipal connection with the mother chiefly in the form of a prelinguistic, presyntactical, prerepresentational "m(other) tongue," similar to what Julia Kristeva has called in a slightly different context the semiotic. Molded by her intense and seemingly unmediated relationship with her widowed mother and especially by a powerful maternal discourse, the Princess's relationships with men—notably her husband, who comes to occupy the position of the mother—remain fixated at the stage of what Jacques Lacan has termed the imaginary, a dual mirroring relationship that precludes the possibility of a normative adult sexuality. Thus one of the standard plots available to the female protagonist in modern European fiction, the so-called marriage plot, is short-circuited by the imperatives of a maternally inflected desire. Unfortunately, of course, the escape from the marriage plot activates the only alternative closure available to the female protagonist, death.

The place of the maternal in feminism, as both Anglo-American and French psychoanalytic theorists agree, is thus at the very least ambivalent: empowering when it involves recovery of and reconnection to a lost maternal body and the resumption of an interrupted mother-daughter dialogue, potentially fatal when it involves unmediated fusion and an inability to enter the paternal cultural order. When the maternal is located in cultural contexts other than the hegemonic white, European one implicit in both Anglo-American and French psychoanalytic theory, a different and even more poignant set of complexities emerges, even as the centrality of the maternal metaphor remains unchallenged. The legacy of slavery, with its violent disruptions of the mother-child bond and its mystifying stereotypical figures of alienated motherhood (the mammy, the matriarch), immensely problematizes the representation of mother-daughter relationships in African American fiction. When Alice Walker goes "looking" for Zora Neale Hurston, the mother through whom, to paraphrase Woolf, so many black women writers think, Walker's quest for origins is frustrated by obstacles peculiar to the African American woman writer, at least until recently: the poverty and invisibility culminating in an unmarked grave. Similarly, in the Asian American context of Maxine Hong Kingston's *Woman Warrior*, the Eurocentric paradigm of ambivalence proves inadequate to account for a mother-daughter relationship embedded in the immigrant experience of clashing Western and Eastern cultures.

What is immediately striking about the readings I have been discussing is their exclusive focus on the female protagonist, on the operations of sexual difference in writing. Maternalist feminist criticism is concerned with identifying the productions of the female imagination, charting female psychosexual development, psychoanalyzing feminine desire, making once again audible a muffled or silenced maternal voice. Though concerned with the operations of gender, such examples of feminist criticism—chosen, of course, for what I take to be their representative status—remain by definition almost exclusively woman-centered; that is, gender is taken throughout these texts to be synonymous with sexual difference, with woman. Even in the early 1980s when the interest in readings of *La Princesse* moved away from the female protagonist and her mother to consider the construction and representation of male subjectivity in the novel and the tradition it inaugurates (Schor, "Portrait"), the underlying presumption of a female specificity in reading and writing remained largely unchallenged. It is perhaps no accident that the only article to approach *La Princesse de Clèves* from a truly bipolar gender perspective is Michael Danahy's "Social, Sexual, and Human Spaces," the sole male-authored text in the cluster I am considering. Danahy fully espouses the feminist critics' concern with the Princess's attempted escape from the oppressive, intrigue-ridden court world, but he subtly shifts the grounds of discussion away from the specificities of women's writing. Instead, he recognizes the novelist's canny representation of the operations of gender in the text's spatial organization. Whereas male characters are given unrestricted access to the various spaces in which the novel deploys its narrative, entering and exiting as they please, the female protagonists, even those with political power such as the Queen, are not free to initiate access and must struggle to find an inviolate space.

To begin to move from feminist to bisexual gender studies necessitates a micropolitical analysis of male power and masculine privilege, a dismantling of the master's house not only with "the master's tools" (Lorde, *Sister* 110–13) but, more important, by the master himself. As it quickly became apparent in the late 1970s and early 1980s, few men were initially willing to open the tool box.

THE RAPE OF FEMINISM

The sudden emergence, in the increasingly competitive "intellectual marketplace" (Jameson 10), of a disruptive critical approach representing a large and politicized constituency within the academy confronted the male-dominated critical-theoretical establishment with a challenge far more threatening than the earlier emergence of black studies, on which women's studies were initially modeled and with which they have often been compared. While feminist critics complained that their male colleagues did not read them (Gilbert), male critics eager to join the movement complained of the "separatism" (Ruthven) of its leading practitioners. What exactly was, and what is, the place of men in feminism (Jardine and Smith)? Should they be in feminism at all? Can they be kept out in the era of reader-reponse criticism, which validates all readers' reponses irrespective of sex, race, or class (Flynn and Schweikart)? What of the sometimes competing claims of race and gender in the race for gender? What was (is) the place of black men in black women's studies or the place of black women in black men's criticism and theory? What did these men and women want?

If adding women authors to the male canon meant nothing less than rethinking the grounds of canonicity itself and inventing a new poetics, a new literary history, and the like, adding male critics to feminist criticism has entailed a similar upheaval. This process follows the familiar logic of the Derridean supplement, wherein all add-ons reveal an inner lack, a difference or, as we shall see in a moment, differences within (Johnson). The emergence of gender studies went hand in hand with the refashioning of feminist criticism into a less provincial, more culturally diverse, more heterogeneous critical approach. But this did not happen all at once.

The understanding that gender is a social construct pinned to a sexed body is fundamental to feminist criticism, and it logically implies that both masculinity and femininity are cultural formations designed to secure the social organization known as patriarchy. Yet, significantly (though it is hardly surprising), most male critics' earliest attempts to deal with feminist criticism and theory did not apply the insights of gender study to deconstructing masculinity. These male critics sought instead to appropriate for themselves the insights of feminist criticism to continue a long tradition of objectifying and othering woman; the privileges of the heretofore unmarked term in a binary opposition—whether it be maleness, whiteness, heterosexuality, or Westernness—are always the last to be interrogated by the members of the privileged class. In some instances, individual male critics—often gay critics in search of a criticism of their own—approached feminist criticism sympathetically, though at first it was hard to see the male "incursions" into feminist criticism as anything but a new ruse of misogyny. Woman remained the object, man the subject.

Symptomatic of this first incursion of men into feminism was the intense critical debate that briefly swirled around Samuel Richardson's *Clarissa*, a text seemingly predestined to serve as an allegory for what I am somewhat melodramatically calling the rape of feminism. Two indissolubly linked features of *Clarissa* made it an appropriate text for simultaneously inviting and mirroring the entry of men into what had heretofore been a critical domain largely occupied by women: Clarissa is, as we know, an inveterate writer and the victim of a particularly sordid rape. By linking rape with the attempt to silence a writing woman—an attempt that, of course, fails spectacularly, since Clarissa continues to produce language and symbols even beyond the grave—*Clarissa* presented a particularly inviting textual body over which to enact the critical battle of the sexes. "Struggle," writes William Warner, "is the pervasive and continuous reality of Richardson's novel *Clarissa*" (*Reading* Clarissa 3). Indeed, as Warner remarks, the struggles for mastery over the interpretation of the novel replicate the struggles for mastery over Clarissa's body that go on within the novel. Inescapably, the issue of rape has always been at the center of the interpretive struggles over *Clarissa*, and critics have long argued over the valence to be attached to this unrepresented act. Yet it was only in the late 1970s, in the light of the women's movement, that this discussion took on major theoretical import.

From the outset of the second wave of feminism, the crime of rape has occupied a central place in feminist theory. Viewed as the physical enactment of the unequal distribution of power under patriarchy, racism, and classism, rape has been the object of countless protest marches and rallies ("take back the night"), articles, and books by such feminist thinkers as Susan Brownmiller, Catharine A. MacKinnon, and many others. Feminist analyses of rape have run the gamut from an ethical protest against all forms of sexual violence, including what is generally viewed as normal heterosexual intercourse, to a radical acknowledgment of the pleasures of danger in sexuality (both heterosexual and homosexual), from a global indictment of rape as a transhistorical crime with interchangeable victims to a historically situated denunciation of the institutionalized rape of black slave women. Most feminists, at least in the United States, would agree that rape is a defining issue of feminism. The argument over "the rape of Clarissa" that burst on the critical scene around 1980 was one whose wider implications far exceeded the specific instance of *Clarissa*. Not the least of these implications was the difficulty of articulating feminism and deconstruction.

Feminism is not a methodology or a theory unified by reference to a single proper noun (e.g., Marx or Freud) or, as has also been suggested, merely a playful eclecticism or pluralism (Kolodny), a female form of what Claude Lévi-Strauss famously called *bricolage*. Rather, it is a radical and always political form of interdisciplinary or transdisciplinary critique; indeed, "women's studies," which began by bringing together historians, anthropologists, and literary scholars, contests by definition the prevailing disciplinary model of the production and transmission of knowledge. This critique can and probably should be applied to all cognitive paradigms whose claims to universal validity are grounded in an indifference to sexual difference. These include Marxism and even, as Irigaray has convincingly shown (*Speculum*), Freudianism, to the extent that Freud continues to dream the old phallocentric dream of symmetry. The conjugal metaphor has been repeatedly enlisted to describe the unhappy marriages (Hartmann) or endlessly deferred nuptials of feminism and other isms, and deconstructionism, which has itself enlisted the hymen as a central metaphor, is no exception to the rule (Bartkowski). As the debate over the status of the female signature has already shown, the intersection of feminism and deconstruction has been the site of some of the most productive and irreconcilable critical exchanges in the 1980s. One primary reason has been the use of deconstruction to critique "essentialism" as a "ruse of metaphysics" (Poovey 57). This association of deconstruction and antiessentialism has led some materialist feminists to enlist deconstruction in their battle against ahistorical essences such as "woman." Others, more drawn to the problematics of sexual difference, resist it, suspecting Derridean antiessentialism as being a ruse of patriarchy, all the while recognizing in deconstruction a powerful lever for unsettling the paradigm of sexual difference and valorizing the previously devalorized term (Schor, *Breaking*; Homans). However, as the debates over *Clarissa* make clear, the tensions between deconstruction and feminism also participate in the tensions between deconstructionist and ideologically based views of language: Deconstruction, as applied by certain of its interpreters, views woman as a trope and sexual difference as a pure language effect, whereas, like other critics unwilling to assent to a disjunction between the world and the text that turns signifiers loose and renders all socially grounded meanings impossible, most feminists would insist that fictional women do bear some relation, however opaque, to historical women and the contingencies of their lives. In a feminist perspective, rape, like woman, can never be just a metaphor.

Interestingly, the first two books to face off against each other in the struggle, Warner's *Reading* Clarissa and Terry Castle's *Clarissa's Ciphers*, share the crucial assumption that *Clarissa* is a text centrally concerned with language. Both critics devote large sections of their studies to charting the ways in which the struggle between Clarissa and Lovelace is in fact a struggle for control over the encoding and decoding of messages, over who shall produce interpretation, and over whether and how meaning will be decided. However, the two critics, operating as they do out of radically incompatible critical frameworks, differ irreconcilably in their readings of Clarissa's enigmatic ciphers. Lining up with the Lovelaceans, Warner attempts to combat what he sees as the dominant traditional reading of Clarissa by deconstructing the seemingly clear-cut and rigid opposition between Clarissa and Lovelace, the innocent virgin and the rake. The inevitable and to my mind regrettable result is that, in the end, the victim is in a sense blamed for her own victimization. Breaking with a tradition of so-called humanist readers stretching back to Richardson himself, Warner sets out to displace the rape from the central meaning-giving position it occupies in the final version of the novel in order to bring out instead Clarissa's redoubtable powers for controlling language and interpretation, and thus snatching her greatest interpretive triumph from the jaws of violent sexual defeat. Warner's language vividly bodies forth his view of Clarissa's powers:

> In raping Clarissa, Lovelace attempts to undermine the power of her wholeness, to break her into parts, to show she's made of the same stuff everyone else is, and therefore can be read by the text of the rake's creed: "once subdued, always subdued." All this will subject Clarissa to Lovelace's interpretation of her, and so the rape becomes Lovelace's venture to master, once and for all, Clarissa's meaning.

> But Lovelace should beware. For even the commonest slut knows how to weave new veils to cover the body with a seeming freshness. And Clarissa is *not* common. (50)

These are fighting words. In *Clarissa's Ciphers*, Castle joins the fray, arguing that Warner forgets a key lesson of feminism: "The battles of interpretation, in the text, in the world, are seldom fair fights." Clarissa and Lovelace are not equal combatants in a political sense: Lovelace has available to him "all the institutionalized advantages of patriarchal power, including the power of sexual intimidation" (193). Warner fails to recognize that struggles for interpretation, whether inside or outside the text, take place in a field where the laws of gender work to disempower some participants while empowering others, and this failure most decisively separates him from politically engaged readers of Clarissa's rape such as Castle and Terry Eagleton. Indeed, lest one assume too hastily that Warner's and Castle's readings differ because of their authors' own positions in the field of gender, Eagleton's aptly named *Rape of Clarissa*, published the same year as Castle's book, complicates the question. Eagleton, a preeminent male Marxist, boldly makes common cause with the feminists and even goes much further in his ideological reading than Castle does, by asserting that *Clarissa* is not only a novel centered on the patriarchal crime against women par excellence but "arguably the major feminist text of the language," "the true story of women's oppression at the hands of eighteenth-century patriarchy" (17).

These strong texts by Warner, Castle, and Eagleton form a curious critical triangle where alliances shift depending on the angle of vision one adopts but where Castle's book occupies the central, mediating position. On the one hand, Warner and Castle share an essentially formalist view of *Clarissa* as a novel about language; on the other, Castle and Eagleton share an essentially ideological view of the relation between the text and the world. If, however, one gives this critical kaleidoscope yet another turn, one sees a crucial third view of this triad wherein Castle disappears, the triangle collapses, and Warner and Eagleton are left fighting over the textual body of a woman; in the end the struggle for interpretation is waged between men. This perspective takes over in Warner's riposte to both Castle and Eagleton, "Reading Rape: Marxist-Feminist Figurations of the Literal," where Warner ends his lengthy review article by focusing all his attention on Eagleton. In turning Eagleton's prose against him, Warner accuses Eagleton of being like Warner himself (like all men?): a Lovelacean who reenacts through his "figuration of the literal"—the lush prose in which he evokes Clarissa's violation—the very rape of Clarissa he seeks to condemn.

In the final section of *The Rape of Clarissa*, however, Eagleton makes an important shift that Warner does not account for and that might be seen as a sort of turning point in the entry of men into feminism. Eagleton, in his postscript, turns briefly to Richardson's final novel, *Sir Charles Grandison*, which he describes as "the production of a new kind of male subject" (96), one constituted through the absorption of the noblest characteristics of female sensibility: chastity and altruism. Though the novel of male sensibility is artistically a dud and the feminization of the male protagonist hardly a cause for feminist rejoicing, Eagleton's last-minute evocation of the ways in which the asymmetries of gender affect the construction of male subjectivity is a crucial and important one. It signals the beginning of a movement away from the attempts by male critics to master feminist criticism even at the cost of phallicizing women—Eagleton's Clarissa is, as Showalter astutely points out, an amazing phallic woman ("Cross-Dressing")—to a more sobering recognition that no one has the critical phallus.

GENDER STUDIES

In the rapidly evolving field of critical theory, it is not always an easy matter to assign precise dates to major shifts, since these shifts occur slowly and in uneven, zigzag patterns. In feminist criticism one must then settle for approximations: "around 1970"—to adopt Jane Gallop's mode of periodization—feminist criticism began to constitute itself on the ruins of New Criticism and in the wake of the social upheavals of the 1960s; "around 1981," again according to Gallop, feminist criticism in the United States attained academic legitimacy as measured by such leading indicators as the exponentially growing list of feminist publications (journals, books, articles), the proliferation of feminist sessions at the annual MLA convention, and, perhaps most significantly, by the tenuring of scholars primarily identified as feminist critics. Though one might argue that feminism's success in the field of literary studies was not as profound as a merely statistical overview might suggest, by the early 1980s feminist criticism and theory were without question no longer marginal activities, practiced by an embattled corps of largely untenured and powerless women.

Around 1985 feminism began to give way to what has come to be called gender studies. As I indicated at the outset, I take it that feminist and gender studies are not coextensive, though they share a central concern with gender. Instead of viewing gender studies as the inevitable transformation of feminist studies, the *end* of feminist literary history as it were, we must for heuristic as well as political reasons hold them apart so that we may grasp their specificities and carefully weigh the risks of prematurely abandoning strictly feminist concerns against the advantages of uncoupling gender from feminist politics (Langbauer).

It is, of course, equally important to subject the very notion of gender studies to close scrutiny, for, like feminism itself, gender studies is not a single entity. In fact, at this transitional moment, gender studies is an ill-defined and undertheorized label covering a heterogeneous set of critical practices whose only commonality appears to be a rejection of a narrowly conceived, woman-centered gynocriticism. Gender studies is, then, a convenient catchall term grouping together such diverse current critical practices as a feminist approach recycled into a new comparativism (what N. K. Miller, in *Subject to Change*, terms "reading in pairs" [129]), a men's studies that knowingly replicates women's studies (Brod), and gay and lesbian studies that increasingly call into question the very notions of sex and gender.

I have chosen 1985 as the date that signals the rise of gender studies in part because it marks the publication of Eve Kosofsky Sedgwick's influential *Between Men*. In that book, Sedgwick articulates the insights of feminist criticism onto those of gay-male studies, which had up to then pursued often parallel but separate courses (affirming the existence of a homosexual or female imagination, recovering lost traditions, decoding the cryptic discourse of works already in the canon by homosexual or feminist authors). This unusual and explosive conjunction both in Sedgwick's book and elsewhere has driven and energized gender studies in the field of literature and has arguably produced the field's finest readings and most significant theoretical advances. Before we examine this most innovative and promising area of gender studies, several other determinants of the shift we are tracing need to be mentioned, for, although Sedgwick's text crystallizes that shift, it is itself caught up in larger trends that need to be sorted out. I mention three in passing—a generational shift, the exhaustion of a paradigm, the emergence of a new constituency—and focus on the fourth, the publication of Michel Foucault's *History of Sexuality*.

By 1985 a first generation of feminist scholars of remarkable daring and creativity had established the indisputable validity of a feminist approach to texts and their interpretations, and a second generation of student-daughters and in some instances student-sons had begun to refine the first generation's pioneering studies. At the same time, as with other paradigms, many of the paradigms of feminism had become familiar, and, in large measure, the results of their application had become predictable. Against this backdrop, highly articulate and increasingly compelling voices that had too long remained marginal within the feminist community of literary studies—chiefly but not exclusively the voices of so-called minority women (African American, Chicana, Native American, Asian American)—began to be heard in a different way by the generally white, bourgeois, liberal, East Coast women who had shaped the early stages of feminist studies. In an era of postcolonialism, of surprisingly acrimonious public debates over the canon and pluralism, and of the flowering of black women's writing, issues of race, class, and ethnicity, long subsumed to the urgent task of creating from whole cloth a new way of reading texts and interpreting culture from a feminist standpoint, could no longer be ignored. In a series of publications (Moraga and Anzaldúa; Hooks; de Lauretis; Hull, Scott, and Smith) the multiple differences that divide women from one another and from themselves returned as a powerful force repressed by a dominant feminism now viewed as dangerously totalizing and exclusionary in its claim to speak for all women. Questions of identity that had been dismissed as pretheoretical were reopened from the standpoints of subjects unaccounted for by dominant theories. The utopian ideal of sisterhood was displaced by the realistic recognition of struggle.

However much women's liberation has been an international movement, for economic, cultural, and structural reasons women's studies has taken off and taken root in the United States as it has in no other country in the world. Because of the overwhelming influence of mainstream feminist studies, other forms of feminist study have found it difficult to constitute themselves without reduplicating some of the stages and gestures of work done "in English" by Americans. Thus canon building has been as central, if not more so, to black feminist studies as it has been to feminist studies in the national literatures (Washington; Gates; N. K. Miller, *Subject to Change*). And yet as the 1980s progressed, the studies of marginal or subaltern subjectivities and cultural productions, without ceasing to follow the lead of mainstream feminist studies in some ways, emerged in others as one of the most powerful forces spearheading the formation of the new interdisciplinary field of cultural studies (Carby; Spivak; Bathrick in this volume).

Meanwhile, other feminists who had struggled to construct subjectivities for women, even in the face of the much touted death of the author-subject, began to come to terms with some of the implications of the poststructuralist or "posthumanist" (Homans) critique of the unified subject. They brought feminism and theory together, legitimating a union long held to be bound by a shotgun marriage (see Culler in this volume). As a consequence of these and other developments, the very ground of feminism—notions such as a universal category of woman or the oppression of women by a universal patriarchy—began to heave and crack, and the temblor's aftershocks continue to be felt today.

Perhaps no single work has proved more unsettling for feminism and more influential in the field of what I would term the new gender studies than *La volonté de savoir*, the first volume of Michel Foucault's four-volume *Histoire de la sexualité*. First published in French in 1976 and translated into English in 1978, this work has provided a tremendous impetus for rethinking not so much the operations of gender—which are not, as many of Foucault's feminist readers have been quick to point out and deplore, his concern—as the distinction between gender and sexuality. The disengaging of sexuality from gender has been a major determinant in the passage from feminist to gender studies as it is emerging today. Whereas gender can be a universal category and has been posited as such, albeit one with culturally inflected variations, sexuality was, according to Foucault, an invention of nineteenth-century Europe. It is, he would argue, from within the prison house of sexuality that we have constructed our views of gender as an intractable binary system of opposites.

By historicizing sexuality, by interrogating sexuality's function as the key to an individual's most intimate and secret identity, by arguing that the association of hysteria with the female body and the association of perversion with the male body are but aspects of the regulation of pleasures and desires effected by the power-knowledge apparatus of the rising bourgeoisie, Foucault made possible a new look at and beyond the sex-gender system, including a questioning of the validity of that foundational distinction. Inspired by Foucault's analyses but also by Monique Wittig's pioneering critiques of the sex-gender system, "postfeminist" theoreticians have begun to argue several issues: First, there is no distinction between sex and gender, in that there is nothing outside or before culture, no nature that is not always and already enculturated; "sex," writes the philosopher Judith Butler, "by definition, will be shown to have been gender all along" (8). Second, the implied correlation or distinction between sex (male/female) and gender (masculine/feminine) and thus the very notion of gender serve to enforce a compulsory heterosexuality. What is at stake, then, in the postfeminist appropriation of Foucault's history of sexuality is a radical questioning of the complicity of the sex-gender distinction and the hegemony of heterosexuality. If it can be shown that gender difference is the product of a series of normative regulatory practices that work to secure a binary sexual model and to marginalize other forms of desire and object-choice, then what needs to be questioned is gender itself. Paradoxically, then, gender studies in its most exciting and genuinely innovative form becomes a kind of cultural studies based on a radical questioning of the very category of gender. It is no accident that this questioning has been carried farthest by gay or gay-identified and lesbian theoreticians bent on disturbing, not to say dismantling, heterosexuality. What gender is or was to feminism, sexuality is to the antihomophobic critical approach Sedgwick seeks to articulate in her most recent work, *Epistemology of the Closet.*

Between Men

If, after Foucault—and he has his detractors—one adopts a periodization that places the invention of homosexuality (as well as hysteria-femininity) in the Victorian era, it follows that works of fiction produced in that era should occupy a privileged position in the study of the engenderment of the novel. The last of Herman Melville's great sea novels, *Billy Budd*, has thus come to occupy a central position in the emerging field of gay studies. In Sedgwick's words, it has "made a centerpiece for gay, gay-affirmative, or gay-related readings of American culture, and for readings by gay critics" (*Epistemology* 92). The Foucauldian matrix of many recent gay or gay-related readings is most apparent in their attention to the presence in late-Victorian and turn-of-the-century works of the very taxonomizing discourses that serve to police and contain a dangerously mobile desire (D. A. Miller). Consequently, Foucault-inspired gender criticism has, like most other forms of applied theory, produced its own distinctive thematics: the thematics of disciplining. Some of the most provocative gay-gender studies today focus on the process whereby what is figured in literature is the very production of homosexuality as a category. Whereas an earlier generation of gay critics denounced the pathologizing of homosexuality (Freudian psychoanalysis fares no better here than it does in early American feminism), more recent critics study its invention, thereby denying the view of homosexuality as a transhistorical essence and provoking a debate on essentialism that is every bit as virulent as that in feminism (Boswell). On the one hand, a gay-affirmative critic such as Robert K. Martin asserts in his reading of *Billy Budd* that the novel is "above all a study of repression" (107), and he takes it as a given that one of the principal things being repressed is homosexual desire: "In this homosocial world, charged with sexual potential, only strict control of the homosexual can prevent a mutiny" (108). On the other hand, Sedgwick in her very Foucauldian reading suggests that what is being produced in *Billy Budd* is homosexuality. She asserts that the same discursive mechanisms that produce homosexuality also work to break down the opposition between the normal and the pathological, the essential and private and the circumstantial and public homosexual male, that is, between Captain Vere and Claggart.

Tragically, much of the energy animating gay-gender studies today derives from the renewed urgency of the fight against homophobia in the age of AIDS (Edelman). As demonstrated by the critical studies of the way fiction sets in place a rigidly binary heterosexual model of human desire, the cost of inventing a stigmatized homosexual male is a form of scapegoating, of which Billy Budd's exemplary punishment is only the most spectacular example. Though no analysis of homophobic discursive practices such as those surrounding AIDS can prevent a single death, one of the remarkable achievements of gay theory is its effectiveness against practices designed to make people with AIDS, chiefly homosexuals, culpable for their illness.

Between Women

At the outset, I alluded to the process of producing this essay; in turning to the question of lesbian studies, I would like to return once again to this process, because part of it involved circulating outlines of nearly all the essays in this volume for commentary among a wide and representative body of MLA members. No section of my essay provoked more spirited responses than the preliminary outline of what follows. What seemed unacceptable was my plan to focus not on the major figures that had emerged from the canon-building stage of lesbian studies—Gertrude Stein, Adrienne Rich, and Monique Wittig—but on the equally important but far more ambiguous (because bisexual?) figure of Colette. These objections are noteworthy because they reveal the controversial nature of this topic. No one contested my equally debatable choice of *Billy Budd* as a focal text for my discussion of gay studies (rather than, for example, Walt Whitman's more obviously affirmative and centrally canonic *Song of Myself*), but my non-choice of texts by Stein, Wittig, and Rich provoked dismay. This dismay points not just to my own difficulties as an "outsider" to get it right but also to important unresolved tensions between feminist and lesbian studies, especially with the emergence of gender studies. What I had failed to make clear in my outline was my reason for wanting to go slightly outside the canon for my exemplum: The canonization of the great lesbian writers, I reasoned, corresponded roughly to the era of gynocriticism and feminist canon building. I was attempting to chart, looking ahead to the future, the effect of gender (and cultural) studies in the area of lesbian criticism and theory. My error, as I see it now, was unwittingly to reduplicate a typical phallocentric gesture by expecting lesbian-gender studies to fit neatly into the template of gay-gender studies.

Not that the two fields do not share crucial assumptions. Lesbian theorists, most notably Wittig, were among the first to point to the imbrication of heterosexuality and gender and to call for an escape from gender, which Wittig describes as "the linguistic index of the political opposition between the sexes" ("Mark" 64). Because a woman is defined through her difference from man within the binary gender system, Wittig, in an essay entitled, in homage to Beauvoir, "One Is Not Born a Woman," concluded that, "Lesbians are not women" (110). Lesbian and gay studies differ significantly, however, in their views on sexuality. In gay studies, the escape from what Barthes called the "binary prison" of sex and gender (*Roland Barthes* 133) goes hand in hand with the embracing of sexuality; in lesbian studies, sexuality is in fact no more a given than is gender. And this brings us to *Sula*.

In her ground-breaking 1977 essay, "Toward a Black Feminist Criticism," Barbara Smith argued that Toni Morrison's 1973 novel *Sula* could be read as lesbian, not because, as she recognized, the central female characters, Sula and Nel, were lovers, but because their relationship was suffused with an eroticized affectivity and furthermore was set in the context of a far-reaching critique of the institutions of heterosexuality (marriage and family). It is perhaps no accident that Smith proposed such a provocative and seemingly perverse interpretation of one of the most popular and widely commented on novels by a contemporary black woman author. As many critics have argued, in a harshly (hetero)sexist and racist society, female bonding or "woman-identification" (Bethel) has offered black women a unique means of survival: hence the prominence of female friendship in such novels as Zora Neale Hurston's *Their Eyes Were Watching God*, Alice Walker's *Color Purple*, and Gloria Naylor's *Women of Brewster Place*; hence also the symptomatic silence surrounding black women's sexuality (Spillers). The eroticization of black female friendship in the modern American black women's novel is the flip side of the appropriation of sexuality by women of the dominant white majority.

Although Smith's classification of *Sula* as a lesbian, indeed an "exceedingly" lesbian, novel is controversial—Morrison herself has registered her dissent—it raises a crucial debate about the definition of lesbianism. Some theorists, following Rich, subscribe to a broad definition of lesbianism that spans a "continuum" from female friendship to sexually consummated woman-woman relationships ("Compulsory"); others, following Catharine R. Stimpson and Barbara Christian among others, define lesbianism as necessarily sexually embodied. The very existence, within the spectrum of lesbian theory, of a significant debate over the centrality of sexuality in defining lesbianism reveals an important difference between lesbian and gay studies, one that mirrors what Sedgwick describes as "an asymmetry in our present society between, on the one hand, the relatively continuous relation of female homosocial and homosexual bonds, and, on the other hand, the radically discontinuous relation of male homosocial and homosexual bonds" (*Between Men* 4–5). In other words, because male homosexuality threatens patriarchal society in a way that female homosexuality does not, male homosexuality is more strictly coterminous with sexual practices than is female homosexuality; there is no gay continuum.

But there is a further, significant trend in much current lesbian theory: Sexuality is not positioned in as unproblematically central a position as it appears to be in gay theory, and gender too is differently sited. It is precisely because of the debates over the proper place of sexuality in defining lesbianism that the place of gender is problematized otherwise. Parting company on this score with Wittig's radical and complete escape from gender, contemporary lesbian theorists seem to want to hold onto at least a shadow of gender, the role-playing inherent in the very notion of gender, as a means of subversion; in a spectacular display of "female fetishism" (Schor), lesbian theorists (Case; de Lauretis, "Sexual Indifference"; Butler) seek to appropriate gender roles simultaneously (e.g., butch and femme), while radically rejecting the fiction of stable gender identities. Thus, Esther Newton, in an influential rereading of what is generally held to be "the single most popular representation of lesbianism in fiction" (de Lauretis, "Sexual Indifference" 161)—Radclyffe Hall's 1928 novel *The Well of Loneliness*—makes the case for the novel's "mannish lesbian" protagonist, Stephen Gordon. Instead of deploring Hall's uncritical acceptance of the discourse of turn-of-the-century sexology that views homosexuality as resulting from tragically mismatched bodies and desires—the so-called trapped-soul paradigm that pervades many contemporary fictional texts—Newton sees it as the only means available to Hall to body forth lesbian desire. In other words, the trappings of gender—including costume and transsexualism, which are areas of crucial significance in lesbian-gender studies—must be donned both to denaturalize gender and to represent lesbian desire adequately.

Feminist and gender studies have been in the vanguard of what we might call the differencing of the American university; the critique of phallocentrism in all its ramifications has changed aspects of our professional activities ranging from the way we define our objects of study to the way we treat the "third women" (Gallop, "Annie Leclerc") who type our manuscripts and clean our offices. This is not to say that the institutions in which we study and teach have become, under the effect of feminism and gender studies, intellectual or workers' paradises or that they have ceased to discipline their subjects as institutions do; for they have not. There is struggle at the seminar table between increasingly fragmented constituencies, and yesterday's marginal subjectivities are always in danger of becoming tomorrow's gatekeepers. But, and for me this *but* makes all the difference, today's students need no longer check their subjectivities at the door. And our readings of all texts are therefore the richer.

Suggestions for Further Reading

The quickest way for the beginner to get her or his bearings in the ever-expanding library of feminist and gender studies is to consult a combination of anthologies, introductory overviews, and a selection of representative or influential works. Many of these sources include substantial bibliographies that can in turn suggest further readings. In addition to those works already mentioned in the essay, I would recommend Toril Moi's *Sexual/Textual Politics: Feminist Literary Theory* and Gayle Greene and Coppélia Kahn's *Making a Difference: Feminist Literary Criticism*, both of which give the reader a sense of the main issues in feminist criticism, before the arrival of gender and postcolonial studies. Elaine Showalter's edited volume *Speaking of Gender* marks the emergence of gender studies as a distinct field. Among the recent anthologies on gender and the question of men in feminism, I suggest two companion books edited by Linda Kauffman, *Gender and Theory: Dialogues on Feminist Criticism* and *Feminism and Institutions: Dialogues on Feminist Theory*, as well as Joseph A. Boone and Michael Cadden's *Engendering Men*. Two works that might provide a useful entry point into the area of Marxist feminist literary and cultural analysis are Judith Newton and Deborah Rosenfelt's *Feminist Criticism and Social Change: Sex, Class, and Race in Literature and Culture* and Cora Kaplan's *Sea Changes: Essays on Culture and Feminism*. For a diverse series of essays on the problems raised by the articulation of feminism and poststructuralism, see Elizabeth Weed's *Coming to Terms: Feminism/Theory/Politics*. Read side by side with Cheryl A. Wall's more theoretical *Changing Our Own Words*, Joanne M. Braxton and Andrée Nicola McLaughlin's *Wild Women in the Whirlwind: Afra-American Culture and the Contemporary Literary Renaissance* provides an excellent introduction to a wide spectrum of current black feminist literary criticism.

Duke University

Works Cited

Barthes, Roland. *The Pleasure of the Text.* Trans. Richard Miller. New York: Hill, 1975. Trans. of *Le plaisir du texte*. Paris: Seuil, 1973.

———. *Roland Barthes by Roland Barthes.* Trans. Richard Howard. New York: Hill, 1977. Trans. of *Roland Barthes par Roland Barthes*. Paris: Seuil, 1975.

———. *S/Z.* Trans. Richard Miller. New York: Hill, 1974. Trans. of *S/Z*. Paris: Seuil, 1970.

Bartkowski, Fran. "Feminism and Deconstruction: A Union Forever Deferred." *Enclitic* 4.2 (1980): 70–77.

Beauvoir, Simone de. *The Second Sex.* Trans. H. M. Parshley. New York: Vintage, 1974. Trans. of *Le deuxième sexe*. 2 vols. Paris: Gallimard, 1949.

Bethel, Lorraine. " 'This Infinity of Conscious Pain': Zora Neale Hurston and the Black Female Literary Tradition." Hull, Scott, and Smith 176–88.

Bock, Gisela. "Women's History and Gender History: Aspects of an International Debate." *Gender and History* 1.1 (1989): 7–30.

Boone, Joseph A., and Michael Cadden. *Engendering Men: The Question of Male Feminist Criticism.* New York: Routledge, 1990.

Boswell, John. "Concepts, Experience, and Sexuality." *Differences* 2.1 (1990): 67–87.

Braxton, Joanne M., and Andrée Nicola McLaughlin, eds. *Wild Women in the Whirlwind: Afra-American Culture and the Contemporary Literary Renaissance.* New Brunswick: Rutgers UP, 1989.

Brod, Harry. "Introduction: Themes and Theses of Men's Studies." *The Making of Masculinities: The New Men's Studies.* Ed. Brod. Boston: Allen, 1987. 1–17.

Brownmiller, Susan. *Against Our Will: Men, Women, and Rape.* New York: Simon, 1975.

Butler, Judith. *Gender Trouble: Feminism and the Subversion of Identity.* New York: Routledge, 1990.

Carby, Hazel V. *Reconstructing Womanhood: The Emergence of the Afro-American Woman Novelist.* New York: Oxford UP, 1987.

Case, Sue-Ellen. "Towards a Butch-Femme Aesthetic." *Discourse* 11.1 (1988–89): 55–73.

Castle, Terry. *Clarissa's Ciphers: Meaning and Disruption in Richardson's* Clarissa. Ithaca: Cornell UP, 1982.

Christian, Barbara. "No More Buried Lives: The Theme of Lesbianism in Audre Lorde's *Zami*, Gloria Naylor's *The Women of Brewster Place*, Ntozake Shange's *Sassafras, Cypress and Indigo*, and Alice Walker's *The Color Purple*." *Black Feminist Criticism: Perspectives on Black Women Writers.* New York: Pergamon, 1985. 187–204.

Cixous, Hélène. "The Laugh of the Medusa." Trans. Keith Cohen and Paula Cohen. *Signs* 1 (1976): 875–94.

Cornillon, Susan Koppelman, ed. *Images of Women in Fiction: Feminist Perspectives.* Bowling Green: Bowling Green UP, 1972.

Crew, Louie, and Rictor Norton. "The Homophobic Imagination: An Editorial." *College English* 36 (1974): 272–90.

Culler, Jonathan. "Reading as a Woman." *On Deconstruction: Theory and Criticism after Structuralism.* Ithaca: Cornell UP, 1982. 43–64.

Danahy, Michael. "Social, Sexual, and Human Spaces in *La Princesse de Clèves.*" *French Forum* 6 (1981): 212–24.

de Lauretis, Teresa, ed. *Feminist Studies/Critical Studies.* Bloomington: Indiana UP, 1986.

———. "Sexual Indifference and Lesbian Representation." *Theatre Journal* 40 (1988): 155–77.

Doane, Mary Ann. *The Desire to Desire: The Women's Film of the 1940s.* Bloomington: Indiana UP, 1987.

DuPlessis, Rachel Blau. *Writing beyond the Ending: Narrative Strategies of Twentieth-Century Women Writers.* Bloomington: Indiana UP, 1985.

Eagleton, Terry. *The Rape of Clarissa: Writing, Sexuality, and the Class Struggle in Samuel Richardson.* Minneapolis: U of Minnesota P, 1982.

Edelman, Lee. "The Plague of Discourse: Politics, Literary Theory, and AIDS." *South Atlantic Quarterly* 88 (1989): 301–17.

Ellmann, Mary. *Thinking about Women.* New York: Harcourt, 1968.

Flynn, Elizabeth A., and Patrocinio P. Schweikart, eds. *Gender and Reading: Essays on Readers, Texts, and Contexts.* Baltimore: Johns Hopkins UP, 1986.

Foucault, Michel. *An Introduction.* Vol. 1 of *The History of Sexuality.* 3 vols. Trans. Robert Hurley. New York: Vintage, 1980. Trans. of *La volonté de savoir.* Vol. 1 of *Histoire de la sexualité.* 3 vols. Paris: Gallimard, 1976.

Fuss, Diana. "Reading as a Feminist." *Differences* 1.2 (1989): 77–92.

Gallop, Jane. "Annie Leclerc Writing a Letter, with Vermeer." N. Miller, *Poetics* 137–56.

———. *Around 1981: Academic Feminist Literary Theory.* New York: Routledge, forthcoming.

Gates, Henry Louis, Jr., gen. ed. *The Schomburg Library of Nineteenth-Century Black Women Writers.* 30 vols. to date. New York: Oxford UP, 1988–.

Genette, Gérard. "Vraisemblance et motivation." *Figures II.* Paris: Seuil, 1969. 71–99.

Gilbert, Sandra M. "What Do Feminist Critics Want? A Postcard from the Volcano." Showalter, *New Feminist Criticism* 29–44.

Gilbert, Sandra M., and Susan Gubar. *The Madwoman in the Attic: The Woman Writer and the Nineteenth-Century Literary Imagination.* New Haven: Yale UP, 1979.

Greene, Gayle, and Coppélia Kahn, eds. *Making a Difference: Feminist Literary Criticism.* New York: Methuen, 1985.

Haraway, Donna. "Geschlecht, Gender, Genre: Sexualpolitik eines Wortes." *Viele Orte überall? Feminisimus in Bewegung: Festschrift für Frigga Haug.* Ed. Kornelia Hauser. Berlin: Argument, 1987. 22–41.

Hartmann, Heidi. "The Unhappy Marriage of Marxism and Feminism: Towards a More Progressive Union." *Capital and Class* 8 (1979): 3–33.

Henderson, Mae Gwendolyn. "Speaking in Tongues: Dialogics, Dialectics, and the Black Woman Writer's Literary Tradition." Wall 16–37.

Hirsch, Marianne. "A Mother's Discourse: Incorporation and Repetition in *La Princesse de Clèves.*" *Yale French Studies* 62 (1981): 67–87.

Homans, Margaret. "Feminist Criticism and Theory: The Ghost of Creusa." *Yale Journal of Criticism* 1.1 (1987): 153–82.

Hooks, Bell [Gloria Watkins]. *Ain't I a Woman: Black Women and Feminism.* Boston: South End, 1981.

Hull, Gloria, Patricia Bell Scott, and Barbara Smith, eds. *All the Women Are White, All the Blacks Are Men, but Some of Us Are Brave: Black Women's Studies.* Old Westbury: Feminist, 1982.

Irigaray, Luce. *Speculum of the Other Woman.* Trans. Gillian C. Gill. Ithaca: Cornell UP, 1985.

———. *This Sex Which Is Not One.* Trans. Catherine Porter and Carolyn Burke. Ithaca: Cornell UP, 1985.

Jameson, Fredric. *The Political Unconscious: Narrative as a Socially Symbolic Act.* Ithaca: Cornell UP, 1981.

Jardine, Alice, and Paul Smith, eds. *Men in Feminism.* New York: Methuen, 1987.

Johnson, Barbara. *The Critical Difference. Essays in the Contemporary Rhetoric of Reading.* Baltimore: Johns Hopkins UP, 1980.

Kamuf, Peggy. "Writing like a Woman." *Women and Language in Literature and Society.* Ed. Sally McConnell-Ginet, Ruth Borker, and Nelly Furman. New York: Praeger, 1980. 284–99.

Kamuf, Peggy, and Nancy K. Miller. "Parisian Letters: Between Feminism and Deconstruction." *Conflicts in Feminism.* Ed. Marianne Hirsch and Evelyn Fox Keller. New York: Routledge, 1990. 121–33.

Kaplan, Cora. *Sea Changes: Essays on Culture and Feminism.* London: Verso, 1986.

Kaplan, E. Ann. *Women and Film, Both Sides of the Camera.* New York: Methuen, 1983.

Kauffman, Linda, ed. *Feminism and Institutions: Dialogues on Feminist Theory.* New York: Blackwell, 1989.

———, ed. *Gender and Theory: Dialogues on Feminist Criticism.* New York: Blackwell, 1989.

Kolodny, Annette. "Dancing through the Minefield: Some Observations on the Theory, Practice, and Politics of a Feminist Literary Criticism." Showalter, *New Feminist Criticism* 144–67.

Kristeva, Julia. *Desire in Language: A Semiotic Approach to Literature and Art.* Ed. Leon S. Roudiez. Trans. Alice Jardine and Thomas Gora. New York: Columbia UP, 1980.

Lacan, Jacques. *Ecrits: A Selection.* Trans. Alan Sheridan. New York: Norton, 1977.

Lafayette, Marie-Madeleine de. *La Princesse de Clèves.* 1678. Paris: Garnier-Flammarion, 1966.

———. *The Princess of Clèves.* Trans. Nancy Mitford. Harmondsworth, Eng.: Penguin, 1978.

Langbauer, Laurie. "Women in White, Men in Feminism." *Yale Journal of Criticism* 2.2 (1989): 219–43.

Lorde, Audre. *Sister Outsider: Essays and Speeches.* Trumansburg: Crossing, 1984.

———. *Zami: A New Spelling of My Name.* Trumansburg: Crossing, 1982.

MacKinnon, Catharine A. "Feminism, Marxism, Method, and the State: Towards a Feminist Jurisprudence." *Signs* 8 (1983): 635–58.

Martin, Robert K. *Hero, Captain, and Stranger: Male Friendship, Social Critique, and Literary Form in the Sea Novels of Herman Melville.* Chapel Hill: U of North Carolina P, 1986.

Melville, Herman. *Billy Budd.* Ed. Harrison Hayford. New York: Library of America, 1984.

Miller, D. A. "*Cage aux folles*: Sensation and Gender in Wilkie Collins's *The Woman in White.*" *The Novel and the Police.* Berkeley: U of California P, 1988. 146–91.

Miller, Nancy K. "Emphasis Added: Plots and Plausibilities in Women's Fiction." N. Miller, *Subject to Change* 25–46.

———, ed. *The Poetics of Gender.* New York: Columbia UP, 1986.

———. *Subject to Change: Reading Feminist Criticism.* New York Columbia UP, 1989.

Millett, Kate. *Sexual Politics.* Garden City: Doubleday, 1970.

Modleski, Tania. "Feminism and the Power of Interpretation: Some Critical Readings." de Lauretis, *Feminist Studies* 121–39.

Moers, Ellen. *Literary Women.* New York: Oxford UP, 1976.

Moi, Toril. *Sexual/Textual Politics: Feminist Literary Theory.* New York: Methuen, 1985.

Moraga, Cherríe, and Gloria Anzaldúa, eds. *This Bridge Called My Back: Writings by Radical Women of Color.* Watertown: Persephone, 1981.

Morrison, Toni. *Sula.* New York: NAL, 1973.

Newton, Esther. "The Mythic Mannish Lesbian: Radclyffe Hall and the New Woman." *Signs* 9 (1984): 557–75.

Newton, Judith, and Deborah Rosenfelt, eds. *Feminist Criticism and Social Change: Sex, Class, and Race in Literature and Culture.* New York: Methuen, 1985.

Poovey, Mary. "Feminism and Deconstruction." *Feminist Studies* 14 (1988): 51–64.

Radway, Janice A. *Reading the Romance: Women, Patriarchy, and Popular Literature.* Chapel Hill: U of North Carolina P, 1984.

Rich, Adrienne. "Compulsory Heterosexuality and Lesbian Existence." *The Powers of Desire: The Politics of Sexuality.* Ed. Ann Snitow, Christine Stansell, and Sharon Thompson. New York: Monthly Review, 1983. 177–205.

———. "When We Dead Awaken: Writing as Re-Vision." *On Lies, Secrets, and Silence: Selected Prose, 1966–1978.* New York: Norton, 1979.

Richardson, Samuel. *Clarissa.* Ed. George Sherburn. Boston: Houghton, 1962.

Rogers, Katharine. *The Troublesome Helpmate: A History of Misogyny in Literature.* Seattle: U of Washington P, 1966.

Rubin, Gayle. "The Traffic in Women: Notes on the 'Political Economy' of Sex." *Toward an Anthropology of Women.* Ed. Rayna R. Reiter. New York: Monthly Review, 1975. 157–210.

Ruthven, K. K. *Feminist Literary Studies: An Introduction.* Cambridge: Cambridge UP, 1984.

Scholes, Robert. "Reading like a Man." Jardine and Smith 204–18.

Schor, Naomi. *Breaking the Chain: Women, Theory, and French Realist Fiction.* New York: Columbia UP, 1985.

———. "Female Fetishism." *The Female Body in Western Culture.* Ed. Susan Suleiman. Cambridge: Harvard UP, 1985. 363–72.

———. "The Portrait of a Gentleman: Representing Men in (French) Women's Writing." *Representations* 20 (1987): 113–33. Rpt. in *Misogyny, Misandry, and Misanthropy.* Ed. R. Howard Bloch and Frances Ferguson. Berkeley: U of California P, 1989. 113–33.

Scott, Joan. "Gender: A Useful Category of Gender Analysis." *Gender and the Politics of History.* New York: Columbia UP, 1988. 28–50.

Sedgwick, Eve Kosofsky. *Between Men: English Literature and Male Homosocial Desire.* New York: Columbia UP, 1985.

———. *Epistemology of the Closet.* Berkeley: U of California P, 1991.

Showalter, Elaine. "Critical Cross-Dressing: Male Feminists and the Woman of the Year." *Raritan* 3.2 (1983): 130–49.

———. *A Literature of Their Own: British Women Novelists from Brontë to Lessing.* Princeton: Princeton UP, 1977.

———, ed. *The New Feminist Criticism: Essays on Women, Literature, and Theory.* New York: Pantheon, 1985.

———, ed. *Speaking of Gender.* New York: Routledge, 1989.

———. "Toward a Feminist Poetics." Showalter, *New Feminist Criticism* 125–43.

Smith, Barbara. "Toward a Black Feminist Criticism." Showalter, *New Feminist Criticism* 168–85.

Spacks, Patricia M. *The Female Imagination.* New York: Knopf, 1975.

Spillers, Hortense. "Interstices: A Small Drama of Words." Vance 73–100.

Spivak, Gayatri C. *In Other Worlds: Essays in Cultural Politics.* New York: Routledge, 1987.

Stimpson, Catharine R. "Zero Degree Deviancy: The Lesbian Novel in English." *Critical Inquiry* 8 (1981): 363–79.

Tompkins, Jane. *Sensational Designs: The Cultural Work of American Fiction, 1790–1860.* New York: Oxford UP, 1985.

Vance, Carol, ed. *Pleasure and Danger: Exploring Female Sexuality.* Boston: Routledge, 1984.

Walker, Alice. "Looking for Zora." *In Search of Our Mothers' Gardens.* New York: Harcourt, 1983. 93–116.

Wall, Cheryl A., ed. *Changing Our Own Words: Essays on Criticism, Theory, and Writing by Black Women.* New Brunswick: Rutgers UP, 1989.

Warner, William Beatty. *Reading* Clarissa: *The Struggles of Interpretation.* New Haven: Yale UP, 1979.

———. "Reading Rape: Marxist-Feminist Figurations of the Literal." *Diacritics* 13.4 (1983): 12–32.

Washington, Mary Helen. *Invented Lives: Narratives of Black Women, 1860–1960.* New York: Anchor-Doubleday, 1987.

Weed, Elizabeth, ed. *Coming to Terms: Feminism/Theory/Politics.* New York: Routledge, 1989.

Wittig, Monique. "The Mark of Gender." N. Miller, *Poetics* 63–73.

———. "One Is Not Born a Woman." *Feminist Issues* 1 (1984): 103–11.

Woolf, Virginia. *A Room of One's Own.* 1929. New York: Harcourt, 1957.

HENRY LOUIS GATES, JR.

"Ethnic and Minority" Studies

A WONDERFUL bit of nineteenth-century student doggerel about the famous Victorian classical scholar Benjamin Jowett nicely sums up the claims of the monoculturalist:

> Here I stand, my name is Jowett.
> If there's knowledge, then I know it.
> I am master of this college:
> What I know not, is not knowledge.
> (McFarland 6)

Unfortunately, as history has taught us, an Anglo-American regional culture has too often masked itself as universal, passing itself off as our "common culture" and depicting different cultural traditions as "tribal" or "parochial." On a more global scale are the familiar claims for a great and integral "Western tradition" containing the seeds, fruit, and flowers of the very best that has been thought or uttered in human history. Conventionally opposed to monoculturalism is multiculturalism, which frequently finds its academic site in so-called ethnic and minority studies. The multiculturalist claims that only when we are free to explore the complexities of our hyphenated American culture can we discover what a genuinely common American culture might look like.

Lately, multiculturalism has been on the defensive. We have been told that it threatens to fragment American culture into a warren of ethnic enclaves, each separate and inviolate; that it menaces the Western tradition of literature and the other arts; and that it aims to politicize the school curriculum, replacing honest historical scholarship with a "feel good" syllabus designed solely to bolster the self-esteem of minorities. The alarm has been sounded, and many scholars and educators—liberals as well as conservatives—have responded to it. After all, if multiculturalism is just a pretty name for ethnic chauvinism, who needs it? Yet common sense reminds us that we are all ethnics, and the challenge of transcending ethnic chauvinism is one we all face.

The society we have made simply will not survive without the values of tolerance, and cultural tolerance comes to nothing without cultural understanding. In short, the challenge facing America in the next century will be the shaping, at long last, of a truly common public culture, one responsive to the long-silenced cultures of color. If we relinquish the ideal of America as a plural nation, we abandon the very experiment that America represents—and we renounce the ideals of humanistic education and scholarship inherent in that experiment.

BACKGROUND

My liberal pluralist preamble is ample evidence that the academic world has radically changed during the past two or three decades. My own graduate students normally greet with polite skepticism the anecdote I relate to them about the day I announced to the tutor at Clare College, Cambridge, that I wanted very much to write a doctoral thesis on "black literature." It was a proposal to which he replied with great disdain, "Tell me, sir, . . . what *is* black literature?" Few, if any, students or scholars of "ethnic and minority" literatures encounter this sort of hostility, skepticism, and suspicion today. In fact, for those of us who were students or professors of such literatures in the late 1960s and on through the 1970s, it is a thing of wonder to behold the various ways in which our specialities have moved, if not from the margins to the center of the profession, at least from defensive postures to a generally accepted validity.

In the United States, the status of African American literature within the academy has been altered astonishingly during the past quarter century. Few English departments have not engaged in, or will not continue to engage in, searches for junior and senior professors of African American literature. We have come a long way since the early 1920s, when Charles Eaton Burch (1891–1941), as chair of the English department at Howard University, introduced into the curriculum a course entitled Poetry and Prose of Negro Life. We have come a long way, too, from the middle 1930s, when James Weldon Johnson (1871–1938), then the Adam K. Spence Professor of Creative Literature and Writing at Fisk University, became the first scholar to teach black literature at a white institution, New York University, where he delivered an annual lecture series on "Negro literature."

What has happened within the profession of literature to elevate the status of African American and other "minority" texts? Multicultural literary studies emerged from social and political movements within the academy in the 1960s, such as black studies, women's studies, affirmative-action recruitment of students and faculty members, and the growth of area and ethnic studies programs. Consequently, and often erroneously, multicultural literary studies has been associated with the academic left. Among the first professional gestures of great importance to this movement was the publication of Dexter Fisher's volume *Minority Language and Literature* (1977), which grew out of a conference sponsored by the Modern Language Association. "In an effort to address the critical, philosophical, pedagogical, and curricular issues surrounding the teaching of minority literature," Fisher explains in her introduction to the book, the MLA in 1972 formed the Commission on Minority Groups and the Study of Language and Literature (8). This group evolved into the current MLA Committee on the Literatures and Languages of America, the charge of which is to support, among other fields, African American, Asian American, Chicano, Native American, and Puerto Rican studies. Until the early 1970s, however, black scholars did not find the MLA a welcoming institution; they formed instead the predominantly black College Language Association, which still thrives today. The commission's establishment was an attempt, in part, to redefine the MLA sufficiently to "open up" its membership to black and other minority professors.

Beginning in 1974, the commission sponsored various colloquiums, funded by the NEH, "to stimulate greater awareness and to encourage more equitable representations of minority literature in the mainstream of literary studies" (8). Fisher's book stemmed directly from a conference held in 1976, at which forty-four scholars, publishers, and foundation program officers came together to consider "the relationship of minority literature to the mainstream of American literary tradition." Fisher continues:

> The question of the "place" of minority literature in American literature raises a deeper, and perhaps more controversial, question: "In what ways does minority literature share the values and assumptions of the dominant culture, and in what ways does it express divergent perspectives?" This question has implications not only for curriculum development and critical theory, but also, and even more important, for the role of the humanities in bringing about a truly plural system of education. (9)

The conference's participants explored the relations between "principles of criticism" and social contexts. As Fisher nicely puts it:

> The emergence of the Black Aesthetics Movement in the 1960s focused attention on the dilemma faced by minority writers trying to reconcile cultural dualism. Willingly or otherwise, minority writers inherit certain tenets of Western civilization through American society, though they often live alienated from that society. At the same time, they may write out of a cultural and linguistic tradition that sharply departs from the mainstream. Not only does this present constant social, political, and literary choices to minority writers, but it also challenges certain aesthetic principles of evaluation for the critic. When the cultural gap between writer and critic is too great, new critical approaches are needed. (13)

Although scholars of minority literatures have concerned themselves with a number of common issues, some of which I discuss later, each field has responded to the issues differently and has evolved in its own way. Because of limitations of space, not to mention expertise, I sketch how the field I know the best—African American literary scholarship—has responded to these issues and has evolved. (For an introductory bibliography to the entire area, see the list of works cited and suggestions for further reading. Ruoff and Ward's *Redefining American Literary History* contains comprehensive annotated bibliographies, as well as illuminating essays on African American, American Indian, Asian American, Chicano, and Puerto Rican literatures.)

We might think of the development of African American criticism over the past three decades in several distinct stages, commencing with the black-arts movement of the mid and late 1960s. The black-arts movement, whose leading theoreticians were Amiri Baraka and Larry Neal, was a reaction against the New Criticism's variety of formalism. The readings these critics advanced were broadly cultural and richly contextualized; they aimed to be "holistic" and based formal literature firmly on black urban vernacular, expressive culture. Art was a fundamental part of "the people"; "art for art's sake" was seen as a concept alien to a "pan-African" sensibility, a sensibility that was whole, organic, and, of course, quite ahistorical. The movement attacked what was identified as European or Western essentialism—masked under the rubric of "universality"—by asserting an oppositional black or "neo-African" essentialism. In place of formalist notions about art, these critics promoted a poetics rooted in a social realism, indeed, on a sort of mimeticism; the relation between black art and black life was a direct one.

Following the great outburst of interest in black studies in the late 1960s, when student protests on its behalf were at their noisiest, the field began to stagnate in the mid 1970s, as many ill-conceived, politically overt programs collapsed or were relegated to a status even more marginal than the one they had previously had. American publishers, ever sensitive to their own predictions about market size, became reluctant to publish works in this field. Forecasts of the death of African American studies abounded in 1975. This outlook would soon change, however, for within the academy a second generation of scholars of black literature was undertaking important projects that would bear directly on the field.

In response to what we might think of as the social organicism of the black-arts movement, a formalist organicism emerged in the mid 1970s. This movement was concerned with directing critical attention away from the "literariness" of the black texts as autotelic artifacts to their status as acts of language first and foremost. The use of formalist and structuralist theories and modes of reading characterized the criticism of this period. The formalists saw their work as a "corrective" to the social realism of the black-arts critics.

In the late 1960s, when black studies formally entered the curriculum, history was the predominant subject; a decade later, literary studies had become the "glamour" area of black studies. While the black-arts movement of the mid 1960s had declared literature, and especially poetry, to be the cultural wing of the black-power revolution, it had little effect on the curricula offered by traditional departments of English. This intervention was dependent on the studies produced by a group of younger scholars—Donald Gibson, June Jordan, Houston Baker, Jr., Arnold Rampersad, Geneva Smitherman, Mary Helen Washington, Carolyn Fowler, R. Baxter Miller, and others—many of whom had been trained by an older generation of African Americanists. That earlier generation included literary critics such as Charles Davis, Michael Cooke, Darwin Turner, and J. Saunders Redding, some of whom had been recruited to previously segregated schools in response to student demands for the creation of black studies.

For a variety of reasons, and in a remarkable variety of ways, these younger scholars began to theorize about the nature and function of black literature and its criticism and, simultaneously, to train an even younger generation of students. While it is difficult, precisely, to characterize their concerns, these scholars seemed to share a concern with the "literariness" of African American works, as they wrestled to make these texts a "proper" object of analysis within traditional departments of English. Whereas black literature had generally been taught and analyzed through an interdisciplinary methodology, in which sociology and history had virtually blocked out the "literariness" of the black text, these scholars, after 1975, began to argue for the explication of the formal properties of writing. If the "blackness" of a text was to be found anywhere, they argued, it would be in the practical uses of language. So, at a time when theorists of European and Anglo-American literature were offering critiques of Anglo-American formalism, scholars of black literature, responding to the history of their own discipline, found it "radical" to teach formal methods of reading.

Further enhancing the study (and status) of African American literary texts and the growth of student interest in the field at this time was the emergence of what we might think of as black women's studies—the meeting, on common terrain, between black studies and women's studies. Since 1970, when Toni Morrison published *The Bluest Eye* and Alice Walker published *The Third Life of George Copeland*, scholars of women's studies have accepted the work and lives of black women as their subject matter in a manner perhaps unprecedented in the American academy. Thus the women's studies movement in the academy helped give new life to African American studies, broadly conceived, in the 1970s.

In the third stage, critics of black literature began to retheorize social—and textual—boundaries. Drawing on poststructuralist theory as well as deriving theories from black expressive, vernacular culture, these critics were able to escape both the social organicism of the black-arts movement and the formalist organicism of the "reconstructionists." Their work might be characterized as a new black aesthetic movement, though it problematizes the categories of both the "black" and the "aesthetic." An initial phase of theorizing has given way to the generation of close readings that attend to the "social text" as well. These critics use close readings to reveal cultural contradictions and the social aspects of literature, the larger dynamics of subjection and incorporation through which the subject is produced. This aspect of contemporary African American literary studies is related directly to recent changes in critical approaches to American studies generally, a subject I return to later.

ISSUES

In what follows I attempt to assemble a (sketchy) catalog of the sometimes interrelated issues that arise under the rubric of "ethnic and minority" or multicultural studies. Among other things, I hope this inventory suggests the practical and theoretical enrichment that can result from bringing together diverse viewpoints. Since the growing attention to minority discourse has fixed on a spatial vocabulary of margin and center and since the formation of the margin has moved to the center of literary history and theory, it is important now to rethink this cartography, for I believe the center-margin topography has started to exhaust its usefulness. My aims, then, in recasting familiar arguments in minority discourse, are to disrupt some of the comforting concepts that seem to foreclose any truly critical inquiry; to encompass the essential continuities among disparate phenomena of marginalization, of center-periphery power relations; and yet to remain responsive to the essential differences within (that other totalizing category) *differences*.

Terminology: Ethnic, Minority, Mainstream, Marginality

We are, of course, all ethnics in America, so that all the separate tributaries of what we might with great profit think of as comparative American literature are, in fact, "ethnic" literatures, including Anglo-American literature. Initial uses of the term *ethnic*, however, connoted "of color" or "minority" in terms of demographic data or political representation. The rubric "ethnomusicology," for instance, curiously refers to all the world's music but that of the West! The implication of "minority" as "minor," "less than," or somehow noncentral to "major" scholarship adheres to all these terms. Even margin-center terminologies, which proved initially enabling in the late 1970s and early 1980s, sometimes served to reinscribe the isolated status of these emerging literatures.

All definitions of ethnic tradition ultimately are both tautological and essentialist. We define such traditions not by texts but by authors—indeed, largely by the ethnic descent of the authors. If Shakespeare, for example, were found to have had even one African antecedent, he would head the list of authors in an anthology of African literature. Danny Santiago—the pseudonym of Daniel James, the Anglo-American author of *Famous All Over Town* (1983)—created a great deal of embarrassment for all those critics who hailed his purportedly "authentic" Chicano novel for capturing the "true voice" of the Mexican American people. Likewise, black authors such as Frank Yerby, who writes "white" historical novels, rarely are taught in black literature courses. Definitions of authors in "national" traditions are equally essentialist, but they have the certain advantage of escaping the pitfalls of biologism. Aleksandr Pushkin is Russian; Nicolás Guillén is Cuban; Ralph Ellison is American; Machado de Assis is Brazilian—despite also all being persons of African descent. Still, defining literatures by nation, a slippery task with writers such as Henry James, T. S. Eliot, James Joyce, Samuel Beckett, Derek Walcott, or Jamaica Kincaid, has served as the essentialist model for most definitions of ethnic literatures, as I discuss later. If the 1970s-style hermeneutics saw the death of the author, the 1980-style cultural politics brought the author back.

Relationship between the Author and an Ethnic Culture

To escape the trap of cultural geneticism, in the broadest sense of that term, several scholars have attempted to categorize ethnic literary traditions on the basis of cultural values or characteristics that demarcate the texts in any given tradition. For instance, the relation between oral poetry and performance and written literature has proved especially fruitful in Native American, Hispanic, African, Caribbean, and African American literary studies. Similarly, the privileging of vernacular speech and vernacular literary forms in written literatures, through direct speech as well as free indirect discourse, has characterized many close readings of this kind. Conventions (call-and-response), genres (signifying, rapping), and forms (code-switching, repetition) have also been identified as cultural elements marking a formal difference between a hyphenated ethnic text and its Euramerican cousins.

While exciting studies using these concerns have appeared in the past decade or two, enabling the charting of specific examples of culturally based language use, studies of this type tend to give rise to the question of "authenticity": Is a text, or its author, less "ethnically sound" or "authentic" if she or he does not draw on these formal devices? Given the essentialist definitions of tradition at play in the construction of ethnically based canons and traditions, perhaps the search for manifestations of a collective ethnic unconscious or transcendent signifiers and signifying practices was inevitable. But the authors in these constructed traditions—all literary traditions are, to some degree, fictional constructs—do not draw on all (or any) of these devices necessarily. A descriptive formalism cannot bring a contrived unity to a "tradition" defined in the first instance by ethnicity. Further, expectations that authors must be accountable spokespersons for their ethnic groups can well nigh be unbearable for an "ethnic" author. If black authors are primarily entrusted with producing the proverbial "text of blackness," they become vulnerable to the charge of betrayal if they shirk their "duty." (The reason that nobody reads Zora Neale Hurston's *Seraph on the Swanee* is not unrelated to the reason that everybody reads *Their Eyes Were Watching God.*) These burdens of representation can too often lead to demands for ideological "correctness" in an author's work, not to mention a prescriptive criticism that demands certain forms of allegiance and uniformity.

Canon Formation and the Construction of Cultural Identity

The twin problematic of canon formation and nation formation is in the background of much debate at the boundaries of literary studies, and it sponsors the ideology of tradition that has long been in the service of minority legitimation. As Kwame Anthony Appiah observes, recent debates have left us "attuned to the ways in which the factitious 'excavation' of the literary canon can serve to hypostatize a particular cultural identity" ("Out of Africa" 161). Self-invention is then depicted as discovery. Emmanuel Wallerstein's observation is to the point:

> Any ethnic group exists only to the extent that it is asserted to exist at any given point in time by the group itself and by the larger social network of which it is a part. Such groups are constantly created and recreated; they also constantly "cease to exist"; they are thus constantly redefined and change their forms at amazingly fast rates. Yet through the physical maelstrom some "names" maintain a long historical continuity because at frequent intervals it has been in the interest of the conscious elements bearing that name to reassert, revalorize the mythical links and socialize members into the historical memory. (qtd. in Higham 199)

Clearly, the endless reconstruction of a "national literature," however subtilized and differentiated, remains the hidden object of much of our literary criticism. It would be easy to demonstrate its operation through the ideology of "tradition," whose tyranny remains little abated even today. And, for better or worse, the margin has borrowed this instrumentality. The German critic Robert Weimann argues, however, that

> when "tradition," or *Erbe*, is defined historically not only by what is preserved but also by what is repressed, not only as liberating but, in the words of Marx, also as burdensome, then the notion of "order" or even the formulation of a canon will, as an act of historicity, appear more deeply heterogeneous and contradictory. (272)

If minority discourses in America seem to embrace the ideology of tradition, it is because they remain at a stage where the anxiety of identity formation is paramount.

This anxiety shows up, for example, in African American literary criticism and theory as the privileging of the vernacular, which is frequently exalted as its *fons et origo*. Such folkish ideology emerges in a variety of contexts; for black nationalism, Adolph Reed, Jr., observes, this folkish essence has been

> hypostatized to the level of a vague "black culture"—a romantic retrieval of a vanishing black particularity. This vision of black culture, of course, was grounded in residual features of black rural life prior to migrations to the North. . . . As that world disintegrated before urbanization and mass culture, black nationalism sought to reconstitute it. (73)

The limitations of the "nationalist elaboration," Reed continues, is displayed "both in that it was not sufficiently self-conscious and that it mistook artifacts and idiosyncrasies of culture for its totality and froze them into an ahistorical rhetoric of authenticity" (74).

If a nationality comes into its own through the production of literature, the apparatus of recognition—the "selection of classics" to which E. R. Curtius tells us canon formation must proceed—remains integral to its realization. Inevitably, the process of constructing a group identity, at the margins as at the very center, involves active exclusion and repudiation; self-identity requires the homogeneity of the self-identical. Ironically, then, the cultural mechanism of minority self-construction must replicate the mechanism responsible for rendering it marginal in the first place. To recur again to Weimann: "the process of making certain things one's own becomes inseparable from making other things (and persons) alien . . ." (qtd. in Krieger 5–6).

Representation versus Articulation

In *Modernism and the Harlem Renaissance* Baker writes:

> Modernist "anxiety" in Afro-American culture does not stem from a fear of replicating outmoded forms or of giving way to bourgeois formalisms. Instead, the anxiety of modernist influence is produced in the first instance by the black spokesperson's necessary task of employing audible extant forms in ways that move clear *up*, masterfully and re-soundingly away from slavery. (101)

Arguably, what is in fact at stake here is the black spokesperson's identity as black spokesperson. The constitution of social groups is politically conceived as a representation of interests; yet as Ernesto Laclau and Chantal Mouffe's analysis suggests, the field of politics can no longer be understood this way, "given that the so-called 'representation' modifies the nature of what is represented," so that "the very notion of representation as transparency becomes untenable" (58). Laclau and Mouffe's intervention becomes of great significance in the discourses of marginality, where we move between the problematic of literary representation and one of representation of interests (the "black spokesperson" paradigm). Some minority intellectuals who would otherwise repudiate the discursive episteme of literary representation as mimesis do not question the model of the transparency of political representation. What Laclau and Mouffe offer as an alternative perspective accepts "the structural diversity of the relations in which social agents are immersed, and replaces the principle of representation with that of *articulation*. Unity between these agents is then not the expression of a common underlying essence but the result of political construction and struggle" (65).

As I argued earlier, if a peripheral ethnicity is to come into its own through the production of literature, the mechanisms of recognition—the "selection of classics"—remains integral to the attainment. But this process too is bound up in the issue of the spokesperson, the dynamism of representation, the site of which is the community of representatives. In fact, at the level of high theory, this whole social struggle is taking place by proxy, with the intellectual community providing the mediation necessary to a "central" reception. Bruce Robbins writes, "As soon as a text is chosen not from the West but from 'the rest,' in fact, attention to its positionality becomes a *sine qua non*: without an act of historical location, it may not 'mean' at all" (156).

The Economy of Authorization

Third World intellectuals, as Gayatri C. Spivak reminds us, are about as organically, indigenously Third World as Third World refrigerators, despite nativist nostalgia largely fueled by Rousseauist sentimentalism bequeathed by the First World. Intellectual formation occurs today in an international arena. In short, we misrepresent the intellectuals, literary critics, and academics of formerly colonized spaces if we ignore that they occupy First World institutions and roles and that they inherit the colonizer's architecture of knowledge and its intellectual structures. The Third World intellectual thus engages willy-nilly in the play of spokesperson or *porte-parole*, the economy of discursive authority that Pierre Bourdieu has incisively explicated through his idea of "l'économie des échanges linguistiques." Since authority comes to language from outside, Bourdieu argues,

> the authorized *porte-parole* can act by words on other agents, and thereby on things themselves, only because his speech concentrates the symbolic capital accumulated by the group which has mandated him and which provides the *basis of power*.
> (qtd. in Thompson 48)

Hence a progressive dialectic of authorization between center and periphery. The empowerment of the periphery, then, logically proceeds from the center, but from there on the colonial relation can easily be reversed.

Production of Agonism

Theorists often imply that the margin or the other is inevitably the endangered target of annihilation or assimilation. Wlad Godzich, for example, contends that "Western thought has always thematized the other as a threat to be reduced, as a potential same-to-be, a yet-not-same." Its paradigm, he argues, is that of the Arthurian quest, in which the "alien domain is brought within the hegemonic sway of the Arthurian world: the other has been reduced to (more of) the same." Indeed, "it is ideologically inconceivable that there should exist an otherness of the same ontological status as the same, without there being immediately mounted an effort at its appropriation" (xiii).

Yet this argument does not acknowledge that the margin is *produced* by the center or that the other is produced by the self or same, and it proceeds as if the two did not define a mutually constitutive system. Our characteristic stance on these matters—as champion of the politically disenfranchised—constantly blinds us to the ways in which the margin (that is, its positionality) is an effect of the cultural dominant rather than an autonomous agency of subversion, the dissolution or co-optation of which is the dominant's dearest wish. Since (as

Pêcheux argues) the very meaning of discourses subsists on such conflictual relations, the periphery is, as it were, never someplace else. A less blinkered view is offered by Sneja Gunew:

> The textual production of marginal minorities exists to confirm hegemonic textualities. And these minority writings have been in general homogenised as the area of plurality, disruption, nonclosure, deferred meaning and process; in other words, as affirming the dynamism of the centre and its ability to accommodate change—change which is safely contained. (142–43)

The threat to the margin comes not from assimilation or dissolution—from any attempt to denude it of its defiant alterity—but, on the contrary, from the center's attempts to preserve that alterity, which result in the homogenization of the other as, simply, other. The margin's resistance to such homogenization, in turn, takes the form of breeding new margins within margins, circles within circles, an ever renewed process of differentiation, even fragmentation. The center has, at least in certain spheres, conferred special authority on the marginal voice. These are the antinomies of center and periphery: where the center constructs the margin as a privileged locale, you assume authority by representing yourself as marginal, and, conversely, you discredit others by representing them as central. This tidy peripeteia is best exemplified in the establishment of what the Brazilian scholar J. G. Merquior calls the "official marginality"(167), which for scholars implies acceptance by the academy but in a role already scripted.

And if we are trading on the margin, whose currency are we using? It is useless to pretend that the discussion takes place in some neutral matrix, that our terms of argument are innocent. When, for example, Harold Bloom writes that "the popular myth of the alienated artist or intellectual is largely based on the late, decadent phase of Romanticism but it is soundly based there" (345), we are reminded that the articulation of marginality has functional significance within modern culture. Obviously, the divide between dominant and adversarial culture is basic to our conception of the intellectual. But the ideology that would thematize the artist or intellectual as adversarial (however reassuring to artists and intellectuals themselves) is, of course, not itself adversarial—far from it. At the same time, the stereotype cannot help but inform our response to the elevation of marginality as not just the stakes or subject but the privileged site of cultural critique.

Margins on the March

But as we saw earlier, the periphery is never someplace else. Where, finally, does this recognition lead? To begin with, we have to examine the strategic function of the conceptual divide between minority (internal) and Third World or postcolonial (external) discourses, which is to deflect the broader implications of what is called "internal colonization." Keeping inside and outside distinct is a means of keeping the other elsewhere. But othering, we might say, starts in the home. The grammarian's term *barbarism* encapsulates the social and linguistic freight of our condition: internal transgression is figured as the savagery beyond our borders; and, projectively, vice versa. John Guillory writes:

> The question of reading and writing belongs to the whole problematic of social reproduction, because what one learns to read is always another language. The internal differentiation of language produced by the classical educational system as the distinction between a credentialed and non-credentialed speech reproduces social stratification on the model of the distinction between the tribe or nation and its sociolinguistic other, the "barbarian." ("Canonical" 501)

At the same time, much theorizing about Europe and its others depicts the production of cultural alterity as an act of self-reflection that requires the complete evacuation of that other's specificity. The other is figured as merely a form or space, a "dingy mirror," as Richard Wright described Africa (158).

Such a view typically takes little interest in the actual effects of such projections on its hapless screens. This indifference is harder to maintain when we shift to the model of internal colonization, the others—sexual, racial, ethnic others—within our cultural borders. At the same time, and conversely, little attention has been paid to the ways in which these tendencies to textualize otherness within certain fixed parameters may operate even in the process of the margin's (self) articulation and construction. The double vision we need here would take in the relation between, on the one hand, how the subjects are constructed or represented to themselves and, on the other, how they are represented within the cultural dominant.

I submit, then, that the ritualized invocation of otherness is losing its capacity to engender new forms of knowledge and that the "margin" may have exhausted its strategic value as a position from which to theorize the very antinomies that produced it as an object of study. Instead, we must prepare to forgo the pleasures of ethnicist affirmation and routinized ressentiment in favor of rethinking the larger structures that constrain and enable our agency.

To recognize the distinctiveness of minority culture is no longer to treat it as a thing apart, isolated and uninformed by the "dominant" culture. To be sure, no culture is without conflict: certainly the zone of minority literary production has always been "multiaccentual." With this idea in mind, recent scholars of African American literature have been able to recuperate the criticism of an earlier generation—which challenged the essentialism of American nationalism, challenged the notion of America as an organic and integrated social regularity founded on the logic of assimilation—without succumbing to the restrictive, rejectionist posture of counternationalism on which the black-arts movement foundered. Recent African American criticism thus resists the contention that texts written by black authors cohere to a tradition because the authors share certain innate characteristics. Opposing the essentialism of European "universality" with a black essentialism has given way to more subtle questions. The critique of essentialist notions that cloaked the text in a mantle of "blackness," replete with the accretions of all sorts of sociological clichés, has brought forth a "postformal" resituation of texts, accounting for the social dynamism of subjection, incorporation, and marginalization in relation to the cultural dominant. Black literature, recent critics seem to be saying, can no longer simply name the margin. Their close readings are increasingly naming the specificity of black texts, revealing the depth and range of cultural details far beyond the economic exploitation of blacks by whites.

Today, as larger myths and narratives of cohesion have fallen under scrutiny, African American literary studies has served as a strategic site of self-critique within American studies, foregrounding the mutually constitutive relations that obtain between such categories as center and periphery, such identities as "black" and "white." As a site where marginal identities can be seen as both provisional and potent, "minority" studies has also been pivotal in retheorizing the politics of canon formation. In this respect, at least, the margin has truly taken center stage. (As Stallybrass and White observe, "what is *socially* peripheral is so frequently *symbolically* center": the "low-Other is despised and denied at the level of political organization and social being whilst it is instrumentally constitutive of the shared imaginary repertoires of the dominant culture" [5–6].) And as the theoretical work of feminist critics of African American literature has turned from a merely additive notion of sexism and racism, we have come to understand that critiques of "essentialism" are inadequate to explain the complex social dynamism of marginalized cultures.

Present and future scholars in "minority" studies will necessarily but also gratefully build on the work of their predecessors, for it is undeniable that many ethnic traditions would have remained buried had earlier scholars not been sedulous in reclaiming them. The challenge ahead, then, seems not to forget about such traditions but to try to be inclusive and extroverted rather than exclusive and introverted in exploring them. Perhaps it is time for scholars to think of a comparative American culture as a conversation among different voices—even if it is a conversation that some of us were not able to join until very recently. Finally, perhaps it is time for us to conceive of an ethnicity, a "blackness," without *blood* and to reconfigure the complex relations among the texts that constitute American literature.

Harvard University

Works Cited and Suggestions for Further Reading

Acosta-Belén, Edna. "Puerto Rican Literature in the United States." Ruoff and Ward 373–80.

Allen, Paula Gunn. *The Sacred Hoop: Recovering the Feminine in American Indian Traditions.* Boston: Beacon, 1986.

———, ed. *Studies in American Indian Literature.* New York: MLA, 1983.

Appiah, Kwame Anthony. "Out of Africa: Topologies of Nativism." *Yale Journal of Criticism* 2 (1988): 153–78.

———. "Race." *Key Words in Contemporary Literary Studies.* Ed. Frank Lentricchia and Thomas McLaughlin. Chicago: U of Chicago P, 1989. 274–87.

Baker, Houston, Jr. *Modernism and the Harlem Renaissance.* Chicago: U of Chicago P, 1987.

———, ed. *Three American Literatures: Essays in Chicano, Native American, and Asian-American Literature for Teachers of American Literature.* New York: MLA, 1982.

Bloom, Harold. *Ringers in the Tower.* Chicago: U of Chicago P, 1971.

Bourdieu, Pierre. *Ce que parler vaut dire: L'économie des échanges linguistiques.* Paris: Fayard, 1981.

Calderón, Héctor, and José David Saldívar, eds. *Criticism in the Borderlands: Studies in Chicano Literature, Culture, and Ideology.* Durham: Duke UP, 1991.

Cheung, King-Kok, and Stan Yogi. *Asian American Literature: An Annotated Bibliography.* New York: MLA, 1988.

Curtius, E. R. *European Literature and the Latin Middle Ages.* Trans. Willard R. Trask. New York: Pantheon, 1953.

Fisher, Dexter, ed. *Minority Language and Literature: Retrospective and Perspective.* New York: MLA, 1977.

Gates, Henry Louis, Jr., ed. *"Race," Writing, Difference.* Chicago: U of Chicago P, 1986.

Godzich, Wlad. Foreward. *Heterologies: Discourse on the Other.* By Michel de Certeau. Trans. Brian Massumi. Minneapolis: U of Minnesota P, 1986. vii–xxi.

Guillory, John. "Canon, Syllabus, List: A Note on the Pedagogic Imaginary." *Transition* 1.2 (1991): 36–54.

———. "Canonical and Non-canonical: A Critique of the Current Debate." *ELH* 54 (1987): 483–527.

Gunew, Sneja. "Framing Marginalia: Distinguishing the Textual Politics of the Marginal Voice." *Southern Review* 10 (1985): 142–56.

Higham, John, ed. *Ethnic Leadership in America.* Baltimore: Johns Hopkins UP, 1978.

JanMohamed, Abdul R., and David Lloyd, eds. *The Nature and Context of Minority Discourse.* New York: Oxford UP, 1990.

Kim, Elaine H. *Asian American Literature: An Introduction to the Writings and Their Social Context.* Philadelphia: Temple UP, 1982.

Krieger, Murray, ed. *The Aims of Representation.* New York: Columbia UP, 1987.

Krupat, Arnold. *The Voice in the Margin: Native American Literature and the Canon.* Berkeley: U of California P, 1989.

Laclau, Ernesto, and Chantal Mouffe. *Hegemony and Socialist Strategy: Towards a Radical Democratic Politics.* Trans. Winston Moore and Paul Cammack. London: Verso, 1985.

Lincoln, Kenneth. *Native American Renaissance.* Berkeley: U of California P, 1983.

Ling, Amy. "Asian American Literature." Ruoff and Ward 353–62.

McFarland, Thomas. *Shapes of Culture.* Iowa City: U of Iowa P, 1987.

McKenna, Teresa. "Chicano Literature." Ruoff and Ward 363–72.

Merquior, J. G. *Foucault.* Berkeley: U of California P, 1987.

Minh-ha, Trinh T. *Woman, Native, Other: Writing Postcoloniality and Feminism.* Bloomington: Indiana UP, 1989.

Pêcheux, Michel. *Language, Semantics, and Ideology: Stating the Obvious.* New York: St. Martin's, 1982.

Reed, Adolph, Jr., ed. *Race, Politics, and Culture.* New York: Greenwood, 1986.

Robbins, Bruce. "Power and Pantheons: Literary Tradition in Some Literary Journals." *Literature and History* 8.2 (1982): 147–58.

Ruoff, A. LaVonne Brown. "American Indian Literature." Ruoff and Ward 327–52.

Ruoff, A. LaVonne Brown, et al. "African American Literature." Ruoff and Ward 290–326.

Ruoff, A. LaVonne Brown, et al. "Minority and Multicultural Literature, Including Hispanic Literature." Ruoff and Ward 287–89.

Ruoff, A. LaVonne Brown, and Jerry W. Ward, Jr., eds. *Redefining American Literary History.* New York: MLA, 1990.

Saldívar, José David. *The Dialectics of Our America: Genealogy, Cultural Critique, and Literary History.* Durham: Duke UP, 1991.

Saldívar, Ramón. *Chicano Narrative: The Dialectics of Difference.* Madison: U of Wisconsin P, 1990.

Sollors, Werner. *Beyond Ethnicity.* New York: Oxford UP, 1986.

Spivak, Gayatri C. *In Other Worlds: Essays in Cultural Politics.* New York: Routledge, 1987.

Stallybrass, Peter, and Allon White. *The Politics and Poets of Transgression.* Ithaca: Cornell UP, 1986.

Thompson, John B. *Studies in the Theory of Ideology.* Berkeley: U of California P, 1984.

Weimann, Robert. *Structure and Society in Literary History: Studies in the History and Theory of Historical Studies.* Rev. ed. Baltimore: Johns Hopkins UP, 1984.

Williams, Raymond. *Marxism and Literature.* Oxford: Oxford UP, 1977.

Williams, William Carlos. *In the American Grain.* 1951. New York: New Directions, 1956.

Wright, Richard. *Black Power.* New York: Harper, 1954.

Paula Gunn Allen

"Border" Studies: The Intersection of Gender and Color

> In his exhaustive opus Irenaeus [Bishop of Lyons] catalogued all deviations from the coalescing orthodoxy and vehemently condemned them. Deploring diversity, he maintained there could be only one valid Church, outside which there could be no salvation. Whoever challenged this assertion, Irenaeus declared to be a heretic—to be expelled and, if possible, destroyed.
>
> . . . In opposition to personal experience and *gnosis*, Irenaeus recognized the need for a definitive canon—a fixed list of authoritative writings. . . .
>
> —Michael Baigent, Richard Leigh, and Henry Lincoln, *Holy Blood, Holy Grail*

NOT only has little changed since I entered the profession in the 1970s, nothing much has changed since Irenaeus, nearly two thousand years ago. They're still pontificating, excluding, and power-tripping, while we're still resisting, dissenting, deconstructing, and subverting. Heresies spring up all around only to die, only to recur persistently like wildflowers, like crabgrass. We still match personal experience and gnosis with canonicity, and those who tenaciously cling to the rotting pillars of Rome dismiss us—or order us purged. It seems that as long as we remain locked into oppositional structures, nothing but "same ol', same ol' " can occur. As long as we avoid the creative, we are condemned to reaction.

The profession when I entered it was much the same as it is today, "Still crazy after all these years," as the song goes. Though I had marched, pamphletted, and taught for peace and social justice, for civil, women's, and lesbian and gay rights, and briefly served as faculty advisor for the Young Socialist Alliance; though I had been writing and publishing for several years; though the poets I published with and read with in coffeehouses and bars, on the streets, and at rallies were fairly frequently not white and on occasion not white men—as far as the academy was, and is, concerned, there was, and is, no literature other than that produced by a Eurocentric formalist elite.

Nearly twenty weary years later, the cops beating African American men is a media sound byte, and the merciless destruction of Native people is largely ignored by all factions in the brawling American polity. Many are glad that "the war has ended," but I am compelled to object: it has not ended; it goes on and on. In the academy we hold rallies, sign resolutions, declare moratoriums, and demand divestiture and withdrawal of American involvement in foreign lands, while the mutilation of people of color at home evokes barely a sigh.

I came of age in the 1960s and by the 1970s was seriously burned out. By 1972 I understood several things: If an issue concerned Native people or women, men, and queers of color, neither the academy nor the intelligensia at large would have a word to say. We are *las disappearadas* (and *desperadas*). We are for the most part invisible, labeled as "marginal," the "poor," the "victims", or we are seen as exotica. Our "allies" adamantly cast us in the role of helpless, hopeless, inadequate, incompetent, much in need of white champions and saviors, dependent upon an uncaring State for every shred of personal and community dignity we might hope to enjoy. Right, left, and center see us as their shadows, the part they disown, reject, repress, or romanticize.

Even our few solid backers in academe perceive us as extensions of the great white way; they fail to perceive us as artists, writers, and human beings-in-*communitas* in our own right. And while some of the despised are recognized, most are not seen as other than a pitiable, amorphous blob. Our capacities as creative, self-directing, self-comprehending human beings are lost in the shuffle of ideology and taxonomy; the contributions of our peoples to the literatures, philosophies, sciences, and religions of the world are ignored. Our proper place in the view of the defining others is that of servant; they have consigned us to their margins, and there we must stay.

In the mid-1960s when I was in graduate school, I was not assigned the work of one woman poet or writer. And while assigned reading included the work of a number of homosexuals, their sexuality was, and largely still is, hidden to the eyes of the self-avowed heterosexual professoriat. In the late 1980s, I envied graduate students in the Ethnic Studies Department at the University of California in Berkeley, where I then taught, who enjoyed the privilege of studying women's literature from every period, every nation, including that of the U.S. of Color, and I sometimes cast envious glances at young colleagues who enjoy a growing body of scholarship and works by lesbians and gay men. It's not true that nothing has changed; there have been some shifts in academic offerings, though for the most part these offerings are not in traditional departments or are included only at the patronizing, cynical sufferance of the academic elite.

For, despite the good intentions and hard work of individuals, the establishment itself, particularly in literary fields, is unrepentantly proud of its constricted intelligence. Even worse is the willful institutional starvation of our students, accomplished by a narrowness of intellect and an insatiable desire for status and prestige. As academics, perhaps we all should concern ourselves with the consequences of institutional mind abuse.

I spent about ten years on the front of a civil war that has raged for centuries and an additional ten years reconnoitering. During that time I came to understand that the position of power for a true Warrior is the Void. It is from the Void that all arises and into that Void that all returns. The most profoundly creative literature of the twentieth century, the most profoundly *literary* literature, is, as it always has been, the literature of the desperadoes (and, in this case, desperadas). It is we who are creating the shape of the new world from the strokes of our pens, typewriter keys, and computer keyboards.

This body of work, literature that rides the borders of a variety of literary, cultural, and ideological realms, has not been adequately addressed by either mainstream feminist scholarship or the preponderance of "ethnic" or "minority" scholarship. However, in the past decade a new field of study has emerged that resists definition by other critics, that seems determined to define itself. This new field raises questions that mainstream feminist and "ethnic" or "minority" aproaches fail to address and simultaneously begins to open before us new possibilities for inquiry.

The process of living on the border, of crossing and recrossing boundaries of consciousness is most clearly delineated in work by writers who are citizens of more than one community, whose experiences and languages require that they live within worlds that are as markedly different from one another as Chinatown, Los Angeles, and Malibu; El Paso and Manahattan's arts and intellectuals' districts; Laguna Pueblo in New Mexico and literary London's Hamstead Heath. It is not merely biculturality that forms the foundation of our lives and work in their multiplicity, aesthetic largeness, and wide-ranging potential; rather, it is multiculturality, multilinguality, and dizzying class-crossing from the fields to the salons, from the factories to the academy, or from galleries and the groves of academe to the neighborhoods and reservations. The new field of study moves beyond the critical boundary set in Western academic circles and demands that the canonical massive walls be thinned and studded with openings so that criticism, like literary production itself, reflects the great variety of writerly lives and thought, particularly those in the American community. For it is not that writers themselves, of whatever color, class, gender, or sexual orientation, have been bound by ideological barriers a mile thick and two miles high but that academics have found the doctrine of exclusion and Eurocentric elitism a necessary tool in the furtherance of Western cultural goals and their own careers.

The work of women of color arises out of the creative void in a multitude of voices, a complex of modes, and most of these women are quite aware of their connection to the dark grandmother of human wisdom. Thus in *The Salt Eaters* the African American writer Toni Cade Bambara draws Velma back from the edge of daylight and heals her through the shadowy presences of Sophia, the dark spirit of wisdom, and the loas, the spirits. Toni Morrison produces a body of work that draws us ever more enticingly toward the great mysteriousness from which human life and significance always arise and to which they inevitably return. Similarly, in *Love Medicine, The Beet Queen*, and *Tracks*, the American Indian writer Louise Erdrich seduces us into the forest of Ojibway women's magic, winding us ever more deeply into the shadows of ancient trees. She leaves not so much as a crumb to draw us back into the light of patriarchal day.

Leslie Marmon Silko reaches into unexplored realms, the gloom of what is long forgotten but that continues to nourish our love and our terror, while Maxine Hong Kingston moves into the deeps of Han myth and memory, who is myth's beloved sister and supernal twin. The Chicana writer Gloria Anzaldúa tells it plainly: The woman in the shadows is drawn again into the world of womankind, and her name is innocence, exuberance, discovery, and passion; her name is our invisible bond.

Women return from the spirit lands to the crossroads over and over; we question, we circle around the center of the fire where the darkest, hottest coals lie. We know it is there—the nothing that bears all signifying, all tropes, all love medicine, all stories, all constructions and deconstructions.

We know this: In the void reside the keepers of wisdom. Women of color are willing and well-equipped to approach the still, dark center of the heart of the gynocosmos where nothing at all exists and whence, paradoxically, all must emerge. Other writers, strangers to the source of meaning, have talked about that mysterious, foreboding place, the dark heart of creation, but it is we—perhaps because we are nothing ourselves—who stalk the void and dance the dervish of significance that is born through our parted lips and legs. Other writers have entered the shadow, but they have named it evil, negation, woman. They have fled, running pell-mell away from her living bounty. They call us woman, other, mother, hooker, maid and believe themselves securely superior, safe from the mournful meaninglessness of our lot. Ah, but our lot is passion, grief, rage, and delight. Our lot is life, however that comes, in whatever guise it takes. We are alive, the living among the dead. Too bad those who see us as shadow, as void, as negation miss it all; so sad they haven't the wit to grieve their loss.

The dark woman has long been perceived as the dumb, the speechless, mother. And while the angrier among us protest that perception, we who are wise welcome and celebrate it. One of our sisters—albeit white and Calvinist but marginalized, closeted, all but disappeared—commented on the humor of the situation, writing:

> I'm Nobody! Who are you?
>
> . . . .
>
> How dreary—to be—Somebody!
> (Dickinson, no. 288)

Only the disappeared can enter the void and, like Grandmother Spider, emerge with a small but vital pot, a design that signifies the power of meaning and of life, and a glowing ember that gives great light. We who are nobody are the alive—and no one knows we're here. We are the invisible—and no one cares. Silly them. They are all at the public banquet hobnobbing with the known, the recognized, the acclaimed. And, as in the history of art in our Western world, they missed the god when she passed by, the god that the ignored and dismissed white lesbian crazy lady HD once so accurately described.

The issue I'm addressing here is not simply a matter of gender: it is fundamentally a matter of the essential experience of non-Western modes of consciousness. For the most part my sisters of the white persuasion are as culture-bound as their more highly prestiged brothers. In the West it is now held that gender (or sex) is a metaphor, a social construct. Further, it is held that since a metaphor can't be used to analyze a metaphorical system, meaning is largely a trick of the mind.

But in other systems—systems not so bound in a self-referencing, nearly psychotic death dance—meaning is derived and ascribed along different lines. This interpretive mode, non-Western to its core, is explored in *The Signifying Monkey*, by Henry Louis Gates, Jr. That work, though Afrocentric in itself, suggests a way out of the Morton Salt box conundrum of Eurocentric patriarchal self-preoccupation. Gates tells us that the meaning of a black text derives from the system of sigificance revealed and shaped by Ifa. The critical task is to render the text comprehensible and by that act assess its quality, by interpreting it through Ifa. According to Gates, that task belongs to Esu, the trickster, who is male and female, many-tongued, changeable, changing and who contains all the meanings possible within her or his consciousness. Thus a text that is malformed or incomprehensible when held up to Ifa as template is a work that has failed. Ifa, Gates writes, "consists of the sacred texts of the Yoruba people, as does the Bible for Christians, but it also contains the commentaries on these fixed texts, as does the Midrash" (10). Esu (or Esu-Elegbara or, in these parts, Papa Legba) is, in Gates's terms, "the dynamic of process," similar to the process of critical interpretation, who "interrelates all the different and multiple parts which compose the system" (38):

> Esu speaks through Ifa, because it is his *ase* that reveals—or conceals—the roadways or pathways through the text to its potential and possible meanings. Whereas Ifa is truth, Esu rules understanding of truth, a relationship that yields an individual's meaning. . . . Esu is the process of interpretation.
>
> (*Signifying Monkey* 38–39)

Similarly, by way of the ceremonial tradition as template, a given work by a native artist can be assessed. In both instances the canon becomes "the sacred," the world of the unseen (but not unheard or unknown), and its primary texts are the myths and ceremonies that compress and convey all the meaning systems a particular cultural consciousness holds. This is not to confuse a relationship to the mysteriousness that underlies and sources the phenomenological with essentialism or absolutism. There is little that is one, holy, catholic, and apostolic in the actual world that lies beyond and within the mundane. Indeed, the true world of the mysteries is more multiplex, polyglot, and free-flowing than any churchman, whether of Christian, Jewish, Muslim, Buddhist, or revolutionary persuasion, can imagine. Its very multitudinousness certainly threatens, even terrifies, the apostles of *mono*tony.

Hortense J. Spillers comments that "the literary text *does* point outside itself—in the primary interest of leading the reader back inside the universe of the apparently self-contained artifact" (244). That is, no cultural artifact can be seen as existing outside its particular matrix; no document, however profoundly aesthetic, can be comprehended outside its frame of reference—a frame that extends all the way into the depths of the consciousness that marks a culture, differentiating it from another. Because Western societies are fundamentally the same—they all arise from the same essential cultural base—Eurocentric critics think that culture is a unified field. French, English, German, Italian, Swiss, Danish, Dutch, Swedish, Russian, and Spanish worldviews are, at their deepest levels, part of the same cultural matrix: they all have the same mother, and that they are governed by members of the same extended family is but one mark of this profound sameness. But though these "cultures" are much alike, others are not of the same configuration, springing in no way from a similar root.

That difference is understood by many who essay to critique literary artifacts, but most assume, wrongly, that the cultural matrix from which all literature derives its meaning is the one described by French critics and other Continental intellectuals. But, to paraphrase Alice Duer Miller, other nations breed other women. Western minds have supposed (wrongly) for some time that language is culture and that without a separate language a culture is defunct. Thus some feminist critics search endlessly for women's language and, failing to discover it, wax wroth. But maybe the idea that language defines ideational identity of a distinct sort is off the mark. Maybe—as many writers have suggested—the use of a language and its syntax, structure, tropes, and conjunctions defines identity in its communitarian and individual dimensions. In this rubric, the external system that a given work points to and articulates and that renders the work significant takes on major importance.

The worlds of experience, knowledge, and understanding, to which the works of women of color point and from which they derive, can clarify the meaning of our texts. At this juncture the critic is faced with a difficult task: The world embodied in Kingston's *Woman Warrior* is hardly the world that gives rise to Morrison's *Song of Solomon*. It is of little use to study critical works concerned with Erdrich's *Love Medicine* if one wishes to explore the significance of Aurora L. Morales and Rosario Morales's *Getting Home Alive*.

To be sure, it may seem that elements of Western literary practice are discernible in work by women of color. But the similarities are likely to be more apparent than actual. The novel itself saw its earliest development in Japan of the eleventh century in *The Tale of Genji* by Lady Murasaki Shikibu. It did not appear in Europe until a few centuries later. Nor is poetry a genre confined to Western literature, though a certain shape has unfolded in recent times that marks it as a modern vehicle. But these modern forms, whether in Middle Eastern, Far Eastern, Native American, African and African American, or Latina communities worldwide, can be shown to derive from preexisting poetic forms in those nations that go back hundreds, even thousands, of years.

Western literary thought is a strong feature of much of the academic criticism produced by scholars of color. The critics who address the work of women writers of color are tightly enmeshed in the training they received in Western-biased universities.

Women of color writing in the United States share the experiences of trivialization, invisibility, and supposed incomprehensibility, but these features characterize the treatment of the critic-less more than that of writers blessed with a critical network that addresses their work within an established critical context. Thus the work of African American women is far more likely to receive appropriate critical treatment than the works of Denise Chávez or Kim Ronyoung are. It seems evident that without a critical apparatus that enables a variety of literatures to be explored within their relevant contexts, the works of las disappearadas are doomed to obscurity. Yet, given the prevailing ethnocentric cultural climate, devising such a system and finding it applied by a great number of critics seems a hopeless task. And if we fail to locate a system that is not ethnically skewed toward the bourgeois male European, the use of which does not obviate the insatiable status needs of literary types who fear loss of promotion and recognition by that same ethnic establishment, separatism seems the only solution.

Nor is the issue simply one of reconstructing the canon or throwing out the concept of canon, literary quality, or aesthetic norms. The recent move toward excising the discussion of these fundamental dimensions of criticism, indeed of thought itself, is hardly a useful response to the conundrum, though one is hard put to imagine creative alternatives to the situation when stuck in Western modes of thought. Perhaps the best course is to begin anew, to examine the literary output of American writers of whatever stripe and derive critical principles based on what is actually being rendered by the true experts, the writers themselves. While we're at it, we might take a look at the real America that most of us inhabit—the one seldom approached by denizens of the hallowed (or is it the hollow?) groves of academe—so that we can discover what is being referenced beyond abstractions familiar to establishment types but foreign to those who live in real time. I am suggesting a critical system that is founded on the principle of inclusion rather than on that of exclusion, on actual human society and relationships rather than on textual relations alone, a system that is soundly based on aesthetics that pertain to the literatures we wish to examine.

A text exists in relation to other texts—particularly, as Gates has demonstrated, to mother-texts, that is, the sacred stories that energize and shape human consciousness—rather than in splendid autocratic, narcissistic, and motherless isolation; as should be fairly obvious, texts are cultural artifacts and thus necessarily derive from, pertain to, and reveal oft hidden assumptions and values. Given that the experience of women as rendered in literature is a societally shaped and conditioned trope, how are we to accurately interpret or illuminate texts written by women of color? Do we see them as arising out of some sort of universalist "woman's world"? Do we look to the social world the writer and text inhabit to locate significance? Do we identify women writers of color in terms of their racial or cultural groups identified in terms of our Eurocentric ideologies? Because such categorizations tend to define colored writers—including those who are women—as "marginal" writers outside the boundaries of "real" literature and thus whose struggles and wishes only are of interest when they serve the goals and fit the preconceptions of those defining us, such an approach can only serve to oppress, distort, and silence. Should we step outside the boundaries placed on us by alien preconceptions of our lot, we are dismissed as crazy.

This is the problem posed by the work of social critics who subscribe to Karl Marx's dictate that the critical act exists as "the self-clarification of the struggles and wishes of the age" (Fraser 253). Nancy Fraser comments that Marx's critical theory "frames its research in the light of contemporary social movements with which it has a partisan though not uncritical identification" (253). She fails to notice that such a narrowly prescriptive (and proscriptive) approach in its narrowness virtually excludes the reality of the voice, text, and human meaning in the work of Third World women. Even the very concept of aesthetics, such a social-movement approach insists, is politically taboo because it is hopelessly engaged in furtherance of the white male supremacist paradigm.

This view might well be valid—but the rendering of beauty as human artifact is hardly an activity exclusive to white males, Western patriarchs, or the bourgeois. In Anna Lee Walters's short story "The Warriors," Uncle Ralph, a homeless alcoholic Pawnee warrior of the old school, counsels his nieces: "For beauty is why we live, . . . [but] we die for it too" (12). In Navajoland the concept of *hojo* 'it beautiful is moving' is central to the ideal of human life, while in the Pueblos we are instructed to "walk in beauty" (it goes this way, iyani). So far as I know, no human society is bereft of devotion to aesthetic principles, though Marxist, bureaucratic, and industrial societies come close.

But though our work draws up the moon from the creative void, signifying our cunning crafting, the critical works concerning our work remain stranded on the far shores of patriarchal positivism. In the world of the patriarchs everything is about politics; for much of the rest of the world, politics occupies little if any part of our preoccupations. Native Americans are entirely concerned with relations to and among the physical and nonphysical and various planetary energy-intelligences of numerous sorts. The idea of expending life force in oppression and resistance strikes most Indians, even today, as distinctly weird. Like Indians, Gnostics the world over, valuing multiplicity, personal experience, community, and simultaneous autonomy, avoid the schizoid dictates of canon-anticanon binary oppositional systems or fixed lists of what is "correct" thought, action, and insight, when the fixing is outside the realm of what is personally known.

For the most part, women of color write from a profound state of gnosis and personal experience, though we refine these in the crucible of community and relationship. But many major feminist critics wish our experience to be otherwise. They deterministically compel it into a mold of their own making, dismissing any work or experience that does not tell the tale they want told. Unhappily, far too many women of color fall into the honeyed trap; having been defined by strangers, many of us accept their definitions and write from the position they have marked out for us. All too unaware, we serve their aim and maintain their comfort—a righteous task for the maid.

In "Marginality and Subversion: Julia Kristeva," Toril Moi suggests that materiality is the point, marginality the key, and subversion the function of the invisibles. Moi praises Kristeva for her outlandishness, her willingness to go to the revolutionary heart of the matter, the mutter, but in extolling the rhetorical pose of the progressive Eurocentric intellectual, Moi reveals her Eurocentric and phallocentric bias. As Moi describes Kristeva's early works, Kristeva wanders hopelessly lost in the master's intellectual house of mirrors, asking and answering her own fantastic ghosts. And while the style of her meanderings is fetching, its self-negating entrancement with patriarchal paradigms is dangerous to writers from the deeps. No patriarch can tell us who we are, nor can any describe the worlds, inner and outer, that we inhabit. Freud, Marx, and Nietzsche—the triumvirate at whose altar Moi and the early Kristeva pay homage—can hardly provide models of intellectual competence that describe and illuminate colored women's works. What they can and do provide are the means whereby gynocosmic energies are bound up in patriarchal structures and thus rendered unusable to ourselves. This situation is well suited to the position of servant we thus occupy. From the confines thus established there is no loophole of retreat; indeed, there is no sense that anything should be retreated from or that there is anywhere to go beyond the servants' quarters.

Interestingly, as Kristeva moves toward consciousness based on some kind of connection to the real, as she goes from the absurdist position of comparing one body of words with another body of words with nary a whiff of human-experienced reality between, Moi rejects her, convinced that "the struggle" is all important. While Moi admits that women's struggle is unique in its various dimensions and is not to be confused with class struggles, she remains wedded to the correct dialectic: we are only to be perceived and authorized when we cast ourselves as marginal, subversive, and dissident, which she characterizes as Kristeva's fundamental theory, though it is more Moi's than Kristeva's. Moi supports a criticism that furthers neopatriarchalism, though as she sees it neopatriarchalism includes feminist struggles carefully interpreted through the lens of the fathers Marx, Neitzsche, and Freud (Moi 164).

To my Indian eyes it is plain that subversion cannot be the purpose or goal for women of color who write, though it likely is a side effect of our creating, our transforming, our rite. For to subvert, to turn under, is only the first step in the generation of something yet unborn; no, even less: it is the last step in the process of death. A truly beautiful clay pot from Acoma or San Juan Pueblo signifies on the emptiness it surrounds; Moi is accurate in her appreciation of Kristeva's unwillingness to dissect emptiness when the approach to somethingness will more than suffice. But what she fails to recognize is that the principles of self-determination and communitarian or autonomous creativity provide the true loophole of escape. Like Moi, one might very entertainingly mistake the menu for the meal and starve thereby, a mistake that for the most part shapes elite criticism and allied fields.

It is au courant to criticize, to interpret and analyze, as if no living processes occur—well enough for those who don't buy, earn, prepare, and serve the meal but who have servants and wives to deal with the tiresome mundanities of life. But our art is not, alas, privy to such alienation from human processes, and thus it must issue from the position of creativity rather than from that of reactivity. Subversion, dissidence, and acceptance of self as marginal are processes that maim our art and deflect us from our purpose. They are enterprises that support and maintain the master, feeding his household on our energy, our attention, and our strength.

In their introduction to *The Feminist Reader*, Catherine Belsey and Jane Moore characterize feminist readers as agents of change, asserting that "specific ways of reading inevitably militate for or against [that] process," thus situating the presumed problem of women squarely in the midst of the oppositional mode (1). Later, they comment:

> In poststructuralist theory meanings are cultural and learned. . . . They are in consequence a matter for political debate. Culture itself is the limit of our knowledge: there is no available truth outside culture with which we can challenge injustice. (10)

Odd, that the concept of adversariness, deeply embedded in patriarchal structures of both the political and the literary kind, requires the aesthetic concerns of literary women to be defined in terms of the culture that oppresses and disappears us. Given that thought, one must say, with Audre Lorde, "the master's tools will never dismantle the master's house."

It is even more peculiar, albeit depressingly common among Western people, that Belsey and Moore cavalierly assume that culture is itself monolithic, worldwide, universal, and impermeable, echoing Irenaeus of eighteen hundred years ago. As a Native woman I am passionately aware that there are a number of available truths outside Eurocentric culture that enable us not only to challenge injustice but to live in a way that enhances the true justice of creating and nurturing life. And as a Native woman I must protest the arrogance of any critical assumption that human society is European in origin and that all power of whatever sort resides within it.

Artists of color can best do something other than engage in adversarial politics, knowing that since we didn't cause patriarchy, we can neither control nor cure it. As recovering codependents of the abusive system under which too many have lived for far too long, we need to invest our energies in our vision, our significances, and our ways of signifyin'. We realize that we are something quite other than Anglo-European critics' definitions of us and that it is at our grave peril that we accept their culture-induced attributions rather than make, shape, and live within our own.

To be sure, women have, as actors, creators, and perceivers, been absented from patriarchal literature—but perhaps that's all to the good. Nor are persons of the female persuasion alone in that exclusion; we belong to a truly massive community of "strangers," one that includes virtually all literary artists on the planet for the past several thousand years. Perhaps, rather than bemoaning our "sorry state" as one of marginality, we might take another look at the actual situation; perhaps, in doing so, we will discover that neither "mainstream" nor "center" is where patriarchal sorts have claimed it to be. In all likelihood, we will discover readily enough that our very exclusion from the old boys club works to our advantage: having never lived in the master's house, we can all the more enthusiastically build a far more suitable dwelling of our own.

When I was growing up I would often go to my mother with some mournful tale of injustice. My plaints were inevitably centered on what the perpetrator had done to me. Sometimes my tale was a wonder of intellectual intricacy. Sometimes it was little more than a virtuoso emotional performance. But my clear-eyed (and intensely aggravating) mother would listen a bit and then pronounce sentence: "Yes, but what were you doing?" Or "You just worry about you." Or "Go do something else, then. If you can't get along with them, go find something else to do."

In this way, she taught me something Native people have long known and American humorists have recently discovered: the way to liberation from oppression and injustice is to focus on one's own interest, creativity, concerns, and community. Perhaps we literary sorts can put the wisdom of the ancients to good use. It is no concern of ours what "they" say, write, think, or do. Our concern is what we are saying, writing, thinking, and doing. In short, we must "get a life!"

In contemporary feminist circles, a debate rages concerning language: whether men own it; whether it is a fixed, immutable force that is reality; or whether it is merely a process that signifies nothing but through which we are all entertained nonetheless. Some feminist critics debate whether we take our meaning and sense of self from language and in that process become phallocentric ourselves, or if there is a use of language that is, or can be, feminine. Some like myself think that language is itself neither male nor female; it is creatively expansive enough to be of use to those who have the wit and art to wrest from it their own significances. Even the dread patriarchs have not found a way to "own" language any more than they've found a way to "own" earth (though many seem to believe that both are possible). However, perusing feminist criticism, I re-realize that patriarchs do own *critical* language, and, sadly, far too many feminist critics sling it as though it had meaning beyond the walls of the literary boys club.

A literary text can be characterized as a "loophole of retreat," the term Valerie Smith uses in her discussion of Harriet Jacobs's trope. "Jacobs' tale is not the classic story of the triumph of the individual will," she writes; "rather it is more a story of the triumphant self-in-relation" (217).

Self-in-relation, rather than the bildungsroman model of self-in-isolate-splendor that drives American civilization, is a primary characteristic of human cultures. I am aware that in the progressive evolution-as-fact paradigm, a main characteristic said to prove elite white male supremacy is precisely the individualistic hero metaphor. But while quite a few enterprises—literary and otherwise—are founded on the concept of individual superiority over relationship, individual heroics characterize but a small portion of literary work and represent an even smaller portion of art in general. As Smith writes:

> [T]he loophole of retreat possesses an ambiguity of meaning that extends to the literal loophole as well. For if a loophole signifies for Jacobs a place of withdrawal, it signifies in common parlance an avenue of escape. Likewise, the garret . . . renders the narrator spiritually independent of her master, and makes possible her ultimate escape to freedom. (212)

In Smith's discussion we see another new critical direction emerging, like Jacobs, from the constriction of belief in ownership. No one can own the sublime and no one can confine the beautiful, the living, or the moving to the tiny regions too many critics reserve for Indians and other "marginalized" peoples. However, we who are seen as borderline writers can erect a criticism that speaks to the kind of spiritual independence Jacobs found in hiding, the kind that must lead to freedom from domination. We can do so by attending to the actual texts being created, their source texts, the texts to which they stand in relation, and the otherness that they both embody and delineate.

The aesthetically profound story for Third World woman writers is necessarily concerned with human relationships: family, community, and that which transcends and underlies human meaning systems. Without benefit of Ifa and Esu, without possession of metatext, without presence of divine interpreter (that tricky familiar of the mysteries), reader and critic are doomed to read the same book over and over, regardless of who wrote it, why they did so, or the circumstances in which the work was embedded and from which it takes its meaning.

The concept in relation or, more "Nativistically," the understanding that the individualized—as distinct from individualistic—sense of self accrues only within the context of community, which includes the nonvisible world of ancestors, spirits, and gods, provides a secure grounding for a criticism that can reach beyond the politicized, deterministic confines of progressive approaches, as well as beyond the neurotic diminishment of self-reflexiveness. To read women's texts with any accuracy, we need a theory that places the twin concepts of I and thou securely within the interconnected matrix of all and everything, one that uses the presence of absence to define the manifest and that uses the manifest to locate and describe the invisible. When such a criticism is forged, the significance of the passive, the receptive, the absent, the dark, the void, and the power that inheres to it will be seen as central to the process of the construction of meaning and the reading of aesthetic texts. Like many women of color who write, Anzaldúa tells us of the habitation and the power of the unseen and its relation to the reality we inhabit. In so describing, she also suggests the direction a new criticism of inclusion can take:

> Where before there'd only been empty space
> She's always been there
> occupying the same room.
> It was only when I looked
> at the edges of things
> my eyes going wide watering,
> objects blurring.
> Where before there'd only been empty space
> I sensed layers and layers,
> felt the air in the room thicken.
> Behind my eyelids a white flash
> a thin noise.
> That's when I could see her. (148)

Suggestions for Further Reading

Assembling this list is a most difficult task: there are so many books—some good, some very good, some mediocre but necessary, some awful but also necessary—that one can hardly find a place to start. I stress here the texts and critical works I have taught, regretting the necessity to neglect much that is wonderful indeed. My major suggestion is simply this: read, read, read.

A good starting place for primary texts is the ground-breaking *Heath Anthology of American Literature* (ed. Lauter et al.). *Redefining American Literature* (ed. Ruoff and Ward) provides helpful literary-historical and critical contexts, as well as extensive bibliographies for each of the literatures discussed in this essay.

Some worthwhile titles by Asian American women writers include *Clay Walls* by Kim Ronyoung, *Seventeen Syllables and Other Stories* by Hisaye Yamamoto, and *The Woman Warrior* by Maxine Hong Kingston. Other important writers are Theresa Cha, Jessica Hagedorn, Cynthia Kadohata, Wendy Law-Yone, Bharati Mukherjee, Sara Suleri, Amy Tan, and Karen Yamashita. Significant critical works include *Woman, Native, Other: Writing Postcoloniality and Feminism*, by Trinh T. Minh-ha; *Articulate Silences*, by King-Kok Cheung (who helped me with this bibliographic appendix); and *Asian American Literature*, by Elaine Kim.

Some of the most important works from the African American side are *Song of Solomon, Beloved, Sula*, and *The Bluest Eye*, all by Toni Morrison; *The Salt Eaters*, by Toni Cade Bambara; *Browngirl, Brownstones* and *The Chosen Place, The Timeless People*, by Paule Marshall; everything by Zora Neale Hurston; and Frances E. Harper's *Iola LeRoy*, the first novel published by a black woman. Other writers to read are Gayl Jones, Jamaica Kincaid, Gloria Naylor, Alice Walker, and Sherley Anne Williams. For critical companions to these works, read Barbara Christian, both *Black Women Novelists: The Development of a Tradition, 1892–1976* and *Black Feminist Criticism: Perspectives on Black Women Writers*, as well as Henry Louis Gates, Jr., *The Signifying Monkey: A Theory of African-American Literary Criticism* and *Reading Black, Reading Feminist: A Critical Anthology*. Christian and Gates bibliographies provide an inquiring reader with a number of works for further study and relishment.

Important writers and works in the Chicana-Latina community include Gloria Anzaldúa, particularly *Borderlands/La Frontera: The New Mestiza*; Ana Castillo, *The Mixquiahuala Letters* and *Women Are Not Roses*; Denise Chávez, *The Last of the Menu Girls*; Sandra Cisneros, *The House on Mango Street*; Cherríe Moraga, *Loving in the War Years: Lo que nunca pasó por sus labios*; Cecile Pineda, *Face*; Alma Villanueva, *Bloodroot*; and Helen Maria Viramontes, *The Moths and Other Stories*. Critical accompaniments should include *Breaking Boundaries: Latina Writings and Critical Readings*, edited by Asunción Horno-Delgado et al.; *Beyond Stereotypes: The Critical Analysis of Chicana Literature*, edited by Maria Herrera-Sobek; and *Chicano Poetry: A Critical Introduction*, by Cordelia Candelaria.

Other works to sample are *Nilda*, by Nicholasa Mohr, a Puerto Rican writer, and *This Bridge Called My Back*, edited by Moraga and Anzaldúa, which contains passionate and dispassionate works that cut across community lines. The volume signals the rise of self-determination and self-definition on the part of women of color across the United States.

Some "must read" works by American Indian women include Louise Erdrich's *Love Medicine, Beet Queen*, and *Tracks* (written in collaboration with her husband, Michael Dorris); *Ceremony* and *Storyteller* by Leslie Marmon Silko; *Spider Woman's Granddaughters*, edited by Paula Gunn Allen; Allen's novel *The Woman Who Owned the Shadows*; Mourning Dove's *Cogewea, The Half Blood*, the first novel published by an American Indian woman; Anna Lee Walters's *Sun Is Not Merciful* and Vickie L. Sears's *Simple Songs*, both short story collections; and Walters's *Ghost Singer*. Critical studies that can be of help include *The Sacred Hoop* by Allen and *Native American Renaissance* and *Ind'in Humor* by Kenneth Lincoln.

And be sure to look for works by Arab American and Indian American (originally from India) women, especially Etel Adnan's novel *Sitt Marie-Rose* and her collection of poetry *The Indian Never Had a Horse*.

University of California, Los Angeles

Works Cited

Adnan, Etel. *The Indian Never Had a Horse and Other Poems*. Sausalito: Post Apollo, 1985.

———. *Sitt Marie-Rose*. Trans. Georgina Kleege. 2nd ed. Sausalito: Post Apollo, 1989.

Allen, Paula Gunn. *The Sacred Hoop: Recovering the Feminine in American Indian Traditions.* Boston: Beacon, 1986.

———, ed. *Spider Woman's Granddaughters: Traditional Tales and Contemporary Writing by Native American Women.* Boston: Beacon, 1989.

———. *The Woman Who Owned the Shadows.* San Francisco: Spinsters, 1983.

Anzaldúa, Gloria. *Borderlands/La Frontera: The New Mestiza.* San Francisco: Spinsters–Aunt Lute, 1987.

———. "Interface." Anzaldúa, *Borderlands* 148–52.

Baigent, Michael, Richard Leigh, and Henry Lincoln. *Holy Blood, Holy Grail.* New York: Dell, 1982.

Bambara, Toni Cade. *The Salt Eaters.* New York: Random, 1980.

Belsey, Catherine, and Jane Moore. *The Feminist Reader.* New York: Blackwell, 1989.

Candelaria, Cordelia. *Chicano Poetry: A Critical Introduction.* Westport: Greenwood, 1986.

Castillo, Ana. *The Mixquiahuala Letters.* Binghamton: Bilingual, 1986.

———. *Women Are Not Roses.* Houston: Arte Público, 1984.

Cha, Theresa. *Dictée.* New York: Tanam, 1982.

Chávez, Denise. *The Last of the Menu Girls.* Houston: Arte Público, 1986.

Cheung, King-Kok. *Articulate Silences: Double-Voiced Discourse in Hisaye Yamamoto, Maxine Hong Kingston, and Joy Kogawa.* Ithaca: Cornell UP, forthcoming.

Christian, Barbara. *Black Feminist Criticism: Perspectives on Black Women Writers.* New York: Pergamon, 1985.

———. *Black Women Novelists: The Development of a Tradition, 1892–1976.* Westport: Greenwood, 1980.

Cisneros, Sandra. *The House on Mango Street.* Houston: Arte Público, 1983.

Dickinson, Emily. *Complete Poems.* Ed. Thomas H. Johnson. Boston: Little, 1960.

Erdrich, Louise. *The Beet Queen.* New York: Holt, 1986.

———. *Love Medicine.* New York: Holt, 1984.

———. *Tracks.* New York: Holt, 1988.

Fraser, Nancy. "What's Critical about Critical Theory? The Case of Habermas and Gender." *Feminist Interpretations and Political Theory.* Ed. Mary Lyndon Shanley and Carole Pateman. University Park: Pennsylvania State UP, 1991. 253–76.

Gates, Henry Louis, Jr., ed. *Reading Black, Reading Feminist: A Critical Anthology.* New York: Meridian, 1990.

———. *The Signifying Monkey: A Theory of African-American Literary Criticism.* New York: Oxford UP, 1988.

Hagedorn, Jessica. *Dogeaters.* New York: Random, 1990.

Harper, Frances E. *Iola LeRoy.* 1892. Boston: Beacon, 1987.

Herrera-Sobek, Maria, ed. *Beyond Stereotypes: The Critical Analysis of Chicana Literature.* Binghamton: Bilingual, 1985.

Horno-Delgado, Asunción, et al. *Breaking Boundaries: Latina Writings and Critical Readings.* Amherst: U of Massachusetts P, 1989.

Hurston, Zora Neale. *I Love Myself When I Am Laughing . . . : A Zora Neale Hurston Reader.* Ed. Alice Walker. Old Westbury: Feminist, 1979.

———. *Their Eyes Were Watching God.* 1937. Urbana: U of Illinois P, 1978.

Jones, Gayl. *Corregidora.* 1975. Boston: Beacon, 1986.

Kadohata, Cynthia. *The Floating World.* New York: Viking, 1989.

Kim, Elaine. *Asian American Literature: An Introduction to the Writings and Their Social Contexts.* Philadelphia: Temple UP, 1982.

Kincaid, Jamaica. *Annie John.* New York: Farrar, 1985.

———. *At the Bottom of the River.* New York: Farrar, 1983.

Kingston, Maxine Hong. *The Woman Warrior: Memoirs of a Girlhood among Ghosts.* New York: Knopf, 1976.

Lauter, Paul, et al., eds. *The Heath Anthology of American Literature.* 2 vols. New York: Heath, 1990.

Law-Yone, Wendy. *The Coffin Tree.* New York: Knopf, 1987.

Lincoln, Kenneth. *Ind'in Humor.* New York: Oxford UP, forthcoming.

———. *Native American Renaissance.* 2nd ed. Berkeley: U of California P, 1985.

Lorde, Audre. "The Master's Tools Will Never Dismantle the Master's House." Moraga and Anzaldúa 98–101.

Marshall, Paule. *Browngirl, Brownstones.* 1959. Old Westbury: Feminist, 1981.

———. *The Chosen Place, the Timeless People.* 1969. New York: Random, 1984.

Minh-ha, Trinh T. *Woman, Native, Other: Writing Postcoloniality and Feminism.* Bloomington: Indiana UP, 1989.

Mohr, Nicholasa. *Nilda.* 2nd ed. Houston: Arte Público, 1986.

Moi, Toril. "Marginality and Subversion: Julia Kristeva." *Sexual/Textual Politics.* New York: Routledge, 1985. 150–73.

Moraga, Cherríe. *Loving in the War Years: Lo que nunca pasó por sus labios.* Boston: South End, 1983.

Moraga, Cherríe, and Gloria Anzaldúa, eds. *This Bridge Called My Back: Writing by Radical Women of Color.* Watertown: Persephone, 1981.

Morales, Aurora L., and Rosario Morales. *Getting Home Alive.* Ithaca: Firebrand, 1986.

Morrison, Toni. *Beloved.* New York: Knopf, 1987.

———. *The Bluest Eye.* 1970. New York: Washington Square, 1972.

———. *Song of Solomon.* 1977. New York: Signet, 1988.

———. *Sula.* 1973. New York: NAL, 1987.

Mourning Dove [Christine Quintasket]. *Cogewea, The Half Blood.* Lincoln: U of Nebraska P, 1981.

Mukherjee, Bharati. *Jasmine.* New York: Grove, 1989.

Naylor, Gloria. *The Women of Brewster Place.* New York: Viking, 1982.

Pineda, Cecile. *Face.* New York: Viking, 1985.

Ronyoung, Kim. *Clay Walls.* Seattle: U of Washington P, 1987.

Ruoff, A. LaVonne Brown, and Jerry W. Ward, Jr., eds. *Redefining American Literary History.* New York: MLA, 1990.

Sears, Vickie L. *Simple Songs.* Ithaca: Firebrand, 1990.

Silko, Leslie Marmon. *Ceremony.* New York: Viking, 1977.

———. *Storyteller.* New York: Seaver, 1981.

Smith, Valerie. "Loopholes of Retreat: Architecture and Ideology in Harriet Jacobs' *Incidents in the Life of a Slave Girl.*" Gates, *Reading Black* 212–26.

Spillers, Hortense J. " 'In Order of Constancy': Notes on Brooks and the Feminine." Gates, *Reading Black* 244–71.

Suleri, Sara. *Meatless Days.* Chicago: U of Chicago P, 1989.

Tan, Amy. *The Joy Luck Club.* New York: Putnam, 1989.

Villanueva, Alma. *Bloodroot.* Austin: Place of Herons, 1977.

Viramontes, Helen Maria. *The Moths and Other Stories.* Houston: Arte Público, 1986.

Walker, Alice. *The Color Purple.* New York: Harcourt, 1982.

———. *Meridian.* 1976. New York: Pocket, 1988.

———. *The Temple of My Familiar.* New York: Harcourt, 1989.

Walters, Anna Lee. *Ghost Singer.* Flagstaff: Northland, 1988.

———. *The Sun Is Not Merciful.* Ithaca: Firebrand, 1985.

———. "The Warriors." Walters, *Sun* 11–26.

Williams, Sherley Anne. *Dessa Rose.* New York: Morrow, 1986.

Yamamoto, Hisaye. *Seventeen Syllables and Other Stories.* Latham: Kitchen Table, 1989.

Yamashita, Karen. *Through the Arch of the Rain Forest.* Minneapolis: Coffee House, 1990.

DAVID BATHRICK

Cultural Studies

VIEWED traditionally, the study of culture in national literature programs has tended to supplement or parallel the study of literature. It has taken the form of cultural history or media courses in existing literature departments. Or it has emerged as shared programmatic activities with one or more established disciplines, such as music, history, psychology, political science, philosophy, anthropology, and biological sciences, sometimes organized as a national ("area") studies offering (e.g., American studies, German studies). In both cases, the objects or areas of cultural expression have been treated as belonging to discrete forms of cultural representation, which require for their study methodological and theoretical systems of inquiry that have evolved within the discursive and institutional histories of a particular discipline or medium. According to this version of cultural studies, interdisciplinarity is conceived as a comparative study of cultural discourses or artifacts coexisting within some shared national or transnational (e.g., European, Latin American, Western) tradition.

What marks a recent departure is the extent to which, in addition to its marginal status as a "subfield" within or between existing disciplines, the rubric *cultural studies* has come to suggest a remapping of the humanities as a whole around new contents, new canons, new media, and new theoretical and methodological paradigms. Some of these elements appear far removed from traditional notions of the literary or of culture or even of the text. The designation *cultural studies* has tended to stake out an area of conflict concerning the very meaning and relation of text and context, representation and the represented, cultural production and the world in which such production takes place. Where once the study of culture was considered ancillary to that of literature, providing at best a background for the literary text, newer approaches have challenged the conceptual models on which such hierarchical organization is based. One such challenge questions the very notion of text and context as stable locations at opposite ends of a spectrum. In the place of the "work" as a sacral, coherent entity to be studied within a complex of mediating, secondary cultural phenomena, cultural studies has sought to problematize the borders of textuality itself and, in so doing, to interrogate the ways in which fields of knowledge are constituted and organized (see Gunn's essay in this volume).

A similar shift in emphasis may be observed in discussions of the canon. Whereas early advocates for the study of working-class, women's, and black literature sought merely to broaden the canon to include neglected works of literary interest, recent debates have questioned the notion of canonicity itself. The intention has not been simply to do away with such a framework but, rather, to make the critique of canon formation an integral part of interpretive and evaluative investigation. Thus central to cultural studies from the outset has been a debate about the organization of knowledge and the role of the intellectual in the process of cultural change. This essay focuses on this latter meaning of the term *cultural studies*.

The historical configuration out of which this recent emphasis in cultural studies has emerged is related to structural, pedagogical, and even ideological changes that have occurred in universities since the 1960s: the rapid expansion of education to include social constituencies previously marginalized or underrepresented in institutions of higher education, together with a rethinking of educational and cultural values in response to challenges raised around issues of political, social, racial, and sexual difference and identity. The two, of course, are related. A generation of students that had grown up on TV and rock and roll, coming from increasingly diverse ethnic and social backgrounds, would be less likely to see culture as simply synonymous with high culture and more apt, if only by their presence, to throw into question the implicit norms of prevailing academic study.

Certainly an important impetus for much of what is occurring as cultural studies within national literature fields today may be found in American studies programs of the 1950s and in the film studies, women's studies, and African American programs started in the 1960s and 1970s. It was in the struggle to realize theses programs that the problem of interdisciplinarity came to be viewed as a curricular as well as cultural issue. More important, women's and African American studies programs evolved directly out of the social and political conflicts in society at large and pressured the academy to reflect such change in educational innovation. Surely the vital theoretical work being done in cultural studies today on questions of gender and race, and their representation in the media, is an outgrowth of this earlier work (see the essays of Schor, Allen, and Gates in this volume).

In literature departments, developments in theoretical practice and curricular organization have called into question the very notion of "literariness" as a discrete discursive or institutional system. This has led to a reinterpretation of cultural texts to include a wide range of subjects from disciplines and even life experiences previously considered foreign to belles lettres, such as medical texts, sporting events, fashion design, and rock music. Thus the use of the term *cultural studies* signifies first and foremost a reorientation of perspective and serves as a kind of terminological mutant. It is broad enough to encompass a vast set of competing yet related theoretical critiques of prevailing assumptions about literature, language, representation, gender, culture, audience, and texts. But it is, at the same time, specific enough to signal one avenue of inquiry within literary studies based on historically oriented cultural criticism and devoted to the redefinition of *literature* to include "nonliterary" materials. Robert Scholes, sensitive to the potential paranoia of the literary faithful, writes:

> Our favorite works of literature need not be lost in this new enterprise, but the exclusivity of literature as a category must be discarded. All kinds of texts, visual as well as verbal, polemical as well as seductive, must be taken as the occasions for further textuality. And textual studies must be pushed beyond the discrete boundaries of the page and the book into institutional practices and social practices. (16; see also Scholes's essay in this volume)

The obvious contradictions and paradoxes that would beset any attempt at redefinition from within are paradigmatic for this project as well. Often one is urged to study "literary" as well as "nonliterary" texts and, simultaneously, to challenge the very concept of an autonomous literary discourse. Or we find the struggle against canonical and theoretical hegemony within literary studies in the name of a model that some critics have seen subsuming existing theories, canons, and even disciplines into a new, more "universal," multicultural, multimedia, gender-critical metadiscourse. Rather than deny its antinomic status, cultural studies often defines itself heuristically as a challenge to all existing systems and structures. In so doing, it functions as a permanent border action, at once within and yet seeking to dissolve the institutional and discursive formations that have been necessary to its emergence and survival in the first place (see Gunn's essay in this volume, in which the notion of interdisciplinarity is explored more in relation to the confrontation of "allied fields" than as a "composite methodological site").

For example, Terry Eagleton, in his "introduction" to literary theory, is forced to conclude that what he has written is

> less an introduction than an obituary, and that we have ended by burying the object that we sought to unearth. . . . I am countering the theories set out in this book not with a *literary* theory, but with a different kind of discourse—whether one calls it of "culture," "signifying practices" or whatever is not of first importance—which would include the objects ("literature") with which these theories deal, but which would transform them in a wider context. (204–05)

With all due respect for Eagleton's dreams of internment, assuredly one other achievement of this "concise, witty and entertaining" introduction may indeed have been to "unearth" (and thereby help *perpetuate*) "the impenetrable world of modern literary criticism for those interested in but with little knowledge of the subject," as the book's dust jacket understandably sought to suggest. My observation in no way discounts the significance of wanting to broaden literary discourse or even of the author's lucid presentation, but it simply reminds us of something central to Eagleton's own position as well as to the function of cultural studies emanating from literature departments today: that the notion of "literature" is not an ontological category but one whose historical *and* institutional evolution will continue to be a legitimizing and transforming dimension of the critical enterprise. Any institutional analysis must understand the extent to which cultural studies is caught between (and is an expression of) two conflicting imperatives that have long been at the center of "professing" the humanities in this country: on the one side, the pressure to establish professionalism through the formation of fields of study and the achievement of theoretical dominance; on the other side, a need to confront precisely such professionalization, compartmentalization, and reification of cultural study by the establishment of greater cognitive unity and a (Arnoldian?) universality for humanistic study as a whole (see Bledstein; Graff; Kaufmann; Weber). Like New Criticism and the post–New Critical theoretical movements (structuralism, deconstruction, recent forms of Marxism, feminism, poststructuralism, etc.), the growth of cultural studies at once concedes to and seeks to subvert competing knowledge interests emanating from field, guild, and market. What some of its practitioners hope distinguishes them from their more traditionalist colleagues is an effort to include in their critical view the conditions of their own existence; to build the very contradictions and diversities underlying cultural representation and its social contingencies into the processes of critical reflection; to understand institutional arrangement and questions of power as integral to the politics of cultural studies itself (see Brenkman).

Given, then, the protean, anti-institutional, and, finally, heuristic suggestiveness of the term *cultural studies*, I should like to proceed by focusing precisely on its nodal points of contradiction, on the programmatic debates and innovations that have emerged under its banner to challenge existing theory and institutional formations in the name of a more relevant and broadened humanistic study.

CULTURAL THEORY AS A CHALLENGE TO LITERARY THEORY

Viewed in relation to the historical formation of literary schools of criticism, cultural studies has pushed generally toward a multiperspectivism that would challenge the notion of one dominant theoretical model as a "master discourse" at the center of the profession. Traditionally, competing schools of literary theory have viewed their evolution as a diachronic history in which one prevailing paradigm is challenged and replaced by another. In the United States, New Criticism is seen to have challenged the "extrinsic" methodologies of the 1930s (Marxism, Freudianism) and, in turn, to have given way to the ascendence of phenomenology, structuralism, and poststructuralism—in that order. Theoretical and methodological struggles rarely questioned this evolutionary model or its center-margin dichotomy; the two are themselves an expression of a particular notion of theory: a total system bound to a particular tradition of literature based on the idea that there is one, "scientific" interpretive model valid for all texts and contexts. The problem of methodological disagreement was often resolved either by retaining the old paradigm or by relegating it to the margins and establishing a new one (see Lentricchia).

Central to the strategic evolution of cultural criticism has been a programmatic effort to challenge what it sees as the claim to universalism at the heart (or at least the practice!) of existing literary theory. This challenge has taken a number of forms. First, there is a tendency to contextualize and desystematize theory itself, as is most evident among new-historicist and anthropologically oriented critics in the United States and in the work of the Birmingham school in Great Britain. Certainly the fact that interdisciplinarity is not only a goal of cultural criticism but in many cases the very condition of its own fragmented evolution has contributed to a changing norm in theory itself. A multiperspective cultural criticism has sought to quarry a broad corpus of theoretical writings from outside the discipline of literature, regardless of their allegiance to a particular deductive, hierarchical system or subject area. Disciplines such as psychoanalysis, anthropology, philosophy, linguistics, sociology, history, political science; writings by Michel Foucault, Jürgen Habermas, Ferdinand de Saussure, Clifford Geertz, Jacques Lacan, Charles Sanders Peirce, Karl Marx, Walter Benjamin, Antonio Gramsci are joined (some would argue eclectically) and brought to bear in ways that severely strain if not jettison established notions of theoretical coherence or compatibility.

Conversely, cultural theorists have applied methods developed for literary textual analysis to challenge theoretical models in other fields. The historian Hayden White (*Metahistory*) and the anthropologist Donna Haraway (*Primate Visions*) have explored how the discourses of history and anthropology have been shaped by a writer's commitment to tropes and narratives. Whereas the more literature-centered have perceived this kind of interdisciplinarity as asserting the "literariness" of nonliterary phenomena and thus extending the relevance of literature as master in the house of a cultural discourse, other cultural critics have argued for the opposite: "intertextuality" as the decentering of the literary within a multitude of equally contending discursive activities. In both the importing of theory into the literary domain and literary criticism's intervention into other territories there is a clear erosion of boundaries and centers, of definitions and suppositions that had once been so crucial in marking the differences between contending critical schools and movements and their ontological starting points as integral theories (see also Gunn's essay in this volume).

Yet despite the claims, intentions, and even achievements, an important epistemological question, experienced perhaps as epistemological double-bind, has fueled the theoretical debates of the cultural studies project in literature departments. Although the emergence of cultural studies clearly results from a breakdown of one kind of theoretical generality, the proposed countermodel—while accepting, and sometimes welcoming, the impossibility of theoretical unanimity—has sought to establish common ground around expanded notions of literature, rhetoric, textuality, theory, culture, discursive practice, or interdisciplinarity. And it is at this point, of course, that the fireworks begin.

While one form of expansion includes a powerful critique of academic theory, it has been aimed at certain kinds and functions of theorizing and thus is to be distinguished from such professional "antitheorists" as Stanley Fish, Steven Knapp, and Walter Benn Michaels (see Mitchell). Where Fish, Knapp, and Michaels would do away with the enterprise of theory altogether (as if such a thing were even possible), advocating instead a version of "pragmatism," the cultural critics take issue with what they see as the ahistorical, apolitical, acontextual, self-referential, and esoteric turn that theory has taken professionally. Moreover, as a theoretical strategy concerned with questions of power and cultural representation, cultural studies has often identified itself polemically with certain social constituencies (women, blacks, Chicanos, the Third World, the "popular"), in relation to a particular politics or as an attempt to reconnect the academic enterprise to more worldly concerns.

Some advocates of cultural criticism see the isolation of much academic literary theory historically as part of a withdrawal of the humanist intellectual from the public world of literary culture into the enclaves of the university, where critics are said to deliver up their findings "for a coterie of specialized professors and graduate students . . . in an esoteric jargon of methodological terms" (Graff and Gibbons 8; see also Jacoby). As an antidote to the "fetishism of technique" and philosophical obscurantism deemed prevalent in much of today's humanistic study, these critics would look to the "New York style" of criticism of the 1930s and 1940s, as practiced in nonacademic journals such as *Partisan Review* and by cultural critics like Lionel Trilling, Philip Rahv, Harold Rosenberg, and Clement Greenberg:

> New York-style criticism is free wheeling and speculative and gets bored easily. It is bored by the close reading of texts; sometimes it is too easily bored with sustained argument altogether. It relies for its authority on the critic's own voice, not an impersonal method or system. (Krupnick, "Two Worlds" 160)

Basic to the New York style is a sense of individual moral and political engagement, of intellectual risk-taking within a larger community of public affairs (see also Graff's essay in this volume). While some proponents of this "unabashedly secular and worldly" role for the university scholar have cautioned against an excessively antiprofessional nostalgia for the bygone days of the metropolitan intellectual (Krupnick 158), Graff and Gibbons's preference for a " 'cultural criticism' based on general ideas" repudiates the overly systematic "superprofessionalism" they associate with linguistically or philosophically oriented methodologies governing literature studies in the academy today (6).

But critiques of "establishment" theory have emerged as well out of the ranks of specialized theory itself. A notable example is Edward Said, who also laments the isolation of literary intellectuals "from the major intellectual, political, moral and ethical issues of the day" (*World* 212). While Said might not describe himself as a cultural critic, his repudiation of what he calls "left" criticism (for the most part deconstruction, but also armchair Marxism and other forms of quiescent liberal humanism) offers a convenient means by which to trace one parting of the ways, within poststructuralism, of cultural and literary critics on questions of intertextuality, history, and politics. The key antagonists in Said's methodological drama are Foucault and Derrida, in particular their differences concerning the ways that texts are situated in relation to other texts. For Said, Derrida, on the one hand, is paradigmatic for a kind of "hermeticism" that limits the activities of the critic to "the search *within* a text for the conditions of textuality" and thereby avoids "making a text assume its affiliations" with other texts and discourses. Foucault's notion of textuality, on the other hand, attempts "by the detail and subtlety of the description to *resemanticize* and forcibly to redefine and reidentify the particular interests that all texts serve" (212). While Said's reading of Foucault certainly reveals his own efforts to graft onto the latter's "micropolitics" a notion of totality seemingly transcendent of individual texts and discourses ("interests that all texts have"), such a move nevertheless allows him to reconfigure the task of the critic not only around issues of professional politics but concerning the methodological complicity in any critical system of language. Despite deconstructionists' left-wing claim to assault the hegemony of "Western metaphysics," Said goes on to argue, the de facto limitation of their practice to the realm of the "literary" and the borders of the text excludes from consideration a broad range of social writings, symbolic formations, and systems of representation.

Of course, one could argue against Said that the essential terms for *any* intertextuality are basic to the very spirit of deconstruction. As Gerald Graff has stated in his plea for "teaching the cultural text," if there is "any point of agreement among deconstructionists, structuralists, reader-response critics, pragmatists, phenomenologists, speech-act theorists, and theoretically minded humanists it is on the principle that texts are not, after all, autonomous and self-contained, that the meaning of any text in itself depends for its comprehension on other texts and textualized frames of reference" (256). But what separates many of the poststructuralist cultural critics from those adhering merely to post-Saussurian truisms concerning the contingency of text is their recasting of the notion of intertextuality. While many of the parties concerned would agree that a purely prediscursive or precultural reality either does not exist or, if it does, is unknowable, Foucault's concept of discursive formation makes possible a textually grounded notion of historical referentiality and political power that is philosophically at odds with most American Derrideans.

The shift in the terms of intertextuality from the notion of discourse as unbounded free play to a process of social signification in a network of contingency and systems of power has marked the move toward cultural criticism in several areas and even disciplines. For the new historicists, to take one prominent American example, it has meant a return to historical scholarship that would reinsert the literary text into a social and cultural matrix, relating it to extraliterary and semiliterary materials: letters, diaries, films, paintings, manifestos; philosophical, political, psychological, religious, and medical treatises (see also Patterson in this volume). Following Foucault, the new historicist would argue for "negotiating" the relation between any and all textual representations as a means of exploring the complex of power within a sociocultural context and of widening the borders of the text itself to indicate how it participates and intervenes in a cluster of neighboring discourses. One may well argue that the new historicist's stress on an indiscriminate assemblage of data and "thick description" (Geertz), coupled with a "relatively weak theoretical overlay in the invocation of the concept of power" (LaCapra 191), merely reproduces many of the troublesome aspects of eclecticism and relativism found in "old" historicism. Yet it is also undeniable that such a critique of both deconstruction (for its textual formalism) and Marxism (for its excessive determinism) has invoked a set of critical concerns that have stimulated the cultural theory debates as a whole (see Veeser).

What has been central theoretically for the new historicism is the insistence with which it has challenged and even swept aside the categorical boundaries between text and context, cause and effect, representation and the represented. Whereas traditional models of historical criticism have organized history around a predetermined, unifying contextual center (e.g., state power, the political economy, patriarchy), which serves, in turn, as explanatory background to a foregrounded cultural text, for new historicists the background itself becomes another source of textual interpretation, made up of written and other forms of representation, to be read, less "spectacularly" we are told, as "a subtle, elusive set of exchanges, a network of trades and trade-offs, a jostling of competing representations, a negotiation between stock companies" (Greenblatt 7).

Which brings us back to the question of relativism. The critique heard most often of both Foucault and the new historicists, by feminists and Marxists alike, concerns precisely their forfeiture of any position—their own as critic; that of an autonomous text or a definable context—from which and on which to generate contingent readings, meanings, or value judgments. If one subsumes undifferentiated texts and contexts into a world of existing representations of power without regard to origin, causation, hierarchy, mediation, temporal or spatial location, so the argument goes, then there is no nonarbitrary way to make judgments about the configuration of contingency at a particular moment—about what, within the intertextuality of linkages, constitutes hegemonic power (vs. powerlessness) or potential resistence or even political meaning (see Cohen).

The question of historical contingency has been particularly important for the various strands of neo-Marxism that have sought to provide a more interdisciplinary basis for cultural studies. The cultural materialism of the British scholar Jonathan Dollimore, for instance, emphasizes specifically the historically rooted nature of all cultural representation in material social forces while at the same time rejecting explicitly any notion of culture as merely reflection of the economic and indicating the extent to which human values and emotions themselves produce specific social formations. Whereas Dollimore, in keeping with his Althusserian orientation, is hesitant to adhere to any grand theory of historical totality that would link causally the differing dimensions of a unified social order, Fredric Jameson looks to a "dialectical" cultural criticism as the "only living philosophy today" that can restore "the notion of a universal object of study underpinning the seemingly distinct inquiries into the economical, the political, the cultural, the psychoanalytic, and so forth" ("Interview" 89). Jameson's *Political Unconscious* represents just such an attempt to establish Marxism as a master code, as a "grand historical narrative" that would subsume and relocate the myriad theoretical voices within a critical paradigm capable of grasping the larger story in all its complexity and richness.

Whether such an attempt is even thinkable under present circumstances is considerably less important than what it says about the need, not only among the Marxists, to lend cohesion to cultural studies around political identities, cognitive linkages, and discursive systems. For certainly the tensions and disparities between the aggressively agnostic "antipositions"—antihumanist, antielitist, antiformalist, antiuniversalist, antiessentialist—of the Foucauldian and anthropological new historicists (or some relative or variant of these) and those who would acknowledge some Archimedian political or epistemological starting point (feminists, cultural Marxists, left deconstructionists, some postmodernists, cultural materialists) are symptomatic of the deeper polemical impulses energizing the cultural studies project as a whole. The critique of essentialism and universalism has been vital in opening up the study of literature and history to a heterogeneity of theme, perspective, constituency, medium; and of political, national, and sexual identities. At the same time, the emergence of once silenced and still oppressed voices within the critical domain of cultural discourse has politicized and helped position and certify those identities as part of a striving for empowerment.

The self-conscious linking of literary and cultural study with questions of cultural identity and political power has encouraged scholars to rethink the social biases and absences within established literature programs. Although cultural studies has resisted identification with any narrow notion of ideological perspective, social constituency, or thematic concern, three areas of cultural experience in particular have provided new directions for the development of its programmatic understanding within the framework of existing disciplines.

In the area of ethnic studies, African American, Third World, and Latin American programs have proffered an internal critique of the ethnocentric Occidentalism of much of humanist scholarly and curricular organization in academic institutions or, more modestly, have sought to resituate prevailing discourses and canons in relation to what and who have been excluded by dominant voices. In many cases, materials and issues previously segregated within ethnic studies have been made a more central and critical part of all literature programs. (See Gates's essay in this volume.) Such a resituating has, in turn, led to a reconsideration of the political dimension of "national" literatures in relation to global changes occurring as a part of postcolonialism and the end of the two-bloc system.

Coming from feminist theory, the critique of essentialism (the feminine as such) and universalism (woman as the new subject of history) has been a vital part of a radical orientation toward the social construction of gender and historicizing of feminist interpretive practice around questions of representation rather than, simply, sexual identity (see Barrett). Moreover, the shift to gender study, as opposed to sexual difference, not only signals the rise of male and gay studies as a component of the study of sex and sexuality but foregrounds the "cultural"—historical and political—framework within which one must explore sexual difference and oppression. (See Schor's essay in this volume.)

A third area of concern has been popular and mass culture, which, in addition to questioning the separations at the root of traditional culture, has incorporated questions of representation of race and gender at every level. Since the first two areas are treated elsewhere in this book, it is to the third that we now address ourselves.

POPULAR AND MASS CULTURE

Certainly one of the major challenges to both the canon and to the "literary" has come through the opening up of literature departments to the study of popular literature and mass media (film, television, video). To be sure, neither the initial efforts of Jungian myth critics like Leslie Fiedler to "cross the border—close the gap" separating high and low culture by embracing provocatively the challenge of "pop" to the canons of genteel culture nor the addition of film courses to literature departments could bring about a fundamental reordering of priorities and evaluation. The structures of institutional containment were tried and true, operating in these instances to extend the border—and critically ignore the gap. By elevating selected icons of the popular into a broadened curriculum, Fiedler's assertion of a "postmodern" (he was one of the first literary critics to use the term) art and criticism merely conferred field and canon status on a newly colonized area of cultural tradition.

A similar process of colonization occurred in the area of film studies. The importation into the United States of "auteur theory," practiced by the French cinematic avant-garde (Jean-Luc Godard, François Truffaut, particularly André Bazin and the *Cahiers du Cinema*), answered well the legitimation needs of a young, burgeoning cinematic subfield within high culture academy criticism. Whereas high criticism had historically ignored Hollywood mass culture for being unworthy of academic concern, auteur theory would help valorize the work of the few "genuine" artist-geniuses (Alfred Hitchcock, John Ford, Orson Welles, Howard Hawks) who were judged to have transcended mediocrity, thereby having the exception confirm the rule. The rule was that most hack directors from Hollywood produced their films in absolute compliance with the formulaic patterns of established cinematic genres (the western, the murder mystery, etc.). The authorship of the chosen artistic few was thus thrown into sharp relief by virtue of their having employed these codes to articulate a personal, artistic vision (see Sarris).

In summation, the containment of mass culture within the American academy operated in a twofold manner. At a methodological level, the privileging of a selectively revised canon effectively prevented new objects of inquiry from throwing into question the critical apparatus as a whole. Such a move, in turn, was reinforced institutionally through curricular quarantine within the safety parameters of the "subfield."

Subsequent developments in mass and popular culture studies have forced a fundamental rethinking of cultural divisions as well as a broadening of intellectual inquiry. Certainly a major impetus has come from Britain, in particular the cultural materialism of Raymond Williams, the cultural studies program at Birmingham University, and the writings in *Screen* magazine. While all three Marxist emanations view language as a "practical material activity" (Williams, *Marxism* 38)—that is, a repudiation of the base-superstructure model of traditional Marxism in favor of a reading of culture itself as a "material force"—their differing strategies, emphases, and, finally, politics and methodologies provide an introduction to the central issues generated by the mass culture debate itself.

In his *Marxism and Literature*, Williams pinpoints the shift in the meaning of the term *literary* from a general designation, in the Renaissance, for the existing body of books and writing to the emergence, in the eighteenth century, of a narrower notion of literature as "imaginative" or "creative" writing. While this codification served initially to express a certain (minority) level of educational achievement, its refinement into a discourse of "sensibility" and aesthetic taste subsequently became a means by which the "para-national profession of literary criticism" was to constitute itself in the nineteenth and twentieth centuries as a discrete and highly elitist discipline within universities. The segregation of literary study along the lines of codified disciplines, Williams would argue, did not evolve as the "natural" compartmentalization of human capacities but, like the changing notions of aesthetics and culture occurring during the same period, was a response "in the name of an essentially general 'creativity' to the socially repressive and intellectually mechanical forms of new social order: that of capitalism and especially industrial capitalism" (50).

Although as a cultural critic Williams had relatively little interest in the reading of textual artifacts, his historicizing of the canon and high literary discourse, together with his call to study popular forms of cultural expression, has helped define a remapping of humanistic study for a generation of British and American cultural critics within and outside the academy. At the Centre for Cultural Studies, for example, a postgraduate program at the University of Birmingham founded in 1964 by Richard Hoggart and devoted primarily to "research of contemporary culture and society," popular culture came to be viewed not simply as a set of values or a collection of texts but also as the practices and experiences of everyday life: the way people make gardens or organize holidays, the ideology of nudist camps, the content and meaning of

British meals, the symbolic world of the motor bike—in short, the cultural and subcultural structures of control and resistance that evolve in and around school, home, street, place of work, recreation, and so on.

The Birmingham model represented above all an institutional as well as intellectual break with the dominant model of cultural studies in traditional literature departments. Yet this endeavor was perhaps least successful in creating a coherent theory to account for the reconfiguration of cultural hegemony in contemporary forms of political domination. The attempts to synthesize a number of seemingly incompatible theoretical paradigms—ranging from the work of E. P. Thompson, Raymond Williams, and Richard Hoggart to that of Louis Althusser, Antonio Gramsci, the Frankfurt school, Walter Benjamin, Friedrich Engels, Georg Lukács, Jacques Lacan, Sigmund Freud, Roland Barthes, and Mikhail Bakhtin—often resulted in a serial linking of names and ideas without any conceptual dialogue or systematic development. If in retrospect the work of Williams, Barthes (of *Mythologies*), and Gramsci (of *Prison Notebooks*) appears particularly influential, it is because of their emphasis on experience as the starting point for social analysis, their shared tendency to view the ideological dimension of culture not as a structuralist abstraction somehow separated from human intentions and practices but rather as a historically determinate part of the give-and-take of political activity, coded and reencoded in a world of representation. "Gramsci massively corrects the ahistorical, highly abstract, formal and theoricist level at which structuralist theories tend to operate," writes Stuart Hall. "His thinking is always historically specific and conjunctural" (36).

Indeed, Hall notes, the strength of the Birmingham project came precisely from having "posed the question of the status of the experiential moment in 'lived' cultures as an irreducible element of any explanation" (24). Paul Willis's study of a male student counterculture and Dick Hebdidge's work on "the meaning of style" within the subculture—despite a tendency to privilege (i.e., romanticize) male working-class youth as the primary subject of revolt (and of history?)—provide fascinating ethnographic accounts of the interpretive schema, linguistic codes, and folk ideologies that social groups employ to survive and resist in the contest for discursive control over cultural meanings of contemporary life. Stuart Hall himself worked out an elaborate model to assess the different ways in which audiences come to terms with the experience of mass-mediated culture. By distinguishing between "dominant," "negotiated," and "oppositional" modes of responding to the media, he sought to differentiate between audiences who simply accept a text at face value (dominant), and the various strategies by which individuals empower themselves through struggles to resist dominant meanings. What is key in this work, beyond its focus on areas of experience often considered marginal to "culture" itself, is an emphasis on the complexity of audience or consumer response to what had been viewed as the manipulation of "cultural dupes" by a dominant culture industry.

Seen from the perspective of reception, then, the work of the Birmingham school was clearly part of a general rethinking of categories within media studies—both in Europe and in the United States—with regard to the complexity and ambiguity of mass cultural communication. Primary here was an effort to question the established either/or positions that had dominated the mass culture debates of the 1950s: either one was for popular culture as a democratic form of artistic expression that would overcome the elitist splits engendered by the creators and defenders of high culture (Edward Shils), or one viewed the entire enterprise as a socioeconomically (Theodor W. Adorno) or popularly (José Ortega y Gasset) orchestrated diminution of culture to its most vulgar common denominator. To be sure, the continued use, particularly among American critics, of the term *mass culture* (as opposed to the English preference for *popular culture*) may reflect a certain skepticism, perhaps even disdain, about the collective potential for creative cultural appropriation by those confronting the infinitely co-opting powers of a consumer industry. Nevertheless, there has emerged within American discussions as well a broadening of textual analysis to include the active role of a potentially critical and resisting spectator in the construction of cultural meaning (see Ross).

Certainly a major theoretical arena in which the reappraisal of the spectatorial role has played itself out within American cultural studies has been the feminist discussions of mass culture, especially within film and television studies (see Modleski). The connection between the oppression of women and the production of stereotypes in mass-mediated culture has long been a central concern of the women's movement. Thus it is not surprising that the move to broaden the notion of textuality, to understand representation not simply as stereotype but as the construction of a subjectivity with profound social, political, and psychological roots, was to bring together gender and culture in an urgent and productive way.

Concerns about representation have been prominent in feminist film studies since its inception—originally as an unarticulated yet vital component in the efforts of feminist critics and filmmakers to confront the degradation of women by searching for alternative or positive female images in films by and/or about women. The limitations of this strategy became evident in the light of what such a focus was refusing implicitly to deal with—the erasure of the feminine and the female as living subject and spectator within mainstream Hollywood films. The film writings based on semiotics, psychoanalysis, and the cinematic apparatus emanating from the French and British discussions of the early 1970s theorized this absence and thereby changed the terms of inquiry and debate. Laura Mulvey's argument in "Visual Pleasure and Narrative Cinema" was as compelling as it was absolute: since the technical and psychic organization of the Hollywood film was founded on voyeurism and fetishism, women could not view the cinematic image without participating in their own humiliation. The only "pleasure" in the classical "narrative" is a male one; the position of the female spectator is marked by absence.

Many American feminists responded to Mulvey's article by contesting its abstract, ahistorical claims concerning the absent female spectator. But it is also true that the article's singleness of intention and radical stance helped shift the debates about female representation in ways that have been immensely useful for cultural studies. Simply at the level of textual analysis, critics were forced to consider the ideological implications of specifically cinematic forms of textual organization. Some theorists, to be sure, disagreed with the notion of a complicity between psychoanalytic theory and Hollywood film. But all critics, regardless of their positions, were compelled to ground their arguments in careful, often imaginative interpretations of individual films. Many of these readings indeed enriched and even implicated theoretical practice in its struggle to bridge the gap between intra- and intertextual explorations of mass cultural material. And key to that bridging, as Mulvey herself has recently reiterated, was the foregrounding of sexual difference: "Feminists came to find in the cinema of the Hollywood studio system, with its rich and disturbing imaging of sexual difference, a gold mine of raw material . . ." (response 249).

What has marked the feminist project as a significant intervention in studies of mass culture is its ability to broaden and resituate theoretically the questions emerging from the initially more narrow, psychoanalytic focus on feminist readings of the cinematic text. In some cases the approach has entailed a historicizing of the cinematic spectator, a response that, in turn, has contextualized and delimited the classical Hollywood paradigm itself. The writings of Mary Ann Doane, Miriam Hansen, Lynne Kirby, Patrice Petro, and Heide Schlüpmann are notable for their attempts to combine insights from psychoanalysis concerning the locus of the female spectator within a system constructed around the male gaze, on the one hand, and historically specific analyses of genres and audiences in a particular period of industrial development, on the other hand. Schlüpmann writes:

> I always see the question of the female spectator in a double perspective, in the context of a production that exploits the female gaze, i.e. addressing it and at the same time repressing it; and in the context of a reception which allows the potential of autonomy, emancipatory tendencies, women's resistances. As a result, both concepts are productive in different ways, that of the empirical spectator and that of the female position inscribed in the filmic discourse. Yet we must further consider that their relation to each other is historical. (response 281)

In her important book on the woman's film of the 1940s, Doane makes a similar point, staging an "interaction" between "audience address" (strategies that are "conscious, explicit and often extremely specific historically") and "spectator positioning" ("basic unconscious positions which establish the very coherence or readability of the text") as a way of contributing to "a more thorough articulation of theoretical and historical approaches to the analysis of spectatorship" (34). Petro's *Joyless Streets* looks to the female spectator of the Weimar cinema precisely in order to mark the intersection of the psychic and the social and to open up a space in which to theorize the place of the historical subject. Hansen's study of the female spectator in a period of transition from early to classical cinema combines an "industrial perspective" with ideological and psychosexual analyses, relating the paradigmatic shift in modes of representation and address with developments in exhibition practice and audience composition (response 170). What marks all their work is the effort to maintain a tension between theoretical and historical lines of inquiry, understanding the relation between the textually constructed modes of representation and the larger configuration of events and discourses in which they are situated and to which they respond.

The resituating of textual representation in the discursive framework of a larger public sphere and in relation to empirical, historical events has helped define and realign a number of different directions within popular and mass culture research. In some cases the original question of the female spectator has created a greater awareness of other modes of "difference," be it of class, gender, or race. For example, the discussions opened up around black filmmaker Spike Lee or the response to the film version of Alice Walker's *Color Purple* have forced a rethinking of cinematic representation in the light of racial and ethnic stereotypes, while providing further means by which the politics of historical representation itself may be given a greater role in university study (Bobo). Similarly, the work of Richard Dyer on gay and lesban film emphasizes the social construction of such representations within a prescribed and enabling historical context: "Like all cultural production, gay/lesbian films exist in and through the confluence of ways of making sense, the terms of thought and feeling available to them. These limit what can be said but also make saying possible; they both form and deform all expression" (1).

Beyond cinematic representation, American scholars influenced by the Birmingham model but informed as well by teachings of the Frankfurt school, have turned to reading other media (television, video, radio, magazines, rock music) and other icons and institutions (Madonna, shopping malls, beach culture, fandoms) to interrogate the ways in which they have become sites of struggle over semiotic meanings. Their work is characterized by a double perspective that can be seen as paradigmatic for the approaches and disagreements guiding much of cultural studies discussions today.

First, there is the attempt to challenge the monolithic approaches that either condemn or uncritically praise mass culture and, in so doing, to explore the contradictory patterns previously associated with the study of high cultural or high modernist texts. For instance, John Fiske's *Reading the Popular* argues for a more nuanced understanding of the way the power of commodity culture remains ultimately a "contested," not a top-down, relationship: "if the cultural commodities or texts do not contain resources out of which the people can make their own meanings of their social relations and identities, they will be rejected and will fail in the marketplace. They will not be made popular" (2). While Fiske's own analysis of "video pleasures" or the evening news indeed offers provocative "readings" of new and important material, his reluctance to place these cultural events in relation to evolving modes of perception and within changing structures of media and commodification leaves his analysis oblivious to the *contextual* dimension of the aesthetic question.

Which brings us to the second consideration in the mass culture debate. What is important about the writings of such theorists as Siegfried Kracauer, Walter Benjamin, Béla Balázs, Theodor Adorno, and, more recently, Alexander Kluge and Hans Magnus Enzensberger is precisely their focus on the specificity of any "medium" within a complex of differing histories: of industrial development, of commodification, of particular genre and narrative traditions, of particular audiences, of discursive performance, of historical and philosophical continuities, and so on. The emphasis simply on active audience appropriation of mass culture (Fiske) conflates reception with critical evaluation, thus obliterating the potential for a more differentiated focus on historically unprecedented modes of consumption, identification, and subjectivity (see Bathrick, Elsaesser, and Hansen).

LOOKING TO THE FUTURE OF CULTURAL STUDIES

The challenge of cultural studies to traditional organizations of knowledge within existing university structures represents more than just the addition of yet another innovative critical strategy for humanistic study. The questions raised touch on fundamental issues concerning how we perceive our educational mission, what we consider worthy of study and debate, who we are as cultural and social human beings. Questions of cultural identity—national, sexual, social—no longer assumed, have become global as well as local issues of political contestation. Not surprisingly, the battle lines of controversy in this country have spilled out of the academy into the legitimating agencies of the cultural public sphere (e.g., controversies surrounding the National Endowments for the Humanities and for the Arts), into institutions of power and political articulation. When former Secretary of Education William Bennett asserts that faculty and college administrators have been guilty of a "collective loss of nerve and faith" that has been "undeniably destructive of the curriculum" (16), he is talking about programmatic developments associated today with the cultural studies movement. For Bennett, the emergence of multiculturalism as a challenge to a unified canon of Western values founded on a set of traditional texts is tantamount to the abandonment of intellectual integrity by a generation lacking the courage to stand up for what it believes: "The curriculum was no longer a statement about what knowledge mattered; instead it became the product of a political compromise among competing schools and departments overlaid with marketing considerations" (19–20). That Bennett and other conservative critics such as Allan Bloom, E. D. Hirsch Jr., and Walter Jackson Bate have attributed the so-called decline of the modern university to the radical upheaval of the 1960s forces us, at the very least, to rethink the categories of present and future discussion.

Critics on both sides of the canon debate would agree with Bennett's assertion that the humanities are currently in crisis and that the curriculum is no longer a "statement" about what knowledge "matters." Disagreement emerges, however, around how to interpret such a breakdown of cultural consensus. Conservatives tend to view the curriculum debate within the humanities as synonymous with the capitulation of traditional authority to intellectual lightweights—a "closing of the American mind" (Bloom) or a compromise to mediocrity—and go on to argue that only an effort to reclaim the legacy of the humanities can save the university. Advocates of cultural studies, for their part, have glimpsed in the crisis a challenge to entrenched social and ethnic divisions as well as an opportunity to register the impact of forms of consumerism and the mass media emanating from economic developments since the 1950s (see Brantlinger). In some cases, their efforts to broaden the canon have led to a lack of cohesion or even the replacement of a traditional canon by an equally narrow and rigid alternative. Furthermore, Bennett is indeed correct in warning about the fashionable, market-driven aspects of the cultural studies boom (see Morris 4–5).

But what is at the heart of the canon controversy, beyond the concern with this or that curriculum, are fundamental differences about the role of culture in modern society and about the responsibilities of academic intellectuals as critics of society. The burgeoning of consumerism and mass-mediated culture since the 1950s has profoundly altered the way we know and see and govern ourselves. For university education, this change has forced scholars to confront problems of visual literacy as an integral part of higher education. The profusion of images in the media, in advertising, and in politics, as well as the expansion of cable television and independent video, has led academic institutions to include the historical and critical analysis of images and visual signs in humanities courses. Such developments have produced a breakdown of boundaries at every level: as a result of marketing all cultural products as commodities circulated in exchange, in the erosion of clear-cut distinctions between high and mass culture; through the influx and broadening of semiological studies, in reformulations of what constitutes a "text"; with the deployment of differing methodological paradigms, in a flow of conceptual models across disciplinary borders. Moreover, the increasing utilization of cultural representation for business and politics has transformed every citizen's relationship to cultural production as a whole. The emergence of cultural criticism as a component of academic study has been, in part, a response to the changing notions of culture in mass-mediated society. We as scholars of culture have been forced to come to terms with the powers of representation in organizing public fantasy for the selling of goods, the packaging of candidates, or the understanding of social difference.

Certainly cultural studies will also have to concern itself with the way strategies of representation work themselves out on a global scale vis-à-vis our shifting relations with Eastern Europe, the Third World, and a postcolonial politics. Here the work of cultural scholars has been vital in posing questions about the performative nature of political organization and the power of representation both to control and to disrupt. In his anthology *Nation and Narration*, Homi K. Bhabha raises fundamental issues about the future of cultural studies in relation to national identity: What forms of narrative express the ideology of the modern nation? How do questions of race and gender, class and colonialism change the boundaries of national identity? How is national identity itself the construction of a particular historical imaginary? Gayatri C. Spivak's *In Other Worlds* and Edward Said's *Orientalism* touch on similar questions and are as important for their methodologies as for their individual textual analyses. What is important about all such work is the extent to which it has redefined the social context of cultural representation as well as the role of intellectuals in the teaching of these ideas.

Cornell University

Works Cited and Suggestions for Further Reading

Adorno, Theodor W. *Negative Dialectics.* New York: Continuum, 1973.

Barrett, Michelle. "Feminism and the Definition of Cultural Politics." *Feminism, Culture, Politics.* Ed. Rosalind Brunt and Caroline Rowan. London: Lawrence, 1982. 37–58.

Barthes, Roland. *Mythologies.* Trans. Annette Lavers. New York: Hill, 1977.

Bathrick, David, Thomas Elsaesser, and Miriam Hansen, eds. *Weimar Film Theory.* Spec. issue of *New German Critique* 40 (1987): 3–240.

Benjamin, Walter. *Illuminations: Essays and Reflections.* Ed. Hannah Arendt. Trans. Harry Zohn. New York: Schocken, 1968.

Bennett, William J. "To Reclaim a Legacy." *Chronicle of Higher Education* 28 Nov. 1984: 16–21.

Bercovitch, Sacvan, and Myra Jehlen, eds. *Ideology and Classic American Literature.* Cambridge: Cambridge UP, 1986.

Bergstrom, Janet, and Mary Anne Doane, eds. *The Spectatrix.* Spec. issue of *Camera Obscura* 20–21 (1989): 5–378.

Bhabha, Homi K., ed. *Nation and Narration.* London: Routledge, 1990.

Bledstein, Burton. *The Culture of Professionalism: The Middle Class and the Development of Higher Education in America.* New York: Norton, 1976.

Bloom, Allan. *The Closing of the American Mind: How Higher Education Has Failed Democracy and Impoverished the Souls of Today's Students.* New York: Simon, 1987.

Bobo, Jacqueline. "Articulation and Hegemony: Black Women's Response to the Film *The Color Purple.*" Diss. U of Oregon, 1989.

Brantlinger, Patrick. *Crusoe's Footprints: Cultural Studies in Britain and America.* New York: Routledge, 1990.

Brenkman, John. *Culture and Domination.* Ithaca: Cornell UP, 1987.

Clifford, James, and George Marcus, eds. *Writing Culture: The Poetics and Politics of Ethnography.* Berkeley: U of California P, 1986.

Cohen, Walter. "Political Criticism of Shakespeare." *Shakespeare Reproduced: The Text in History and Ideology.* Ed. Jean E. Howard and Marion F. O'Connor. London: Methuen, 1987. 18–46.

Doane, Mary Ann. *The Desire to Desire: The Woman's Film of the 1940s.* Bloomington: Indiana UP, 1987.

Dollimore, Jonathan. *Radical Tragedy: Religion, Ideology, and Power in the Drama of Shakespeare and His Contemporaries.* Chicago: U of Chicago P, 1986.

Dyer, Richard. *Now You See It: Studies on Lesbian and Gay Film.* London: Routledge, 1990.

Eagleton, Terry. *Literary Theory: An Introduction.* Oxford: Blackwell; Minneapolis: U of Minnesota P, 1983.

Fiedler, Leslie. *Cross the Border—Close the Gap.* New York: Stein, 1964.

Fiske, John. *Reading the Popular.* Boston: Unwin, 1989.

———. *Television Culture.* New York: Methuen, 1987.

Gates, Henry Louis, Jr., ed. *Black Literature and Literary Theory.* New York: Methuen, 1984.

Geertz, Clifford. *The Interpretation of Cultures.* New York: Basic, 1973.

Graff, Gerald. *Professing Literature: An Institutional History.* Chicago: U of Chicago P, 1987.

Graff, Gerald, and Reginald Gibbons, eds. *Criticism in the University.* Evanston: Northwestern UP, 1985.

Gramsci, Antonio. *Prison Notebooks.* Trans. Quintin Hoare and Geoffrey N. Smith. New York: International, 1971.

Greenblatt, Stephen J. *Shakespearean Negotiations: The Circulation of Social Energy in Renaissance England.* Berkeley: U of California P, 1988.

Habermas, Jürgen. *The Philosophical Discourse of Modernity.* Trans. Frederick G. Lawrence. Cambridge: MIT P, 1987.

Hall, Stuart. "Cultural Studies and the Centre: Some Problematics and Problems." *Culture, Media, Language.* Ed. Hall et al. London: Hutchinson, 1983. 15–47.

Hansen, Miriam. *Babel and Babylon: Spectatorship in American Silent Film.* Cambridge: Harvard UP, 1991.

———. Response. Bergstrom and Doane 169–74.

Haraway, Donna. *Primate Visions: Gender, Race, and Nature in the World of Modern Science.* London: Routledge, 1990.

Hebdidge, Dick. *Subculture: The Meaning of Style.* London: Routledge, 1979.

Huyssen, Andreas. *After the Great Divide: Modernism, Mass Culture, Postmodernism.* Bloomington: Indiana UP, 1987.

Jacoby, Russell. *The Last Intellectuals: American Culture in the Age of Academe.* New York: Basic, 1987.

Jameson, Fredric. "Interview." *Diacritics* 12 (Fall 1982): 72–91.

———. *The Political Unconscious: Narrative as a Socially Symbolic Act.* Ithaca: Cornell UP, 1981.

Johnson, Richard. "What Is Cultural Studies Anyway?" *Social Text* 6.1 (1987): 38–80.

Kaufmann, David. "The Profession of Theory." *PMLA* 105 (1990): 519–30.

Kirby, Lynne. "Male Hysteria and Early Cinema." *Camera Obscura* 17 (1988): 113–31.

Krupnick, Mark. *Lionel Trilling and the Fate of Cultural Criticism.* Evanston: Northwestern UP, 1986.

———. "The Two Worlds of Literary Criticism." Graff and Gibbons 158–69.

LaCapra, Dominick. *Soundings in Critical Theory.* Ithaca: Cornell UP, 1989.

Lentricchia, Frank. *After the New Criticism.* Chicago: U of Chicago P, 1980.

Mitchell, W. J. T. *Against Theory: Literary Studies and the New Pragmatism.* Chicago: U of Chicago P, 1985.

Modleski, Tania, ed. *Studies in Entertainment: Critical Approaches to Mass Culture.* Bloomington: Indiana UP, 1986.

Morris, Meaghan. "Banality in Cultural Studies." *Discourse* 10.2 (1988): 3–29.

Mulvey, Laura. Response. Bergstrom and Doane 248–52.

———. "Visual Pleasure and Narrative Cinema." *Screen* 16.3 (1975): 6–18. Rpt. in *Visual and Other Pleasures.* By Mulvey. Bloomington: Indiana UP, 1989. 14–26.

Nelson, Cary, and Lawrence Grossberg, eds. *Marxism and the Interpretation of Culture.* Urbana: U of Illinois P, 1988.

Ortega y Gasset, José. *The Dehumanization of Art.* Trans. Helene Weyl. Princeton: Princeton UP, 1968.

Penley, Constance. *The Future of Illusionism: Film, Feminism, and Psychoanalysis.* Minneapolis: U of Minnesota P, 1989.

Petro, Patrice. *Joyless Streets: Women and Melodramatic Representation in Weimar Germany.* Princeton: Princeton UP, 1989.

Radway, Janice. *Reading the Romance: Women, Patriarchy, and Popular Literature.* Chapel Hill: U of North Carolina P, 1984.

Ross, Andrew. *No Respect: Intellectuals and Popular Culture.* New York: Routledge, 1989.

Said, Edward. *Orientalism.* New York: Pantheon, 1978.

———. *The World, the Text, and the Critic.* Cambridge: Harvard UP, 1983.

Sarris, Andrew. *The American Cinema: Directors and Directions, 1929–1968.* New York: Dutton, 1968.

Schlüpmann, Heide. Response. Bergstrom and Doane 279–82.

Scholes, Robert. *Textual Power: Literary Theory and the Teaching of English.* New Haven: Yale UP, 1985.

Shils, Edward. "Mass Society and Its Culture." *The Intellectuals and the Powers and Other Essays.* Chicago: U of Chicago P, 1972.

Spivak, Gayatri C. *In Other Worlds: Essays in Cultural Politics.* New York: Routledge, 1987.

Veeser, H. Aram, ed. *The New Historicism.* New York: Routledge, 1989.

Weber, Samuel. *Institutions and Interpretation.* Minneapolis: U of Minnesota P, 1987.

White, Hayden. *Metahistory: The Historical Imagination in Nineteenth-Century Europe.* Baltimore: Johns Hopkins UP, 1974.

———. *Tropics of Discourse: Essays in Cultural Criticism.* Baltimore: Johns Hopkins UP, 1978.

Williams, Raymond. *Culture and Society, 1780–1950.* New York: Harper, 1966.

———. *Keywords: A Vocabulary of Culture and Society.* New York: Oxford UP, 1983.

———. *The Long Revolution.* Harmondsworth, Eng.: Penguin, 1965.

———. *Marxism and Literature.* London: Oxford UP, 1977.

Willis, Paul, et al. *The Youth Review: Social Conditions of Young People in Wolverhampton.* London: Gower, 1988.

Epilogue

Gerald Graff

The Scholar in Society

> English and literary studies have reached a point in their theoretical development when they've become incapable of communicating to the layman at the very historical moment when they've most needed to justify their existence. The brightest and most innovative young people in literary criticism are as impenetrable as nuclear physicists. The Left-wing intelligentsia is trapped in a kind of ghetto that only they understand, and so can't bring leverage to bear on the body politic.
>
> —David Lodge

WHAT kind of "leverage" can literary and linguistic scholarship bring to bear on the "body politic"? What, if anything, has humanistic scholarship to say to the lay person? What is the social function of humanistic research? These questions have been troubling as long as scholarship has existed, but they have acquired a new urgency as scholarship has come to be publicly supported by academic institutions and tied to the mission of democratic higher education. The comment by David Lodge (qtd. in Atlas 57), a well-known novelist and until recently a professor of English himself, succinctly reflects the belief of many today that the distance between the scholar and society is growing.

Complicating the issue is the emergence since the 1960s of the academic "Left-wing intelligentsia" referred to by Lodge. Though this intelligentsia claims to put its scholarship in the service of social change, it often seems to pursue this project, as Lodge suggests, in languages that are impenetrable to those who presumably are to benefit from the changes. And yet, the current public battle over the state of the academic humanities is a sign of a certain convergence of interests between scholars and society.

People do not wage war unless they care about the same things, and the eruption of what has been called a "culture war" over the humanities has opened a discussion between scholars and the public that did not exist previously. Though the popular accounts of the new academic trends have often been hostile and inaccurate, the effect has been to make language and literary studies a bit less mysterious to the outside world than they were before. If nothing else, the public at least knows that academic experts on language and literature vigorously disagree about fundamental questions in their discipline.

To make this point is not to minimize the vast and disturbing gulf that still separates the discourses of humanities scholars from those of the public at large as well as the urgent need for humanists to bridge this gulf. But as I argue in this essay, major changes have been taking place in humanities research, changes that call into question long-held assumptions about academic specialization and the separation of scholars from society. The common charge that the academic humanities are narrowly "specialized" and deal only in esoteric matters has not been true for over a generation.[1] The charge overlooks the fact that narrow specialization in the humanities has increasingly been penalized, that the highest professional rewards have gone to work that advances ambitious theories and broad cultural and interdisciplinary generalizations—as many of the essays in this volume demonstrate. What is mistaken for overspecialization is a set of new languages of generalization that many either dislike or do not understand.

IS HUMANITIES RESEARCH NECESSARY?

When Lodge observes that English and literary studies have "become incapable of communicating to the layman," one might ask when in the past was there easy communication between scholars and nonscholars? The concept of the scholar has always assumed a certain necessary and salutary distance from the immediate concerns of the body politic.

This distance first started to be felt as a major problem, however, when scholarship came to be organized on a large scale in the new research universities of the late nineteenth century, a development that brought the scholarly function into partnership with democratic education. It is as academic scholars have come to be publicly supported in mass educational institutions that the question of how "to justify their existence," in Lodge's phrase, has become urgent.

When the fields of English and other modern languages first emerged in the newly established universities of the late nineteenth century, they were inspired by a broad social and educational mission. Though most research produced by the first modern language scholars was highly specialized, consisting of minute philological investigations into the etymology, grammar, and history of the modern languages, this research was felt to be a contribution to a larger literary and national culture. In this respect, the philologists harked back to the literary nationalism of late-eighteenth- and early-nineteenth-century writers such as Johann Gottfried Herder, Friedrich Schlegel, and Jules Michelet, who popularized the doctrine that the distinctive greatness of a nation was expressed in the quality of its language and literature.

It followed from this literary nationalism that the philologist, no less than the poet and the man and woman of letters, was a social leader, a creator of the national character and consciousness. James Wilson Bright, as president of the Modern Language Association, declared in his address to the 1902 annual convention that "the philological strength and sanity of a nation is the measure of its intellectual and spiritual vitality." The philologist, Bright added, must share in "the work of guiding the destinies of the country" (lxii).

It was this broad social mission that had enabled modern language studies to break the centuries-old educational grip of classical Greek and Latin and to give modern language studies a central place in the college and school curriculum. In combining the seemingly opposed impulses of scientific method and romantic cultural nationalism, the new modern language philology promised to reconcile the scholar and society, the professional and the amateur, graduate research and undergraduate education.

As narrow as the early philologists' investigations often were, taken together these investigations were thought to compose a grand and inspiring picture of the Western cultural and literary tradition.[2] In theory at least, even the most seemingly trivial research fact was a part of a larger cultural whole; research was thus a force for cultural unity in a nation where such unity had always seemed precarious at best and where it was now threatened by massive European immigration.

In practice, however, the performance of academic philologists fell short of their missionary cultural pretensions. Philologists might describe themselves as cultural leaders, but few outside the academy took their claims seriously,[3] and they themselves were often forced to concede that the industrious accumulation of research facts did not often add up to any edifying cultural meaning. Some of them wondered publicly if their research actually served any larger educational and humanistic purpose.

The distinction hardened between the "scholar," concerned chiefly with more or less quantifiable facts, and the journalistic or belletristic "critic," concerned with more elusive personal interpretations and judgments. That an unhealthy gulf had grown up between the two became a frequent observation both inside and outside the academy. The scholar, it was said, commanded professionalism, expertise, and rigor, but produced few interesting conclusions, while the critic abounded in facile and amateurish generalizations, but lacked solid evidence for them. This schizoid condition was reproduced in the working lives of many professors: after being specialists in their research and their graduate seminars, they were expected to become generalists when they entered the undergraduate classroom.

Few made the transition successfully, and their failures left language and literature departments vulnerable to harsher critics, who charged that the very existence of these departments rested on a misconceived attempt to apply rigorously scientific methods to subjects inherently resistant to them.[4] Since the beginnings, then, academic humanities scholarship has had to face public skepticism about its very reason for being. Though research in the sciences is often obscure and highly specialized, it has a commonly assumed social rationale that legitimates it in the public mind. Because humanities research lacks such a rationale, obscurity and specialization in its scholarship can easily seem merely frivolous or perverse.

News articles on the Modern Language Association annual convention that satirize bewilderingly opaque session and paper titles are a relatively benevolent manifestation of this response. But the mood has lately begun to take an angrier turn as the magnitude and the costs of the humanities-research enterprise have steadily grown without a visible increase in its contribution to the public good. This anger overlays the already long-standing fear that research draws humanists away from the teaching of undergraduates. As Wayne Booth asked in his essay "The Scholar and Society" in the 1981 edition of *Introduction to Scholarship in Modern Languages and Literatures*, "[How] can we justify a national educational system that rewards and encourages scholarly specialization . . . , often at the expense of simple essential matters like teaching the young how to read and write?" (125).

The target of Booth's criticism was not humanities research itself but the failure of humanists to make the larger implications of their research clear to students and the general public. Booth went on to argue that "most of our important work deserves also to be translated into a language that will, by its nature, teach the public that we are serious and that what we do can be important to more than a priestly cult" (126).

That most humanities research is even worthy of being translated has always been questioned, however, by harsher critics, who say that this research is so trivial that it inherently conflicts with the values officially promoted by the humanities. (As one critic called it, playing on a traditional Latin tag, humanities research is a kind of "*litterae inhumaniores*" [Foerster].) According to such critics, the standard forms of humanities research dampen the creative spirit when they do not stifle it entirely. The implication is that literature and the arts would be better off without an army of academic scholars attached to it. "When I was an undergraduate in Chicago," Saul Bellow has said, "we were told not to bother with humanist scholars but to study the Great Books themselves" (qtd. in Atlas 83).

The suspicion, moreover, is that academic humanists themselves secretly share this view and that much of their research would not be produced if it were not for the compulsion of publish-or-perish requirements. Even Booth complains "that our profession has, for complex reasons, developed a strange capacity to generate a kind of research that is not only irrelevant to society but irrelevant to the interests of the researcher" (129). The source of this strange capacity, of course, lies in tenure and promotion requirements that measure the competitive ranking of universities by their annual research production rather than their excellence in teaching.

In all these criticisms, the aspect of scholarly research that draws the most persistent condemnation is its supposed specialization. Scholarly specialization, in the title of an official report by Lynne V. Cheney, current chair of the National Endowment for the Humanities, is seen as part of a "tyrannical machine," a legacy of the nineteenth-century German university in which "the scholar's proper role lay in producing 'bricks' for the rising temple of knowledge" (*Tyrannical Machines* 27). Research, it is said, not only results in the neglect of teaching and the subversion of the values of the humanities but undermines the common ground of the curriculum and the commonly shared values in the culture. Though the accusation that research specialization subverts "the common culture" goes back at least a century, it has resurfaced as an especially persistent theme in the wave of critical books, reports, and polemical exposés on higher education that have appeared since the mid-1980s.[5]

As Allan Bloom put it in his 1987 best-seller, *The Closing of the American Mind*, "most professors are specialists, concerned only with their own fields, interested in the advancement of those fields in their own terms, or in their own personal advancement in a world where all the rewards are on the side of professional distinction" (339). A 1987 editorial in the *New Republic* put it this way: "the energy needed to churn out the cutting wedges of ephemeral research means less time and effort devoted to teaching. . . . Once unitary truths are scorned, there's no reason to distinguish between the important and the trivial in education" ("Case" 7–8).

The implication of such comments is that research is essentially selfish, placing the personal advancement of the researcher and the advancement of the field ahead of education and the common culture. The effect of research is seen as divisive, undermining the "unitary truths" that supposedly bind us together (though the editorialist does not specify what these truths are or who should be empowered to define them). And as the imagery of cutting wedges and tyrannical machines suggests, research is thought of as a mechanical product that is impersonally and soullessly "churned out," not an activity with its own forms of skill and creativity.

Certainly a good many of these charges against humanistic research have been justified. But in my view they are increasingly misleading as descriptions of the current state of the academic humanities. Booth argued in 1981 that, with respect to institutional expectations about research, "what must be changed are the rules of the house. . . ." ("Scholar" 130). Yet the rules of the house were already undergoing significant change at the moment Booth was writing, though it is easier to see this today than it was then. Far from glorifying specialization, the humanities for over a generation have regarded the narrower forms of specialization with disfavor and have gone in search of large cultural, theoretical, and interdisciplinary overviews.

Here a great deal hinges, of course, on how protean words like *specialization* and *generalization* are used. In one sense, as Catharine R. Stimpson points out, "specialization is a feature of every complex organization, be it social or natural, a school system, garden, book, or mammalian body." After all, "no single entity can survive within its environment if it must perform every task that must be done." So the question, Stimpson says, "is not whether we are specialists but how we specialize—in what, for whom, with whom, and to what end" (3).

As Stimpson also observes, the critics of research conflate at least "four distinct terms . . . as if they were synonyms: specialization, theory, radical, and flight from undergraduate teaching."[6] In other words, *specialization* has become an ideological buzzword, useful for denigrating new forms of politically oriented theory, scholarship, and teaching. Scholars in women's studies, minority literatures, and multicultural studies are accused of subordinating scholarship to political causes and promoting the values of "special interest groups." (See, among others, the essays by Schor, Allen, Gates, and Bathrick in this volume.) These scholars retort that those who make these charges are themselves a special interest group, despite their claim to speak from a universal viewpoint, and that they have their own kind of investment in a political "cause"—acceptance of the status quo being as much a cause as desire to change it.

In *Tyrannical Machines*, Cheney adduces "the importance of new theoretical approaches" as her primary example of how narrow specialization is taking over the humanities, causing courses in "increasingly narrow topics" to be substituted for ones in broadly general ones. Cheney cites one university that replaced ten courses in Western civilization by three new courses, Discourse and Society, Text and Context, and Knowledge and Power, and another that allows a general requirement to be filled by a course called Sexuality and Writing (31–32). But it is not clear from these titles that the changes to which Cheney refers are indeed toward greater narrowness and specialization: what could be more general in scope than "discourse and society," "knowledge and power," and "sexuality and writing"? Insofar as those topics may bring several different cultures into play, they could be construed as less narrow than the particularistic "Western" civilization. Obviously, what is objectionable about the new courses is not a difference in degree of specialization but a difference in ideology.

Here one sees a contradiction in current criticism of alleged specialization, for it is clearly the general import of political issues like "knowledge and power" that arouses uneasiness from opponents, not specialization or obscurity. One suspects that underlying the attacks on the specialization and obscurity of research dealing with these issues is a fear that the import of this research may become *all too clear*, that it may bring all too much "leverage to bear on the body politic," in Lodge's phrase, especially if its implications continue to be taught to undergraduates. After all, if the new theories and methods were merely specialized and obscure, it is doubtful that people would be getting so worked up over them.

This is not to suggest there is no truth in Lodge's observation that "the brightest and most innovative young people in literary criticism" are often impenetrable to the lay person. But that their efforts are stirring up so much public controversy is itself a sign of a certain kind of "leverage," or at least an ability to attract a degree of public attention and debate that is unprecedented for humanities scholarship. When an unfamiliar idiom such as "discourse and society" baffles students and others, this is a problem needing attention. But the problem still cannot be described as a problem of narrow specialization. It is one thing for an academic subject to be so narrow or trivial that no one but another expert can take an interest in it. It is another for a subject to possess potentially broad interest that it fails to receive because it has not been effectively translated into lay terms.

Take, for example, the scholar who writes an article for *Critical Inquiry* or *PMLA* on the politics of interpretation in seventeenth-century French painting and the journalist who writes an editorial on spin control as a new feature of the climate of public life—where what has come to matter, it is now often felt, is not just the event itself (a presidential debate, the war in the Persian Gulf) but the "spin" placed on the event by the communications media. The editorialist who writes about spin control is in some ways concerned with the same phenomenon as the scholar—the political struggle to control meaning. Both are testifying in their different ways to the proposition that whoever controls language controls much more than language. Insofar as recent humanities scholarship is concerned with drawing out and advancing the implications of this proposition, it is less esoteric, rarefied, and remote from journalistic interest than it seems to be.

Yet the different discourses of scholars and journalists can easily prevent the two sides from recognizing that their concerns overlap. These discourses are not neutral, entailing as they do very different and often antagonistic assumptions about language and the politics of language. Yet a dialogue may be possible once the terms of the one discourse begin to be translated into those of the other. Academic scholars in the 1990s who hope to close the gap between themselves and society will need to be more concerned with this sort of translation than were their predecessors. In fact, this project figures to be crucial at a moment when some of those scholars are coming under unprecedented journalistic attacks.

WHAT COUNTS AS "RESEARCH"?

I have said that recent attacks on the specialization of humanities research echo a litany of complaints that was already well established a century ago. What is usually overlooked is that the litany has not gone completely unheeded. When critics of research like Cheney attack the view that "the scholar's proper role lay in producing 'bricks' for the rising temple of knowledge," it does not occur to them that this model of knowledge, and hence their criticisms of it, has been out of date for decades. Though Cheney borrows for the title of her report the phrase "tyrannical machines," from a 1903 essay by William James, she does not consider that what was true of scholarly research in 1903 may no longer be true in 1990. Humanists who only gather "bricks" of information no longer compete effectively with colleagues who can put their knowledge into larger contexts.

It is true, as Stimpson notes, that most professors of literature have continued to concentrate "on a period, figure, nation, or problem" (2). But it is also true that the context has expanded in which a particular scholarly specialty now tends to be considered. Stimpson points out that recent critics of Gertrude Stein's writing range far beyond Stein's texts: "they [have] studied modernism, genre theory, psychoanalysis, linguistics, Parisian society" (3). Not only would an experimental writer like Stein not have been studied at all in a literature department a generation ago, but critics are not likely to make an impact today unless they can place Stein in a broadly cultural or philosophical context.

This change is seen in the language used to evaluate scholarly work for academic positions and grants, where approval is now signaled by terms like *broad-gauged, wide-ranging*, and *interdisciplinary* and where it is becoming difficult even to imagine work being commended for its minute specialization. That grant application forms now ask applicants to justify the larger significance of their project also indicates where our values have come to lie.

Any history of research in language and literature since the turn of the century would be a story of the progressive expansion and transformation of the concept.[7] In literary studies after World War II, the growth of the New Criticism, myth criticism, and other interpretive schools was accompanied by a significant broadening of the definition of what could be counted as academic research, which now included the analytical "close reading" of texts. Though textual "explication" eventually succumbed to the same mechanization that had often marked the older work in philology and literary history, it encouraged academics in their teaching and publishing to raise the sorts of broad questions about literature and culture that had previously been associated with journalism. One sees this broadening in the many essays and books by academic critics in the 1940s and 1950s on the general functions of literature and its mode of knowledge in a culture dominated by science and materialism.

Other changes around the same time similarly helped broaden the scope of humanities research. These included the expansion of the academic canon to include modern and contemporary literature (a revision almost as dramatic as the one being fought over today, and often bitterly resisted) and the establishment of creative writing as a field, followed by film and other media studies, popular culture, and ethnic and gender studies. The legitimation of contemporary culture as a field across numerous disciplines—marking the dissolution of traditional antiquarian restrictions on the culture thought fit to be studied in universities—brought the concerns of the humanities far closer than they had been before to the concerns of the surrounding society.

Contributing to this loosening of restrictions on what could count as humanities research were demographic changes that increasingly democratized American education after the war. As new ethnic constituencies entered the postwar university, including previously excluded or marginalized groups, student bodies and faculties were infused with people who were often intellectually more restless and iconoclastic than the previous academic generation and less at home with traditional literary culture. Postwar academic culture was less genteel and more contentious than it had been earlier, and a contentious climate favored those academics who commanded interpretive and theoretical skills and who were more inclined to be reflective about the public functions of the humanities. A new general discourse about the public role of the humanities dates from this period. It was a reflection of this trend when, in the early 1960s, "criticism" itself became a research field with its own courses.

To mention still another type of democratization, the new forms of textual close reading proved to be applicable to texts that were not considered literature at all. Though the study of film and popular culture would not become prevalent in literature departments until the late 1960s, in retrospect one can see how the way for such study was paved by the earlier academic critical revolution, whose techniques of close analytical reading could locate complex meanings in a comic strip or popular film as easily as in a canonical novel or poem (see Bathrick in this volume). Myth critics like Northrop Frye and Leslie Fiedler pointed out that the same structural and mythical patterns that underlay the Bible and the literary classics could be found in all narratives including those of advertising and popular culture. Fiedler dramatized the point in a 1955 study, in which he gave historical events such as the Rosenberg spy case and the Joseph McCarthy hearings "the same careful scrutiny we have learned to practice on the shorter poems of Donne." The critics of the 1950s thus anticipated the theorists of the 1980s in the practice of thinking of historical events as "texts" (Fiedler ix).

Therefore, though the postwar interpretive methodologies helped to consolidate a hierarchical literary canon, there was something about these methodologies that unwittingly subverted canons and hierarchies. The mere application of the same set of interpretive conventions to a classical tragedy and a popular film tended to level the status differences between these objects and make them seem commensurable. In this respect, one could argue that it was the critics of the 1940s and 1950s who began to undermine canonical hierarchies of culture long before today's canon revisionists arrived on the scene. It was also the critics of that period, with their interests in anthropology and psychology, who initiated the transgression so much lamented by many today in which models borrowed from the behavioral sciences impinge on the humanities.

None of these changes occurred without a fight, of course. Interpretive criticism and the study of modern literature, creative writing, and popular culture became legitimate research activities only after acrimonious battles. Such battles continue today over the tenure qualifications of teachers of women's and ethnic studies and rhetoric and composition.

As a consequence of the changes I have been tracing, a great part of the research done by humanists today would not have been recognized as "research" at all according to the criteria in force before the war. Once the word *research* (and *scholarship*) could mean anything from a philological study of the passive voice in Old Icelandic to a critical reading of Gertrude Stein or a contemporary experimental novel, it became an administrative catchall for measuring faculty production rather than a precise or meaningful indicator of the kind of work being produced. In this respect, the fate of words like *research* and *scholarship* in the academy resembles the fate of words like *art* and *literature*, which have become open-ended categories whose meanings are continually redefined as new works and styles emerge.

This state of affairs can easily leave administrative review bodies perplexed about the criteria for evaluating research. As in the art world, there are those who complain that standards have been abandoned in the desperate pursuit of trendiness. Though such criticisms are sometimes justified, those who hold up earlier forms of research as a model of integrity from which we have fallen forget how often those forms were criticized for their pedantry, intellectual timidity, and irrelevance to contemporary life. In its greater engagement with contemporary culture—even the more antiquarian fields increasingly acknowledge that interpretations of the past inevitably reflect the interests of the interpreter—postwar research has brought the academic humanities potentially closer than they were before to the concerns of students and lay people. Though academic humanists have too often been reluctant to recognize the fact, the university's growth into an instititution servicing great masses of people necessarily turns it into an agency of cultural popularization. It is even fair to call today's university a form of popular culture, in competition with journalism and other media as an alternative interpretation of experience.

Certainly, the widening of the range of options for professional work means that there is less and less excuse for scholars in the 1990s to feel caught in the forced-labor syndrome described in 1981 by Booth, in which they feel pressure to produce "a kind of research that is not only irrelevant to society but irrelevant to the interests of the researcher." In my own experience, most academics who pursue research and publication do so not because they feel forced but because they feel the excitement—rare in any occupation—of creating an intellectual project and contributing to a research community. To be sure, some scholars still take up projects in which they lack personal conviction. But the point is that there is increasingly less institutional compulsion to do so.[8]

On the contrary, if there is pressure on humanists today, it is not to specialize narrowly but to transcend specialization—by making large cultural and theoretical claims and transgressing field boundaries. As Bruce Robbins puts it, the highest academic rewards now go to "those who have the vision to retool professional procedures and protocols in response to or anticipation of great historical shifts and newly emergent visions of the public interest. . . ." Those who "set the professional agendas" today, according to Robbins, are those who "force professional paradigm-shifts, re-align the competing disciplines among themselves and (in so doing) in new relation to worldly power."

Jonathan Culler makes a similar point in his essay "Literary Theory" in this volume, where he notes that the growth of theory bespeaks the emergence of a new "notion of generality as theoretical significance. . . . As publishers and their blurbs tell us, a theoretical point or claim has come to be what you aim for when you are trying to reach a broad audience in literary studies. . . . [P]oints of general interest are taken to be theoretical positions even if they do not rely on anything like theoretical argument." It is this new theoretical generality described by Culler that has made possible the recent interdisciplinary mergers of literary studies with philosophy, religion, sociology, popular culture, the history of science, anthropology and ethnography, and the law.[9] The recent development of the much discussed new field of literary and legal interpretation

(Levinson and Mailloux) would have been inconceivable had literary studies remained confined within the older specialist discourse. The same general ideas and debates now circulate across the most diverse fields and create possibilities of common discussion that did not exist when positivistic specialization defined the norm (see Gunn in this volume).

Of course, it is one thing to overcome boundaries between the academic disciplines and quite another to overcome the boundary between those academic disciplines and the lay public. The general ideas that circulate freely across law and literature—the debate over "critical legal studies," for example, which has been influenced by deconstruction and poststructuralism—are often mysterious to nonacademics. But the blurring of internal boundaries tends to affect external boundaries as well. Once literary scholars become part of a common discussion with lawyers and legal theorists, they are speaking to concerns that a wider public may come to recognize it has a stake in.

Critics who see the growth of theory, then, as the ultimate surrender to the narcissistic specialization that has supposedly overcome the humanities generally, have things exactly backward. What these critics mistake for specialization are in fact new languages of generalization, languages that have so far resisted popularization but are not intrinsically incapable of it.

Changes in academic publishing have also had a hand in raising the prestige of generality while devaluing specialization. In the early 1970s, when government financial support for higher education was markedly curtailed, university presses were forced to think more commercially in deciding what to publish. Previously, the role of the university press had been to subsidize the kind of scholarly work whose prospective market figured to be too small to interest a commercial publisher. Without completely abandoning this role and entering into competition with trade houses for huge sales, university presses began to market their lists more aggressively and to copy trade-press advertising techniques. The effect of the new conditions was to reduce the publishability of the scholarly book that speaks solely to specialists and to increase that of the book that addresses a wider audience, even if still usually a predominantly academic one. The book addressed chiefly to specialists could still be published, but only if its author demonstrated larger implications of the subject for readers beyond the immediate field. These conditions obtain less widely in scholarly journal publishing, whose less stringent economic constraints allow it to remain more receptive to field-specific writing.

In the wake of all these changes, then, the graduate student who in 1945 might have written a dissertation on the topic Certain Aspects of Robert Southey's Juvenilia would be likely in 1990 to write one on Robert Southey and the Construction of Gender in the Discourse of Romanticism, in which a claim might be made about the roots of our present views about sexuality. Is this a bad thing, as many believe? There is obviously the danger of confusing profundity with trendiness and hype, and it is unfortunate when premature expectations of a "major contribution" fall on scholars hardly out of graduate school. Furthermore—contrary to charges that standards are declining—faculty publication expectations have become progressively more demanding, sometimes unreasonably so. It is untrue, as folklore has it, that pure quantity often overrides considerations of quality in the evaluation of professional work, but it is true that the crass requirement of a *book* for tenure is often rigidly applied when several excellent articles would be a more reasonable expectation.

Then, too, in an intensely competitive employment market, the premium placed on "professional paradigm shifts" and "newly emergent visions" of history and culture can easily make young scholars feel that getting a teaching position (or a research grant or even a graduate fellowship) depends on making extravagant claims. Again rather like avant-garde artists, today's scholars may think they risk losing caste unless they can plausibly represent their work as a breakthrough on the frontiers of thought or perception.[10] The breakthrough ethos is not new—its logic was implicit in the old "brick accumulation" model of the positivist era. But the dissolution of that positivist model has left scholars vulnerable to a new revisionism that blurs the boundaries between the scholarly "cutting edge" and the political and cultural vanguard. The effect is further to exalt scholarship that addresses the big picture and to devalue that which does not.

A case in point is the declining status of textual editing, a vital and highly challenging kind of work that at one time was the staple of doctoral dissertations but is too often now discounted as positivistic. This situation may be changing as a result of recent interest in the theoretical implications of editing,[11] but then it seems symptomatic that an alliance with theory was needed to reverse the downward fortunes of editing. Of course, if editing has always had important theoretical implications, as the new editing theorists point out, then it does not seem unreasonable to expect these implications to become a central concern of the field (see Greetham in this volume). Yet this should not diminish the currency of valuable work that is not particularly theoretical. A new set of problems, then, has arisen for prospective humanities scholars precisely because they are no longer encouraged to crawl into their specialties and turn their backs on larger public concerns.

Yet if it is no longer true that humanities research is narrowly specialized and technical in scope, it is impossible to deny that this is the way such research still tends to *look* to nonacademics. The issues now treated by academic humanists have the potential of greater interest to nonacademics than those treated in the past, but humanists as a group remain poor at making the general implications of this work available to their constituencies. Academic discourse tends to look more hopelessly specialized and remote from the interests of the general society than it actually is, enabling its journalistic detractors to represent it as absurdly esoteric.

To put it another way, academic humanists need to take some responsibility for controlling the way their ideas and projects are represented to a wider public. It is true that since academics rarely have direct access to the mass media, they are vulnerable to being caricatured there. But it is also true that caricatures of the academy flourish when academics fail to explain themselves in terms the public can understand. As long as academic humanists are unable or unwilling to make their debates accessible in the public sphere, it will continue to be their detractors who speak for them.

I have argued that transformations in research over the last several decades have put humanities scholarship into a more promising relation to the concerns of the general public than it was half a century ago, more promising but also more controversial and antagonistic. These changed conditions make it possible to envisage a new and healthier relation between research and teaching. If I am right that the charges of specialization against humanities research are anachronistic, then there is less need than in the past for a conflict between the interests of research and the interests of general education.

The inevitability of this conflict has been deeply imbedded in our inherited concept of general education, which sees itself as a sphere of "general" concerns that are somehow more humane, universal, and common than the "special interests" of disciplinary research. This defensive and compensatory conception of general education has always been self-defeating in the past, and it has even less chance of succeeding today, now that universities and colleges are irreversibly invested in the research enterprise, where the sources of intellectual vitality in academic culture more than ever lie.[12] As long as general education is seen as protecting the interests of some imagined general realm against the incursions of professional discourse, the disabling conflict between undergraduate teaching and research can only continue.

The broadening of the concept of research makes it possible to foresee an end to the conflict between research and teaching. Instead of trying to protect the interests of general education from those of research, it would be more productive for academic institutions to take advantage of whatever in research is potentially of general interest to nonprofessionals. Instead of discouraging scholars from letting their research obtrude into their undergraduate teaching, institutions would begin encouraging scholars to *teach their research*, as many scholars have in fact been doing successfully for some time, particularly in the fields influenced by new theories of culture and society.[13]

It is significant, in this regard, that many liberal arts colleges have begun to encourage faculty research, that, as Cheney notes, "even at liberal arts colleges . . . the emphasis on research is growing," so that some liberal arts schools "are considering calling themselves 'research colleges.' " Cheney, who views this trend toward research with dismay, can account for it only as a symptom of the corruption of higher education, an unfortunate sellout to competitive and financial pressures (*Tyrannical Machines* 26). What Cheney seems unable to imagine is that some liberal arts college teachers might actually want to pursue research and that a liberal arts college might see increasing its commitment to research not as a betrayal of its educational ideals but as a way of fulfilling them more effectively, by enlivening and broadening an otherwise provincial intellectual environment.

Teaching our research in undergraduate classrooms (and even making undergraduates copartners in that research) clearly places us under an obligation to do better than we have in clarifying the general implications of our work to students and other lay audiences. If humanities scholars of the 1990s will be engaging issues of general public interest to an unprecedented degree, we need to take seriously the possibility that people out there will be listening.

University of Chicago

Suggestions for Further Reading

On a topic as vast as the scholar in society, any bibliography must be selective and somewhat arbitrary. One place to begin would be with classic nineteenth-century statements such as John Henry Newman's *Idea of a University*, Matthew Arnold's *Culture and Anarchy*, and Thomas Henry Huxley's essays on science, education, and culture. These works first defined the issues and reference points that persist in discussions today: the function of the humanistic scholar in a mass democratic society increasingly subject to utilitarian pressures; the extent to which it is possible or desirable for scholarship to be disinterested; the competing cultural and educational claims of the sciences and the humanities.

Raymond Williams's *Culture and Society, 1780–1950* remains a masterful summing-up of this "culture and society" tradition, whose concepts still frame speculation on the social role of the scholar. Questions about the scholar in society have increasingly come to concern the organization of scholars in the modern university. The standard history of the American university is Laurence R. Veysey's *Emergence of the American University*, which usefully distinguishes three functions whose coalescence and collision shaped the institution: liberal culture (later called humanities), research, and vocationalism. See also Veysey's important forthcoming article, "The Humanities in American Universities since the 1930s: The Decline of Grandiosity."

Standard studies of academic professionalism include Burton Bledstein, *The Culture of Professionalism*; Magali Sarfatti Larson, *The Rise of Professionalism*; and Pierre Bourdieu, *Distinction*. Histories that discuss the social functions envisaged for "English" and other language and literature disciplines by their founders include Stephen Potter, *The Muse in Chains*; E. M. W. Tillyard, *The Muse Unchained*; and, the most pertinent today, Chris Baldick, *The Social Mission of English Criticism, 1848–1932*. Essays start with William Riley Parker's classic "Where Do English Departments Come From?" See also Michael Warner's "Professionalization and the Rewards of Literature, 1875–1900," and Gerald Graff and Michael Warner's *Origins of Literary Studies in America*.

The 1960s and their aftermath have seen an immense outpouring of work—impossible to acknowledge comprehensively—arguing for the unavoidably political dimensions of scholarly production even when (or especially when) that production is ostensibly unconcerned with questions of politics and power. Much of this work has sought to explain the origin and institutionalization of academic language and literature studies in ideological terms, often seeing the establishment of these studies as a compensatory response to the threats of democratization, immigration, labor agitation, and other sources of social conflict. Richard M. Ohmann's *English in America: A Radical View of the Profession* sets forth such a historical overview, dealing centrally with the teaching of writing as well as of literature. A chapter in this book by Wallace Douglas, "Rhetoric for the Meritocracy," provides a telling account of the meritocratic social values that underlay the establishment of English composition in the American curriculum during the nineteenth century.

A succinct Marxist critique of the social influence of academic English is Terry Eagleton's influential *Literary Theory*, especially chapter 1, "The Rise of English" (which is avowedly indebted to a dissertation by Baldick). Frank Lentricchia's *After the New Criticism* is a historical study of recent literary theory, with emphasis on the social functions served or not served by them, and his *Criticism and Social Change* calls for a more socially committed literary scholarship. Jane Tompkins in *Sensational Designs* and Russell Reising in *The Unusable Past* offer incisive critiques of the political implications of canon making by American anthology editors and the New Criticism.

In the voluminous literature reflecting on the status of women and feminism in the university, particularly relevant work includes Angela Simeone, *Academic Women*; Linda Kauffman, editor, *Feminism and Institutions*; and (with respect to literary studies) the anthology edited by Elaine Showalter, *The New Feminist Criticism*.

These left-leaning critiques have recently provoked a backlash, which often asserts the need to divorce humanistic culture from questions of politics, even though many of the critics associated with the backlash avow neoconservative allegiances. The most widely discussed expressions of this backlash include Allan Bloom, *The Closing of the American Mind*; Richard J. Sykes, *Profscam*; and Roger Kimball, *Tenured Radicals*; and numerous polemical articles in neoconservative journals such as *Commentary, New Criterion*, and *American Scholar*. Much of this writing reiterates arguments usually developed with less vituperation and more rigor in earlier works such as Irving Babbitt's *Literature and the American College*; Julian Benda's *Treason of the Intellectuals*; and José Ortega y Gassett's *Mission of the University*. A recent critique from the Left that coincides on a number of points with those from the Right is Russell Jacoby, *The Last Intellectuals*.

Notes

[1] In a forthcoming essay, "The Humanities in American Universities since the 1930s: The Decline of Grandiosity" Laurence R. Veysey points out that though we have come to think of the "humanities" as the natural category that links such subjects as history,

philosophy, and the arts, the use of humanities as an administrative category for subsuming these and other subjects is recent, dating only from the mid-1930s. Veysey observes that the fortunes of humanities as an academic administrative category were paradoxically boosted by a sudden stream of laments that humanistic values had been thrown on the defensive by the cultural and disciplinary gains of the physical and especially the social sciences.

Veysey quotes statements by administrators through the 1920s indicating that they did not think of literature, art, history, and philosophy as belonging to any common concept of "humanities" and in fact did not see these subjects as necessarily possessing common ground at all. Veysey does not quite put it this way, but I draw the conclusion from his essay that humanities became a privileged administrative category only when it came to be felt that *some* term was needed to group departments that did not fit either of the two major divisional groupings, the physical and the social sciences, that developed in the early university. It is as if humanities, that is, answered the need for a name for everything that was left over after factoring out the sectors of the university concerned with technology, money, and political power.

[2]For an early American academic's eloquent expressions of the larger cultural rationale of philology and literary history, see Cook; for a slightly later restatement, see Greenlaw. For an excellent study of the often virulently nationalist and racist political attitudes informing nineteenth-century Anglo-Saxon philology (as well as many of the ideas of Matthew Arnold), see Faverty; for a more recent study of the political contexts of Anglo-Saxonism in "Old English," see Frantzen.

[3]In an MLA address in 1902, a year before Bright declared philologists to be national leaders, James Taft Hatfield complained that language and literature scholars were "largely shut out" from the leadership role in the country that the importance of their work merited. As Hatfield put it, "the practical man would hardly conceal his amusement at the assumption of a company of mere philologists that they were identified with the true progress of the community, and were the custodians of its higher fortunes; he would see some vanity in this belief, and yet we cherish it" (391–94). Hatfield and many of his colleagues blamed the commercial and philistine temper of American culture for this separation between the scholar and society. As a later scholar, Edward C. Armstrong, put it in 1920, though "the aggregate of knowledge" had become "greater than ever before, . . . the large share-holders in this knowledge are no longer in control. Leadership has been assumed by the untrained host, which is troubled by no doubt concerning its competence and therefore feels no inclination to improve its judgment" (xxxix).

[4]For two of the most influential attacks, both from a new-humanist perspective, see Babbitt and Foerster.

[5]Among the most prominent of the official reports are several from the National Endowment for the Humanities: Bennett, "To Reclaim a Legacy" (1984); Cheney, *Humanities in America* (1988) and *Tyrannical Machines* (1990). For reports taking a similar line, see the Association of American Colleges, *Integrity in the College Curriculum* (1985), and Boyer, *College: The Undergraduate Experience*, a 1987 publication of the Carnegie Foundation for the Advancement of Teaching.

[6]To this list I would add the habit of confusing specialization with departmental compartmentalization, something quite different: the fact that on a given campus the professors of literature, foreign languages, philosophy, and history have little regular contact with one another does not necessarily mean that they are too specialized for such communication to be possible.

[7]For documentation relevant to this discussion, see my *Professing Literature*.

[8]Booth's account of his own scholarly career tends to belie his picture of a profession that forces scholars to practice kinds of research that are irrelevant to their real interests. Describing his early years in the profession after World War II Booth says, "I spent most of my time investigating the history of the self-conscious narrator in comic fiction before *Tristram Shandy*." Noting that he has "since read many articles and even a book on something like the same subject" and that "there are hundreds of scholars now working on topics related to that one novel," Booth wonders if such work constitutes a justifiable use of the public's trust ("Scholar" 124).

What is noticeable, however, is that the study of narrative conventions that Booth adduces as an example of his own narrow specialization would before the war have probably been discouraged for being all *too* interpretive and "critical," not sufficiently objective and scholarly. (Booth, who kindly read and commented on a draft of this essay, tells me that the subject was indeed considered risqué when he took it up in the 1950s.) And Booth's major book, *The Rhetoric of Fiction*, which nobody would think of calling specialized, grew out of this earlier narrower interest. Such a work would not have been thinkable in an academic department before the war.

[9]Then, too, the heightened contentiousness of present-day academic culture (a further result of the demographic democratization that I describe above) is another factor that tends to call forth new discourses of generality. In literary studies, it is in large part the climate of increased dispute, contention, controversy, and internal self-division described in Culler's essay that has generated the proliferation of "theory." For as fewer common premises are shared among scholars, there becomes more need to formulate and debate premises. When we no longer agree on what "literature" is, anyone who uses the term is likely sooner or later to be plunged into a debate about it and thus forced to "do theory" whether he or she wants to or not (Graff 250). The collapse of tacit agreement on first principles creates a conflict of theories, which perforce are less concerned with formulating agreed-upon laws than with analyzing and debating contested premises.

As Culler suggests, "theory of literature" in the era of René Wellek and Austin Warren's influential 1949 book of that title denoted a foundational discourse that defined "the mode of existence" of the "literary" (see Wellek and Warren's central chapter, "The Mode of Existence of a Literary Work of Art"). Today, by contrast, "theory of literature" tends to be concerned not with defining literature but with "problematizing" such definitions by pointing out their contested or historically contingent status.

[10]These insecurities are further intensified by changes in the supervisory relations of faculty members to graduate students. In an earlier era, the senior professor in "the period" exercised a kind of ownership of the field, dispensing patronage to his (or in rare cases, her) graduate students. In this quasi-feudal arrangement, the student's dissertation topic was often assigned by the director (an academic equivalent of arranged marriage), who from a central position in the field advised on which topics had not yet been covered. "Nobody has done Southey's juvenilia," the senior professor would point out to the prospective dissertation writer who had just passed the qualifying examination. "Why don't you work that up?" True to the best paternalistic traditions, the patriarch was considered responsible for his apprentices, looking out for them after the PhD, suggesting them for job openings and research opportunities. Graduate students might joke privately about the uninspiring topics they had been assigned (it is this kind of situation Booth doubtless had in mind when he referred to research that is irrelevant to the interests of the researcher), but the arrangement worked in the students' interest insofar as it virtually

guaranteed them a position and the makings of a small but secure niche in the specialized area they had written about.

The collapse of this quasi-feudal structure has occurred at an uneven rate from field to field and institution to institution. But as the once tightly defined structure of fields has dissolved, the old-boy network of job placement has weakened, transforming PhD students from apprentices in a master's shop into wage-laborers selling their skills in a deregulated free market. The new conditions bracingly liberate students from faculty authority in their choice of subjects and methods—and I doubt that many would wish to see the older arrangements restored—but they also leave them on their own, unprotected from the vicissitudes of the market.

[11] See recent work by Hayford; Parker; McGann; Shillingsburg; Mailloux; and Tanselle, among others.

[12] For a recent restatement of the "defensive and compensatory" traditional general education philosophy here described, see Boyer.

[13] "Undergraduate research" has been advanced by the National Conferences for Undergraduate Research, initiated in 1987 by faculty members and administrators at the University of North Carolina, Asheville, and sponsored by the Association of American Colleges.

Works Cited

Armstrong, Edward C. "Taking Counsel with Candide." *PMLA* 35, app. (1920): xxiv–xliii.

Arnold, Matthew. *Culture and Anarchy.* Ann Arbor: U of Michigan P, 1965. Vol. 5 of *Complete Prose Works.* Ed. R. H. Super. 11 vols. 1960–77.

Association of American Colleges. *Integrity in the College Curriculum: A Report to the Academic Community.* Washington: AAC, 1985.

Atlas, James. *The Book Wars: What It Takes to Be Educated in America.* New York: Whittle, 1990.

Babbitt, Irving. *Literature and the American College: Essays in Defense of the Humanities.* Boston: Houghton, 1908.

Baldick, Chris. *The Social Mission of English Criticism, 1848–1932.* London: Oxford UP, 1983.

Benda, Julian. *The Treason of the Intellectuals.* Trans. Richard Aldington. New York: Morrow, 1928.

Bennett, William J. *To Reclaim a Legacy.* Washington: NEH, 1984.

Bledstein, Burton. *The Culture of Professionalism: The Middle Class and the Development of Higher Education in America.* New York: Norton, 1976.

Bloom, Allan. *The Closing of the American Mind: How Higher Education Has Failed Democracy and Impoverished the Souls of Today's Students.* New York: Simon, 1987.

Booth, Wayne C. *The Rhetoric of Fiction.* Chicago: U of Chicago P, 1961.

———. "The Scholar in Society." *Introduction to Scholarship in Modern Languages and Literatures.* Ed. Joseph Gibaldi. New York: MLA, 1981. 116–43.

Bourdieu, Pierre. *Distinction.* Trans. Richard Nice. Cambridge: Harvard UP, 1984.

Boyer, Ernest L. *College: The Undergraduate Experience.* Report of the Carnegie Foundation for the Advancement of Teaching. New York: Harper, 1987.

Bright, James Wilson. "Concerning the Unwritten History of the Modern Language Association of America." *PMLA* 18, app. 1 (1903): xli–lxii.

"The Case for Book Burning." *New Republic* 14 and 21 Sept. 1987: 7–9.

Cheney, Lynne V. *Humanities in America: A Report to the President, the Congress, and the American People.* Washington: NEH, 1988.

———. *Tyrannical Machines: A Report on Educational Practices Gone Wrong and Our Best Hopes for Setting Them Right.* Washington: NEH, 1990.

Cook, Albert S. *The Higher Study of English.* Boston: Houghton, 1908.

Douglas, Wallace. "Rhetoric for the Meritocracy." Ohmann 97–132.

Eagleton, Terry. *Literary Theory: An Introduction.* Oxford: Blackwell; Minneapolis: U of Minnesota, 1983.

Faverty, Frederick E. *Matthew Arnold the Ethnologist.* Northwestern Univ. Studies 27. Evanston: Northwestern UP, 1951.

Fiedler, Leslie. *An End to Innocence: Essays on Culture and Politics.* Boston: Beacon, 1955.

Foerster, Norman. *The American Scholar: A Study in "Litterae Inhumaniores."* Chapel Hill: U of North Carolina P, 1929.

Frantzen, Alan J. *Desire for Origins: New Language, Old English, and Teaching the Tradition.* New Brunswick: Rutgers UP, 1990.

Graff, Gerald. *Professing Literature: An Institutional History.* Chicago: U of Chicago P, 1987.

Graff, Gerald, and Michael Warner, eds. *The Origins of Literary Studies in America: A Documentary Anthology.* New York: Routledge, 1989.

Greenlaw, Edwin. *The Province of Literary History.* Johns Hopkins Monographs in Literary History 1. Baltimore: John Hopkins UP, 1931.

Hatfield, James Taft. "Scholarship and the Commonwealth." *PMLA* 17 (1902): 391–409.

Hayford, Harrison. "Historical Note." *Moby-Dick.* By Herman Melville. Evanston: Northwestern UP; Chicago: Newberry Lib., 1988. 581–85.

———. "Unnecessary Duplicates: A Key to the Writing of *Moby-Dick.*" *New Perspectives on Melville.* Ed. Faith Pullin. Edinburgh: Edinburgh UP, 1978. 128–61.

Howe, Irving. "What Should We Be Teaching?" *Dissent* (Fall 1988): 477–79.

Huxley, Thomas Henry. *Huxley on Education: A Selection.* Ed. C. Bibby. Cambridge: Cambridge UP, 1971.

Jacoby, Russell. *The Last Intellectuals.* New York: Basic, 1987.

James, William. "The Ph.D. Octopus." *Harvard Monthly*, 1903. Rpt. in *Educational Review* 55 (1918): 149–57.

Kauffman, Linda, ed. *Feminism and Institutions: Dialogues on Feminist Theory.* New York: Blackwell, 1989.

Kimball, Roger. *Tenured Radicals: How Politics Has Corrupted Our Higher Education.* New York: Harper, 1990.

Larson, Magali Sarfatti. *The Rise of Professionalism: A Sociological Analysis.* Berkeley: U of California P, 1977.

Lentricchia, Frank. *After the New Criticism.* Chicago: U of Chicago P, 1980.

———. *Criticism and Social Change.* Chicago: U of Chicago P, 1984.

Levinson, Sanford, and Steven Mailloux, eds. *Interpreting Law and Literature: A Hermeneutic Reader.* Evanston: Northwestern UP, 1988.

Mailloux, Steven. *Interpretive Communities: The Reader in the Study of American Fiction.* Ithaca: Cornell UP, 1982.

McGann, Jerome J. *A Critique of Modern Textual Criticism.* Chicago: U of Chicago P, 1983.

———, ed. *Textual Criticism and Literary Interpretation.* Chicago: U of Chicago P, 1985.

Newman, John Henry. *The Idea of a University.* Ed. Martin J. Svaglic. Notre Dame: U of Notre Dame P, 1982.

Ohmann, Richard M. *English in America: A Radical View of the Profession.* New York: Oxford UP, 1976.

Ortega y Gasset, José. *The Mission of the University.* Trans. H. L. Nostrand. Princeton: Princeton UP, 1944.

Parker, Hershel. *Flawed Texts and Verbal Icons: Literary Authority in American Fiction.* Evanston: Northwestern UP, 1984.

Parker, William Riley. "Where Do English Departments Come From?" *College English* 28 (1967): 339–51.

Potter, Stephen. *The Muse in Chains: A Study in Education.* London: Cape, 1937.

Reising, Russell. *The Unusable Past: Theory and the Study of American Literature.* New York: Routledge, 1986.

Robbins, Bruce. "The East as Career: Edward Said and the Logics of Professionalism." *Edward Said: A Critical Reader.* Ed. Michael Sprinker. London: Blackwell, forthcoming.

Shillingsburg, Peter. *Scholarly Editing in the Computer Age: Theory and Practice.* Athens: U of Georgia P, 1986.

Showalter, Elaine, ed. *The New Feminist Criticism: Essays on Women, Literature, Theory.* New York: Pantheon, 1985.

Simeone, Angela. *Academic Women: Working toward Equality.* Westport: Begin, 1986.

Stimpson, Catharine R. President's Column. *MLA Newsletter* 22.4 (1990): 2–3.

Sykes, Richard J. *Profscam: Professors and the Demise of Higher Education.* Chicago: Regnery, 1988.

Tanselle, G. Thomas. *Textual Criticism since Greg: A Chronicle, 1950–1985.* Charlottesville: UP of Virginia, 1988.

Tillyard, E. M. W. *The Muse Unchained: An Intimate Account of the Revolution in English Studies at Cambridge.* London: Bowes, 1958.

Tompkins, Jane. *Sensational Designs: The Cultural Work of American Fiction, 1790–1860.* New York: Oxford UP, 1985.

Veysey, Laurence R. *The Emergence of the American University.* Chicago: U of Chicago P, 1965.

———. "The Humanities in American Universities since the 1930s: The Decline of Grandiosity." Forthcoming.

Warner, Michael. "Professionalization and the Rewards of Literature, 1875–1900." *Criticism* 27 (1985): 1–28.

Wellek, René, and Austin Warren. *Theory of Literature.* New York: Harcourt, 1949.

Williams, Raymond. *Culture and Society, 1780–1950.* New York: Harper, 1966.

Index